NATIONAL
GEOGRAPHIC

TRAVELER

colombia

by Christopher P. Baker

National Geographic
Washington, D.C.

CONTENTS

Pages 2–3: A horse-drawn carriage in historic Cartagena
Opposite: Colombia is renowned for its festive joie de vivre, best experienced at Carnaval.

TRAVELING WITH EYES OPEN

Alert travelers go with a purpose and leave with a benefit. If you travel responsibly, you can help support wildlife conservation, historic preservation, and cultural enrichment in the places you visit. You can enrich your own travel experience as well.

To be a geo-savvy traveler:

- Recognize that your presence has an impact on the places you visit.

- Spend your time and money in ways that sustain local character. (Besides, it's more interesting that way.)

- Value the destination's natural and cultural heritage.

- Respect the local customs and traditions.

- Express appreciation to local people about things you find interesting and unique to the place: its nature and scenery, music and food, historic villages and buildings.

- Vote with your wallet: Support the people who support the place, patronizing businesses that make an effort to celebrate and protect what's special there. Seek out local shops, restaurants, and inns. Use tour operators who love their home—who love taking care of it and showing it off. Avoid businesses that detract from the character of the place.

- Enrich yourself, taking home memories and stories to tell, knowing that you have contributed to the preservation and enhancement of the destination.

That is the type of travel now called geotourism, defined as "tourism that sustains or enhances the geographical character of a place—its environment, culture, aesthetics, heritage, and the well-being of its residents." To learn more, visit National Geographic's Center for Sustainable Destinations at *travel.nationalgeographic.com/travel/geotourism.*

colombia

ABOUT THE AUTHOR & THE PHOTOGRAPHER

After earning degrees in geography at the University of London and Latin American Studies (including a thesis on Colombia) at the University of Liverpool, **Christopher P. Baker** settled in California and established a career as a travel writer, photographer, lecturer, and tour leader. In addition to the *National Geographic Traveler: Colombia* guidebook, he has authored and photographed guidebooks to Costa Rica, Cuba, the Dominican Republic, and Panama in the National Geographic Traveler series, as well as more than two dozen guidebooks for other publishers. He is also the author of the award-winning *Mi Moto Fidel: Motorcycling Through Castro's Cuba*, published by National Geographic Adventure Press; plus the coffee-table books *Cuba Classics: A Celebration of Vintage American Automobiles* and *Enchanting Costa Rica*. Recipient of the 2008 Lowell Thomas Travel Journalist of the Year award, Baker is one of the world's foremost authorities on Costa Rica and Cuba. He has also written and photographed for more than 200 publications, from *National Geographic Traveler* to *Newsweek*. He has given talks at National Geographic headquarters, the National Press Club, and the World Affairs Council, among other prestigious organizations, and he has been profiled in *USA Today* and featured on CNN, the National Geographic Channel, NPR, and dozens of other radio and TV outlets. He escorts National Geographic Expeditions' "Discovering Colombia," "Costa Rica and the Panama Canal," and "Cuba: Discovering Its People and Culture" tours. Visit his website at *christopherpbaker.com*.

Charting Your Trip

Visitors to Colombia discover all that's best in South America packed into one country. Its terrains range from Amazon rain forest to Andean peaks. The country is physically stunning, ecologically astounding, and culturally vibrant. Add the sophistication of Bogotá, Cali, Medellín, and Cartagena. Plus, most of the country is safer than in its violent past, thanks to a crackdown initiated in the early 2000s.

How to Get Around

Colombia is a large country—at 440,000 square miles (1.14 million sq km) about the size of California and Texas combined. Its internal air network is well developed, and flying is the preferred way of getting between distant cities and within the Amazonía region. Five major airlines (see Travelwise p. 262) compete, and together, they serve the entire country. Service isn't cheap.

Many tour companies offer the relative security of group travel. Comfortable buses operate frequently between most towns (see Travelwise p. 263). *Colectivos* (shared mini-vans or pickups) and *chivas* (colorful trucks converted to open-air buses) connect some remote rural towns. They're uncomfortable, but fun if you don't mind sharing space with chickens and pigs. Extensive bus and taxi systems make getting around easy in major cities, and Medellín's Metro and MetroCable are acclaimed.

For the intrepid, renting a car (see Travelwise p. 263) is a great way to see more of Colombia. Although a decade ago, many of the nation's highways were considered too dangerous, Colombia's military now guards the main roads to ensure safety. Major highways and *autopistas* (motorways) are well paved, although many are extremely mountainous, winding, and subject to landslides. Expect tolls on major roads.

Three main highways run north–south. One links Cartagena with Medellín and Cali, and continues south as the Pan-American Highway to Ecuador. From Bogotá you can follow a road through the Magdalena River Valley north to Santa Marta

Bronze statue of Spanish conquistador
Sebastián de Belalcázar

or south to San Agustín. A more scenic road claws up through the Cordillera Oriental. To explore remote Colombia, including Los Llanos, an off-road vehicle is mandatory, although be cautious of straying too far off the beaten path because of bandits and narco-terrorists. Always check on road conditions ahead. Motorcycling is also a popular way to see the country.

If You Have One Week

The great distances make it difficult to see many different parts of Colombia on a short trip. It makes sense to plan an ideal one-week itinerary around either Bogotá or Cartagena. Both cities are served by direct flights from North America and Europe.

For a **Bogotá**-based trip, **day one** could be spent exploring Plaza Bolívar and La Candelaria. On **day two,** you'll want to continue strolling La Candelaria, being sure to include the Museo Botero, which displays works by Colombia's foremost artist; and Parque Santander, with the world's preeminent pre-Columbian gold museum.

Day three can include a funicular ride to Cerro de Monserrate for a stupefying view over the city. At its base, Quinta de Bolívar is worth a stop. Spend the afternoon around Parque de la Independencia, including visits to the Museo de Arte Moderno and Museo Nacional. On Friday nights and weekends, you can take the elevator to the top of Torre Colpatria for unsurpassed city views.

Rent a car (or take an excursion tour) to spend the next several days exploring Cundinamarca and Boyacá. **Day four** should include a visit to the salt cathedral at Zipaquirá (30 miles/50 km to the north). Continue via the winding mountain road to Chiquinquirá and Villa de Leyva two to three hours beyond. Spend **day five** roaming the cobbled streets of this village. **Day six,** return to Bogotá via Tunja and Laguna del Cacique Guatavita, setting for the myth of El Dorado. On **day seven,** you might spend your time in Parque Metropolitano Simón Bolívar.

NOT TO BE MISSED:

Visiting the Museo del Oro in Bogotá **71**

The thrill of white-water rafting at San Gil **111–112**

Walking through Cartagena's colonial streets **127–133**

Celebrating Carnaval in Barranquilla **144**

Relaxing on Tayrona beach **151**

The yesteryear atmosphere of Popayán **203–204**

Scuba diving off Isla de San Andrés **238**

Macaws in Amazonas **258–259**

Tourist Information Sources

ProColombia, the government tourism promotion agency, has an informative website *(colombia.travel)* plus offices in the following international locations:
• United States: 601 Brickell Key Dr., Suite 608, Miami, FL 33131, tel 305/374-3144
• Canada: 2 Bloor St. W, Suite 902, Toronto, ON M4W 3E2, tel 416/363-9225
• United Kingdom: 2 Conduit St., London W1S 2XB, tel 020/7491-3535

The **Bogotá Tourism Institute** *(Cra. 24 #40-66, Chapinero, tel 57-1/217-0711, bogotaturismo.gov.co)* has information kiosks throughout the city, and you'll find similar bureaus in most other *alcaldías* (municipalities).

The **National Parks Office** *(Cra. 10 #20-30, Bogotá, tel 1/353-2400 or toll free 0-1800-012-9722, parquesnacionales.gov.co)* has an excellent website.

Staying Safe

Travel within Colombia requires that you adhere strictly to safety precautions.
- Don't wander into working-class areas, especially *tugurios* (slums).
- Dress modestly and forsake wearing watches and jewelry.
- Carry your wallet and other valuables in a secure money belt.
- Hide your camera when not in use.
- Carry purses and bags across the shoulder.
- Use radio-dispatched taxis only.
- Use only ATMs associated with banks.

- Never accept a drink or food offered by strangers—it might be laced with *burundanga*, a chemical that causes victims to lose their will and memory.
- Don't stray too far off the beaten path. Most main roads are now safe for travel. Paramilitaries and armed rebel groups have retreated to remoter areas; even so, criminal elements still operate in cities, and guerrilla groups are especially active in the regions bordering Ecuador, Venezuela, and Panama.
- Register with your embassy in Bogotá.

If you choose to base yourself in **Cartagena,** begin with a horse-drawn coach ride around the old city. Spend the rest of **day one** and **day two** exploring on foot, taking in the squares and museums. Build in time for a taxi ride or guided tour to Castillo de San Felipe de Barajas and Cerro de la Popa. After dining on Plaza de San Diego, a *chiva rumbera* party bus is a fun way to explore the city by night. On **day three,** take an excursion boat from the city dock to Islas del Rosario archipelago. **Day four,** take a bus or taxi to Volcán de Lodo El Totumo to steep in hot mud. After rinsing off, continue along the coast via Barranquilla, arriving at Parque Nacional Natural Tayrona in time for a spectacular sunset. Spend **day five** on the beach, and **day six** exploring the park, including a climb to the pre-Columbian site of El Pueblito. **Day seven,** make the five-hour return drive south to Cartagena for your homebound flight.

Best Times to Visit

Colombia has an equatorial climate; thus, seasonal variations are minimal. Swings in temperature coincide with differences in elevation, which range from sea level to 18,947 feet (5,775 m). Colombians refer to the area under 3,000 feet (914 m) as the hot zone *(tierra caliente),* between 3,000 and 6,500 feet (1,981 m) as the temperate zone *(tierra templada),* between 6,500 and 11,500 feet (3,505 m) as the cold zone *(tierra fría),* and above that the frozen zone *(tierra helada).* Coastal cities and Leticia simmer with average daily temperatures in the 70s and 80s (23°–32°C). Bogotá, by contrast, has a year-round temperature averaging 44° to 68°F (6.7°–20°C).

In general, Colombia has two seasons—dry or *verano* (summer, coinciding with northern winter), and wet or *invierno* (winter, coinciding with northern summer)—with variations throughout the country. The Andean region typically has both a main dry season December to March and a shorter dry period July and August. The Amazon has a uniform climate that is quite wet year-round.

December to March is high season in coastal resorts; hotel rates go up accordingly, as well as during Semana Santa (Holy Week), and June through July. Many festivals take place during the dry periods.

Parque Nacional Natural Tayrona has some of the most beautiful beaches in Colombia.

If You Have More Time

One week isn't enough time to scratch the surface. A second week would allow you to take a 1.5-hour flight between Bogotá and Cartagena and combine the itineraries.

For a **third week** or your next trip, you could focus on the mountain towns of Santander Department, where adventure seekers find thrills in San Gil and in Parque Nacional Natural El Cocuy. Medellín makes a great base for exploring the Cordillera Occidental to the west. Here, the draws include the allure of the Zona Cafetera, where you can visit coffee haciendas. The Quibdó region to the southeast is studded with colonial towns, as is Antioquia. Farther south (350 miles/560 km), you'll want three days to explore the Valle de Cauca, the colonial gem of Popayán, and nearby Silvia. Returning to Bogotá via San Agustín, stop to admire the pre-Columbian stone statues and the desert of Tatacoma on your ten-hour drive back.

With **additional days,** consider taking a two-hour flight to San Andrés island for an immersion in Afro-Caribbean culture and in ocean waters renowned as a dive paradise. To include the Amazon, you would need at least a month in Colombia, budgeting a minimum of three days to visit the Amazon. Plan to fly into Leticia, perhaps for overnight before a riverboat transfer to Parque Nacional Natural Amacayacu for wildlife viewing, birding, and an immersion in indigenous culture.

Money Matters

The national currency is the peso; although the official symbol is $, it's sometimes written as COP. U.S. currency is rarely accepted, except in Cartagena and heavily touristed areas. Plenty of places to change money exist; avoid doing so on the street. Exchange rates are fickle; check before leaving for your trip.

Most banks have ATMs that work with U.S. and European bank cards. Traveler's checks are difficult to cash due to widespread fraud. Credit cards are widely accepted.

Carry small peso bills for tips and purchases, as change for larger bills may be hard to come by.

History &
Culture

Santuario de Las Lajas, a Gothic
church in southern Colombia

Colombia Today

Colombia is a South American giant awakening to its vast potential. In this diamond-shaped tropical nation, you will find a cornucopia of natural wonders side by side with sleepy villages and vibrant cities. A place where tourism is now booming, and turmoil and guerrilla conflict are yesterday's news.

Word is getting out (tourist arrivals jumped 14 percent in 2014 alone). The cruise ships have returned to swashbuckling Cartagena, where ancient fortresses still echo with the clash of cutlasses and the roar of cannon. This Caribbean gem full of cathedrals, convents, and ancient mansions painted in soft tropical colors— guava green, papaya yellow, tangerine—reflects Colombia's positive future while

Revelers dance and have fun aboard Colombian party buses called *chivas rumberas*.

showcasing the best of a picturesque past. The cobblestone plazas of Villa de Leyva, Popayán, and Bogotá, the capital city, still echo with the boot steps of Spanish conquistadores. And tiny time-warp colonial villages color Colombia's rural highways. Here, folkloric traditions run deep: Women sewing lacy *polleras* (skirts) and men wearing *sombreros aguadeños* and *vueltiao* (straw hats from Aguado and the lower Magdalena River Basin, respectively) make the living past seem cinematic. Cali, Medellín, and Bogotá are modern metropolises pinned by glittering skyscrapers, hotels, and trendy nightclubs that are settings for midnight-to-dawn marathons of sizzling salsa.

The lingering perception of a nation in turmoil is now outdated, thanks to a decade-long pacification campaign. True, urban wealth contrasts sharply with grinding poverty and misery. And Colombia still has more than its fair share

> **The cobblestone plazas of Villa de Leyva, Popayán, and Bogotá, the capital city, still echo with the boot steps of Spanish conquistadores.**

of drug-trafficking and guerrilla-related problems. Although caution is still required when exploring cities and the more remote regions, the narco-traffickers' presence is usually nothing more than a newspaper note for tourists, who thrill to discover a destination as exciting, diverse, and welcoming as any in Latin America.

Contrasts Abound

Geographically, Colombia is a triptych of coastal plain, soaring mountains, and velvety jungle. Rivers teem from the Andes into the Amazon Basin and the seamless sponge of Chocó's Pacific coast—vast rain forest homes to jaguar, monkey, poison dart frog, and other wildlife species of every stripe, spot, and hue. The central highlands of Antioquia are flanked by corduroys of glossy green coffee bushes, conjuring images of a smiling Juan Valdéz leading his burro laden with beans. In La Guajira Peninsula on the far north Caribbean coast, the tapestry changes to a dusty, cactus-studded landscape that is home to flamingos and the welcoming Wayúu indigenous people. The beach-fringed Caribbean island archipelago of San Andrés y Providencia—embroidered with offshore coral reefs and cays licked by turquoise waters—appeals, too, for its distinctive, English-speaking Afro-Caribbean culture.

Colombia's indigenous heritage is as diverse as anywhere in the Americas. Pre-Columbian stone statues and ancient cities still peek forth from the jungled terrain. Bogotá's world-class Museo del Oro gleams with a jaw-dropping display of gold relics. And the living indigenous cultures range from the nomadic Nukak of the deepest Amazon to the Andes' Guambiano peoples, whose

women are garbed as flamboyantly as the most exotic of scarlet macaws.

Nature lovers will not be disappointed. Visitors speak in raptures of phenomenal birding, with more species than any other country in the world. Hikers are delirious from mountain highs in snow-tipped Parque Nacional Natural El Cocuy and Parque Nacional Natural Los Nevados. Scuba diving abounds, in both Caribbean and Pacific waters. So, too, do other adrenaline-boosting sports, from paragliding to white-water rafting. San Gil, in Santander, is the extreme-sports capital of South America, known for, among other things, its exhilarating white-water runs. Suesca, outside Bogotá, plus El Cocuy are acclaimed as rock climbers' nirvanas. Opportunities to saddle up exist throughout the nation, especially on the cattle ranch-resorts of Los Llanos. You can even top off your adventure tour by whale-watching off Bahía Solano and Isla Gorgona. Meanwhile ashore, wildlife viewing comes easily in national parks from Tayrona to Amazonas, where sighting a freshwater dolphin is a virtually guaranteed highlight.

Only a 3.5-hour flight from Miami, this accessible and affordable country has an astonishingly well-developed tourist infrastructure, thanks in part to a large and sophisticated domestic travel market. Cartagena's restoration showcases stylish boutique hotels and chic restaurants hidden behind antique facades. In fact, the sophistication of Colombia's dining is reason enough to visit. Then there's the irresistibly infectious music and dance. You'll find an afternoon siesta a wise investment to prepare for Colombia's notorious nightlife—from twangy *vallenato* rhythms to furiously fast-paced salsa, seemingly the undercurrent of Colombian life. A glance at the calendar reveals a nonstop colorful calliope of festivals honoring the nation's traditions and irrepressible passions, culminating in the biggest two bashes of all: Barranquilla's high-octane Carnaval and the Concurso Nacional de Belleza, when the entire nation takes off work to celebrate the crowning of Miss Colombia, in Cartagena.

No wonder more and more foreign travelers are returning home with breathless tales of a land with a lively Latin spirit, a gracious people, and an amazing story of transformation.

Colombia at a Glance

Land area: 439,737 square miles (1,138,914 sq km)
Population: 46.7 million (2015 est.)
Literacy: 94.7 percent
Life expectancy: 75 years
Government: Democratic republic
Independence: July 20, 1810
Capital: Bogotá
Highest point: Pico Cristóbal Colón 18,947 feet (5,775 m)
Currency: Colombian peso (COP$)
Gross domestic product (GDP): $640 billion (2014 est.)
GDP per capita: $13,400
Population below poverty line: 32.7 percent (2012 est.)
Language: Spanish, plus 64 indigenous languages
Religion: 90 percent Catholic
Time: GMT, minus 5 hours EST

Demography

If ever a country were a melting pot, Colombia—whose population tops 46 million (exceeded in Latin America only by Brazil and Mexico)—is it, with every conceivable

Bulls are still used today as beasts of burden throughout rural Colombia.

ethnicity thrown into the *sancocho* (traditional meat and vegetable stew). Elaborately costumed Guambiano Indians. Barely costumed Emberá-Wounaan Indians. White-clad Arhuaco. Afro-Caribbeans. Pure-blood Spanish elite sipping cocktails.

The early Spanish colonialists who came in search of gold encountered thriving and diverse indigenous cultures numbering perhaps two million individuals. Many of these tribes quickly succumbed to European diseases and the ruthlessness of 16th-century Spanish conquistadores, though more than 80 pure-blood indigenous groups survive today. The mixing of native Indian and Spanish blood produced an exotic mestizo population today comprising 58 percent of the nation. Large numbers of African slaves imported to Colombia between the 16th and 18th centuries infused their singular traits into the bouillabaisse. Today, blacks compose 18 percent of Colombia's population.

An entire potpourri of Europeans arrived during the 19th century, primarily settling the Caribbean alongside Lebanese (Colombian pop diva Shakira, a native of Barranquilla, has Lebanese heritage). Syrians, Jews, Gypsies, and even a few Koreans and Japanese. Germans settled Santander. Chinese indentured laborers were brought in to lay the Panama Railroad and, later, the railways and roads between Cali and Buenaventura and between Bogotá and the Caribbean. Lithuanians, Croatians, Poles, and English arrived during World War II and the Cold War to stitch their customs into the cultural quilt of the nation. The past few years have witnessed a growing influx of North Americans and Europeans seeking to retire in the sun.

Unlike most Andean countries, Colombia is highly urbanized; about 77 percent of the population lives in cities: Cali and Medellín exceed 2.5 and 3.9 million, respectively; Bogotá has a population of 9.8 million.

The National Identity: Proudly and fully Latino, perhaps more than other Latin American people, white Colombians cling tightly to their Spanish heritage. Spanish colonists introduced their social system and imposed their conservative values on the indigenous population and African slaves, whose descendants remain segregated economically, geographically, and socially. Diverse geography, rugged terrain, and a heterogeneous population fostered extreme regionalism in cultures, societal mores, and ways of life, resulting in only a limited sense of national identity and cohesion outside the white elite. For example, the Afro-Caribbeans of San Andrés and Providencia (which Colombia acquired from Britain at the end of the colonial period) are Protestant, continue to speak English, and resist the notion that they are Colombian. It is said that the only time that the regional cultures unite for a common goal is during elections, sporting events, and the Miss Colombia pageant.

Independence reinforced the colonial status quo. Continuing political anarchy, a lack of road and rail networks, and slow evolution of other infrastructure tempered economic development and inhibited the evolution of a viable middle class (today composing perhaps 20 percent of the population), whose emergence is a relatively recent phenomenon. Colombian society remains highly stratified according to class and color. "Whiteness" is considered an ideal (as is the "refined" dialect of Bogotá) and an unofficial racial pecking order exists, closely related to socioeconomic status: The country's

EXPERIENCE: Volunteer Opportunities

Little is as soul-satisfying as knowing you have contributed to the local ecological and cultural welfare while traveling. Hiring guides, for example, is one way to help hard-pressed locals. You can also give your time and skills to projects in Colombia that are seeking volunteers. By doing so, you create bonds, learn about traditional customs, and contribute to the care and development of local communities. Here are some key organizations seeking volunteers in Colombia:

Friends for Colombia (*336 Upper Point Dr., Manson, WI 98831, tel 509/590-1401, friendsforcolombia.org*) includes community service in low-income projects during one-week trips to Cartagena.

Fundación ProAves (*Cra. 20 #36-61, Bogotá, tel 57-1/340-3229, proaves.org*), Colombia's foremost conservation nongovernmental organization, has an eco-volunteer program, with efforts focused on protecting endemic bird

species. Projects range from reforestation to reserve maintenance.

Hands Up Holidays (*61 Parkstead Rd., London SW15 5AN, England, 201/984-5372 in North America or 0207/193-1062 in the U.K., handsupholidays.com*) includes a 5-day volunteer component in its 14-day upscale holidays in Colombia. Volunteers help develop skills among former coca-leaf farmers.

Let's Go Volunteer (*Calle 85 #19A-25, Bogotá, tel 57-310/884-8041, letsgo volunteer.info*) weds volunteer programs in underprivileged communities with Spanish tuition in Ibagué. Options range from working in shelters to environmental projects.

United Planet (*11 Arlington St., Boston, MA 02116, tel 617/267-7763, unitedplanet .org*) seeks volunteers for programs working with disabled and disadvantaged children in Colombia. Teaching computing, language, music, or sports are among the skills sought.

peasants, indigenous people, and blacks continue to face discrimination. The department of Antioquia, with its history of miscegenation, is an exception: Economic achievement is valued above ethnicity.

The majority of rural people live a simple life, tending coffee and arable farms in the highlands and cattle on the lowlands, especially in Los Llanos, where everyday life evokes the cowboy spirit. Rural society is still rigidly hierarchical and strongly influenced by Spanish traditions; urban society less so, although family background, perceived social class, and personal connections—termed *palanca* (leverage)—trump most other considerations in business and politics. Dynasties and elitist white old-boy networks—called *roscas*—are evident, where blood connections open doors and shape almost every aspect of economic and political life.

Gender roles are defined by tradition: Machismo (the public personification of the male as sexual conquerer, head of household, and defender of family pride) and *marianismo* (the veneration of feminine "virtues" like purity, compliance, and reliance on men) are ingrained, especially in rural communities. The younger urban generations have begun to cast off these traditional bonds, and middle- and upper-class women today hold powerful positions within society. Ninety percent of Colombians identify themselves as Catholics who put great faith in God, and in many rural communities the local priest is still the primary authority figure.

> ## Local Phrases to Know
> Colombians have their own regional slang and idioms. These common phrases will help you fit in like a local:
>
> **A papaya dada, papaya partida**
>   A papaya given, papaya taken. Give someone the chance to take something from you, and they will.
> **El parche** The happening place to be
> **Ese plan pega** That sounds great
> **¡Qué chevere!** How cool or awesome!
> **¡Suerte!** Good luck! Depending on tone of voice, it can mean "Go to hell!"
> **Traqueto** Head honcho involved in the drug trade who has lots of money
> **¿Vientos o maletas?** How are you? Literally "winds or suitcases," a play on **bien o mal** (good or bad).

Standards of Living: Colombia ranks midway down the world's chart for life expectancy (75 years average), and infant mortality is triple that of the United States. About half the population is covered by the public health-care system; other state entities and private medicine serve another 30 percent, and one-fifth lack access to medical treatment entirely. Huge regional disparities exist. Officially, only 5.3 percent of the populace is illiterate—a significant drop over the past decade, thanks to local library initiatives.

Education is free and compulsory only at the primary level nationwide. Most departments also provide public-funded secondary education, and children in pin-neat uniforms in even the remotest of rural communities are one of the joyful sights in this land. Nonetheless, lack of public secondary schooling in many regions is one of Colombia's greatest failings and challenges.

Colombia's per capita income is approximately $13,400, but society displays extreme (and growing) inequality, surpassed in the Americas only by Bolivia and Haiti. Almost half the population officially lives below the poverty line, and 12 percent live in extreme poverty, which disproportionately affects Afro-Colombians, indigenous groups, displaced persons, and rural communities. Although Colombia has a sizable middle class, there is no avoiding the impoverishment found nationwide, especially in urban slums riddled with unemployment, crime, and despair. Most of Colombia's predominantly white wealthy elite, secluded in deluxe high-rise condos of Bogotá and Medellín, is out of touch with the impoverished masses in their tumbledown huts without electricity, running water, and sewers. Almost every city has slums called *comunas,* or *barrios de invasión,* sprinkled throughout—"invaded neighborhoods" populated by people (at least 3.3 million nationwide) displaced by armed conflict.

The Wayúu people of La Guajira Peninsula continue to follow a traditional lifestyle.

Extreme inequality in land distribution (5 percent of landowners own 70 percent of farmland) exacerbates rural poverty–a root cause of Colombia's sociopolitical violence. President Juan Manuel Santos has pledged to correct the extreme inequality and restore land to the millions of peasants dispossessed by right-wing paramilitaries, left-wing guerrillas, and drug traffickers.

Indigenous Peoples Today: Colombia has 87 indigenous groups totaling 1.4 million people–about 3.4 percent of the country's total population, composing one of the most diverse indigenous populations in the world. Most live within *resguardos indígenas* (semiautonomous districts), where indigenous groups are guaranteed rights to self-government. Although Colombia's 644 resguardos indígenas cover 116,692 square miles (302,231 sq km)–almost one-third of the national territory—less than one-tenth is suitable for agriculture, and education in resguardos is of poor quality; the level of illiteracy and dropouts is high. Another 445,000 or so indigenous people live outside resguardos, and they have no legal rights over the land on which they live.

Although widely dispersed throughout Colombia indigenous groups are concentrated on the margins of the country and in the high Andes, notably in the departments of Amazonas, Cauca, Guainía, La Guajira, Nariño, Vaupés, and Vichada—these regions are populated by at least 50 percent indigenous people. Linguistically Colombia's indigenous peoples are divided into 13 families and speak 64 distinct languages. For example, the rain forest–dwelling Emberá-Wounaan (who despite living in northern Chocó are culturally related to Amazonian tribes) are referred to jointly, yet the two groups speak different languages. The tribal groups range from the Baro, whose fewer than 900 members barely represent a quorum, to the 144,000 members of the Wayúu.

According to Colombia's National Indigenous Organization (ONIC), at least 32 groups are at risk of extinction. Despite the passage of laws intended to safeguard their heritage, invasions by powerful oil, mining, and logging companies whittle away at indigenous lands. And the fight to control territory and Colombia's natural resources has put indigenous groups in the crossfire of armed conflict. ONIC has recorded the murders of more than 2,000 indigenous people since 1998. Members of the Emberá tribe, for example, live under constant threats by FARC (see sidebar p. 30) and the Águilas Negras (Black Eagles) paramilitary group. Few indigenous groups have escaped arbitrary killings and forcible recruitment by armed groups.

Meanwhile, the government's coca crop fumigation operation is contaminating the land and contributes to displacement from ancestral homelands and the disintegration of traditional ways. Indigenous peoples account for 7 percent of Colombia's three million internally displaced persons. The Awá people of Nariño, in the extreme southwest of the country, have been especially brutalized and suffer the highest rate of forced displacement in the country.

Most groups are caught in a cycle of poverty. Many indigenous communities practice destructive slash-and-burn agriculture, while others migrate to work seasonally as coffee pickers or plantation workers. Suffering high rates of malnutrition and politically disempowered on a national level, these groups are often suspicious of outsiders. Thousands of indigenous people struggle to survive in cities, estranged from their communities and prey to drugs, prostitution, and exploitation.

Cultural Faux Pas to Avoid

- **Don't wear shorts in cities if you're male. It's considered improper.**
- **Don't insult Colombian culture. Colombians are proud of their country and are especially touchy about past U.S. imperialism.**
- **Don't refer to the United States as America or yourself as an American. Colombians, like all Latin Americans, regard America as the continent; its inhabitants are all Americans. You should refer to the United States (Estados Unidos) as such, and to a U.S. citizen as an Estadounidense.**
- **Do maintain personal hygiene. Colombians appreciate cleanliness.**
- **Do feel free to use *piropos*, "compliments" meant to woo women; unless vulgar, Colombian women appreciate them.**
- **Don't denigrate drug lords such as Pablo Escobar, who is considered a hero by many poor Colombians.**

In 2009, Colombia endorsed the UN Declaration on Human Rights of Indigenous Peoples, reversing a controversial abstention in 2007. In recent years, the Constitutional Court has issued decrees to safeguard indigenous freedoms, adding strength to the Constitution of 1991, which recognized the rights of indigenous peoples to manage the political, economic, and administrative affairs of their traditional lands.

Government & Politics

Colombia is defined by the Constitution of 1991 as a democratic republic run by an elected president and a cabinet of ministers. Presidents may serve a maximum of two consecutive four-year terms (an attempt by Álvaro Uribe to change the constitution to permit a third term was overruled by the Supreme Court). Legislative power resides in the bicameral *congreso* (congress), which consists of a 102-member Senado (Senate), elected by direct vote, and 166-seat Camara de Representantes (House of Representatives), elected by proportional representation.

Members serve four-year terms and sit in the neoclassical Capitolio Nacional overlooking Plaza de Bolívar in Bogotá. Voting is universal for all citizens age 18 or above. Elections are held in March every four years and overseen by the National Electoral Council. The Supreme Court is one of four roughly co-equal bodies that oversee interpretation and implementation of laws; judges are elected by peers for eight-year terms.

Colombia is divided into 32 *departamentos* (departments) plus the *distrito capital* (Bogotá). The departments are overseen by an elected governor and regional assembly, and are broken into a total of 1,120 municipalities headed by mayors, as is the distrito capital. Five seats in congress are reserved for representatives of indigenous groups. Their legally recognized reserves take up nearly one-quarter of the national territory and are administered by semiautonomous *cabildos*—indigenous authorities—that coexist with Colombian state bodies.

Juan Manuel Santos

Inaugurated on August 7, 2010, as Colombia's president, Juan Manuel Santos comes from a political dynasty. His great-uncle, Eduardo Santos, was president 1938–1942; his cousin served as vice president 2002–2010; and his family owned Colombia's most important newspaper, *El Tiempo*, until its sale in 2007. Santos, who holds multiple degrees (including from Harvard and the London School of Economics), previously served in various ministerial posts, including defense minister (2006–2009) under President Álvaro Uribe. He oversaw the Colombian Army's controversial raid against the FARC camp in Ecuador in March 2008, and Operation Checkmate, the rescue of Ingrid Betancourt and 14 other hostages, in July 2008.

Parties & Issues: For a century and a half following the republic's independence from Spain, power alternated between the Conservative and Liberal parties. The former supported Simón Bolívar and his advocacy of strong centralized government allied to the Catholic Church; the Liberals followed Bolívar's rival, Francisco de Paula Santander, and decentralized secular government. Their sustained rivalry spawned two civil wars.

Today, Colombia has five major political parties, and more than a dozen smaller parties that are represented in congress and span the political spectrum. Despite the past century having been characterized by periods of violent conflict, the nation is now considered to

Popular President Juan Manuel Santos, elected in 2010, greets some of his supporters.

be a stable democracy with a strong respect for free elections and the institutions of a civilian government.

President Álvaro Uribe, elected president in 2002 as an independent Liberal, broke the two-party system that had ruled the country since 1958; his administration was a coalition of the three major parties. He ended his second term in 2010 with unprecedented approval ratings. Uribe was succeeded by his defense minister, Juan Manuel Santos, of the Liberal Party, who received 69 percent of the vote in the June 2010 runoff election against eccentric former Bogotá mayor Antanas Mockus, of the centrist Green Party.

The past two decades have witnessed a significant decrease in violent defense of sectarian party affiliations. But government is plagued by corruption. Scores of lawmakers have been investigated and indicted for "parapolitics"—involvement with vote-buying paramilitary narco-traffickers. In recent years, the Autodefensas Unidas de Colombia (AUC, or United Self-Defense Forces of Colombia)—an umbrella of right-wing paramilitary groups that controlled pockets of the country—has demobilized but morphed into armed bandit groups.

Even so, President Juan Manuel Santos promised to continue the Uribe administration's fight to eradicate corruption and stamp out widespread murders and human rights abuses by Colombia's security forces. His first year in office was marred by a severe uptick in FARC attacks, followed by a year of successful counterstrikes, culminating in November 2011 with the killing of FARC leader Guillermo León Sáenz. Santos returned to office in 2014 dedicated to advancing negotiations with FARC to end the armed conflict, earning the bitter opposition of Uribe. Colombia retains an active military and heavily armed police, which together number about 250,000 uniformed personnel and consume about 6 percent of the national budget. Military service is compulsory. ■

History of Colombia

Although Christopher Columbus (1451–1506) never set eyes on the land named for him, his chancing upon the Americas in 1492 set in motion a convoy of conquistadores seeking El Dorado. Spain quickly asserted sovereignty over the land, beginning a bitter history of upheavals lasting five centuries. Following independence in 1810, the republic suffered a century and a half of turmoil and civil war. In recent years, Colombia has risen above its troubled past.

First Peoples

Humans may have occupied the region we know today as Colombia as early as 12,000 years ago following the first crossing by hominids of the Bering Strait around 40,000 B.C. More than two million indigenous peoples are thought to have inhabited the region at the time of the Spanish conquest. Separated by distance and daunting terrain, scores of diverse tribes evolved distinct languages and cultural forms. They varied from nomadic hunter-gatherer groups to stratified agricultural chiefdoms.

Dozens of archaeological sites also have been uncovered throughout the region, although no massive pyramids and few major cities have been unearthed, and most sites date back no more than 2,000 years. An exception is Teyuna—better known today as Ciudad Perdida (Lost City)—founded around A.D. 800, high in the Sierra Nevada de Santa Marta, by the Tayrona of northern Colombia.

The indigenous people never unified to form kingdoms or empires such as those of the Inca of Peru or the Maya of Mesoamerica.

The indigenous people never unified to form kingdoms or empires such as those of the Inca of Peru or the Maya of Mesoamerica. Nonetheless, the Muisca, who settled the Cordillera Oriental of modern-day Cundinamarca, Boyacá, and Santander, evolved one of the most complex sociopolitical structures of the Americas.

The Muisca: The Muisca comprised two tribal confederations, called *cacicazgos:* Hunza in the north, around today's Tunja, and the larger, more powerful Bacatá, with its capital in today's Bogotá. Each tribe was headed by a *cacique* (chieftain) who ruled over competing areas; tribes warred with each other for control of the most productive land. They lived in circular huts constructed on pole frames atop stone bases, with walls of cane and roofs of thatched palm, similar to those in which many of their Amazonian descendants live today.

The Muisca (like the Tayrona, they spoke Chibcha) were skilled weavers who also developed sophisticated irrigation and used salt, emeralds, and gold as currency for trade with neighboring regions. They were also the most masterful of pre-Columbian goldsmiths. They shaped animal figurines and decorative body items, such as bracelets, pendants, and chest plates, reserved for the use of caciques, who were buried with their wives, servants, and possessions when they died. Among the stunning gold Muisca items to be seen in Bogotá's Museo del Oro is the "Balsa Muisca"—a 19-inch-long (48 cm) depiction of a raft bearing a cacique and 12 attendants performing an initiation ceremony that gave rise to the legend of El Dorado.

Colombia is also speckled with giant stone statues chiseled with scowling faces, standing guard outside ancient tombs. Parque Arqueológico Nacional de San Agustín, near San Agustín in Huila Department, and Parque Arqueológico Nacional Tierradentro, near Popayán, protect the greatest concentrations, which date from between A.D. 500 and 1300. Little is known about the mysterious tribe that created the statues and hypogea. Meanwhile, the Chibcha tribes of the eastern lowlands were being supplanted by warlike Caribs on the eve of the Spanish invasion.

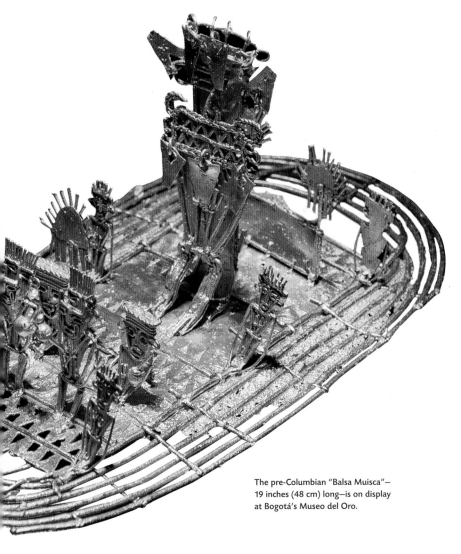

The pre-Columbian "Balsa Muisca"— 19 inches (48 cm) long—is on display at Bogotá's Museo del Oro.

The Arrival of the Spanish

The Caribbean cultures were the first to experience the brutality of early Spanish conquistadores, who enacted a policy of extermination. The first European to sight Colombia was Spanish explorer Juan de la Cosa (1460–1509), who landed in 1499 at Cabo de la Vela (Cape of Sails), at the tip of La Guajira Peninsula. During the next two years, de la Cosa, accompanied by Rodrigo de Bastidas (1460–1527) and Vasco Núñez de Balboa (1475–1519), explored the Caribbean coast of present-day Colombia and Panama. (In 1502, Christopher Columbus also explored the coast of Panama during his fourth and final voyage to the New World). The first attempt at settlement—San Sebastián de Urabá—founded by Alonso de Ojeda (1466–1515) in 1508, in the Golfo de Urabó, was short-lived; so, too, was Santa María la Antigua del Darién, founded the following year by Bastidas and Balboa.

Francisco Pizarro (1475–1541)

Destruction of Local Culture: The Spaniards' arrival spelled doom for the region's indigenous peoples, who greeted the *arrivistes* while adorned in their finest gold bracelets, earrings, and chest plates. The Spanish conquistadores were not on a holy mission: They were compelled by a quest for riches, and hastened their cultural lessons with the musket and cutlass. Thus began the country's long, often brutal colonial history. When, in 1509, Juan de la Cosa landed an expedition near today's Cartagena to take possession as governor of Nueva Andalucía (the territory between the gulfs of Urabá and Maracaibo), he met fierce resistance by natives. De la Cosa was killed by poison-tipped arrows; supposedly only Alonso de Ojeda and one other man survived.

On September 25, 1513, Balboa crossed the Panamanian isthmus and became the first European to catch sight of the Pacific Ocean—clad in armor, Balboa famously waded into the ocean (which he named Mar del Sur, Southern Sea) to claim it for Spain. The momentous discovery positioned Panama as a staging point for the conquest of the Pacific Americas, followed by the founding of Santa Marta (1525) and Cartagena de Indias (1533), which became strategic cities for rapid subjugation and colonization of Colombia's interior via the Cauca and Magdalena Rivers. The ensuing decades were marked by a brutal tyranny and exploitation. Entire indigenous communities were put to the sword, while others were enslaved to extract gold from the mountains and jungles. Whole tribes withered and died under the intolerable hardships of forced labor. European diseases—smallpox, measles, tuberculosis—against which they had no resistance hastened their demise. Many groups fought long bitter struggles against the Spanish but gradually retreated into the thickly forested mountains and coastal plains.

Colonial Era

After the conquest of Peru by Francisco Pizarro (1475–1541) in 1532, the plundered wealth of the Inca began filling the vaults of Panama City and Cartagena—founded the following year by Pedro de Heredia (1520–1554). In 1536, an expedition led by

Gonzalo Jiménez de Quesada (1496–1579) navigated the Magdalena Valley and entered the Muisca region. Taking advantage of the rivalry between Hunza and Bacatá, the Spanish soon conquered the Muisca, and on August 6, 1538, Santa Fé de Bacatá (present-day Bogotá) was established. Tales of the Muisca's initiation ceremonies at Guatavita (in which vast quantities of gold were tossed in the lake) rapidly evolved into the legend of El Dorado. An obsession with finding the fabled hidden city of gold fostered rapid colonization throughout the region. Nikolaus Federmann (1505–1546) explored the eastern plains and Cordillera Oriental from Venezuela, while Sebastián de Belalcázar (1479–1551) ventured north from Peru and established the cities of Popayán and Santiago de Cali (today's Cali).

In 1550, Bogotá became the seat of the Real Audiencia, which governed Nuevo Reino de Granada (New Kingdom of Granada), comprising modern Colombia, Ecuador, Panama, and Venezuela. Although relatively isolated, the city became one of the main centers of Spanish colonial power. Meanwhile, Cartagena grew as the chief entrepôt for the looting of the Muisca and Inca cultures. Unimaginable quantities of silver, gold, and emeralds were transported north by river and mule for shipment to Spain.

The vast wealth drew the larcenous attention of pirates–cold-hearted cut-throats capable of astoundingly inhumane deeds. English slave trader turned pirate Sir Francis Drake (1540–1596) ransacked Cartagena in 1586. Thereafter, Cartagena gained fortifications. The Spanish also developed a flotilla system to guard the creaking treasure ships, with one galleon for every ten merchant vessels.

Seeds of Long-lasting Conflict:

In 1717, the Virreinato de Nueva Granada (Viceroyalty of New Granada) superseded Nuevo Reino de Granada and incorporated additional territory. However, difficulties of communication throughout the vast entity granted de facto autonomy to subordinate political bodies whose rivalries contributed to regional factionalism that erupted in frequent violence. Napoleon Bonaparte's (1769–1821) occupation of Spain in 1808 led, in 1810, to declarations of independence by cities and regions throughout the Virreinato. First, Valledupar, then Cali, Cartagena, Santa Marta, and other cities all formed their own juntas (ruling bodies), which declared themselves sovereign and resisted centralist efforts by Bogotá. It was a time of confusion. The period became known as the Patria Boba (Foolish Fatherland) as battles raged between federalist, centralist, and royalist interests.

In 1811, the province of Bogotá transformed itself into a state—Cundinamarca—loyal

Treasure Routes

Between 1566 and 1790, twice-yearly treasure fleets *(flotas de indias)* arrived in Cartagena following a ten-week journey from Spain. Scores of galleons laden with supplies, goods, and emigrants converged on Cartagena and split into the two flotas, bound respectively for Portobelo and Veracruz, while couriers were sent ahead to inform the king's agents and merchants of the fleets' impending arrival. Armies of clerics and royal accountants arrived alongside soldiers employed to guard mountains of gold, silver, and emeralds piled high in the streets. Merchants held massive trade fairs. The ships returned to Spain via Havana, guarded by naval escort and groaning from the weight of their bullion. Storms sank far more vessels than were lost to pirates.

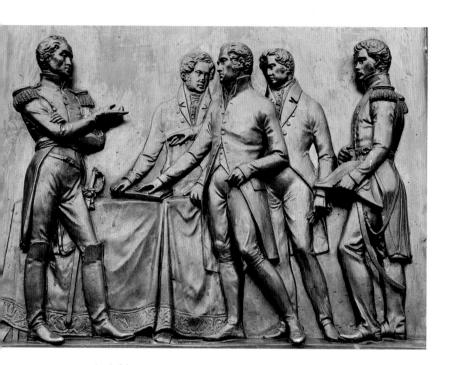

A relief depicts representatives meeting at the Congress of the United Provinces.

to the Spanish throne. Delegates from the competing regions met under the Congress of the United Provinces, officially known as Juntas de Gobiernos Provinciales. Their proposed confederation was rejected by Bogotá. Declarations of independence by various provinces sparked civil wars in 1812 and 1814. The stillborn nation was too fractured to resist when, in 1815, Spanish troops arrived and quickly retook New Granada.

Independence

The independence movement was thereafter led by Venezuelans Simón Bolívar (1783–1830) and Francisco de Paula Santander (1792–1840). After retaking Caracas in 1814, Simón Bolívar—now called El Libertador (The Liberator)—commanded forces of the United Provinces. His campaign culminated at the Battle of Puente de Boyacá on August 7, 1819, after which Bolívar swiftly secured defining victories in Ecuador and Venezuela. On September 7, 1821, he was named president of Gran Colombia, with Santander as vice president. However, regional jealousies and differences resisted Bolívar's unification efforts. In 1826, Bolívar initiated an ultimately unsuccessful congress to create a Pan-American union of all the independent republics. Gran Colombia dissolved in 1830, and Bolívar resigned.

Thereafter, Panama proclaimed independence, but neighboring Colombia—then called Nueva Grenada—forced it to reunite, with Panama becoming one among Colombia's many provinces (the union was uneasy, however, and three attempts to sever the union were violently suppressed). Meanwhile, Venezuela, Peru, and Ecuador formed their own republican governments. Colombia and Peru briefly warred over territorial rights, while the country itself was riven by internal uprisings. Eventually the republic dissolved in 1858, replaced by a brief confederation of sovereign provinces. Civil war led to another attempt, in 1863, to unite the factions as the Estados Unidos de Colombia (United States of Colombia), modeled on the United States. The strife-ridden entity finally adopted its current name, the Republic of Colombia, in 1886.

Thousand Days War: Politics of the era were dominated by the Conservative Party (founded by Bolívar), which supported a strong central government in hand with the Catholic Church, and the Liberal Party (founded by Santander), which believed in secular, decentralized government. In 1899, their bitter and intractable rivalry ignited the Thousand Days War (1899–1902), which claimed an estimated 100,000 lives and ended in a Conservative Party victory.

Meanwhile, the United States, for whom a shortcut between the seas had become crucial to its evolving naval power, had grown determined to build a canal. Once it settled on a route across the province of Panama, the United States was determined to bully the Colombian government into negotiating a canal treaty on its own terms. When a weakened Colombia refused to agree to Uncle Sam's terms, a plot was hatched to sever the province. On November 3, 1903, Panama declared independence. The United States instantly recognized the breakaway republic. On May 4, 1904, the French-owned assets in Panama were handed over to the United States, and the Stars and Stripes was raised—the beginning of a long animosity between a chagrined Colombia and the United States.

The 20th Century

The Conservatives held office until 1930, when the Liberals were returned to power. Colombia remained plagued by poverty and social problems. The gains of limited economic prosperity accrued to a relatively small white minority. Liberal reforms failed to resolve the country's problems. In 1948, charismatic Liberal leader Jorge Eliécer Gaitán (1903–1948) ran for the presidency as a champion of the people. On April 9, 1948, he was assassinated in Bogotá on the eve of the Tenth Pan-American Conference, in which heads of states had gathered to sign the founding charter of the Organization of American States. Tens of thousands were swept up as the city erupted in a wave of unbridled looting and violent mayhem. The Palacio de Justicia, the historic San Carlos palace, and scores of schools, churches, and other important buildings went up in flames and more than 3,000 people were killed in the fatal day known as Bogotazo.

> After retaking Caracas in 1814, Simón Bolívar—now called El Libertador (The Liberator)—commanded forces of the United Provinces.

La Violencia: The maelstrom overcame Cali, Medellín, and soon the entire country, which was ripped apart by the polarizing fault line in Colombian society. A decade-long strife—La Violencia (The Time of Violence)—ensued as peasant guerrilla groups, self-defense groups, and party-affiliated death squads (pejoratively called *bandoleros*) tortured, murdered, and raped. The brutality was unprecedented. Many people were killed with machetes and other crude implements, and their bodies mutilated in unimaginably cruel ways. More than 300,000 people died in the partisan violence. Millions more abandoned the countryside for the relative safety of cities.

In 1953, the army under Gen. Gustavo Rojas Pinilla (1953–1957) toppled the authoritarian Conservative government of Laureano Gómez in an attempt to end the violence, which endured through 1958. Although Roja's repressive operations against bandoleros (including amnesty for groups that demobilized) succeeded, he was overthrown by military dissidents on May 10, 1957, following a popular call for his ouster, and civilian rule was restored. The Conservatives and Liberals agreed to a 15-year bipartisan coalition known as the Frente Nacional (National Front), in which the presidency was to alternate between the parties every four years and government posts would be shared.

Rise of Guerrilla Movements: The National Front attempted to address the urgent social problems and underdevelopment that had fueled La Violencia. Well-meaning efforts to institute far-reaching agrarian and other economic reforms accelerated following the Cuban Revolution in 1959. The United States, seeking to preempt communist uprisings throughout South America, initiated a massive economic aid program under the Alliance for Progress, which called for far-reaching reforms, notably in inimical land-tenure arrangements. Success proved chimerical; the vested Conservative interests were too entrenched, allowing serious problems to fester. In the ensuing two decades, various administrations shifted their efforts to vain attempts to suppress the radical left-wing rural insurgencies undermining the social, economic, and political system, while the root causes fueling the insurgencies went unresolved.

Fidel Castro's example in Cuba was instrumental in the metamorphosis of Colombia's partisan rural violence into a more radical left-wing form. In 1959, the founding of the revolutionary Movimiento Obrero Estudiantil Campesino (Peasant Student Workers Movement), or MOEC, marked the beginning of communist guerrilla insurgency in Colombia. Three years later, MOEC merged into the nascent Ejército de Liberación Nacional (National Liberation Army, ELN), a Cuban-trained Marxist guerrilla group. Other peasant-based guerrilla groups born during La Violencia had established independent communist

ABC of Extremists

AUC (Autodefensas Unidas de Colombia). Formed in 1997, United Self-Defence Forces of Colombia is a group of right-wing paramilitary factions funded by drug cartels and wealthy landowners. It has formally disbanded, but groups still exist.

ELN (Ejército de Liberación Nacional). The left-wing National Liberation Army derives its inspiration from the Cuban Revolution. Its numbers have fallen from about 4,000 to less than 2,000. It often wars against FARC, but there has been a recent truce between the two groups.

FARC (Fuerzas Armadas Revolucionarias de Colombia). Founded in 1964, the Marxist Revolutionary Armed Forces of Colombia was once the largest and wealthiest rebel group. It controls large swathes of territory and earns millions of dollars a year by taxing cocaine transactions in its territory. Its leader was killed in October 2011. Its numbers have dropped from about 35,000 in 2002 to about 8,000–10,000 today.

M-19 (Movimiento 19 de Abril). The April 19 Movement laid down its arms and renounced armed struggle in 1990. Today, it is a political party espousing nationalist revolutionary socialism.

enclaves in remote mountain valleys of Marquetalia and Sumapaz. In 1964, the Colombian National Army attacked the bases as part of Plan LASO (Latin American Security Operation), a U.S. military initiative to crush leftist rebels. From the ashes arose a new rural-based group: the Marxist-inspired Fuerzas Armadas Revolucionarias de Colombia (Revolutionary Armed Forces of Colombia, FARC), which rapidly rose to preeminence.

In 1974, claims of fraud in the final National Front presidential election—won by Misael Pastrana (1970–1974)—led to the formation of a nationalist urban guerrilla group: Movimiento 19 de Abril (April 19 Movement, M-19). Whereas ELN and FARC initially were limited to small-scale confrontations in rural regions, M-19 enacted a series of daring attacks in Bogotá. On February 27, 1980, for example, it stormed the Dominican Republic Embassy during a cocktail party and seized as hostages 14 ambassadors, including the ambassador of the United States.

Drug Cartels: The 1970s witnessed the rise of another scourge, as Colombia's marijuana smugglers graduated to trafficking in cocaine to feed a new worldwide demand. The vast profits led to a massive increase in domestic production of coca. By the 1980s, producers and traffickers had evolved into powerful criminal cartels headed by ruthless kingpins based in Cali and Medellín. Chief among them was Pablo Escobar (1949–1993), billionaire head of the Medellín cartel—he was even elected to the Congress of Colombia in 1982, having successfully cultivated a Robin Hood image by doling out millions to the poor. U.S. pressure to extradite Escobar and other cartel bosses led to a wave of intimidation and assassination. The Medellín cartel murdered hundreds of journalists, judges, police, and politicians, including Justice Minister Rodrigo Lara Bonilla (1946–1984). Thousands of others were bought off through a policy of *plata o plomo* (silver or lead). By the early 1980s, the cartels virtually controlled the country.

> **The National Front attempted to address the urgent social problems and underdevelopment that had fueled La Violencia.**

FARC also gradually morphed into a militarized narco-terrorist organization. It grew wealthy based on kidnapping, extortion, and control of cocaine production on remote rural terrain. By 1982, FARC was powerful enough to stage large-scale attacks on Colombian troops. That year it adopted a new strategy. Seizing power militarily replaced that of building conditions for mass insurrection. FARC began closing in on major cities. The leftist groups also struck at the drug cartels, unleashing another twist to the surreal setting. When, in 1981, M-19 kidnapped the sister of Medellín cartel co-founder Jorge Luis Ochoa, the cartel founded the Muerte a Secuestradores (Death to Kidnappers) death squad—a precursor to the many right-wing paramilitary groups that soon emerged to protect the interests of wealthy landowners and entrepreneurs against left-wing guerrillas.

Negotiating With Rebels: The Conservative Belisario Betancur Cuartas (1923–) administration (1982–1986) pursued high-profile negotiations with M-19 and FARC, as a result of which the Unión Patriótica (Patriotic Union) was set up to permit leftists to participate in government. Elements of Colombia's security forces, however, refused to honor a cease-fire, and many party candidates were murdered by rightists. In response, on November 6, 1985, 35 M-19 guerrillas stormed Bogotá's

Palace of Justice and took 300 lawyers and judges hostage. Eleven of the country's 21 Supreme Court justices were among more than 100 people killed in the battle, in which the building and key criminal records were destroyed by fire. Shortly after, M-19 demobilized and its leaders were pardoned; it thereafter became a nonviolent political party. The peace accords with FARC, meanwhile, eventually crumbled.

The assassination of presidential candidate Luis Carlos Galán (1943–1989) by Pablo Escobar's hit men, and the bombing in 1989 of Avianca Flight 203 in an attempt to kill presidential candidate César Gaviria Trujillo, prompted a new crackdown on drug lords. Offered leniency, Escobar surrendered in 1991 and was confined to a luxurious private prison from where he maintained his criminal enterprise. Believing that the government intended to extradite him, he escaped and in 1993 was hunted down and killed on December 2, 1993. (More than 300 of Escobar's associates were later slain by a vigilante group called Los Pepes—People Persecuted by Pablo Escobar.) The highly sophisticated Cali cartel filled the vacuum left by the end of Escobar's empire. It enjoyed close ties with high government and banking officials before being eradicated in 1995.

> **President Uribe is credited with transforming Colombia from a guerrilla-infested narco-state into a stable democracy.**

The New Millennium

On the eve of the new century, Colombia was on the verge of becoming a failed state. FARC controlled an area the size of France, had 16,000 combatants, and had begun kidnapping soldiers and politicians. An ill-fated attempt at appeasement by President André Pastrana (1998–2002) ceded FARC de facto control of a demilitarized zone in Caguán. Pastrana also initiated Plan Colombia, an effort to empower democratic institutions, stimulate the Colombian economy, and combat endemic violence and drug trafficking. A $1.3 billion U.S. military aid package was earmarked for counternarcotics training and coca eradication. The controversial aid program strengthened right-wing death squads, supported by paramilitary sympathizers within the armed forces. Ostensibly operating as counterinsurgency forces, but financed by cocaine earnings, the paramilitary groups organized into the Autodefensas Unidas de Colombia (United Self-Defense Forces of Colombia, AUC), headquartered in Monteria.

In 2002, newly elected President Álvaro Uribe (1952–)—who ran as an independent Liberal candidate and whose own father was kidnapped and killed by FARC—launched a get-tough campaign, Plan Patriota, to crush the AUC, ELN, and FARC. Uribe's plan for democratic security pushed back the guerrillas from around Bogotá and seized back huge swathes of territory, while most paramilitary units were disbanded. Annual murder rates in Bogotá and Medellín have since fallen below those of Washington, D.C. Colombians have been able to take to the roads again for the first time in years. Uribe's popularity was boosted on July 2, 2008, when former Colombian presidential candidate Ingrid Betancourt (1961–) and 14 fellow hostages were rescued by the Colombian Army (Betancourt was captured in 2002 by FARC and held for six brutal years).

President Uribe is credited with transforming Colombia from a guerrilla-infested narco-state into a stable democracy. He led several free-trade agreements, fought corruption, and vastly increased social spending. He campaigned successfully to get the constitution altered,

James Rodriguez and the Colombia team thrilled fans and neutrals alike at the 2014 FIFA World Cup.

permitting him to serve a second term, but failed in a bid to rewrite the constitution to allow a third term. Uribe left office on May 30, 2010, with astronomic approval ratings (since tarnished by revelations of extrajudicial procedures). His successor, former defense minister Juan Manuel Santos (1951–), vowed to continue Uribe's policies, including a hard-line approach to guerrillas, while simultaneously negotiating with FARC to end their armed struggle. Santos also worked to reestablish diplomatic ties with Venezuela and to resolve many of Colombia's urgent social and economic problems affecting the poor. In 2011, he enacted the Law of Victims to compensate victims of the violence. ∎

Food & Drink

Colombia has long been a cultural crossroads, and the fusion of international flavors is reflected in the restaurant scene. Every town has its Chinese restaurant, South American *parrillada* (steak house), and pizzeria. Hip fusion restaurants abound in Bogotá, Cali, and Medellín, which compete with international cities around the world for the variety and quality of their cuisines. And regional varieties honor indigenous and peasant traditions that make the most of this fertile land.

Blood sausage, a traditional Colombian dish, is served at Cali's La Galería market.

Flavorful native cuisine melds indigenous, Spanish, and African influences into a mouth-watering mélange of dishes defining *comida criolla*—creole food—which differs between the uplands and coast. The dish most associated with the country is *bandeja paisa*, a hearty Antioquian dish made with various meats, black beans, rice, fried eggs, plantains, and avocado.

Colombians are big on meats and tend to shun green vegetables in favor of starch. They're fond of roast pork and *patacón con puerco*, pork with banana-like plantain. *Pollo asado* (roast chicken) is a staple. *Bistec* (steak) is also popular. In *fritanga*, a smorgasbord barbecue of meats and offal are served with *arepas*—unleavened corn patties—a streetside staple. In Los Llanos, barbecued meat is common. *Arroz con pollo*

(rice and chicken) is another favorite, often served with peas or crumbled boiled egg yolk at breakfast. More often, Colombia's breakfast includes thick arepas with fresh cheese, roast meats, and eggs.

Seafood abounds in Colombia, notably on the Caribbean and Pacific coasts. Almost every seafood restaurant features ceviche, raw fish marinated with chopped onions and peppers. The fish of choice is *róbalo* (sea bass), often served with garlic; dorado (mahimahi) and *pargo* (snapper) are also favored. The Caribbean coast simmers its lobster, shrimp, and other seafood in special spices and coconut milk. Trout is a local delicacy in the highland, as are freshwater fish such as *amarillo* in the Amazon. During bullfighting season *(Jan.–Feb.)*, many local restaurants offer specials of paella and sangria—paeans to the nation's Spanish heritage.

Colombians' use of corn reflects indigenous traditions, as in *tamal,* a cornmeal pastry stuffed with chicken or pork stewed with peppers, garlic, and onions, then wrapped in a banana leaf and boiled.

Many locals have a weakness for sweets, such as *arequipe,* or *dulce de leche,* made of boiled and sweetened condensed milk. Milk is also used in *arroz con leche* (sweetened rice with milk, sugar, and cinnamon) and flan.

Other Dishes

Ajiaco, a typical Andean soup made of corn, chicken, and potatoes, with *guasca* (a local herb), is one of the local favorites. Another regional speciality is *sancocho,* soup that may contain corn, yucca, and any other number of vegetables depending on the locale. Or try *buñuelos,* fried round cheese fritters.

Regional markets are cornucopias of tropical fruits, such as mangos, melons, papayas, pineapples, and strawberries. These, and local favorites such as *maracuyá* (passion fruit) and *guanábana* (soursop), find their way into *batidos,* iced shakes made with water or milk. *Agua de pipa* from a green coconut is the perfect pick-me-up on hot days, as is *suero,* a sweet-and-sour yogurt drink introduced by Arab immigrants 200 years ago. Colombia's lager-style brews (see sidebar p. 84) are also perfectly suited to the tropical climate when served chilled.

Drinks

The urban working man's drink is *aguardiente,* a harsh anise-flavored sugarcane liquor, up to 30 percent proof. The country's prize rums are light-bodied and smooth in flavor, and often mixed with sugar, lemon, *panela* (raw cane sugar), and boiling water to make *canelazo,* a hot alcoholic beverage of the Andes.

Colombia's arabica coffee is world class, and individual labels regularly make the top-ten list of international coffee critics. Ironically, Colombians—who prefer hot chocolate—are not big coffee drinkers and like it weak, American style, or thick and heavily sugared, espresso style.

EXPERIENCE: Colombian Cooking Classes

Colombia's menu of regional cuisines is impressive. Add to that its fertility and abundance, and the imagination of chefs who meld globe-spanning influences with traditional native Colombian ingredients. The result is a potpourri of exotic flavors as befits dedicated gourmands.

Take home more than mere memories of delicious *bandeja paisa* and *sancocho* (traditional Colombian dishes) by signing up for cooking classes.

In San Andrés, **Lucy Trigidia Chow Robinson** *(tel 57-8/513-2233, e-mail: lucy trgidia@yahoo.com)* hosts cooking classes focused on Afro-Caribbean dishes, such as *rondón*—a coconut-milk stew with tubers and fish or meat. You even go shopping for ingredients at local markets.

In Cartagena, **Hotel Anandá** *(Calle del Cuartel #36-77, Cartagena, tel 57-5/664-4452, anandacartagena.com)* hosts cooking classes. At **La Cevichería** *(Calle Stuart #7, Cartagena, tel 5/664-5255, lacevicheria cartagena.com),* owner Jorge Escandon offers culinary tours that include cooking classes. The head chef of **Hotel LM** *(Calle de la Mantilla #3-56, Cartagena, tel 57-5/664-9100, hotel-lm.com)* also teaches in an interactive kitchen.

The following culinary schools offer more formal courses, in Spanish:
Gato Dumas Colegio de Cocineros
Cra. 18 #89-39 Chicó, Bogotá, tel 57-1/610-2593, gatodumas.com
Verde Oliva Academia de Cocina
Calle 102 #14A–40, Bogotá, tel 57-1/257-7909, academiaverdeoliva.com.

Land & Landscape

Colombia packs a potpourri of landscapes and climates into its 439,737 square miles (1,138,914 sq km). Occupying the northwest corner of South America, at the juncture with Panama, the country also borders Venezuela, Brazil, Ecuador, and Peru. Terrain varies from coral-encrusted shorelines and lush rain forests to glacier-capped volcanic peaks. Mists sift through coffee country at mid-elevation, and Andean mountains appear as dazzling as movie creations.

Colombia comprises two great territorial zones. The eastern half is a vast and relatively flat extension of the Amazon Basin. The western half is dominated by the Andes Mountains, which splinter into three ranges, the product of geological upheavals caused by the jostling of three tectonic plates: the Caribbean, Nazca, and South American plates.

Despite Colombia's location in the tropics, extremes of elevation spawn a profusion of microclimates. The smothering heat of the lowlands contrasts with the crisp cool of the highlands and freezing nights of the upper Andes. In general, there are two seasons: dry *(la sequía)* and wet *(época de lluvia)*, though the nation is a patchwork of variations.

About 12 percent of Colombia is sheltered in 56 national parks and reserves comprising 52,517 square miles (136,017 sq km). Several marine parks ring islands that stud the ocean close to shore, some surrounded by coral reefs.

The smothering heat of the lowlands contrasts with the crisp cool of the highlands and freezing nights of the upper Andes.

The Colombian government has long been an advocate of ecological preservation. Even so, during the past century, swathes of forest have disappeared for logging, cattle ranching, and slash-and-burn agriculture. The Río Magdalena Valley has lost 50 percent of its forest, and the "green lung" of the Amazon is being felled to make way for the coca plant.

Caribbean Lowlands

The Caribbean lowlands extend east from the Golfo de Urabá to the Cordillera Central. The blunt northern face of the Cordillera Central rises sheer to the south. Between coast and mountain, the flatlands are pitted with lakes and broken into a puzzle by myriad rivers. The colonial city of Mompox sits in the center of the area. Fortresses still guard the entrance to the ancient port of Cartagena, which remains a commerce center, along with Barranquilla (Colombia's fourth largest city) and Santa Marta (Colombia's equivalent of Rio de Janeiro).

Many beautiful beaches line Parque Nacional Corales del Rosario y de San Bernardo and Parque Nacional Natural Tayrona. Tayrona's sands are hemmed against a backdrop of lush mountains—the Sierra Nevada de Santa Marta, clawing skyward to 18,947 feet (5,775 m) atop Pico Cristóbal Colón, Colombia's highest peak.

Although enfolded by sea, this is Colombia's dry quarter. Cacti punctuate the landscape, studded at its tip by Parque Nacional Natural Serranía de Macuira, an island of dwarf cloud forest. Marine turtles crawl ashore to lay eggs on beaches.

Thermal cascades tumble down the Cordillera Occidental near Pereira.

Andean Highlands

Marching north into Colombia from Ecuador, the Andes split into the Cordillera Occidental, Cordillera Central, and Cordillera Oriental. Broken into peaks and troughs, these rugged chains are the setting for Colombia's three major cities: Bogotá, Cali, and Medellín. Rising to 9,840 feet (2,999 m), the relatively low Cordillera Occidental is separated from the Cordillera Central by the Valle de Cauca. The Río Cauca flows north between the two cordilleras in a deep, intensely farmed gorge. Higher up, mid-elevation slopes are clad in rows of coffee. The Eje Cafetero is sprinkled with alpine towns beneath volcanoes that stud the towering 500-mile-long (800 km) Cordillera Central. Rising 112 miles (180 km) north of the Ecuadorian border, the 994-mile-long (1,600 km) Río Magdalena cleaves the Cordillera Central and Cordillera Oriental as if with an ax. The Cordillera Oriental—longest and widest of the chains—extends almost the full length of Colombia. The cordillera peaks at 17,487 feet (5,330 m) in Parque Nacional Natural El Cocuy.

Natural Highs: Avoiding Altitude Sickness

When traveling in Colombia, you're apt to be in higher elevations than you're used to. The higher you climb, the less oxygen is in the air. Above about 8,000 feet (2,438 m), you could become sick. Early signs of altitude illness are headache, dizziness, lethargy, nausea, and trouble sleeping.

So, if you're heading into Colombia's mountains, here's how you can avoid potentially lethal high-altitude illness:
• Take your time traveling to the higher altitudes to let your body adjust to lower levels of oxygen.
• Drink lots of water plus coca tea; also avoid coffee and alcohol.
• Climb high, sleep low (at least 1,000 feet/ 300 m below where you hike).
• Take it easy. Don't exert yourself.

Pacific Zone

The western slopes of the Cordillera Occidental fall to coastal plains that unfurl inland like a great green carpet—a sparsely inhabited world of jungle and swamp. Colombia's wettest region stretches 450 miles (724 km) north–south, yet barely reaching 75 miles (121 km) wide. This lowland belt is home to 3 percent of Colombia's population.

In the far north, the serrated shore of Chocó Department is backed by the Serranía del Baudó, a low mountain range tight up to the coast. Beaches like ribbons of silver lamé unspool along the wild shoreline. The Serranía del Baudó and the Cordillera Occidental are located on the cusp of a huge lowland basin drained by the Río Atrato, which snakes north to the Golfo de Urabá and is dotted with remote settlements. The network of rain forest and rivers and swamps extends north to the Darién gap, the frontier between Colombia and Panama. The rivers form liquid highways for communities that live under threat of attack by FARC and other extremist groups.

South of Buenaventura, the shore is thick with mangroves forming a maze that comprises the largest such complex in South America. Parque Nacional Natural Sanquianga protects 309 square miles (800 sq km) of mangroves, swamps, and bamboo forests.

Los Llanos

Los Llanos (the plains) extend east from the foot of the Cordillera Oriental in a seemingly endless sea of rolling prairies and seasonally flooded grasslands, which take up

Frailejónes **thrive on the bitterly cold upper slopes of Parque Nacional Natural El Cocuy.**

one-quarter of the national territory. The region, a huge saucer-shaped depression extending north into Venezuela, is a vast floodplain of the mighty Orinoco, which forms part of the border between the two countries. Flat and mostly treeless, the region is exposed to the northeast trade winds, whose desiccating effect from December to April is countered from May to November by torrential rains.

The few settlements concentrate close to the Andean foothills. The expansion of population eastward is a recent phenomenon, and settlements—sleepy cowboy towns—lie along the numerous rivers that snake east in lazy curls to the Orinoco. The term *llaneros* (plainsmen) is synonymous with cowboys, and Los Llanos is cattle country roamed by millions of heads of cattle on Texan-scale estates. Nonetheless, commercial agriculture has gained a grip as wetlands have been drained for rice and other crops. Los Llanos is renowned for its swamp-based wildlife.

Amazon Basin

Covering an area of 156,000 square miles (404,000 sq km), equal to 35 percent of Colombia's territory, the sparsely populated Amazonía region makes up the nation's southeast. The region is divided into two zones. To the west, a huge plateau known as the *piedemonte* extends east of the Andes. Except for a single road running parallel to the mountains, the region is virtually uninhabited and FARC controls much of it. Nonetheless, Parque Nacional Natural Amacayacu and Parque Nacional Natural La Paya have facilities for those wishing to explore a mosaic of wetland and forest.

East of the piedemonte is the Amazon proper, where rain is almost a daily occurrence. In the spongy heat, the vegetation is as luxuriant as anywhere on Earth. Giant *cedro* trees tower 100 feet (30 m) in the air, and orchid species are counted in the thousands. Cloaked in a dozen shades of green, the dense Amazon forest is invisible from the air through the canopy. There are no roads, just airstrips and river transport.

Home to dozens of indigenous tribes, the Amazonía region also harbors a mind-boggling array of birdlife and wildlife species. Much of the jungle is protected within Parque Nacional Natural Amacayuca. ■

Flora & Fauna

Colombia is a pivotal region at the apex of the two Americas. Profuse in wildlife, the environment is a veritable tropical Eden–a cornucopia of biodiversity. With its wild extremes of terrain and microclimates, Colombia boasts more than a dozen distinct ecological zones, from coastal mangrove forests and swampy wetlands to polar deserts and desert-dry deciduous forests.

Tropical Greenhouse

Acre for acre, Colombia—one of the world's 17 megadiverse countries—is as rich in species as anywhere in the world. The country hosts more than 55,000 known plant species, second only to Brazil, including the world's highest species endemism. Much of Colombia is steeped in humidity and near-constant high

Colombia's tropical lowland rain forests steep in heat and humidity.

temperatures, with the sun overhead throughout the year. Combined with profuse rainfall that tops a drenching 200 inches (500 cm) in many places, the heat fuels luxuriant growth.

The country is rich in orchid species: More than 3,500 species have been identified so far, including the *flor de mayo,* the beautiful national flower whose blue, red, and yellow petals display the colors of the Colombian flag. Thriving on moisture, these plants are found at every elevation, from sea level to the upper slopes of the Sierra Nevada de Santa Marta. Most orchid species are epiphytes, arboreal nesters that root on other plants, drawing their moisture through sponge-like roots from the air. Other epiphytes include bromeliads: Their tightly whorled spiky leaves form cisterns that trap water and detritus whose decay sustains the plants.

The landscapes flare with color. Orange and purple angel trumpet vines. Anthuriums in whites, reds, and pinks.

Acre for acre, Colombia—one of the world's 17 megadiverse countries—is as rich in species as anywhere in the world.

Heliconias (almost 100 species). Yellow *papilio amaryllis.* Carnal red passionflowers and *labias ardentes* (burning lips) looking like Marilyn Monroe's kiss-me pout. Even the tropical dry broadleaf deciduous forests of the lowlands explode in colors in dry winter months, when yellow *corteza amarilla,* purple jacaranda, and flame red *spathodea* emblazon the landscape before dropping their petals like colored confetti.

Mangroves & Wetlands: Colombia's shorelines are home to eight species of *manglares* (mangroves; see sidebar p. 42). These halophytic plants–terrestrial species able to survive with roots in salt water–thrive in alluvium washed down to the coast. Colombia has a relatively large area of mangroves–protected within eight parks and reserves–including forests that stretch for almost 400 miles (645 km) from Juradó on the border with Panama to Ecuador on the Pacific.

The mangrove forests of the Pacific littoral reach 160 feet (50 m) in height–taller than anywhere else in the world. Standing over the dark waters, mangroves rinse silt from the slow-flowing rivers to form new land by the shore–their interlocking stilt roots forming a tangle among the braided channels. Thus, they fight tidal erosion and trap nutrients that nourish a profligate world.

Water hyacinths crowd the innumerable bayous of the Amazon and Orinoco Basins. Other grassy wetlands, swamp forests, and freshwater pools speckle the Río Magdalena's northern floodplain, drawing migratory shorebirds.

Páramo: Treeless alpine plateaus called *páramos* (wastelands) dominate the windswept Andean landscapes between 10,000 and 14,500 feet (3,050–4,020 m). These mountain savannas are remarkable for a high percentage of endemic species: Up to two-thirds of the tussock grasses, dwarf shrubs, and ground-hugging cushion plants that typify the zone are found nowhere else. Most notable are the *frailejónes,* of the spiky-leafed, fire-resistant *Espeletia* genus, first described by botanist Alexander Von Humboldt in 1801. Forests of *frailejónes* dominate the bleak landscapes between tree line and snow line.

Formerly glaciated, the lake-studded *páramo* is marshy. Plants have adapted to thin, peatlike soils, intense desiccation and ultraviolet radiation, and summer-by-day/winter-by-night extremes in temperature. Many have evolved crafty techniques to avoid freezing, such as mucilaginous fluids to act as a thermal buffer.

Mangroves

Each mangrove species has evolved its own unique way for ridding itself of salt—from secreting it through leaf glands to preventing it from being taken up by the roots. The glutinous mud they call home is so dense that it contains almost no oxygen. Thus, most mangroves form aerial roots, drawing oxygen through spongy bark and giving the appearance that they are walking on water. Black mangroves send out underground roots that sprout lines of offshoots called pneumatophores, which stick up like upturned nails.

The interlocking roots help protect land against erosion while acting as pioneer landbuilders by filtering out silt brought down to the sea by rivers.

Several species of mangroves produce fleshy seedlings resembling plumb bobs. After germinating on the branch, they drop like darts. At low tide, they stick upright in the mud and instantly send out roots. Seeds that hit water float upright on the tides like half-filled bottles; they can survive sea journeys of hundreds of miles.

Rain Forests: Rain forests are among the most complex ecosystems on Earth. Biologists recognize at least 13 types of rain forest, ranging from the lowland jungle to high-mountain cloud forest at elevations around 4,000 feet (1,220 m), where branches drip with mosses and epiphytes thrive in the near-constant mists. Differences are determined by altitude, rainfall, and soil. Thus, the same latitude in Colombia may be marked by tropical evergreen rain forest on the Pacific coast and seasonally dry evergreen forest in the Sinú Valley. All rain forests receive in excess of 100 inches (250 cm) of rainfall per year. The true lowland rain forests that smother the *llanuras* (plains) of Chocó and the Amazon and Orinoco Basins may receive up to 300 inches (750 cm).

The lowland rain forest is a multilayered riot of green so densely shaded that little undergrowth grows on the floor. Trees of Gothic proportion grow to 100 feet (30 m) or more before merging like giant umbrellas, forming a solid canopy. Some species with trunks like great Corinthian columns, such as the mahoganies and ceiba or silk cotton, soar past their neighbors.

In the hot, humid tropics, plants grow year-round. Dead leaves decompose quickly, and nutrients are recycled into the forest canopy. Thus, tropical soils are thin, and the massive hardwood trees spread their great roots wide, like giant serpents;

In dry season, Colombia's deciduous forests flare with colorful blooms.

the huge trees are flanged at their bases, like rockets, to prevent their toppling over.

Only about 10 percent of sunlight reaches the cool, dank forest floor, where plants such as the poor man's umbrella *(sombrilla de pobre)* put out broad leaves to soak up the subaqueous light. The lack of sunlight precludes growth so that the saplings of many canopy species stop growing once they reach about 10 feet (3 m) in height, then wait until a tree falls before erupting into explosive growth.

Tropical Ark

Colombia is home to 1,885 bird, 471 mammal, 524 reptile, and 754 amphibian species, including *Phyllobates terribilis*—the endemic and infamously deadly poison dart frog. Insect species number in the tens of thousands. The staggering profundity stems from Colombia's remarkable diversity of terrains and microclimates, and its position at the juncture of two major continents: Over eons, life-forms from both have migrated across the narrow land bridge and diversified remarkably as an adaptation to vastly varied local relief and climate.

> Colombia is home to 1,885 bird, 471 mammal, 524 reptile, and 754 amphibian species, including *Phyllobates terribilis*—the endemic and infamously deadly poison dart frog.

Birds: Ornithologists' hearts take flight in Colombia, which boasts an astounding 1,885 or so known species of birds— 73 are endemics found only here. Several hundred species are migrants—the country is a node for birds migrating between the Americas. Colombia's coastal and lowland wetlands are particularly rich in migratory shorebirds, such as sandpipers, willets, and whimbrels. White ibises, spoonbills, and herons pick for morsels on the shore, where coastal mangroves prove ideal nesting sites for boobies, pelicans, and frigate birds.

The forests are alive with the squawks and screeches of parrots barreling overhead in jet-fighter formation. Colombia has 51 species of parrots, from the diminutive

EXPERIENCE: Birding at Its Best

Wherever you are in the country, the birding is sure to astound. Colombia has a wide network of qualified tour guides, and it is a favorite destination for tour companies that specialize in birding. With so many distinct ecological zones, you're spoiled for choice. A perfect tour would visit several habitats, perhaps combining montane cloud forest, lowland rain forest, mangroves, coastal wetland, and offshore islands.

The keel-billed toucan boasts a rainbow-hued beak.

Many visitors to Colombia come specifically to spot such rare birds as the Perijá parakeet, yellow-eared parrot, and four species of quetzals. The coastal wetlands draw waterbirds in the millions. Pink flamingos stomp around in the lagoons of La Guajira. And the rain forest and montane habitats are unsurpassed for checking off an A to Z of avian species—from the aracari, antpitta, and Andean condor to the blue-billed curassow and harpy eagle, not to mention the great green macaw.

The websites of **Fundación ProAves** (proaves .org) and **Colombia Birding** (colombiabirding.com) are excellent resources, as is the **Asociación Bogotana de Ornitología** (Bogota Ornithological Association; avesbogota.org).

Here are a few of the best places to see the more than 1,880 species:

Reserva de las Aves El Dorado (see pp. 150–151) in the Sierra Nevada de Santa Marta spans 3,000 to 8,500 feet (900–2,600 m) elevation and protects the habitat of more than 400 bird species.

Reserva Natural de las Aves El Paujil (see p. 96) was created by Fundación ProAves in 2003 to protect the critically endangered blue-billed curassow. This marquee forest and wetland reserve in the Magdalena Valley also protects dozens of other endemic species.

Reserva Natural de las Aves Loro Orejiamarillo (see p. 177) is named for the yellow-eared parrot. The endangered bird is commonly seen here. The reserve, in Chocó, also boasts other sought-after endemics, such as the black-billed mountain toucan.

Santuario de Fauna y Flora Los Flamencos (see pp. 157–158), just 20 minutes west of Ríohacha, is the place to see West Indian flamingos, scarlet ibises, and roseate spoonbills. Inland, the reserve features dry-forest scrub that is home to many highly local endemics, including the rufous-vented chachalaca.

The following companies specialize in birding tours: **Birding Tours Colombia**, tel 57/315-585-7937, birdingtourscolombia.com **Colombia Birding**, tel 57/314-896-3151, colombiabirding.com **EcoTurs Colombia**, tel 57-1/287-6592, ecoturs.org **Manakin Nature Tours,** tel 57-8/743-6914, manakinnaturetours.com **Victor Emanuel Nature Tours,** tel 512/328-5221 (in U.S.), ventbird.com.

spectacled parrotlet to the giant green-winged macaw, one of seven macaw species found here. Large flocks of scarlet macaws (*guacamaya roja*) can be seen in the Amazon Basin, plunging between the treetops like flying rainbows.

Toucans, with their banana-like beaks, are common throughout the country; Colombia has 21 species. So, too, are cattle egrets, easily seen in pastures. And quetzals— the emerald jewels of the cloud forest—are more numerous here than anywhere else in the region; Colombia is the only country to boast four species. The handsome black-and-gray harpy eagle can be seen in lowland rain forests. It nests atop the tallest trees, keeping a sharp eye out for monkeys and other potential snacks. Colombia's national bird is the massive Andean condor. The largest of the nation's 77 or so raptor species, it soars over the Andes. Although the bird is endangered throughout its range, the Zoo-logical Society of San Diego spearheads a successful breed-and-release program.

There are dozens of species of tanagers and trogons and doves, plus bellbirds, umbrella birds, and antbirds scavenging on insects and lizards flushed out by columns of army ants. Previously unknown or extinct species pop up, such as Fenwick's antpitta, first discovered in 2008; it lives only in a remote patch of cloud forest in the Reserva Natural de las Aves Colibrí del Sol in Colombia's western Andes.

Mammals: Colombia's six species of elusive tropical cats, found from shoreline to the highest mountain slopes, are shy and not easily seen by visitors. Deep in the cobalt shadows, jaguars move silent as a cloud. Four species—the jaguar, margay, ocelot, and oncilla—have spotted coats; all are listed as endangered or threatened due to hunting, deforestation, and poaching. The puma and weasel-like jaguarundi, with their single-colored coats, fare slightly better.

Far more easily seen are the country's 36 species of monkeys, from the endan-gered cotton-top tamarin and omnivorous white-faced capuchin to large-eyed

Capybaras—the world's largest rodents—inhabit watery lowlands.

Squirrel monkeys are among the most gregarious of Colombia's 36 species of monkeys.

night monkeys and herbivorous howlers. Male howlers are heard as often as seen. Two- and three-toed sloths are commonly seen snoozing in treetops or moving along branches at a languorous pace. And capybaras, the world's largest rodents, inhabit watery sloughs.

The raccoon-like brown coati *(pizote)* is ubiquitous. Agoutis (large rodents), armadillos, and anteaters—from the small slothlike silky anteater to the 7-foot-long (2.1 m) giant anteater—are among the other commonly seen mammals. Baird's tapirs inhabit lowland forests. The mountain tapir, a furry cousin, has adapted to the high Andean cold. So, too, the jet-black spectacled bear, named for its white-and-black spectacled face. Manatees—endangered herbivores—inhabit coastal lagoons and Amazonia rivers, home to the endangered neotropical river otter and pink Amazon dolphin.

Amphibians & Reptiles: Amphibians and reptiles thrive in the hot, damp tropics. Snakes, of which Colombia has more than 240 species, are ubiquitous, although often well camouflaged. A swaying vine turns out to be an eyelash pit viper, so green as to be almost iridescent. Anacondas up to 20 feet (6 m) long slither through the marshes of Amazonas. Most snake species are small, preying on small birds, lizards, and rodents. Fewer than 10 percent are venomous.

The viper family includes the much feared, burnished brown fer-de-lance (locally called *mapanare*), an aggressive giant that accounts for most of the fatal snake bites

in Colombia. Banded coral snakes account for many of the others.

Frogs abound, including red-eyed tree frogs and gaily colored poison dart frogs, secure in their Day-Glo liveries meant to ward off predators. No one knows how many species await discovery: In 2009, a three-week expedition to the Tacarcura region turned up 60 new species of amphibians, including 10 previously unknown species of frogs. In recent decades a deadly fungus has killed off many frog and toad species and threatens countless others, such as the endangered and transparent Colombian giant glass frog (*Centrolene heloderma*).

American crocodiles *(cocodrilos)* infest coastal estuaries, though this giant reptile is dwarfed by the endemic Orinoco crocodile, which reaches lengths of up to 17 feet (5 m) and is one of the most critically endangered reptiles on Earth. Its diminutive cousin, the caiman, rarely grows beyond 6 feet (1.8 m). The tree-dwelling iguana inhabits both wet and dry lowland forest and can grow to 3 feet (0.9 m). Dozens of smaller lizards are highlighted by the Jesus Christ lizard, a lowland dweller named for its ability to run across water on its hind legs.

Marine Life: The warm waters off Colombia's coasts are prodigiously populated by fish and marine mammals. The Pacific gulf waters and, farther out, the nutrient-rich deeps around Isla Gorgona and Isla de Malpelo teem with fish. Humpback whales and even sperm whales and orcas frolic in the nutrient-rich Pacific waters, where they gather to mate and give birth.

Harmless manta rays. Whale sharks. Octopuses, crabs, and spiny lobsters the size of house cats. These and other creatures thrill scuba divers in Colombia's Pacific pelagic playpen. On the Caribbean side, an extravaganza of fish play tag in the coral-laced waters of the San Andrés archipelago and around the Islas del Rosario. Five species of marine turtles come ashore to lay their eggs at beaches on the shores of both the Caribbean Sea and Pacific Ocean. The Golfo de Urabá, for example, is a major nesting site for leatherbacks, although the green turtle population has been so reduced by harvesting that only one major nesting site remains in the region.

> **Five species of marine turtles come ashore to lay their eggs at beaches on the shores of both the Caribbean Sea and Pacific Ocean.**

Insects: Incalculably rich in insect fauna, Colombia resounds to a cacophonous buzz. The rain forests are thought to have about 20,000 insect species per acre (50,000 per ha), from microscopic flower mites that hitch rides inside the nostrils of hummingbirds to giants such as the 6-inch-long (15 cm) titan beetle. A single acre of Amazon rain forest may house millions of ants, from vast swarms of army ants to the less aggressive leaf-cutters scurrying along well-worn pathways with shards of scissored leaves above their heads. Some 3,500 species of butterflies flit about the country, including the scintillating morpho butterflies in varying shades of electric blue. ■

Culture & Arts

Colombia's vibrant cultural scene stirs the imagination of visitors. From Afro-Caribbean rhythms and Latin tunes to classical music, Colombianos are proud of their vibrant cultural scene. So fertile are the arts that Colombia's performers set the world abuzz, and not just with their infectious music. Colombia is a trendsetter in literature, the fine arts, and fashion. The cultural menu spans a full spectrum that arouses the admiration of the rest of the world.

Colombia's culture has its roots in the fusing of indigenous, Spanish, and African cultures: a synthesis where different worlds of identity become merged in exotic romanticism and Rabelaisian excess, like a palpitating novel by Nobel Prize–winning novelist Gabriel García Márquez. The country's national identity and vibrant spirit in the arts draw inspiration from a passionate and turbulent history—an expressive searching over centuries of a creative people attempting to overcome violent forces. The literary scene, for example, has long found its inspiration in Colombia's continuum of struggle. And the nation's talented painters and sculptors have produced a visceral and dynamic collection of work that provides a visual commentary on Colombia's aspirations and social tensions.

Visual Arts

Colombia has an art tradition dating back 8,000 years, to a time when pre-Columbian peoples adorned their ceramics with stylized red, black, and ocher motifs. Artistic expression remains an important part of Colombian life. Much of the country is a magical mystery tour of home-spun studios selling everything from indigenous pieces conveying scenes of simple indigenous and peasant lifestyle to striking, sometimes haunting, contemporary paintings. And Bogotá, Cali, and Medellín are world-class in their range of museums and galleries displaying works of great complexity and beauty. No pueblo is without its provincial equivalents.

The country's national identity and vibrant spirit in the arts draw inspiration from a passionate and turbulent history.

Fine arts evolved only slowly during the early colonial period, when most Colombian art was imported from Spain. Colombia's homegrown artists of the period produced mostly for the Catholic Church in the European Renaissance and medieval styles of the period, although with occasional elements borrowed from indigenous culture. Churches and ancient mansions throughout Boyacá and Cundinamarca display extant examples in the form of colorful albeit faded murals. The 17th century witnessed an evolution of a homegrown creole style of baroque painting, led by Gregorio Vásquez de Arce y Ceballos (1638–1711). In time, realism, romanticism, neoclassicism, and other schools of European art jumped the Atlantic to infuse the works of such native Dominican artists as Martín Tovar y Tovar (1827–1902) and Ricardo Acevedo Bernal (1867–1930).

The evolution of the muralist movement in postrevolutionary Mexico became a primary inspiration for Colombian artists during the 1920s and 1930s. Artists such as Pedro Nel Gómez (1899–1984), Santiago Martínez Delgado (1906–1954), and Ignacio Gómez Jaramillo (1910–1970) founded the Colombian muralist movement, which fused Mexican, neoclassical, and art nouveau styles. Together, they blessed the country with striking murals of a political nature, such as Gómez's "La República" in the Museo de Antioquia, Medellín; Martínez's mural of Simón Bolívar and Francisco de Paula Santander in the elliptic chamber of the Capitolio Nacional in Bogotá; and

Cartagena's Museo de Arte Moderno displays contemporary art on two levels.

Gómez's "The Liberation of Slaves and the Insurrection of the Commune" in Bogotá's Capitolio Nacional.

Colombian art didn't find its own expression until the 1950s, as the nation came under the sway of Europe's avant-garde movement. Colombian painters adapted international styles to local themes. The influence of Gauguin and Van Gogh are apparent in Pedro Nel Gómez's "Self-Portrait in a Hat" (1941), and his admiration for Cézanne informs his 1949 self-portrait. Following Jorge Eliécer Gaitán's assassination in 1948, a period of social and political turmoil inspired Colombian artists, often resulting in wildly imaginative works such as the often disquieting work of Alejandro Obregón (1920–1992), considered the father of modern Colombian painting. Although his expressionistic and pictographic style—his paintings typically were divided horizontally—often depicted Colombian landscapes featuring Andean condors and other emblematic creatures, he never shied away from depicting political violence. For example, his prize-winning works for the 1956 Guggenheim International Exhibition commemorated popular leaders killed in the Bogotazo and its aftermath.

> **Colombian art didn't find its own expression until the 1950s, as the nation came under the sway of Europe's avant-garde movement.**

Obregón was, with Enrique Grau (1920–2004), Édgar Negret (1920–2012), Ramírez Villamizar (1923–2004), and Fernando Botero Angulo (1932–), among the Big Five of contemporary Colombian art. Today, Botero enjoys an international fame equivalent to that of Gabriel García Márquez and Shakira. Although renowned for portraying universally chubby figures, Botero often employs them as weighty criticism of ecclesiastics and other politically powerful figures. Colombia's finest artists today compete artistically and commercially on an international level—their works fetching tens of thousands of dollars apiece. In Botero's case, make that millions. Lesser known figures walk a line between worlds of optimism and grim reality: Contemporary artist Carlos Uribe's (1964–) "Horizons" reproduces Francisco Antonio Cano's (1865–1935) pastoral idyll of the same name, though with the addition of a military plane spraying defoliants.

The nation's largest collection of works by Colombian artists is found in permanent and revolving exhibits at Bogotá's Museo de Arte Colonial, Museo de Arte Moderno, and Museo Botero; Medellín's Museo de Antioquia and Museo de Arte Moderno; and Cali's Museo La Tertulia.

Earning international recognition for his photojournalism, Nereo López Meza (1924–2015) was considered Colombia's foremost photographer. His six decades of work are condensed into *Nereo: Images From Half a Century* (2009).

Sculpture: Fernando Botero's situational portraits are most dramatically hewn in three dimensions. His voluptuous nude women recline in cities nationwide, while pudgy bureaucrats in top hats and suits straddle equally girthy bronze horses. His mirthful marble, granite, and mostly bronze pieces—many weigh several tons—carry on a tradition of exaggerated sculpture dating back 2,500 years. Beginning around 200 B.C., an enigmatic culture of today's southern Huila Department evolved masterful stone-cutting skills. Their monolithic statues—intricately carved with anthropomorphic and zoomorphic motifs—stud the Andean lowlands around San Agustín.

Throughout the colonial period, sculpture was limited to religious icons and to monuments and other sculptural representations of public figures. Patriotic allegory reached an apogee of dramatic expression in the enormous bronze casts of Rodrigo Arenas Betancourt (1919–1995). His monumental statues adorn almost every Colombian city, including the 38-foot-tall (11.6 m) "Monumento a la Raza" ("Monument to Race"), outside the Centro Administrativo de la Alpujarra in Medellín. Arenas was kidnapped by FARC guerrillas in 1987 and held captive for three months.

Sculptor Hector Lombana (1930–2008) copied Arenas's trademark style in his somber "Monumento a la Democracia," in Panama City; although he is more fondly remembered for "Los Zapatos Viejos" ("The Old Shoes"), a beloved city icon in his hometown, Cartagena. It took Botero to lift the mood with his sensual and rotund naked women. Few others have followed: Themes of eroticism aren't the constant in Colombia that they are in other Latin American countries. Instead, the viewer is constantly drawn back to more disturbing aspects of the country's reality. Recently, Doris Salcedo (1958–) has earned international stature for her installation artwork that often transforms household items into moving and esoteric memorials to victims of narco-terrorism and Colombia's civil war.

Meanwhile, an outpouring of contemporary jewelry crafted from emeralds and gold carries on a tradition with a lineage of 5,000 years.

Literature

Colombia was slow to evolve a literary culture, which was spawned by the clenched fist call for independence. Early literary works tended toward polemic poetry in the tradition of the romantic verses of Spain. The 19th century fostered the evolution of a nationalist spirit in Colombian literature, notably in the works of Simón Bolívar, who decried injustice and espoused the cause of independence. The subsequent fight for independence helped nurture criollo expression, epitomized by sentimental depictions of peasant life, native culture, and roots of the Colombian identity, in a style of literature known as *costumbrista,* espoused by such authors as Tomás Carrasquilla Naranjo (1858–1940).

The hard years of civil war in the late 19th century proved a precursor of Colombian *modernismo*—an early 20th-century reaction to the romanticism of the costumbristas. Modernism cast off prior formalities in favor of free expression, espoused by such writers as León de Greiff (1895–1976), who wed experimental style to themes of solitude, tedium, and pain. The 1940s brought new repression to Colombia, spawning a nihilistic literary phase called the Nadaísmo (Nothingness), led by Gonzalo Arango Arias (1931–1976).

Gabriel García Márquez

Affectionately known as Gabo, journalist, novelist, and screenwriter Gabriel García Márquez is considered a Colombian national hero. He was born March 6, 1927, in Aracataca, in Magdalena Department. After leaving his law studies, he pioneered the magic realism style of literature in such novels as *Love in the Time of Cholera* and *Autumn of the Patriarch*. His most famous novel, *One Hundred Years of Solitude,* chronicles several generations of the Buendía family from the time they founded the fictional village of Macondo—a setting he used for several novels. He was awarded the Nobel Prize in literature in 1982. His esteem permitted him to act as a negotiator between the Colombian government and the ELN and FARC guerrillas. He lived in Mexico from 1961 to his death in 2014.

As political turmoil spread throughout Latin America during the 1960s and 1970s, young Latin American novelists blossomed. Carlos Fuentes (Mexico), Mario Vargas Llosa (Peru), and Colombia's Gabriel García Márquez (1927–2014) spearheaded the Boom Latinoamericano (Latin American Boom) movement. Writing against a troubled and troubling backdrop, they broke down the barriers between the mundane and the fantastical, escaping from a preimposed straightjacket to produce spontaneous, sexually charged, surrealist novels full of endless layers of experience and meaning. With García Márquez's publication of *One Hundred Years of Solitude* in 1966, the movement became known as magic realism.

García Márquez (see sidebar p. 51) dominated Colombia's literary scene thereafter with a string of limelight successes, including *Autumn of the Patriarch* (1975) and *Love in the Time of Cholera* (1985). Nonetheless, Colombia continues to produce an endless stream of gifted writers. Chief among them is Héctor Abad Faciolince (1958–), best known for his novel *Angosta* (2004), a dark depiction of Colombia's violence, and for his autobiographical *El Olvido que Seremos* (2006), recalling the life and circumstances of his father's murder by Colombian paramilitaries in 1987. Historically, women have not been well represented in Colombian literature. A modern exception is journalist Laura Estrepo (1950–), who fictionalizes real-life stories with great success; her first novels were written in exile in Mexico, where she fled to escape death threats by M-19 guerrillas.

Colombians love literature, and there is no shortage of bookstores. Bogotá hosts an International Book Fair each spring.

Music, Dance, & Film

Music, the pulsing undercurrent of Colombian life, plays a pivotal role in the nation's culture. Meanwhile dance—from the early *pasillo* to the latter-day salsa craze and Latin pop—has always been a potent expression of Colombians' sensuality. Big city nightclubs explode on weekends to the *vida loca* (crazy life) vibe. Despite the infectious popularity of contemporary forms, Colombians also hold fast to their roots: The seductive rhythms and soulful beats pulsing through the streets owe much to the marriage of Spanish and African sounds, with infusions of indigenous influences, depending on genre.

> **Music, the pulsing undercurrent of Colombian life, plays a pivotal role in the nation's culture.**

Colombia's folkloric tradition runs deep, although *música folclórica* in its original form is performed today only in festivals and stage presentations. Colombia's *música típica* fuses the sound of the five-string *mejorana* guitar with *tambores* (African bongo drums) and pre-Columbian musical instruments such as tagua seedpods and *churucas* (gourd rattles). Dances are typified by toe-and-hole stomps for couples dressed in traditional clothing—the *vueltiao* hat and white shirt for men, and the ankle-length, lace *pollera colora* for women. Traditional

Dancers in traditional costume perform a folkloric show at Parque Nacional del Café.

dancing—known in Colombia as pasillo—is based on the stylized Spanish *paseo,* with men and women circling each other, accompanied by much "yip-yipping" and tossing of hats and scarves. Pasillo derives from the European waltz and became popular in the 19th century. There's no better way to experience traditional *música Colombiana* than at the Festival Nacional del Pasillo Colombiano, held in Aguadas each August; or at a *fiesta patronal*—festivals hosted by each of the country's municipalities.

Many típico dances of the Caribbean lowlands are derived from African culture, such as the flirtatious *mapalé,* popular around Turbó and Chocó, performed by couples whose sensual swaying of hips and fast-paced, rhythmic, almost acrobatic movements recall the West African origins of the nation's Afro-Colombian people. *Cumbia,* which evolved in the Caribbean as a derivative of the *cumbe* dance of Equatorial Guinea, is also performed by men and women dressed in traditional fashion. In San Andrés and Providencia, calypso, Jamaican-derived reggae, and other Caribbean island tunes infuse the culture. And indigenous communities throughout the nation—the Awá, Emberá, U'wa, Wayúu, and scores of other groups—cling proudly to their centuries-old traditional dances, performed to the accompaniment of drums, clarinets, and Pan-style flutes.

Ever adaptive, the traditional music genres have morphed into dozens of variants. Cumbia spawned *champeta* and *vallenato,* while champeta has evolved its own contemporary forms by adapting reggae and recently reggaeton, as performed by Dexter Hamilton and his band BIP. Each region also has its own forms, such as the drum-, guasá- (a hollow gourd filled with seed), and marimba-based *currulao* of the Pacific's Chocó; the harp-led *joropo* of Los Llanos, full of lament about hardship and betrayed love; and the slow, melancholic *bambuco* of the Andean regions, derived from a fusion of early pasillo and indigenous music.

Meanwhile, by the 1940s, cumbia was influenced by U.S. big band sounds, such as mambo, and evolved into a more refined "golden age." In Cuba, the formation of homespun brassy big band sets opened the way for the evolution, in the 1960s and '70s, of a Latin-jazz dance-oriented sound called salsa. Danced to an impossibly fast and infectious beat, high-spirited, hip-swiveling salsa exploded on the Colombian scene. Performers such as Joe Arroyo invented a distinctively Colombian form, which flourished in the city of Cali, where nightclubs still explode on weekends to the vida loca vibe.

Colombia also has its own rock, punk, and heavy metal artists. Recently the country has exploded onto the Latin pop scene thanks to Shakira and Juanes. Born in Barranquilla in 1977, Shakira emerged as a musical prodigy two decades ago. Her big break came in 1996, with her multiplatinum album *Pies Descalzos (Bare Feet)*. Today, the pop megadiva, philanthropist, and UNICEF Goodwill ambassador is the highest selling Colombian artist of all time. Colombia's other undisputed ambassador of contemporary sound is Juanes (born Juan Esteban Aristizábal Vásquez, in 1972, in Carolina del Príncipe, Antioquia), who fuses classic rock and pop with such Colombian rhythms as cumbia and vallenato. Dubbed by *Vanity Fair* as the "Bono of Latin America," Juanes, whose cousin was murdered by leftist rebels in 1990, has attained national hero status for his socially conscious lyrics and for his humanitarian work focused on peace and reconciliation.

EXPERIENCE: *Fiestas Patronales*

Colombia's annual calendar is a whirligig of *fiestas patronales*. Almost every town has its patron saint's day. There's always a religious parade, often side by side with an irreligious bacchanal in Carnaval fashion. Other towns feature traditional rodeos and *tope* (a display of horse-riding skills), and a pageant to crown a beauty queen. Fireworks sometimes explode over town while partygoers jive in the streets to *vallenato, cumbia,* and other traditional music. Plan your calendar in Colombia around these key patron saint festivals:

Fiesta Patronal de San Andrés (*Nov. 30, San Andrés y Providencia*). This four-day festival features a float parade, church choirs, and regional cuisine. It sometimes coincides with the **Reinado Internacional del Coco** beauty pageant.

Fiesta Patronal San Francisco de Asís (*Oct. 4, Quibdó, Chocó*). The Afro-Caribbean populace parties for 20 days as a figure of St. Francis heads parades through the city, with bands playing cymbals, drums, tubas, and clarinets. The last day culminates with a procession of statues, as locals dressed in Franciscan costume offer prayers.

Fiestas Patronales de Santa Bárbara (*Oct. 4–8, Arauca, Los Llanos, porta laraucano.com*). The fiesta begins with an homage to St. Barbara, followed by four days of fireworks, bullfights, and a pageant to crown the Reinado Llanera beauty queen.

A salsa band performs the popular style of music at a beauty pageant.

On the classical front, the country has been neither an inspirational locale nor a breeding ground for composers and instrumentalists, although the classical genres are popular with urban sophisticates. Bogotá is home to the Orquesta Sinfónica Nacional de Colombia, and the city's Orquesta Filarmónica de Bogotá is acclaimed for its eclectic repertoire spanning classical European through contemporary Colombian genres, including bambucos and mapalés. Colombia's virtuoso classical guitarist Ricardo Cobo (1962–) debuted at the age of 17 with Bogotá's philharmonic. And Medellín hosts the Orquesta Filarmónica, and an International Classical Music Season. The Fundación Batuta promotes classical music training among young underprivileged children and youth at risk nationwide with the motif of swapping violence for violins.

Colombia has no classical ballet company. However, the Ballet de Colombia, founded in 1960 by Sonia Osorio (1928–2011) and today under the direction of her son Rodrigo Obregón Osorio, fuses modern techniques of ballet and spectacle to cumbia, mapalé, joropo, and other ancestral roots of Colombian culture. Cali has hosted an annual international ballet festival since 2007.

Colombia hosts the Iberoamerican Theater Festival, the largest such festival in South America. The few Colombian-born actors to gain stardom include Catalina Sandino Moreno, nominated for an Academy Award for her role in the 2004 Colombian-U.S. movie *María Full of Grace*. Colombia's nascent filmmaking industry has been boosted since 2003 by government funding. Cartagena hosts the annual Bogotá Film Festival and the Cartagena Film Festival, founded in 1960 and Latin America's oldest of its kind. ∎

A vibrant capital teeming with sizzling nightlife, world-class hotels and restaurants—enveloped in a gorgeous natural setting

Bogotá

The *teleférico* (cable car) heading up
Cerro de Monserrate above Bogotá

Bogotá

European in character, Latin American in soul, Colombia's capital city of 9.7 million people is a cosmopolitan center of sophistication. In two decades, Bogotá has transformed itself into a surprising tourist destination and welcoming city that is Colombia's epicenter of business, politics, and entertainment. Thanks to its location and international airport, it also functions as the main gateway to attractions throughout the country.

Skyscrapers scratch a nighttime sky in Bogotá's Centro Internacional district.

Occupying a plateau in the geographic heart of the country, the world's third highest metropolitan area is hemmed in tight against the bottle green Cordillera Oriental. Most zones of touristic interest lie along this eastern fringe, centered on La Candelaria—the historic core founded as Santa Fé de Bacatá in 1538.

Bogotá is divided into 20 districts, with more than 1,200 barrios. Much of the metropolis is a hodgepodge of redbrick and concrete buildings as well as sectors of public housing. Different architecture—from art deco and modernist to Gothic and Renaissance—lines the city's streets. Bogotá today is being hailed as the "Athens of South America"—a sophisticated tableau of architecture, action, and art.

The high-rise condominiums of Los Rosales, stylish shopping malls of Santa Barbara, trendy restaurants and boutiques of Zona Rosa—all point to Bogotá as the resurgent capital of Colombian cool.

Local citizens are equally proud of the city's past, concentrated in the 400-year-old *centro histórico*, or old district, in the Plaza de Bolívar and La Candelaria. Full of cathedrals and museums, the colonial district is also the headquarters of government. To the north, the districts of Chapinero and Chicó boast faux-Tudor homes, courtesy of English immigrants who came to lay railroads in the late 19th century.

Most of the essential sights can be seen in two or three days. Proximity makes exploring easy. Freethinking mayors and urban planners have blessed Bogotá with enviable transit networks: the *ciclorutas* network of more than 214 miles (320 km) of bike paths and the TransMilenio bus system. The numbering of streets is based on a grid—*carreras* (abbreviated cra.) run north to south; *calles* run east to west. Even so, Bogotá's sheer scale adds to the daunting task of navigating the enormous city, which is about the same size as New York or London.

What of Bogotá's reputation? Two decades of tough-on-crime security has reduced murders from a peak of 4,378 in 1993 to a low of 1,283 in 2014—it has the lowest murder rate of Colombia's main cities. However, don't be fooled into thinking because La Candelaria is quaint, the tourist hub is entirely safe. When exploring, know where you're heading. And *never* walk the city streets alone at night.

Just north of Bogotá is the city of Zipaquirá, founded in the 1600s, and neighboring areas that are the domain of climbers and birders.

The region south of Bogotá is enveloped by the Cordillera Oriental, which protects waterfalls and climbing peaks, and offers two terrific zoos. ∎

NOT TO BE MISSED:

The changing of the presidential guard   65

Strolling the streets of La Candelaria   66–67

Enjoying oversize art at the Museo Botero   69–70

Admiring pre-Columbian gold at the Museo del Oro   71

A look at the Museo Nacional   76

Joining a night tour aboard a *chiva rumbera*   78

Sipping a seasonal brew at Bogotá Beer Company   84

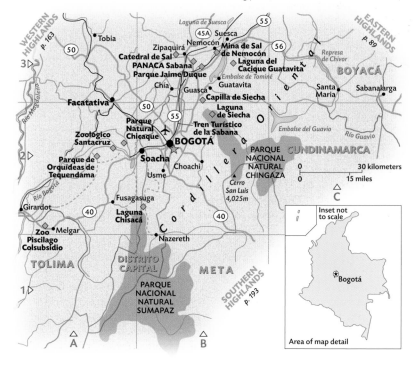

Historic Bogotá

Rising gently eastward toward the base of Cerro Monserrate, the city's historic core is composed of various parishes—La Catedral, La Concordia, La Merced—which evolved around early colonial churches. The district, known as La Candelaria, was declared a national monument in 1963. Its buildings come in an amalgam of styles: Humble colonial ones abut regal neoclassical buildings as well as stunning examples of art deco and 1950s modernist styles.

A family feeds birds in La Candelaria's Plaza de Bolívar, Bogotá's foremost social gathering spot.

Growth of the City

Santa Fé de Bogotá was founded on August 6, 1538, by Spanish conquistador Gonzalo Jiménez de Quesada on the site of a Teusa-quillo indigenous settlement in the shadow of the Andes. In 1550, the Real Audiencia de Nueva Grenada—the Royal Court—was established here. Churches and public works went up, and the Catedral de Santa Fe was begun in 1572. Although initially ruled from

Lima, in 1717 Santa Fé was named the capital of the newly created viceroyalty of Nueva Granada.

By the beginning of the 19th century, Santa Fé had attained a sophistication to rival many cities in Spain. It was also at the forefront of the revolutionary movement for independence and witnessed great violence, followed by Spain's brutal recon-quest and rule (1816–1819). After independence, it was renamed

Don't forget to take an umbrella; afternoon storms can come up quickly, even if the sun is shining earlier in the day.

—JEFF JUNG
National Geographic contributor

Bogotá and became the capital of Gran Colombia, the republic that encompassed much of today's northern South America. Despite continued political strife, Bogotá acquired fine public buildings, aqueducts, a tramway, rail connections to elsewhere in Colombia, and in 1927 an airport. The city today owes much to a modernization plan initiated in 1938.

Much of downtown Bogotá was destroyed during the Bogotazo of April 1948, massive riots sparked by the murder of populist presidential candidate Jorge Eliécer Gaitán. Progressive dictator-president Gen. Gustavo Rojas Pinilla (1953–1957) oversaw a rebuilding program. Bogotá was rocked again on November 6, 1985, when guerrillas of the M-19 revolutionary movement seized the Palace of Justice and took more than 300 civilians hostage. One hundred and fifteen were killed in the ensuing battle and fire that consumed the palace.

In recent decades, Bogotá has expanded to become a metropolis and model of urban reinvention, thanks to two-term mayor Antanas Mockus Šivickas (1995–1997, 2001–2003), whose initiatives

reduced homicides 72 percent and traffic fatalities by half. Mockus's budgetary surpluses allowed Enrique Peñalosa (1998–2001), who served in between Mockus's two terms, to finance the groundbreaking TransMilenio bus system.

In the last ten years, La Candelaria, which had been among the city's seediest neighborhoods, has recovered considerably and is being gentrified with boutique hotels, cafés, and bohemian galleries adjoining old restaurants that serve traditional dishes.

Plaza de Bolívar

The logical starting place is Plaza de Bolívar *(inside back cover map D1 & map p. 67)*, a vast square occupying a city block at the western edge of La Candelaria. Laid out in 1539 as Plaza Mayor (Main Square), it was used for military parades, and as a bullring and marketplace. It has since been the city's main magnet of social life as well as its seat of national power.

Bogotá
- 59 B2 & inside back cover

Visitor Information
- Instituto Distrital de Turismo, Cra. 24 #40-66
- 57-1/217-0711
- Cra. 8 & Calle 10
- 57-1/283-7115
- Free walking tours Tues. & Thurs. 10 a.m. & 2 p.m.

bogotaturismo.gov.co

NOTE: For information about cultural activities in Bogotá, contact the Secretary of Culture, Recreation, and Sport, Cra. 8 #9-83, tel 57-1/327-4850 ext. 500.

Tipping Tips

In Colombia, tipping is used to reward good service, rather than given automatically. Most Colombians tip little or not at all—at most, about 10 percent in restaurants. Many places add a 10 percent service charge to the bill; this is voluntary—there's no obligation to pay it. On tours, it's recommended you tip guides US$2 per day; US$10 per day per person is an appropriate fee for private guides. Tip bellboys US$1 a bag. Chambermaids are often overlooked—US$2 per day is the norm. Taxi drivers don't expect tips, and they should never receive a tip if they display aggressive or disrespectful driving.

Museo de la Independencia

- ▲ Map p. 67
- ✉ Cra. 7 #11-28
- ☎ 57-1/334-4150
- ⏱ Closed Mon.
- 💲 $

www.museo
independencia.gov.co

Catedral de la Inmaculada Concepción

- ▲ Map p. 67
- ✉ Cra. 7 & Calle 10
- ☎ 57-1/234-9794

catedraldebogota
.org

Capitolio Nacional

- ▲ Inside back cover D1
- ✉ Calle 10 bet. Cra. 7 & 8
- ☎ 57-1/382-4000
- ⏱ Open Fri. by appt.

senado.gov.co

The first cry for independence rang out here on July 20, 1810: The "Grito de Independencia" (Cry of Independence) occurred at La Casa del Florero (Vase House)—a late 16th-century Mudejar-style home on the park's northeast corner—when a Creole vendor refused to sell a vase to a Spanish noble. This sparked a spontaneous revolt against Spanish rule. Today, the house, called the **Museo de la Independencia** (also known as Museum 20 de Julio), is dedicated to the independence movement.

The square took its modern form in 1960, when it was remodeled for the 150th anniversary of independence. At its center is a bronze **statue of Simón Bolívar.** Cast in 1846, Bolívar looks down figuratively on events and on children chasing pigeons and riding donkeys and llamas.

Rising over the east side of the plaza, the **Catedral de la Inmaculada Concepción,** completed in 1823, is the fourth church to stand at this site. Inside, the triple nave is supported by twin rows of Corinthian columns, with domed vaults between. A gray marble floor glistens underfoot. Don't miss the chapel on the right containing the tombs of Gonzalo Jiménez de Quesada and independence hero Antonio Nariño (1765–1824).

The cathedral adjoins the **Capilla del Sagrario,** a side chapel completed in 1700 and restored after the 1827 earthquake. Richly decorated, its interior features a Mudejar-style vaulted ceiling and an ebony-and-marble altar inlaid with tortoise shell.

The **Palacio de Justicia** *(inside back cover map D1)* takes up the plaza's north side. Its facade is formed by two planar blocks framing a pavilion topped by a cupola. Completed in 1998, it replaced the former Palace of Justice destroyed in November 1985, when troops stormed the building to free the civilians and Supreme Court justices that were held hostage by M-19 guerrillas. Access is restricted.

Across the plaza, triple rows of six fluted Ionic columns front the sandstone, H-shaped **Capitolio Nacional,** the nation's seat of

---

EXPERIENCE: Dance Until Dawn

Bogotá has an amazing nightlife. Whether seeking mellow jazz, hard rock, or sizzling salsa, you have a wide range of venues to choose from. Here are some of the best:

Armando Records *(Calle 85 #14-46, Chapinero, tel 57-1/530-6449, armando records.org).* A three-in-one nightclub with live acts, superb DJs, and separate spaces for electronica to salsa.

Centro Cultural Planetario *(Cra. 6 #26-07, Teusquillo, tel 57-1/379-5750).* The city planetarium is an unlikely venue for free Thursday folk-jazz-fusion concerts.

El Salto del Ángel *(Cra. 13 #93A-45, tel 57-1/654-5454, saltodelangel.com.co).* The disco bar is a cool spot for partying the night away.

Exchange Salsa Bogotá *(La Villa, Cra. 14A #83-56, Chicó, tel 311-492-0249).* Friday night groove where gringos and locals learn salsa for free, then party until 3 a.m.

Theatron *(Calle 58 #10-18, tel 57-1/235-6879).* This large and popular gay disco features electronic music.

Patrons visit a Bogotá club and bar, one of many that contribute to the city's sizzling nightlife.

government. Started in 1847 but not completed until 1926, its long evolution melded Ionic, neoclassical, and Renaissance influences. The central block—the Salón Eliptico—hosts the plenary sessions of the Congress of Colombia, while the Senate and House of Representatives are to each side. Guided visits on Fridays let you admire the triptych fresco by Santiago Martínez Delgado (1906–1954) in the Salón Eliptico, which depicts Bolívar and Francisco de Paula Santander exiting the Congress of Cúcuta that created Gran Colombia. It is considered Colombia's foremost 20th-century mural.

Stretching the length of the plaza's west side, the **Alcaldía Mayor** (Town Hall) occupies the three-story French Renaissance–style Palacio Lievano. Completed in 1905, it features a Mansard

roofline. A portico supported by heavy rectangular columns runs along its lower level, providing protection from sun and rain. Tucked into the southwest corner is the Instituto Distrital de Turismo's PIT Centro Histórico Tourist Information Bureau. Across Calle 10, the colonial building with balconied upper windows is the **Casa de los Comuneros.** Today housing the Secretariat of Culture, Recreation, and Sport, it displays early 19th-century architectural details, including frescoes.

South of the Plaza

The Capitolio Nacional is the northernmost of a three-block government complex that extends south of Plaza de Bolívar, framed by Carreras 7 and 8. The latter is lined with intriguing buildings, including the **Iglesia Museo de Santa Clara,** dating from 1674.

Alcaldía Mayor
✉ Cra. 8 #10-65
☎ 57-1/381-3000
bogota.gov.co

Iglesia Museo de Santa Clara
▲ Map p. 67
✉ Cra. 8 & Calle 9
☎ 57-1/337-6762
⊕ Closed Mon.
www.museocolonial.gov.co

Beating Pickpockets at Their Game

Like in any city, thieves here are looking for easy targets. Here are a few precautions to help you avoid becoming a victim.
• Wear your shirt over your fanny pack; make sure the clasp isn't exposed.
• Don't carry your camera loosely on your shoulder; sling it around your neck.
• Keep your smartphone or iPod hidden under your shirt, along with any cords.
• Stick to well-lit main streets, especially after dark.

• Carry money and documents in a money belt worn inside the waistband of your skirt or pants.
• Make photocopies of important documents. Leave the originals in the hotel safe.
• Use a purse that zips; wear it around your neck inside your clothing.
• Leave your jewelry at home.
• Educate yourself on problem areas and avoid them.

Museo del Siglo XIX
🅰 Map p. 67
✉ Cra. 8 #7-93
☎ 57-1/281-9948
💲 $
🕐 Closed Sun.

Casa de Nariño
🅰 Map p. 67
✉ Cra. 8 #7-26
☎ 57-1/562-9300
🕐 Tours Mon.–Fri. 9 a.m., 10:30 a.m., 2:30 p.m., & 4 p.m.; Sat.–Sun. 2:30 p.m.–4 p.m.

visitas.presidencia
.gov.co

Templo de San Agustín
🅰 Map p. 67
✉ Calle 7 & Cra. 7
☎ 57-1/209-6011

The church's austere facade and heavy Renaissance-style doors belie the ornate interior. Now a museum, it displays a vast collection of art from early colonial days on, but it is the wall murals and Moorish roof that most enchant.

Back on Carrera 8, the next block offers views of the Plaza de Armas and the **Observatorio Astronómico** (map p. 67). The white octagonal tower was built in 1803 as the continent's first astronomical observatory. It can be visited by prior arrangement through the **Claustro de San Agustín** (Cra. 8 #7-21, tel 57/311-292-5100, e-mail: claustro@unal.edu.co). A former convent, now administered as a museum with temporary exhibitions, it's at the end of the block on your right.

A few steps to the south, make sure not to miss the **Museo del Siglo XIX** (Museum of the 19th Century), occupying a beautiful two-story house furnished in period fashion as if the building were still lived in. Exhibits include female costumes, a small pharmacy, and a huge doll collection.

Security is strict on this block

INSIDER TIP:

INSIDER TIP:

Pedal Bogotá on Sunday mornings, when 70 miles (113 km) of streets close to cars. Rent bikes at Bogotá Bike Tours (bogota biketours.com).

—JOHN ROSENTHAL
National Geographic
Traveler magazine writer

as you pass **Casa de Nariño**, the formal name for the presidential palace—the official home of Colombia's presidents since 1908. It stands on the site where Antonio Nariño (translator of The Rights of Man) was born in 1765, in a home demolished to make way for the palace, which was inaugurated in 1918 and remodeled with its neoclassical exterior in 1979. It is lavishly decorated with antiques and contemporary art. A free one-hour tour by prior arrangement is a treat.

The palace's southern facade faces the **Templo de San Agustín**, remarkable for its rare elliptical roof. Originally part of an Augustine convent, the church tempts visitors inside to admire a delicately worked pulpit, musicians' gallery, baroque gold-gilt altar, and coffered ceiling.

If you turn left onto pedestrianized Carrera 7, you'll pass wide-open **Plaza Armas,** providing a view of Casa de Nariño. This is the place to witness the **Changing of the Guard** (Mon.–Wed., Fri., & Sun. 4 p.m.), featuring more than 200 soldiers in period and ceremonial costume.

La Candelaria Core

The heart of La Candelaria, with its bustling brick-cobbled streets and wealth of attractions, extends uphill from the plaza along Calles 10 and 11. The major sites are packed along a four-block axis.

Calle 10: Immediately north of Plaza de Bolívar, your eye is drawn toward the whitewashed mannerist facade of the **Iglesia de San Ignacio** (map p. 67), begun by the Jesuits in 1610. Its massive redbrick pillars support a semicircular barrel vault roof with a dome decorated with a representation of heaven.

Facing the church, tiny **Plazoleta de Cuervo** (map p. 67) is named for Colombian linguist Rufino José Cuervo (1844–1911).
(continued on p. 68)

The recently restored Teatro Colón is one of La Candelaria's most graceful Renaissance buildings.

A Walk Through La Candelaria

Bogotá is a sprawling city, but a three-hour walk around its historic core takes in many of Bogotá's most important sites, including churches, government buildings, and museums that span the spectrum from regional costumes to the artwork of Fernando Botero.

Intriguing murals line Callejón de Embudo in Bogotá's La Candelaria.

Start at the Tourist Information Office on the southwest corner of **Plaza de Bolívar ❶** (see pp. 61–63). After admiring the Capitolio Nacional and Alcaldía Mayor, stroll down Carrera 8 to the **Iglesia Museo de Santa Clara ❷** (see pp. 63–64), a 17th-century church that today is a religious art museum. Exiting, turn west onto Calle 9 and walk one block to visit the **Museo Histórico de la Policía Nacional** *(Calle 9 #9-27, tel 57-1/233-5911, policia.gov.co)*. Housed in the baroque former police headquarters, the Museum of Police History traces the force's evolution with exhibits including a dummy of Pablo Escobar's bullet-ridden corpse.

Return to Carrera 8. On your left is **Plaza de Armas ❸**, the parade ground where the changing of the presidential guard takes place four times a week. Passing the octagonal **Observatorio Astronómico** (see p. 64) on your left, you'll reach the **Museo del Siglo XIX ❹** (see p. 64), with displays replicating life in the

NOT TO BE MISSED:

Casa de Nariño • Iglesia del Carmen • Museo de la Independencia • Biblioteca Luis Ángel Arango • Museo Botero

19th century. A few steps beyond is the entrance to **Casa de Nariño ❺** (see p. 64), the presidential palace.

Turn left onto Calle 7 to visit **Templo de San Agustín** (see pp. 64–65). Walk east past the **Archivo General** (National Archives) on your right; turn left on Carrera 6 for the **Museo Arqueológico ❻** *(Cra. 6 #7-43, tel 57-1/243-1690, museoarqueologicomusa.com, closed Sun.)*. Beyond the carriage doors, a huge collection of pre-Columbian pottery is displayed in *salas* opening to a paved courtyard.

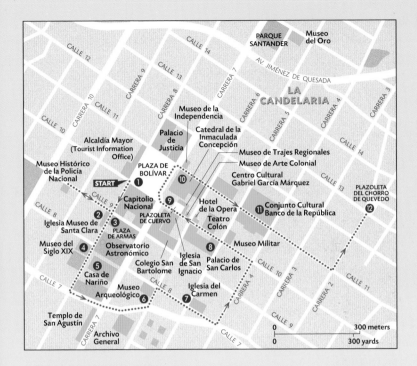

From here, Calle 8 leads one block uphill to **Iglesia del Carmen** . Completed in 1938, the Byzantine-inspired Gothic church is an eclectic building decorated in red and white stone. Follow Carrera 4 west two blocks to Calle 10. Don't miss the **Museo Militar** (see p. 68) on the northeast corner. Next head downhill, passing the **Teatro Colón, Hotel de la Opera,** and **Palacio de San Carlos** (see p. 68). The next block includes **Museo de Arte Colonial** (see p. 68) and **Museo de Trajes Regionales** (see p. 68), both worth a stop. The latter enfolds the **Plazoleta de Cuervo** (see p. 65). Note **Iglesia de San Ignacio** (see p. 65) across the street. The Jesuit church adjoins **Colegio San Bartolomé.**

You're now back in Plaza de Bolívar. Stop in at the **Catedral de la Inmaculada Concepción** (see p. 62). Exiting, visit the **Museo de la Independencia** (see p. 62) to learn about the argument over a vase that spawned Colombia's quest for independence. From here, turn up

> ◪ See also map p. 59 & inside
>   back cover
> ► Plaza de Bolívar
> ⊕ 3 hours
> ⬌ 1.75 miles (3 km)
> ► Plaza del Chorro de Quevedo

Calle 11. Stop to admire the **Centro Cultural Gabriel García Márquez** (see pp. 68–69), a modernist structure by Colombian architect Rogelio Salmona. Ahead awaits the **Conjunto Cultural Banco de la República** (see pp. 69–70): The **Biblioteca Luis Ángel Arango** (a library, exhibition, and concert space) on your left faces buildings that integrate the **Museo Botero, Museo de Arte del Banco de la República,** and **Casa de Moneda.** After visiting the museums, continue to Carrera 2 and turn left. You are now in an area of colonial homes. The street leads to **Plazoleta del Chorro de Quevedo** (see pp. 65, 68), a plaza where Bogotá was founded in 1538, completing your route tracing the city's history.

Museo de Trajes Regionales

◮ Map p. 67
✉ Calle 10 #6-36
☏ 57-1/282-6531
◷ Closed Sun.
$ $

museodetrajes
regionales.com

Museo de Arte Colonial

◮ Map p. 67
✉ Cra. 6 #9-77
☏ 57-1/341-6017
$ $

museocolonial.gov.co

Palacio de San Carlos

◮ Map p. 67
✉ Calle 10 #5-51
☏ 57-1/381-4000
◷ Closed Sat.–Sun.

Museo Militar

◮ Map p. 67
✉ Calle 10 #4-92
☏ 57-1/281-2548
◷ Closed Mon.
$ $

centrohistoricoejc
.mil.co

Museo de Bogotá

✉ Cra. 4 #10-18
☏ 57-1/352-1865
◷ Closed Mon.
$ $

museodebogota
.gov.co

Centro Cultural Gabriel García Márquez

◮ Map p. 67
✉ Calle 11 #5-60
☏ 57-1/283-2200

fce.com.co/CCGGM

He's shown poised in bronze, legs crossed in a chair atop a stone pedestal shaded by palms and other tropical foliage. The colonial home behind the square is where independence activist Antonio Nariño printed *The Rights of Man,* for which he was jailed for ten years. Today, the house forms part of the **Museo de Trajes Regionales** (Museum of Regional Costumes). Colombia's diverse and colorful indigenous and regional costumes are displayed here.

A stone's throw east, the weathered 16th-century building adjoining the church is occupied by the **Museo de Arte Colonial,** accessed on Carrera 6. Its vast collection of tapestries, paintings, sculptures, and Spanish relics is displayed in galleries that surround a spacious courtyard.

On the next block, **Hotel de la Opera**—a restoration of two colonial homes—abuts the recently restored **Teatro Colón** *(map p. 67, Calle 10 #5-32, tel 57-1/381-6380),* designed by Italian architect Pietro Cantini and completed in 1895 with an Italian Renaissance facade. Opposite, the somber late 17th-century neoclassical **Palacio de San Carlos** began as a seminary. It was converted into the presidential palace in 1828, and that September bore witness to an attempt to assassinate Simón Bolívar, who escaped through a window. Today, it houses the Ministerio de Relaciones Exteriores (Ministry of Foreign Affairs). Its sumptuously furnished salons can be explored on guided tours.

Across Carrera 5, the grandiose two-story colonial building on the left is the **Museo Militar.** Run by the Colombian Army, it traces the nation's military history and exhibits uniforms, armaments, tanks, and aircraft.

From here, Calle 10 steepens as it leads three blocks through a residential area lined with colonial buildings. Stop at the **Museo de Bogotá.** Its exhibits interpret the history and culture of the city. Beyond Carrera 3, the street ends at **Iglesia Egipto** (Egypt Church), which is worth a visit to view the coffered ceiling adorned with a mural of Mary's flight from Egypt.

INSIDER TIP:

Fernando Botero's one stipulation upon donating his pieces to the Museo Botero was that entrance to the museum be free, and so it has remained.

—AARON RETIG
Colombia Whitewater *co-author*

Calle 11: The block leading east from Plaza de Bolívar is a charmer for its tiny restaurants and pastry shops *(pastelerías),* such as **Antigua Santafe** (see Travelwise p. 275).

Crossing Carrera 6, pause to admire the **Centro Cultural Gabriel García Márquez.** This modernist cultural complex was designed by Colombia's most celebrated architect, Rogelio Salmona, and features a

Pre-Columbian gold glitters in the modernist Museo del Oro's circular Sala de la Ofrenda.

library, three auditoriums, and a superb bookstore.

Conjunto Cultural Banco de la República:
No tour of La Candelaria would be complete without a visit to the Conjunto Cultural Banco de la República *(map p. 67)*, one block north. The complex takes up two blocks and includes many of the city's most important cultural centers, including on the north side of the street the **Biblioteca Luis Ángel Arango** *(Calle 11 #4-14, tel 57-1/343-1224, banrepcultural.org/blaa)*, the nation's largest library.

Opposite, pass through the huge nail-studded oak doors of the **Casa de Moneda** to explore the history behind the minting of colonial money. The bank's impressive gold and silver coin collection spans four centuries.

The courtyard connects to the **Museo de Arte del Banco de la República,** which depicts Colombian art from the 16th century to the present day. Temporary exhibits by contemporary artists such as Wilfredo Lam and Andy Warhol hang in counterpoint to the dour yet historically important body of early religious works. Don't miss the three solid gold and silver Catholic monstrances encrusted with emeralds and other jewels. These invaluable relics (the largest features 1,485 emeralds, plus amethysts, diamonds, pearls, sapphires, and topaz) are kept in a special bank vault.

The galleries merge into those of the **Museo Botero,** dedicated to the works of Fernando Botero. He opened the museum in 2000 and donated most of the 123 sculptures, drawings, and paintings that trace his evolution as Colombia's leading living artist. The westernmost *salas* exhibit pieces by Monet, Picasso, Renoir, Salvador Dalí,

Casa de Moneda
✉ Calle 11 #4-93
☎ 57-1/343-1331
🕐 Closed Tues.

**banrepcultural.org
/museos-y-colecciones**

Museo de Arte del Banco de la República
✉ Calle 11 #4-15
☎ 57-1/343-1316
🕐 Closed Tues.

**banrepcultural.org
/coleccion-de-arte-
banco-de-la-republica**

Museo Botero
✉ Calle 11 #4-21
☎ 57-1/343-1316
🕐 Closed Tues.

**banrepcultural.org
/museo-botero**

Plazoleta del Chorro de Quevedo

⚠ Map p. 67 & inside back cover D1

✉ Calle 13 & Cra. 2

Parque Santander

⚠ Map p. 67 & inside back cover D1

✉ Calle 16 & Cra. 7

and other artists of the 19th- and 20th-century art world.

Bogotá's humble origins can be traced to **Plazoleta del Chorro de Quevedo,** a tiny brick-paved square at the top of La Candelaria. It marks the spot where in 1538 Gonzalo Jiménez de Quesada is thought to have established the foundation of what would become Bogotá. A tiny church—the **Ermita de Humilladero**—tucked in the southeast corner is a copy of a church that once stood in Plaza Santander. The plaza is ground zero for Bogotá's alternative street culture, drawing skateboarders, jugglers, and students to the *chicha* (drink made of fermented corn) bars and off-beat clubs along alleys that radiate out from the plaza. The most interesting is **Callejón de Embudo** (Funnel Alley), a sloping cobbled

lane adorned with creative graffiti and murals. (This area of upper La Candelaria requires caution both day and night.)

Avenida Jiménez & Around

West of Plaza de Bolívar, Carrera 7 widens into a broad and busy thoroughfare packed with street vendors. After four blocks, it meets Avenida Jiménez, dividing the historic city core and Bogotá's commercial center. The snaking boulevard is lined with ecclesiastical buildings, government offices, and universities. The city's cultural pride and joy—the Museo del Oro (Gold Museum)—is here, but the area has many other sites of interest often overlooked by tourists.

Parque Santander: This lively tree-shaded plaza is named

A sculpture by Fernando Botero stands in the entrance to the Museo Botero.

for Gen. Francisco de Paula Santander. A bronze statue by Italian sculptor Pietro Costa shows Santander holding a sword in his left hand and the constitution in his right. Today, the square is ringed by modern buildings, including the graceful Avianca tower to the north. Take the elevator to the 23rd floor for the **Museo de la Esmeralda** (Emerald Museum). Less a museum than an exhibition hall of gleaming emeralds attached to a sales showroom, it features a faux mine where re-creations of emerald veins from three different locations provide an insight into the gemstone's formation.

The **Museo del Oro** (Gold Museum) is reason enough to visit Bogotá. On the plaza's east side, it occupies a modernist building built to display the Banco de la República's 34,000-piece pre-Columbian gold collection. Galleries on three levels display exquisitely crafted pieces dating back nearly 2,500 years, with rooms named the Working of Metals, People and Gold in Pre-Hispanic Colombia, and Cosmology and Symbolism. The exhibits are themed also by region, noting distinctions between different cultures. The main collection is housed in a vast vault. Don't miss the "Balsa Muisca"–an intricate 19-inch-long (48 cm) gold raft. The tour ends in the circular Sala de la Ofrenda. You enter the pitch black Offering Room, the doors close, haunting pre-Columbian music begins, and wraparound glass panels representing the waters of Lake Guatavita light up to display a remarkable

collection of gold offerings. Pick up a free English audio guide.

The plaza opens west onto **Iglesia de la Veracruz,** a 16th-century church rebuilt after an earthquake in 1827. It displays its original Mudejar-influenced altar. Many independence heroes are buried here. It is open only during Mass. More impressive is the **Iglesia de San Francisco de Asis** (tel 57-1/341-2357), immediately south at the corner of Avenida Jiménez and Carrera 7. Begun in 1575 (but rebuilt after an earthquake in 1785), Bogotá's oldest surviving church boasts one of the most ornately decorated interiors in the country, including beautiful green-and-gold Mudejar *alfarje* ornamentation and an elaborate baroque gilt altar.

Museo de la Esmeralda

✉ Edificio Avianca, Calle 16 #6-66, Piso 23

☎ 57-1/2836-4268

🕐 Closed Sun.

museodelaesmeralda .com.co

Admiring Rogelio Salmona

Rogelio Salmona (1927–2007), Colombia's most significant 20th-century architect, graced Bogotá's skyline with striking redbrick buildings infused with whimsical spirals, curves, patios, and canals. Born in Paris, Salmona moved to Bogotá as a youth and studied architecture under French architect Le Corbusier. He was heavily influenced by the Islamic brick architecture of Granada, Spain.

Here are five of his buildings you should not miss:

Centro Cultural Gabriel García Márquez (Calle 11 #5-60)
Museo de Arte Moderno (Calle 24 #6-04)
Archivo General (Cra. 6 #6-91)
Torres del Parque & Plaza de Toros (Cra. 6 #26-50)
Biblioteca Pública Virgilio Barco (Cra. 60 #57-60).

Museo del Oro

🅰 Map p. 67

✉ Calle 16 #5-41

☎ 57-1/343-2222

🕐 Closed Mon.

💲 $$

banrepcultural.org /museo-del-oro

Palacio de San Francisco

✉ Av. Jiménez #7-50

☎ 57-1/243-9931

urosario.edu.co

Quinta de Bolívar

🅰 Inside back cover D1

✉ Calle 20 #2-91 Este

☎ 57-1/336-6410

🕐 Closed Mon.

💲 $, Sun. free

www.quintadebolivar
.gov.co

Avenida Jiménez: The former Franciscan monastery that adjoined the San Francisco church on its north side was replaced in 1917 by the **Palacio de San Francisco.** This imposing neoclassical building is now part of Universidad del Rosario. Note the magnificent ground level statuary. The south side of the avenue at the corner with Carrera 7 is usually thronged with emerald traders selling their gems. Populist Liberal

INSIDER TIP:

Colombia is an amazingly hospitable place. Don't be surprised if locals stop you to say thanks for visiting their country.

—ERIC KRACHT
National Geographic Channels staff

Party leader Jorge Eliécer Gaitán was assassinated here on April 5, 1948, sparking the Bogotazo.

Avenida Jiménez channels east between office buildings towering over **Plazoleta del Rosario** *(Av. Jiménez & Calle 6),* the setting for the open-air craft market and a statue of Gonzalo Jiménez de Quesada. This is a great place to sip coffee or beer at one of the plaza's café bars, bustling with students from Rosario University, which occupies the old Claustro de Nuestra Señora del Rosario convent on the plaza's south side.

From here, the avenue winds east, sloping gently to **Parque de los Periodistas** at Carrera 3. It

was once a hangout for speakers and intellectuals, hence its name: Journalists' Square. The plaza is studded with a circular, sandstone monument—**Templete de Libertador**—created in 1883 by Florentine architect Pietro Cantini to honor the centenary of Simón Bolívar's birth. A bronze figure of the Liberator stands in the monument, surrounded by Doric columns. The grandiose neoclassical building to the northeast is the **Real Académia de la Lengua,** headquarters of the Royal Academy of Spanish Language.

Here, the avenue broadens into an airy tree-lined boulevard, free of traffic except for articulated TransMilenio buses. If you cross to the east side of Avenida Jiménez, you'll pass **Policarpa Salavarrieta** *(cnr. of Calle 18),* a bronze statue depicting the eponymous heroine (1795–1817) who spied for independence forces and was shot for treason by Spanish royalists. A stone's throw beyond, the gracious whitewashed facade of the **Parroquia Nuestra Señora de las Aguas** (Church of Our Lady of the Waters), dating from 1644, is topped by a triform bell tower with seven small bells.

Quinta de Bolívar: From the church, Avenida Jiménez (which becomes Calle 20) swings east some 440 yards (400 m) to Quinta de Bolívar. This expansive estate belonged to José Antonio Portocarrero until 1820, when it was given by the government of Nueva Grenada to Simón Bolívar as an expression of gratitude. He used it during his five-year presidency. In 1830, he gave the house to his friend José Ignacio Paris. In 1922, the state established a museum in it.

Now a national monument, it has been restored to resemble its original appearance and is furnished as it was when Bolívar lived here. The quinta includes the salon, game room, Bolívar's bedroom, the kitchen—plus the apartment of Bolívar's mistress and political adviser, Manuelita Saenz.

lucky—snowcapped Nevado del Tolima far off to the west. For this reason, Monserrate is one of Bogotá's most visited sites. On Sunday, throngs of pilgrims puff up the more than 1,000 steps, now patrolled by police to combat past incidences of muggings. You're wise to ascend by cable car or funicular. (The Cerro Monserrate tram station is only 220 yards/200 m east and uphill of Quinta de Bolívar, but

Cerro de Monserrate

 Inside back cover E2

✉ Cra. 2 Este #21-48, Paseo Bolívar

☎ 57-1/284-5700

$ $$

🚠 Funiculars & cable cars run daily but schedules vary.

cerromonserrate.com

The game room at Quinta de Bolívar retains its original furnishings.

Cerro de Monserrate: The thickly forested mountains that soar over Bogotá rise to Cerro Monserrate, topped by a white church perched at 10,341 feet (3,152 m). The site has been a center of worship since 1657 when a Carthusian monastery was built; the current church dates from 1920. A 17th-century carving of the Señor Caido (Fallen Christ) adorns the altar.

On clear days, you're granted a panoramic view of the city and—if

muggings have been reported. Take a taxi.)

You can satisfy your hunger at Casa San Isidro. Perched on the hillside, it offers views over the city through wraparound windows.

To the south, you look across a valley to **Cerro de Guadalupe** (10,882 feet/3,317 m), the highest point in the capital. It, too, has a chapel, plus a 49-foot-tall (15 m) marble statue of Nuestra Señora de Guadalupe (Our Lady of Guadalupe). ∎

Beyond the Historic Core

Beyond the historic core, interesting sites for tourists concentrate along a narrow belt running north, roughly corresponding with Carrera 7. Centro Internacional boasts the world-class Museo Nacional. Farther north, gentrified Chapinero, Chicó, and bohemian Usaquén are graced by well-kept parks and faux-Tudor houses, plus some of the city's hippest bars, restaurants, and nightclubs. To the west, Parque Simón Bolívar is Bogotá's amoeba-shaped equivalent of New York City's Central Park.

The Iglesia de Las Nieves, built in 1922, represents a fine example of Byzantine architecture.

Parque de la Independencia

Visitor Information

✉ Cra. 7 & Calle 26
☎ 57-1/284-2664
🕐 Closed Sun.

✉ Cra. 13 #26-62
☎ 57-1/286-2248
🕐 Closed Sun.

Las Nieves

Extending north of Avenida Jiménez to Calle 26, the pulsing commercial and working-class barrio of Las Nieves evolved around the **Iglesia de Las Nieves** (inside back cover D2, Cra. 7 & Calle 20), a pink-and-cream banded Byzantine church built in 1922. The bronze statue across the street in

Plazoleta de Las Nieves is that of scientist and independence martyr Francisco José de Caldas (1768–1816).

Nearby, the art deco **Teatro Jorge Eliécer Gaitán** (Cra. 7 #22-47, tel 57-1/379-5750 ext. 200, teatrojorgeeliecer.gov.co) opened in 1940 as the city's first movie house, and is now home to the

Bogotá Symphony and Santa Fé de Bogotá Choir. Art deco devotees will also appreciate the **Museo Art Déco** (Calle 21 #5-59, tel 57-1/341-1855), housed appropriately in an art deco apartment building.

The ultimate statement in Colombian art deco architecture is the **Biblioteca Nacional** (National Library). The nation's principal library was completed in 1938. The sober, four-story building has courtyards, plus a soaring study hall in the center, bathed in sunlight streaming down from above. To its west stands the somber redbrick **Museo de Arte Moderno,** better known to locals as MAMBO. Six exhibition rooms—designed by iconic architect Rogelio Salmona (see sidebar p. 71)—display works by Colombia's most important artists, alongside those of Pablo Picasso, Salvador Dalí, Max Ernst, and Andy Warhol.

The museum stands in the shadow of **Torre Colpatria** (Cra. 7 #24-89, tel 57-1/609-0052, $, ID needed to enter). Dominating the local skyline, the 50-story skyscraper soaring 653 feet (199 m) is the tallest building in Colombia. The rooftop **Mirador Colpatria** is open to visitors on Friday evenings and on weekends. The 360-degree view places the entire city in panoramic perspective.

Centro Internacional

The Torre Colpatria looms over the Centro Internacional, immediately north of Calle 26. This buzzing business district is pinned by glass-and-concrete tower blocks padded with falling fog. The Hotel

Crowne Plaza Tequendama makes a great base for exploring. To its north is the **Recoleta de San Diego** (inside back cover map D2, Cra. 7 #26-47, tel 57-1/341-2476), a charming counterpoint to the modernity that surrounds it. The tiny church is all that remains of a Franciscan monastery dating from the early 17th century. Stop in to admire the church's decoratively carved altar and ornate silverwork.

Immediately north of the church, the **Planetario** (Planetarium) offers projections of the universe onto an 82-foot-wide (25 m) dome, the largest in Latin America. Be sure to visit the rooftop sundial.

Steps away, the circular **Plaza de Toros La Santamaría**—the city's bullring—draws you uphill. Its metaphorical gravitational pull is owed to its striking Mudejar redbrick design by Spanish architect Santiago Mora. Completed in 1940, it seats 14,500 spectators.

EXPERIENCE:
Biking on *Ciclorutas*

Bogotá has **208 miles (334 km)** of *ciclorutas,* bicycle paths—more than any other Latin American city. Many follow major boulevards but are separate from car lanes; some feed into the TransMilenio bus system, while others weave through parks. Join in the world-famous Ciclovia—a ride every Sunday and holiday, when major avenues are closed to cars and cyclists take to the streets. The similar Ciclopaseo de los Miércoles is held alternate Wednesdays. **Bogotá Bike Tours** *(Cra. 3 #12-72, La Candelaria, tel 57-1/281-9924, bogotabiketours .com)* rents bicycles and offers cycling tours.

Biblioteca Nacional

- 🅰 Inside back cover D2
- ✉ Calle 24 #5-60
- ☎ 57-1/381-6464
- 🕐 Closed Sun.

bibliotecanacional .gov.co

Museo de Arte Moderno

- 🅰 Inside back cover D2
- ✉ Calle 24 #6-04
- ☎ 57-1/286-0466
- 🕐 Closed Mon.

mambogota.com

Planetario

- 🅰 Inside back cover D2
- ✉ Cra. 6 #26-07
- ☎ 57-1/281-4150
- 🕐 Closed Mon.

planetariodebogota .gov.co

Plaza de Toros La Santamaría

- 📍 Inside back cover D2
- ✉ Cra. 6 #26-50
- ☎ 57-1/334-1482

Museo Nacional

- 📍 Inside back cover D2
- ✉ Cra. 7 #28-66
- ☎ 57-1/381-6470
- 🕐 Closed Mon.
- 💲 $

museonacional
.gov.co

Cementerio Central

- 📍 Inside back cover D2
- ✉ Calle 26 bet. Cra. 17 & 20
- ☎ 57-1/269-3141 ext. 9
- 💲 Free tours

bogotaturismo.gov
.co/cementerio
-central

In 2012 the city mayor banned bullfighting, but was overruled in 2015 by the Constitutional Court. The plaza has been used since 2012 for public events that celebrate "life," and at time of publication the plaza's future use is unclear.

A short walk up Carrera 7 leads to the **Museo Nacional** (National Museum), housed in the imposing fortress-like former prison, El Panóptico, itself a national monument dating from 1874. The museum's 17 salas on three levels synthesize Colombia's history, packing in the centuries with everything from pre-Columbian mummies and the standard used by conquistador Francisco Pizarro (1478–1541) to

iconography about Simón Bolívar. Upstairs is a superb collection of artwork, including modernist paintings by Fernando Botero. Don't miss the gold objects in the museum's banklike vault.

The hilly residential neighborhood immediately east is **La Macarena,** a gritty bohemian sector popular with artists and intellectuals. It's renowned also as a zona gastronómica, drawing foodies to restaurants that concentrate around Carrera 4 and along Calle 27B, off Carrera 7, a sloping cobbled alley lined with converted colonial homes.

Centro Internacional extends north 0.6 mile (1 km) to **Parque Nacional Olaya Herrera** (inside back cover E2, Cra. 7 bet. Calles 35 & 39). This forested park laid out in 1934 with a plethora of sports facilities gets packed on weekends. A monumental fountain honoring liberal party Gen. Rafael Uribe Uribe (1859–1914) stands alongside Carrera 7.

Cementerio Central: Avenida Eldorado—Calle 26—connects Centro Internacional to Bogotá's international airport (TransMilenio buses operate from one end to the other). One of the city's major thoroughfares, this broad boulevard unfurls northwest past Cementerio Central, the city's somewhat decrepit main cemetery, declared a national monument in 1984.

Here, the great men of Colombian history slumber within a fascinating assemblage of baroque, neoclassical, and modernist tombs. The cemetery was laid out in

TurisBog Bus

Introduced in 2013, the green double-decker Turis-Bog Bus (Parque Central Bavaria, tel 57-1/250-6225 or 467-4602, turisbog.com, Wed.–Sat. 9 a.m.–5 p.m.) is a city icon, offering a splendid overview of Bogotá. The narrated tour takes in many of the key tourist sights, from Quinta Bolívar to the Jardín Botánico, on a grand city circuit four times daily. Optional walking tours of La Candelaria can be combined with the bus tour, which offers an audio-guide service, the ability to hop off and hop on any of the nine stops at will, plus a bracelet good for discounts at specific restaurants and shops along the route.

1831 in three sections according to social status. The Tuscan-style main gate, crowned by a statue of Cronos, the Greek god of time, opens to **Globo A,** containing the most noteworthy tombs.

The **Central Alley** leads to a VIP section, including the chapel and a cenotaph in honor of Gonzalo Jiménez de Quesada, founder of Bogotá. To the left side is the tomb of Francisco de Paula Santander, the nation's first constitutional president.

To the right, look for the flower-strewn tomb of Leo Siegfried Kopp (1858–1927), a philanthropic German-Jewish immigrant who founded the Bavaria brewery. After his death, a cult developed around his grave, topped by a sculpture that resembles French sculptor Auguste Rodin's "The Thinker."

The poorest folks were traditionally buried in rows of vaults in **Globo C,** north of Carreras 20 and 22. The site was paved with red bricks in the 1990s to create **Parque del Renacimiento** (Renaissance Park; *inside back cover map D2*), a recreational park featuring a statue by Fernando Botero, plus the **Centro de Memoria, Paz y Reconciliación,** a landscaped Modernist monument with solemn underground exhibition halls that honor and keep alive the memory of Colombia's six million victims of decades of internal armed conflict.

Parque Metropolitano Simón Bolívar:

Bogotá's vast Central Park *(inside back cover map C4)* equivalent takes up 920 acres (372 ha) of western Bogotá and is the largest green recreational area in the city. Carrera 60 and Calle 63 bisect it and form a cross through its heart. The quadrangular park and its satellite attractions compose a complex of landscaped zones, amusement and sports centers, plus entertainment and venues that are a setting for many of Bogotá's leading festivals. A large lake at its heart has rowboats, paddleboats, and canoes.

On the park's northwest side, across Carrera 68, is the **Jardín Botánico José Celestino Mutis.** The lush tropical garden is named for José Celestino Mutis (1732–1808), a Spanish scientist

The tomb of Leo Siegfried Kopp in Cementerio Central

Centro de Memoria, Paz y Reconciliación

- 🅰 Inside back cover D2
- ✉ Cra. 22 #24-52
- ☎ 57-1/381-3000 ext 4610
- 🕐 Guided visits Mon. 11 a.m.– 2 p.m. *&* Tues.– Fri. 8 a.m.–5 p.m.

centromemoria.gov.co

Jardín Botánico José Celestino Mutis

- 🅰 Inside back cover C4–C5
- ✉ Calle 63 #68-95
- ☎ 57-1/437-7060
- 💲 $

jbb.gov.co

Maloka

- 🅰 Inside back cover B4
- ✉ Cra. 68D #24A-51
- ☎ 57-1/427-2707
- 🕐 Closed Mon.
- 💲 $

maloka.org

Plaza de Lourdes

- 🅰 Inside back cover D4

Quinta Camacho

- 🅰 Inside back cover D4–E4
- ✉ Bet. Cra. 5 & 14 & Calles 68 & 74

who led the first botanical expedition in the New World. Founded in 1955 and spanning 50 acres (20 ha), the garden displays more than 2,300 species of native and exotic plants arranged in 35 ecological zones representing hot, dry, and wet climates. The collection of 50 palm species is noteworthy. The arboretum comprises rooms displaying bromeliads and orchids; ornamental flora; tropical moist climates; desert species; plus the

---

Party Time!

Strobe lights flicker. A traditional *vallenato* band pumps out dance music. And liberal pourings of free rum and *aguardiente* help lubricate the festivities as celebrants party aboard a *chiva rumbera*. These party buses ply the streets of Colombia's major cities by night. A bilingual director with a microphone takes charge as the bus combines a city tour with free-flowing liquor and music (and sometimes fried plantain, yucca, and other snacks), typically ending at a nightclub, where you can kick up the party a notch.

Chivas Tours *(Calle 100 #49-07, tel 57-1/481-4444, chivastours.com)* offers various tours plus charter buses for groups.

---

hot, humid conditions of the Amazon, where lotuses the size of dinner tables float atop a black pool. A rose garden is ablaze with the blooms of 73 species. The garden also has bilingual guides to help translate.

Nearby, west of Avenida El Dorado, **Maloka** is an interactive center dedicated to teaching children about science, technology, and culture. More than 200 fun exhibitions in nine halls are

themed for the universe, life, biodiversity, man, electricity and electromagnetism, technology, and molecular structures.

Chapinero

North of Centro Internacional, the Chapinero district (between Carreras 7 and 13) displays a European style and sensibility, exemplified by redbrick mock-Tudor houses that transport you metaphorically to London. **Plaza de Lourdes** is the pulsing heart of Chapinero—a 24/7 venue for street vendors and devout Catholics who come to pray at the **Iglesia de Nuestra Señora de Lourdes.** Dating from 1875, but consecrated in 1937, this Gothic church features a German pipe organ and stained glass.

Northeast of Plaza de Lourdes, **Quinta Camacho** is among the most pleasant of Bogotá's zones, with many upscale redbrick mansions converted into fine-dining restaurants. For a true immersion in coffee culture, seek out **Amor Perfecto** *(Cra. 4 #66-46, tel 57/248-5796, amorperfectocafe.net)*, an educational center and coffee lounge with the intent to expand appreciation of coffees.

A major spot for Bogotá urbane sophisticates, the area nicknamed **Zona G** *(inside back cover map D4, Calles 69 & 70 bet. Cra. 4 & 7)* is a center for globe-spanning fine-dining restaurants: The "G" stands for "gourmet."

Chicó

Chapinero merges north into the Chicó district *(bet. Calles 80 & 90 & Cra. 7 & 15)*. This is ground zero for all things trendy and modern, centered on the **Zona Rosa** (bet. Cra. 7 & 14 & Calles 80 & 85), which resounds at night with the percussion of the city's hottest nightspots

Zona Rosa's up-and-coming competitor is **Parque 93,** a leafy park that also lends its name to the surrounding district in Chicó Norte. **Museo de El Chicó,** three blocks east of Parque 93, displays valuable antiques and art donated to the city by its last owner, Mercedes Sierra de Pérez, as was the 18th-century hacienda in which the antiques and art are housed.

Usaquén

The northernmost of the tourist zones, Usaquén evolved in the 18th century as an upscale retreat for wealthy residents. The village has since been swallowed up by the ever expanding city. Glass-faced office towers and commercial plazas envelope narrow cobbled streets lined with charming colonial homes.

INSIDER TIP:

Some of the best people-watching is around the T-Zone and Parque 93, especially after work and on weekends.

—JEFF JUNG
National Geographic contributor

At its heart is **Parque de Usaquén,** a village-like green with tree-shaded benches. On the park's north side, Calle 119 is lined with bistros and bars. To the east rises the well-preserved **Iglesia de Santa Bárbara** *(inside back cover map F6),* begun in 1775, and the adjoining cloister, added in 1914. Carrera 6A, on the west side, is the Sunday setting for a vibrant flea market focused on eclectic art and crafts. The pedestrian-only street leads to **Hacienda Santa Bárbara** *(inside back cover map F6)*—a modern commercial center built within a 19th-century hacienda. ∎

Parque 93
- Inside back cover E5
- ✉ Calle 93 bet. Cra. 11A & 13

Museo de El Chicó
- Inside back cover E5
- ✉ Cra. 7 #93-01
- ☏ 57-1/623-1066
- 🕐 Closed Sun.

museodelchico.com

Parque de Usaquén
- Inside back cover F6
- ✉ Cra. 6 & Calle 118

EXPERIENCE: Dining Like a Local

When it comes to seeking out hearty fare at bargain prices, head to Calle 11 in La Candelaria, where **Antigua Santafe** (*Calle 11 #6-20; see Travelwise p. 275*) is as authentic as it gets. The quaint eatery fills up quickly at lunchtime, in which case try **La Puerta Falsa** (*Calle 11 #6-50, tel 57-1/286-5091*) next door.

Arepas—corn-based doughs—are a Colombian staple. Some of the best are served at **Aqui in Santa Fé** (*Cra. 7 #62-63, Chapinero, tel 57-1/235-6216*). It serves

arepas with a choice of a dozen fillings.

In the El Retiro commercial plaza in Zona Rosa, **Plaza de Andres** (*Calle 81 #11-94, tel 57-1/863-7880, andrescarne deres.com*) is a Disneyland of food courts from the creator of the festive Andrés D.C. (see Travelwise p. 275). Take your pick from a coffee station, bakery and delicatessen, sandwich and burger stations, seafood and grill areas, and a rice station that serves everything from ceviche to paella.

Around Bogotá

Outside the city boundaries, several towns and rural regions deserve a visit: Chía, where a meal at the one-of-a-kind Andrés D.C. restaurant is not to be missed; the nearby colonial town of Zipaquirá, with its remarkable underground salt cathedral; Laguna de Guatavita, supposed source of the legend of El Dorado; and a trio of national parks to the south that give birders and hikers a taste of the Andes.

The underground Catedral de Sal, 25 acres (10 ha) in size, was carved inside a salt mine.

Chía
🄼 59 B3

Zipaquirá
🄼 59 B3

The Autopista Norte (Avenida Caracas) leads north from downtown Bogotá to the town of **Chía.** While known for the **Puente del Común,** an arched stone-and-brick bridge dating from 1792, Chía is legendary for a one-of-a-kind steak house— **Andrés D.C.** (see Travelwise p. 275)—which has to be experienced to be believed. With more than 700 staff and seating for 3,000 people, this sprawling, eccentric temple of kitsch

is a cross between a restaurant, nightclub, and circus. The classic Colombia fare is sublime, but it's the contagious party mood, crazy paraphernalia and decorations, and zany entertainment that make this experience a must.

North of Bogotá
Zipaquirá: This city, 12 miles (19 km) north of Chía and 31 miles (50 km) north of Bogotá, was founded in 1600 and clings tight to its colonial heritage. The

INSIDER TIP:

At FunZipa Restaurant
(Calle1 #9-99) near the
Zipaquirá salt mines,
you can eat potatoes
cooked in the ovens
used to evaporate salt.

—JOHN ROSENTHAL
National Geographic Traveler
magazine writer

on the west side of town.

Next, follow Carrera 6 uphill
to the **Catedral de Sal,** a remarkable underground salt "cathedral."
Allow at least one hour to explore
this surreal and stunning piece of
engineering and artistry covering
25 acres (10 ha) on three levels.
The cathedral was carved inside
an active salt mine from halite
deposits that formed 250 million
years ago.

**Museo
Arqueológico**
✉ Calle 6 & Cra. 6,
   Zipaquirá
☎ 57-1/852-3499

Catedral de Sal
✉ Calle 3 #8-36,
   Zipaquirá
☎ 57-1/852-9890
💲 $$
catedraldesal
.gov.co

historic core has been preserved
more or less in its entirety, with
whitewashed houses uniformly
decorated with olive-green
trim and base. Its somber main
square—**Plaza de los Comune-
ros**—is surrounded by beautiful
buildings. Most striking is the
Palacio Municipal *(Cra. 7 #4-11),*
the city hall, built in 1929 in clas-
sic French style. On weekdays you
can step inside to admire paint-
ings of Simón Bolívar.

Towering over the square, the
weathered **Catedral Diocesana**
took 111 years to build (it was
consecrated in 1916) with a
remarkable interior of red brick
and stone. One block to the
north, the recently remodeled
Plaza de la Independencia is
ringed by small bars and restau-
rants and is thronged at night,
when salsa and merengue music
crank up.

Zipaquirá was a stronghold
of the pre-Columbian Muisca.
The **Museo Arqueológico** is
filled with their ceramic and
carved-stone antiquities, includ-
ing instruments used to mine
salt from tunnels dug into the
hillside behind the museum,

Still Puffing Away

Colombia's once extensive rail network is
now used mostly for freight. However, two
venerable steam trains still puff away, com-
bining sightseeing with a dose of nostalgia.
Tren Turístico de la Sabana *(tel 57-1/375-
0557, turistren.com.co)* departs Bogotá's
Estación de la Sabana and Estación de
Usaquén for Zipaquirá and Nemocón on
Sundays aboard Baldwin 2-8-2 or 4-8-
steam locomotives. In 2015, plans were
announced to resurrect the **Tren Turístico
del Café y Azúcar** between Cali and
Buenaventura, and La Teblaida, in the
Eje Cafetal. The Tren del Pacífico offers
commercial service.

On the upper level, made
between 1991 and 1995, broad
corridors lead past 14 stations of
the cross bathed in eerie blue,
green, and red light. The lower
level features a sanctuary carved
by miners in 1932. It also features
the main cathedral (dating from
1954), which measures 394 feet
(120 m) long by 72 feet (22 m)
tall, with a huge cross cut directly
from the rock above the high
altar. Here, don't miss the "Cre-
ación del Hombre" ("Creation of
(continued on p. 84)

Pre-Columbian Gold

The people of the Americas began to master goldsmithing as early as 2000 B.C. In time, the Aztec and Andean cultures crafted some of the finest gold sculptures ever produced. Weighted with symbolism and religious significance, their glittering masterpieces—headdresses, pendants, face masks, and figurines—reflected an appreciation for gold far exceeding mere wealth.

A pre-Columbian gold adornment shows a *cacique* with giant nose ring and ear pendants.

When Christopher Columbus arrived on America's shores in 1492, many New World cultures were already highly developed. The vast Aztec and Inca Empires, with their awesome displays of gold, silver, and precious jewels, had evolved metallurgical skills that rivaled those of the Spanish conquistadores.

The foundations of advanced metallurgy were laid by the Chavín, who evolved in the northern coastal region of modern-day Peru around 900 B.C. They mastered gold smelting and casting and excelled at hammering gold into wafer-thin sheets, which they embossed with decorations. The Early Horizon (900 B.C.–A.D. 200) cultures

also discovered the use of alloys. Fully developed smelting evolved during the Moche culture (200 B.C.–A.D. 600), when metallurgists began to experiment with fluidity, color, and strength. Thereafter, most pre-Columbian gold was actually *tumbaga*—a copper-gold alloy. The cultures applied citric acid to dissolve copper from the surface, leaving a sparkling layer of pure gold atop an alloy base.

Meanwhile, northern Andean civilizations evolved the more elaborate lost-wax technique, in which a model of the desired sculpture is made of wax then coated in clay. This is then fired to melt the wax, which drains through

Bogotá's Museo del Oro displays the world's largest collection of pre-Columbian gold.

a small hole and is replaced by molten gold; the ceramic mold is later broken to reveal the sculpture. The skill spread throughout the Americas and reached a high level of sophistication with the Quimbaya (A.D. 300–1550) of Colombia—an area rich in gold deposits. The Quimbaya were renowned for exquisite and masterful gold objects using a wide range of metalworking techniques, including filigree gold thread.

The culture of gold reached its zenith with the Inca, especially prolific goldsmiths whose short-lived empire (A.D. 1400–1532) extended from today's Ecuador to northern Chile. They developed advanced mining techniques and even created a garden populated with life-size gold animals, plants, and people at the temple of the sun in Cusco.

The polytheistic pre-Columbian cultures revered gold as the sweat or tears of the sun—the supreme deity. They fashioned items in an abundance of anthropomorphic and zoomorphic figures, produced for ceremonial or religious function, including funerary and other face masks. Jaguars, bats, frogs, and crocodiles were prevalent. Other items were produced as symbols of status or purely for aesthetic value. Eroticism was a feature of South American (but not Mesoamerican) doll-like figurines, often shown masturbating with gross exaggerations of genitalia—an artistic expression of fertility.

The arrival of the conquistadores witnessed the demise of gold production and the decimation of 2,500 years of cultural achievement. Vast quantities of gold treasure were seized, melted down, and shipped to Spain. Most Andean mines eventually fell into disuse, although *oreros* (prospectors) still work Colombia's streams and hillsides seeking the eternally elusive nugget that will land them on easy street.

Myth of El Dorado

In pre-Columbian times, the Muisca people initiated their *zipa*—tribal chief—by covering his body with gold dust during a ritual at Lake Guatavita, into which *tunjos* (pendants inscribed with wishes) and other gold objects were tossed as an offering. Tales of this "golden king" inspired Spanish conquistadores to imagine *el dorado* (the golden one) as a place and eventually a legendary and elusive lost city of gold. The quest to find El Dorado has inspired European explorers for five centuries, giving rise to the term's metaphorical reference to anywhere wealth can be rapidly acquired, or as a kind of holy grail that one might fruitlessly seek during a lifetime.

Mina de Sal de Nemocón

🗺 59 B3
✉ Nemocón
☎ 57-1/854-4120

minadesal.gov.co

Man") bas-relief sculpture by Carlos Enrique Rodríguez, which is based on "The Creation of Adam" by Michelangelo. Visitors must join guided tours, which depart regularly.

The cathedral is the highlight of **Parque de la Sal,** which includes the **Museo de la Salmuera** (Brine Museum), plus a climbing wall.

Which Brew Is Best?

Colombians love their beer, such as the popular yet undistinguished Águila and the more palatable Club Colombia.

Bogota Beer Company (tel 57-1/702-9999, bogotabeercompany.com) produces eleven handcrafted beers, from its classic English-style Candelaria Clásica light-bodied pale ale to its Guinness-like Tequendama Negra stout. It is found in trendy pubs around Bogotá.

In Medellín, **3 Cordilleras** (Calle 30 #44-176, tel 57-4/444-2337, 3cordilleras .com) microbrewery supplies Medellín's discerning bars and restaurants. Brewmaster Juanchi Velez leads 3.5-hour tours each Thursday at 5:30 p.m. ($$), including five beers.

PANACA Finkana

✉ Vía Briceño km 4
☎ 57-1/307-7002
🕐 Closed Mon.– Thurs.
💲 $$$

parquefinkana.com

While the salt cathedral gets crowded on weekends, the **Mina de Sal de Nemocón,** 9 miles (15 km) to the north in the colonial town of Nemocón, is a more intimate carbon copy with a subterranean chapel, mirror lake, plus mineralogy museum.

A fun way to visit Zipaquirá and Nemocón is aboard the Tren Turístico de la Sabana (see sidebar p. 81) that operates from Bogotá on weekends, with options for inclusive tours

of the salt cathedral or Nemocón's salt mine.

Families with children might enjoy **PANACA Finkana,** a farm-focused theme park with more than 2,000 animals, plus equestrian and other shows; and **Parque Jaime Duque,** an adventure theme park that also has a zoo exhibiting such native species as spectacled bear, capybara, and various monkeys. Both are on the road that links Zipaquirá to the Autopista Norte via Briceño.

Laguna del Cacique Guatavita: This high-rimmed circular lake studs a mountain at 9,842 feet (nearly 3,000 m) in elevation. En route, you pass through emerald meadows reminiscent of England's upland countryside, with sheep grazing the margins on each side. The lake, 35 miles (56 km) northeast of Bogotá, resembles a meteor crater or volcanic cone. It was sacred to the pre-Columbian Muisca, who supposedly tossed gold into the jade-colored waters as part of their rituals (see sidebar p. 83). An unsuccessful attempt in 1580 to drain the lake left a deep notch visible on the lake's western side. A more concerted effort in 1898 by English entrepreneurs succeeded in draining the lake by means of a bore, but the project went bankrupt before it bore fruit.

Well-maintained trails lead uphill from a visitor center to a mirador (lookout) atop the steep-sided meniscus, lipped with bamboo, bromeliads, and foxglove. Interpretive signs in English and

Spanish line the route, and bilingual guides are available.

The lake is 11 miles (18 km) northeast of the town of **Guatavita,** created in the 1960s in colonial Spanish style to house residents displaced by the creation of the Embalse de Tominé reservoir, which supplies Bogotá with water and electricity.

Suesca: The Embalse de Tominé is fed by the Río Bogotá, which flows past the colonial village of Suesca, marked with a sign on the Autopista Norte at Tres Esquinas. The river flows at the base of a natural rock wall—**Las Rocas de Suesca**—in a canyon that has evolved as an activity center for rock climbing, rappelling, and rafting. The sheer-faced sandstone wall reaches

410 feet (125 m) high, runs for 2 miles (3 km), and is Colombia's premier destination for climbing. Climbers of all levels can choose from more than 400 routes, many of them bolted. To get there, walk from the hamlet of **Cacicazgo** along a railway track that runs along the scarp's base (a single train runs early in the morning). In Cacicazgo **Monodedo** (tel 57/316-266-9399, monodedo.com) sells climbing equipment and offers beginning classes in climbing and rappelling. **Colombia Extreme** (tel 57-331/661-5122, colombiaextrema.com/suesca.htm) also offers climbing trips from Bogotá.

Suesca is also a base for canyoning in the **Chocoancia ravine,** for mountain biking, and for spelunking. **Suescalada** (tel

Parque Jaime Duque

🗺 59 B3

✉ Autopista Norte km 34

☎ 57-1/620-0681

💲 $$

parquejaimeduque .com

Laguna del Cacique Guatavita

🗺 59 B3

✉ 11 miles (18 km) NE of Guatavita

☎ 57-1/320-9000

💲 $$

www.car.gov.co

Zipaquirá's colonial core is preserved in entirety; founded in 1600 the city clings to its heritage.

Suesca is acclaimed as Colombia's premier rock-climbing and rappelling site.

Parque Natural Chicaque

- 🗺 59 A2
- ✉ Vía Soacha–La Mesa km 8
- ☎ 57-1/368-3114 (Bogotá) or 57/316-469-6542
- 💲 $$

chicaque.com

Zoológico Santacruz

- 🗺 59 A2
- ✉ Vía Mesitas del Colegio km 16, 5.5 miles (9 km) W of Salto de Tequendama
- ☎ 57/310-329-8880
- 💲 $

zoosantacruz.org

57/604-3637, *suescalada.com*) can get your adrenaline pumping with multiactivity excursions. Birders can head north to **Laguna de Suesca,** one of several remnant bodies of water from a vast lake that once covered the Sabana de Bogotá. Waterfowl can be spied picking amid the reeds for fish and insects.

South & East of Bogotá

The mountains that envelop Bogotá to the south and east offer an invitation to nature lovers. Within a 30-minute drive of the capital, you can hike amid mists that swirl through forest primeval. For this, take the Autopista Sur south from Bogotá through the suburb of Soacha; from there the road north to

Mosquera passes the turnoff for **Parque Natural Chicaque.**

Reached via a 2-mile-long (3 km) unpaved road, this park protects seven different forest types, including swathes of endangered ancient Andean oak. Ancient Muisca trails through the cloud forest unveil waterfalls and lead to **El Pico del Águila,** a mountaintop lookout that offers a sweeping panorama of the Magdalena Valley and toward snowcapped peaks in the distance. The park has a restaurant and lodge, plus guided hikes.

Nearby, off the highway to Girardot, the **Zoológico Santacruz**—considered to be "Bogotá's Zoo"—spans 79 acres (32 ha) and exhibits almost 400 animals, including 136 mammal species, of which 85 percent are native species, including jaguars and tapirs. The zoo is run by the Fundación Zoológico Santacruz, formed in 2001 with a mission to save endangered Andean species and to educate the public about conservation. Nearby, **Parque Orquídeas del Tequendama** displays thousands of orchids, and the garden is splendid for birding.

Colombian native fauna is also a highlight at **Zoo Piscilago Colsubsidio,** a children's theme park and zoo, where you can see such species as the giant anteater, jaguar, and four species of monkey. It's a short distance east of Girardot.

Parque Nacional Natural Chingaza—east from Bogotá via the La Calera-Guasca road—is a stunning example of high-Andean wilderness. However, check with Colombia's National Natural Park System headquarters (*Cra. 10 #20–30, Bogotá, tel 57/353-2400 ext. 102, 138, 139, parquesnacionales.gov.co*) before visiting the park, as it has been closed for security reasons in past years.

Frailejónes (tree-like shrubs) stud this high-altitude *páramo,* (alpine tundra). Andean condors soar above sapphire blue lakes framed by craggy peaks that reach 13,205 feet (4,025 m) atop Cerro San Luis. **Laguna Siecha,** a necklace of once sacred lakes named for the Muisca goddess of fertility, can be reached via **Guasca,** a southern gateway to Laguna del Cacique Guatavita (see pp. 84–85) in the midst of dairy country.

Stunning wilderness also abounds in **Parque Nacional Natural Sumapaz,** a larger carbon copy of PNN Chingaza. Check with the park system headquarters before planning a visit, as the park has been closed for security reasons in past years.

Draped across 59 square miles (153 sq km) of the Cordillera Oriental, this vast mountain wilderness is a realm of endangered endemic species, such as the spectacled bear and Andean condor. In winter months, its peaks are dusted with snow. A trail near **Laguna Chisacá** ascends to a 12,835-foot (3,912 m) peak. Farther in, beyond the dirt track at Nazareth, lies a boggy savanna called Ciénaga Andabobos, studded with ancient glacial lakes. ■

Flower Industry

Colombia exported $1.34 billion of flowers in 2013, making it the second largest supplier of flowers in the world, behind the Netherlands. Anthuriums, carnations, roses—Colombia grows them all, thanks to an ideal climate perfect for year-round cultivation in the fertile Andean plateaus around Bogotá and Medellín, the two primary centers of cultivation. The country's flower industry, which began in the 1960s, today employs about 172,000 people. Production peaks in February, when about 450 million flowers are exported for Valentine's Day.

Zoo Piscilago Colsubsidio
- 🅰 59 A2
- ✉ Vía Bogotá–Girardot km 105, Melgar
- ☎ 57-1/317-510-5647
- 🕐 Closed Mon.–Tues., and daily Dec.–Jan. & June–July
- 💲 $$

piscilago.co

Parque Orquídeas del Tequendama
- 🅰 59 A2
- ✉ Bogotá-Mesitas del Colegio km 19
- ☎ 57/300-464-5960
- 💲 $

orquideasdel tequendama.com

Parque Nacional Natural Chingaza
- 🅰 59 B2–C2

Parque Nacional Natural Sumapaz
- 🅰 59 A1–B1

A region marked by soaring peaks and fertile valleys, where the traditional lifestyle of Colombia thrives and adventurers find thrills

Eastern Highlands

Iglesia de Nuestra Señora de
La Candelaria, Macheta

Eastern Highlands

Northeast of Bogotá, the Cordillera Oriental forms a convoluted backbone that separates the lowlands of Los Llanos to the east from the broad basin of the Río Madgalena to the west. Spanning the departments of Cundinamarca, Boyacá, Santander, and Norte de Santander, the region is considered the historical heart of Colombia. Dotted with time-capsule colonial pueblos, it has become a haven for those in search of a traditional way of life, as well as a haven for high-mountain trekkers and adventurers.

In traditional dress, men from the region wear fedoras and woolen ponchos called *ruanas*.

The region was a center for the pre-Hispanic Muisca culture, whose abundant use of gold and emeralds primed the Spanish conquistadores' quest for a mythical El Dorado. Tunja, the Muisca seat of power, is today the architecturally rich capital of Boyacá Department and the main hub from which roads radiate to cities and sites throughout the region.

Settled at an early stage of Spanish rule, the region contains some of Colombia's best preserved colonial towns, notably Villa de Leyva and Barichara. These architectural jewels are among the most visited sites in the nation and boast boutique hotels that combine the best of both worlds, old and new.

No other region in the nation played such

an important part in the liberation from Spanish rule. The most hallowed ground in the nation is Puente de Boyacá, where a republican army led by Simón Bolívar and Francisco de Paula Santander won the decisive battle that ended Spanish rule in South America.

The Eastern Highlands are also replete with off-beat tourist draws, from the prehistoric kronosaur and other fossils of Monquirá to the emerald mines of Chivor and the thermal spas of Paipa. Meanwhile, San Gil has evolved as the extreme-sports epicenter of Colombia, drawing thrill seekers for white-water rafting and other adventure activities.

Geography swings to extremes in this region, from the plunging canyon of

Chicamocha, where cacti grow at its base, to the glacier-capped peaks of Parque Nacional Natural El Cocuy, which tempt hikers for some of the most rewarding trekking in the Andes. Just getting to Cocuy from Tunja takes the better part of a day as the broad vales of Boyacá give way to mountain chains pleated into ridges cleaved by gorges of ever increasing height and depth. These lushly forested heights span a half dozen or so national parks that climax out at 17,497 feet (5,333 m) atop Ritacuba Blanco in Parque Nacional Natural El Cocuy.

Climatic variations also run to extremes. Most of the highland area enjoys a temperate climate. However, you'll need plenty of cold-weather gear for exploring Cocuy, which bears the brunt of rain-bearing winds from the east.

Most sites can be easily reached within a day's drive of Bogotá via a secure and well-maintained highway that connects the capital to Tunja and, at the region's extreme north, the major city of Bucaramanga. Frequent intercity buses ease travel between major cities, from where regional buses *(chivas)* and taxis can get you to your final destination. If you plan to drive, be prepared to negotiate precipitous switchback passes. ■

NOT TO BE MISSED:

Visiting an emerald mine 95

Watching the guards in period costume at Puente de Boyacá 99

Villa de Leyva's cobbled streets 100–101

Soaking in a curative thermal spa at Paipa 103

A trek in Parque Nacional Natural El Cocuy 108–109

White-water rafting at San Gil 111

Snacking on *hormigas culonas* in Baricharā 120

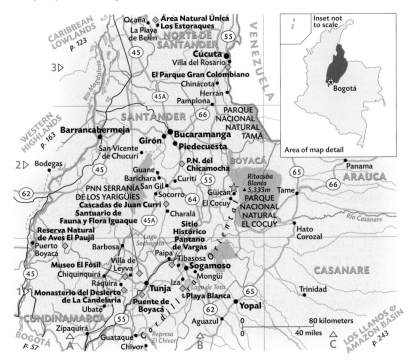

Boyacá

The department of Boyacá boasts the lion's share of the Eastern Highlands attractions. The region is sprinkled with convents, haciendas, and colonial villages, reflecting a history that spans almost five centuries. In addition, kaleidoscopic landscapes span cactus-studded deserts to high-mountain *páramos* (alpine tundra) and peaks that glisten with snow.

A classic car navigates the cobbled streets in Villa de Leyva, Boyacá.

Boyacá

🅐 91 B1

Visitor Information

✉ Calle 20 #9-90,
   Casa de la Torre,
   Tunja

☎ 57-8/742-0150

**boyaca.gov.co
/SecCultura**

Centuries of History

At the time of the Spanish arrival, this area was the heartland of the Muisca indigenous people, whose twin spheres of influence centered on rival tribal confederations led by the *caciques* (chiefs) Tisquesusa (near today's Bogotá) and Nemequene (Tunja). The Muisca evolved communities that were specialized in artisanal production of textiles, ceramics, and metal goods, and were the most advanced indigenous group the Spanish encountered in the territory that constitutes present-day Colombia. In 1536, Spanish conquistador Gonzalo Jiménez de Quesada entered the region and subdued the confederations. Muisca culture was swiftly exterminated under the brutal subjugation of Spanish rule. Tunja was founded in 1539 by Gonzalo Suárez

Rendón and evolved as one of the most important administrative and economic centers of the Viceroyalty of New Grenada. Nonetheless, the 19th-century flames of independence were stoked here, and the sequence of battles between nationalists and Spanish royalists culminated in the decisive battle at Puente de Boyacá, near Tunja, on August 7, 1819.

The Western Route

Two routes lead north from Bogotá, granting access to the sites of Boyacá and, beyond, Santander. The vast majority of visitors speed along the dual highway (Hwy. 55) that leads to Tunja. A more scenic and less congested westerly route (Hwy. 45A) begins at Zipaquirá (see pp. 80–81, 84) and runs via Ubaté, Chiquinquirá, and Barbosa. Perfect for travelers heading directly to San Gil and Bucaramanga, the latter route also grants easy access to the numerous sites to be seen west of Villa de Leyva.

The countryside is a patchwork of arable fields and pastures conjured into a jigsaw puzzle by meandering hedgerows. Roadside signs around **Ubaté** tempt a brief stop to admire the **Iglesia de Santa Barbara** before continuing through a fertile valley to Laguna de Fúquene—an important source for the reeds used for weaving *paja* (straw) into hats, as well as a great birding site. Least bitterns and spot-flanked gallinule are especially common. The lake seasonally floods its plain. It was once

Colombia's largest freshwater lake, but irrigation and drainage to supply Bogotá has reduced it to only one-third of its original size.

Chiquinquirá: This market town—also a major religious center—sprawls on the west side of the Río Suárez Valley at a brisk 8,432 feet (2,570 m) elevation. Religious tourism is big business. The lovely main square—**Plaza de Bolívar**—is framed by shops selling religious trinkets; *cañitas,* the city's famous pink candy-cane sticks; and brightly colored guitars. A

INSIDER TIP:

Play *tejo* [see sidebar p. 117] in Boyacá Department, its birthplace, where tradition holds that the losing team picks up the beer tab.

–THOMAS CLYNES
National Geographic
magazine writer

bronze statue of Simón Bolívar in the square depicts him in working clothes, his sleeves rolled up, knee cocked, and hands on his hips.

The town's main draw is the **Basilica de Nuestra Señora del Rosario.** Pilgrims flock here each July 9 and December 26 to ask for miracles (or forgiveness of their sins) by lighting a candle at "La Chinita," a painting—the "Virgin of the Rosary" (1563),

(continued on p. 96)

Emeralds

For 400 years, Colombia has produced the bulk of the world's supply of emeralds. Since 2007, Brazil leads the world in emerald exports, yet Colombia still sets the standard for quality. Sought-after for 4,000 years as a symbol of fidelity and good health, and for their radiant beauty, the purest and greenest of emeralds are more precious even than diamonds.

Emeralds are extracted from narrow tunnels that follow veins in Colombia's emerald mines.

Emeralds–from the Latin *esmaraldus,* via the Greek *smaragdos* (green gem)–are a rare form of beryl and derive their intense green color from traces of chromium and vanadium. They were formed millions of years ago when beryllium silicates and chromium, which are rarely located together, came together in veins deep beneath the Earth's crust. After the minerals cooled and crystallized to form exquisite gemstones, geologic forces took eons to push the gems toward the surface.

They range in color from slightly yellowish green to deep blue-green. Only the darker gems are considered emeralds; light-toned gems are called green beryls. The value of an emerald depends on cut, color, clarity, and carat. The most precious combine a pure and vivid verdant hue with flawless transparency. Though emeralds are not as hard as rubies, sapphires, or diamonds, the finest and rarest emeralds–called *gota de aceite* (oil drop, which refers to a visual effect due to structure)– surpass all in value at up to $30,000 per carat. Such flawless clarity is extremely rare. Natural mineral inclusions often mar purity, although they may add to a stone's character. A rare type of Colombian emerald known as a trapiche, for example, exhibits dark carbon impurities that give the stone a six-pointed radial pattern, like the spokes of a *trapiche,* or mill wheel.

Holy Gemstone

Since about 2000 B.C., emeralds from Egypt were traded throughout ancient cultures. Cleopatra, among others, believed the stones held magical properties and lent her name to Cleopatra's Mines, near the Red Sea town of Berenice. The Inca and Aztec also regarded the emerald as a holy gemstone and began mining crystals around A.D. 500. Following the Spanish conquest, vast quantities of emeralds were shipped to Europe. Spain traded the gems for gold to Egypt, India, and Persia, filling the treasure chests of emperors, sultans, and maharajas.

Ever since, Colombian mines have produced the bulk of the world's emeralds, being overtaken only in recent years by slightly inferior gems from Brazil and Africa. Colombia's emerald production fell from 5.73 million carats in 2006 to 2.12 million carats in 2008. (Emeralds also come from mines as far afield as Afghanistan and Zimbabwe.) Colombia has about 150 known deposits; those from the Muzo region,

Emeralds embedded in quartz (upper); a cut emerald is partnered with diamonds (lower).

EXPERIENCE: Visiting the Emerald Mines

Colombia has three main emerald mining areas–Chivor, near Tenza, 56 miles (90 km) northeast of Bogotá; and the twin sites of Coscuez and Muzo, in western Boyacá and Cundinamarca. Together, they compose the Emerald Belt in the Cordillera Oriental. The Muzo mine, 75 miles (120 km) north of Bogotá, is owned by Swiss-based Muso International Group and cannot be visited. Municipio Chivor's Asociación Sendero Verde Esmeralda *(tel 57-1/314-382-4901, e-mail: hugo.san .chivor@hotmail.com, $$$$$)* **offers a full-day guided tour of the Chivor region, including a visit to the mines.**

including the mines of Muzo, Coscuez, and La Pita, account for three-quarters of production. Each mine produces slightly distinct types of crystals. Those from Muzo, for example, have more saturated color; those from Chivor have a slightly more blue cast and are typically found in a brownish matrix of calcite and iron oxide, or in marble-like shale.

Emeralds are extracted by open-pit mining or in narrow tunnels that follow veins tightly sandwiched in shale. Modern mining regulations have made cave-ins a rare occurrence. Even so, mining emeralds is a job for young men with strong bodies. Locals, called *guaqueros,* dig in the slag or scour the rivers for emeralds washed downstream with tailings.

Jewelers have developed a special cut because of the gem's hexagonal shape: the rectangular emerald cut with beveled corners.

Reserva Natural de Aves El Paujil

🅰 91 A1

by Spanish artist Alonso de Narváez—whose deteriorated condition they believe to have been restored by the prayers of a pious woman in 1586. In 1829, Pope Pius VII declared the Virgen de Chiquinquirá the patron saint of Colombia. The painting is displayed at the cathedral's impressive altar.

Now walk northwest one block to **Parque Julio Flórez,** where you'll see the **Iglesia La Parroquia de la Renovación,** built on the site of the original church (toppled by an earthquake) where legend says the "La Chinita" miracle took place; a staircase near the altar leads down to the supposed site. The park is named for a local poet, whose bust adorns the square.

Fundación ProAves

In 1998, a group of Colombians hatched an initiative to save the yellow-eared parrot from extinction. Fundación ProAves *(tel 57-1/340-3229, proaves.org)* has since become one of the most effective conservation groups in the tropics. ProAves owns 26 reserves that serve to protect endangered species in partnership with local communities. And the yellow-eared parrot now numbers more than 1,000.

Two blocks to the southeast of Plaza de Bolívar, **Parque Papal** honors the visit in 1986 of Pope John Paul II to the area. Nearby, the lovely republican-style former train station with a green mansard roof now houses the **Palacio de la Cultura Rómulo Rozo** *(Av. Julio*

Always check before assuming you can use your credit card. Many merchants are willing to shave the price a little if you use cash (en efectivo).

—RACHAEL JACKSON
National Geographic Channels researcher

Sálazar & Calle 21), with a library and small art museum.

Reserva Natural de Aves El Paujil: One of the last refuges for many endangered lowland species, including the Magdalena tapir and the variegated spider monkey, this 2,406-acre (974 ha) nature reserve was created by ProAves in 2003 to protect the only known habitat of the critically endangered blue-billed curassow (locally called *el paujil*). The reserve spans 558 to 2,297 feet (170–700 m) in elevation on the western slopes of the Cordillera Oriental, near the village of Puerto Pinzón. Highway 60 leads west from Chiquinquirá and drops down to Puerto Boyacá; from there, it's two hours on convoluted lanes to reach Puerto Pinzón. The reserve has accommodations and extensive trails.

Valle de Tenza: Midway between Bogotá and Tunja, there's a sign on Highway 55 for the town of Guatague via Machetá, the gateway via an

Period icons from the colonial era fill Tunja's Casa Museo del Fundador.

exquisite gorge to one of the most beautiful mountain zones in the region. The road winds downhill via Guataque to **Represa El Chivor,** a man-made lake measuring 21 miles (33 km) end to end. You can circle the lake, passing through primitive tunnels with water cascading down from above.

Passing over the dam at the eastern end of the lake, turn right for the small town of **Chivor,** gateway to the second major emerald mining zone in Colombia. Visits to the mines can be arranged with advance notice (see sidebar p. 95).

Tunja

One of the oldest cities in Colombia, and also the coldest (average temperature is 52°F/11°C), Tunja occupies a sloping mountain plateau 85 miles (137 km) north of Bogotá. It was founded in 1539 by Gonzalo Suárez Rendón atop Hunza, the pre-Hispanic seat of the Zipa—the ruler of the northernmost of the two Muisca confederations. Today, it's the capital of Boyacá; this sizable city (pop. 150,000) has a large student population.

Most sites of interest surround or are within one block of Tunja's vast and treeless **Plaza de Bolívar** (Cra. 9 & Calle 19). It has a life-size statue of the namesake hero atop his horse at its center and is ringed by imposing colonial buildings. Begin with the **Casa Museo del Fundador,** on the plaza's east side. It was built in 1540 in Mudejar style for Gonzalo Suárez Rendón. The city's tourism office is on the ground floor. Upstairs, Rendón's former living quarters display suits of armor, religious vestments, and period furnishings, but the highlight is the magnificent ceiling frescoes of mythical

Chivor
🗺 91 B1

Tunja
🗺 91 B1
Visitor Information
✉ Secretaría de Cultura y Turismo, Casa del Fundador, Cra. 9 #19-68
☎ 57-8/742-6547

Casa Museo del Fundador
✉ Cra. 9 #19-68, Tunja
☎ 57-8/742-3272
💲 $

Casa de Don Juan de Vargas

✉ Calle 20 #8-52, Tunja

☎ 57-8/742-6611

🕐 Closed Mon.

💲 $

fondocultura.org /casa-museo.html

scenes. Similar motifs adorn the ceiling of the **Casa de Don Juan de Vargas,** around the corner to the northeast. The Mudejar theme repeats in the panel-beamed ceiling of the plaza's **Catedral Santiago de Tunja.**

The city abounds with colonial churches. Top billing goes to the **Iglesia Santo Domingo** *(Cra. 11 #19-55),* one block west of the plaza. Initiated in 1559, its simple exterior belies the extravagance of its baroque wood carvings, most remarkably in the Capilla del Rosario—a New World Sistine Chapel that drips with gilt and is layered with mother of pearl.

The **Templo y Convento de San Francisco** *(Cra. 10 #22-23),* completed in 1572, is not to be missed for its baroque cedar Altar de los Pelíanos and lovely cloister. Another glorious interior

adorns the **Convento y Templo de Santa Clara de Real** *(Cra. 7 #19-58).* Completed in 1574, it was the first convent established in Colombia. Note the facade's pilasters adorned with grapes, garlands, and pelicans; and the golden sun on the ceiling, used to trick the *indígenas* (indigenous people) into conversion to Catholicism.

The tourism office in Tunja can provide a complete list of other sites. Don't miss the **Paredón de los Mártires** *(Cra. 11 & Calle 14),* four blocks southwest of the plaza at Parque Bosque de la República. This Wall of Martyrs—a sloping paved walkway studded with busts and statues—honors independence fighters executed by Spanish royalists in November 1816. Note the bullet holes in the wall, protected by a glass screen.

Puente de Boyacá: One of the

At Puente de Boyacá, the Monumento a la Gloria de Bolívar honors the independence hero.

Scams to Watch Out For

Although the vast majority of tourists return home without mishap, many are victims of scams large and small. Crafty scam artists are incredibly inventive and apply basic psychology to part naive and inattentive visitors from their money and/or possessions. Use a healthy dose of skepticism, especially when dealing with "Good Samaritans" and anyone who approaches you with a strange request. Here are some scams to watch out for.

If your credit card transaction is processed incorrectly, make sure incorrect imprints are destroyed. Keep your credit card in sight during transactions to avoid "skimming."

Someone sprays you with what resembles bird droppings, then a partner appears and starts wiping you down. Presto! Your pockets are picked. Make sure to remain vigilant.

If you get a flat tire, drive to a secure place where there are other people. Many victims are robbed by "Good Samaritans" offering to help change a tire.

Never trust a plainclothes policeman, even if he shows you identification. Such scams are common in Colombian cities.

Decline drinks, cigarettes, gum, et cetera offered by strangers; they may be tainted with *burundanga* (scopolamine), a hypnotic drug that erases free will and short-term memory. It is commonly used in robberies and rapes in Colombia.

Arguments are often a ruse to distract your attention. Whether the argument involves you or not, make a retreat.

You pay with a 50,000 peso note (about US$28). The waiter or merchant or taxi driver disappears, then returns and hands it back claiming it's a fake. In fact, he's just handed you a counterfeit. Mark all high denomination bills in advance to avoid being scammed.

Never accept unsolicited help with your luggage.

Beware of foreign residents (or anyone else) selling you an unbelievable real estate deal. If it's too good to be true, it's just that.

---

significant events in Colombian history took place 9 miles (15 km) south of Tunja. Here, on August 7, 1819, a makeshift patriot army led by Simón Bolívar and Francisco de Paula Santander defeated Spanish troops under Gen. José María Barreiro in a battle that closed the door on Spanish rule. The main Bogotá–Tunja highway bisects the hilly site, which is studded with various monuments.

The battle's epicenter was a tiny bridge—the Puente de Boyacá—that spans the Río Teatinos (it can be crossed with a running leap). To the north side, a statue of Santander looks over the **Plaza de Armas.** Note the large rock

inscribed with a plaque that honors a legion of British volunteers, to whom Bolívar credited victory. South of the bridge, the **Plazoleta de las Banderas** is ringed with the flags of Bolivia, Colombia, Ecuador, Panama, Peru, and Venezuela fluttering over an eternal flame: **La Llama de la Libertad.** Soldiers in period costume often stand guard.

The hill immediately east of the bridge rises to the grandiose neoclassical **Monumento a la Gloria de Bolívar,** which dominates the historic site. It stands 59 feet (18 m) tall and features five caryatids representing the liberated nations. Angels stand at each corner, blaring their trumpets

Puente de Boyacá
🅰 91 B1

Villa de Leyva

🅰 91 A1

Visitor Information

✉ Oficina de Turismo, Cra. 9 #13-04

☎ 57-8/732-0232

Casa Museo de Antonio Nariño

✉ Cra. 9 #10-25, Villa de Leyva

☎ 57-8/732-0342

🕐 Closed Wed.

www.museos colombianos.gov.co

Museo de Arte Religioso del Carmen

✉ Cra. 10 & Calle 14, Villa de Leyva

☎ 57-8/732-0214

🕐 Closed Mon.– Fri.

💲 $

in proud proclamation of the triumph of liberty.

Villa de Leyva

Picture-perfect in every way, Villa de Leyva is Colombia's poster child of architectural preservation. Founded in 1572 by Hernán Suárez de Villalobos, this lovely colonial town 24 miles (39 km) west of Tunja was declared a national monument in 1954. It has been preserved in its entirety, including its stone-paved, uneven streets embedded with fossils from the surrounding area. Every building is whitewashed, with terra-cotta

INSIDER TIP:

Head to the Plaza Mayor at dusk to watch the orange lights come up as the sun goes down.

—JEFF JUNG
National Geographic contributor

tile roofs, plus bottle green doors, trim, and balconies, many decorated with flowerpots overflowing with geraniums. Such beauty is particularly remarkable given the town's setting in the semiarid Valle de Saquencipá, which is studded with cacti and thorny scrub nibbled by goats.

The town is laid out in a near-perfect grid around the vast cobbled **Plaza Mayor.** Squat and unremarkable by Colombian standards, the **Iglesia de Nuestra Señora del Rosario** dates from

1608, but it is rarely open. The flags fluttering over the **Casa del Primer Congreso** (*Cra. 9 & Calle 13, closed Sun.*), on the park's northwest corner, recall the first congress that met here on October 4, 1812, to set up the brief-lasting Provincias Unidas de la Nueva Grenada. Facing it, on the south side of Carrera 9 is the town hall, or **Alcaldía,** housing the official Tourist Information Bureau.

History buffs might enjoy the **Casa Museo de Antonio Nariño,** where the forefather of independence spent his last days; and the **Casa Natal de Antonio Ricuarte,** a restored mansion in Parque Ricuarte where the eponymous independence martyr was born. Both serve as history museums.

The real pleasure is in simply strolling the streets and savoring the past through the soles of your shoes. Allow two days for taking in all the sights, including the **Museo de Arte Religioso del Carmen** in the **Iglesia de Nuestra Señora del Carmen,** which adjoins the still functioning **Monasterio de las Carmelitas Descalzas** (Convent of the Shoeless Carmelites) on Plazuela del Carmen. The museum displays an impressive collection of religious art and icons.

Around Villa de Leyva:

Villa de Leyva is a base for horseback riding, mountain biking, and excursions to a half dozen or so sites that make for intriguing day trips. Most are northwest of town, along the road to Santa Sofia.

The badlands about 1.2 miles

The graveyard at Convento del Santo Ecce Homo, a convent founded by Dominicans in 1620

(2 km) northwest of town are pitted with Pozos Azules, jade blue pools whose color is attributed to sulfur minerals. The pools ($) can be visited on horseback. Just beyond the pools, the road divides at the Amonita, a large ammonite set in a crossroads monument. Families will enjoy visiting the **Granja de Avestruces** (*Zoocriadero Finca El Carmen, tel 57/313-442-7796, espexoticas.com .co, $$*), an ostrich farm that also has horses, llamas, and sheep.

Turn right at the Amonita for the **Museo El Fósil** to view a nearly complete kronosaur—an ancient marine reptile resembling a giant alligator—preserved as it was discovered in 1977. The fossil measures 23 feet (7 m) and dates from the Cretaceous period, when the area was a shallow saltwater sea. Opposite, and more impressive, is the modern **Centro de Investigaciones**

Paleontológicas, a research and education center displaying dozens of dinosaur skeletons. You can watch scientists at work through a glass wall.

Nearby, **Parque Arqueológico de Monquirá** preserves 30 or so stone monoliths, many of them phallic. This mini-Stonehenge dates back almost 2,000 years and served as a Muisca ritual site and astronomical observatory.

Another 2.5 miles (4 km) along the Santa Sofia road, signs point the way to **Convento del Santo Ecce Homo** ($). Founded by Dominicans in 1620, its walls include giant ammonites and other fossil stones. Flanking a garden courtyard, the cloisters open to rooms laid out by themes that display farming instruments, friars' quarters, a library, and sacred relics. Its chapel is notable for its gilded retable, plus parchment musical manuscripts in the choir loft.

Museo El Fósil
- 🅰 91 A1
- ✉ Vía Santa Sofia km 4
- ☎ 57/310-570-0243
- 💲 $$

Centro de Investigaciones Paleontológicas
- ✉ Via Santa Sofía km 4
- ☎ 57/314-219-2904
- 🕐 Closed Mon.
- 💲 $$
- http://on.fb.me /1tzNqIF

Parque Arqueológico de Monquirá
- 🕐 Closed Mon.
- 💲 $

Ráquira
 91 A1

Monasterio del Desierto de la Candelaria
91 A1
✉ La Candelaria, 3.7 miles (6 km) SE of Ráquira
☎ 57-8/257-7837
💲 $

The Sáchica–Sutamarchán road leads west to **Ráquira** (19 miles/30 km from Villa de Leyva). The "city of pots" is well named, as virtually the entire community exists on making earthenware vases, piggy banks, dwarfs, and other pottery. The dirt road that clambers up over the desertified hills east of Ráquira drops to the colorful hamlet of Candelaria

de Arcabuco mountains are enshrined within this 16,680-acre (6,750 ha) wildlife sanctuary, which ranges between 7,875 and 12,500 feet (2,400–3,800 m) in elevation. This compact park offers sensational hiking and birding. It is made up of two massifs, different in character. The southern and lower massif is dry, with opuntia cactus. The

A group of horseback riders explore the sites around Villa de Leyva.

Santuario de Fauna y Flora Iguaque
91 B1
✉ 8 miles (13 km) NE of Villa de Leyva
☎ 57/312-585-9892
💲 $$$

naturariguaquesp
.weebly.com

and the **Monasterio del Desierto de la Candelaria,** an Augustine monastery founded in 1604 and still in use. You can visit the chapel, a small museum, and hermit-like grotto, and join monks in the cloisters and courtyard.

Santuario de Fauna y Flora Iguaque: Rising northeast of Villa de Leyva, the **Alticlinal**

northern range rises to a *páramo* studded with *frailejónes* (see sidebar p. 104), drawing the bulk of visitors. A local community organization administers the reserve at **Naturar Iguaque Lodge**, with a restaurant and accommodations.

A steep and sometimes muddy 3-mile (4.7 km) trail with interpretive signs ascends from Naturar Iguaque Lodge to

Laguna Iguaque, one of eight glacial lagoons in the northeast corner of the reserve. It was sacred to the Muisca. Allow six hours round-trip. You'll pass through moist subtropical forest. Above, cold mists swirl through dwarf forest, where mosses and ferns thrive in the sodden mists haunted by the whistles of quetzals and Andean siskins. Beyond lies the páramo.

The signed turnoff for the park is 1.2 miles (2 km) south of Arcabuco; from there, it's 12 miles (20 km) via dirt road to the visitor center. The reserve (but not Naturar Iguaque Lodge) can also be accessed on the road north from Tunja to Moniquirá via a dramatic gorge. Tour operators offer trips from Villa de Leyva (see Travelwise pp. 310–311).

Paipa

Framed by forested mountains, the town of Paipa, 28 miles (45 km) northeast of Tunja, looks southeast over a large man-made lake sparkling in a broad valley famous for its *aguas termales* (thermal mineral springs), which have made Paipa a renowned center for health tourism. Paipa, founded in 1568, is worth a stop to admire its historic core with whitewashed houses adorned with pink doors and green windows.

The historic main square, **Parque Jaime Rook,** was laid out in 1602 and named for the Englishman Col. James Rook, leader of the British Legion of volunteers who sided with Simón Bolívar at Puente de Boyacá

(see p. 99). The sandstone **Iglesia Catedral San Miguel Arcángel** with a neoclassical facade adjoins the handsome **Casa Cultural,** mingling colonial and republican styles.

Lago Sochagota, 1.2 miles (2 km) south of town, is popular for angling, boating, and waterskiing. A more intimate experience can be enjoyed at the must-see **D'Acosta Hotel Hacienda del Salitre** (see Travelwise p. 279).

Chivas

Chivas—the traditional mode of transportation in rural Colombia—are a quintessential element of Colombian culture. Chivas (the word means "goats") are typically old school buses or trucks with parallel bench seats and cutaway sides, with doors to the sides for each row. They're painted in various combinations of yellow, blue, and red (the colors of the Colombian flag) and gaudily adorned. Colombian peasants call them *escaleras* (stairs) because of the ladder for accessing the rooftop luggage rack.

Originally a Jesuit convent dating from 1736, this national monument is now an atmospheric boutique hotel on a working dairy estate. Visitors can use the open-air thermal pool. Simón Bolívar slept here after the battle of July 25, 1819.

Sitio Histórico Pantano de Vargas: The Battle of the Vargas Swamp occurred in a broad valley surrounded by hills and was a prelude to the final, decisive battle at Puente de Boyacá (see p. 99). The battle site, 4 miles (7 km) southeast of Paipa, is a national shrine and features a

Paipa

 91 B1

Visitor Information

✉ Cortupaipa, Edificio Sede Cultural, Calle 24 #21-31, on SE side of plaza

☎ 57-8/785-2910

E-mail: cortupaipa @turismopaipa.com

Lago de Tota

🏔 91 B1

paved plaza with artisans' stores and a chapel. Steps lead up to the **Monumento a los Catorce Lanceros,** the largest monument in Colombia. Erected in 1970 by Rodrigo Arenas Betancour, it measures 330 feet (100 m) long and 131 feet (40 m) tall and features a massive spearlike spire overhanging a bronze sculpture that depicts 14 mounted lancers. Trails lead to **Cerro de Bolívar,** the hill from which Bolívar directed the battle; **Piedra Hueca,** a large rock with a cave where Bolívar supposedly prayed for victory; the **Casa de las Seis Ventanas,** an adobe mansion where the Spanish general José María Barreiro was headquartered; and the **Casa Museo de La Libertad,** a museum displaying armaments from the battle.

Lago de Tota

Colombia's largest alpine lake occupies a basin dramatically framed by a mountain meniscus at 9,892 feet (3,015 m) above sea level. Stocked with rainbow trout, it is fringed by reeds that are a habitat for the Colombian grebe and Colombian ruddy duck. Hotels line its northeast shore. The lake is reached via the ungainly industrial city of Sogamoso, with its **Museo Arqueológico Sogamoso** *(Calle 9a #6-45, tel 57-8/770-3122, closed Mon.),* which has a re-creation of an indigenous Muisca village, plus exhibits on goldsmithing and mummification.

Lago de Tota comes into view at El Crucero, 10 miles (16 km) southeast of Sogamoso. The paved road extends along the east shore, where campesinos (peasant farmers) cultivate onions in fields that extend to the steely blue waters. Beyond the village of Aquitania, the now unpaved road (four-wheel-drive vehicle recommended) climbs up and around the lake's south side, passing

Frailejón

Of the tropical Andes' approximately 45,000 plant species, none is so emblematic as the *frailejón* (*Espeletia* genus) of the treeless high-altitude *páramo* grasslands of Colombia, Ecuador, and Venezuela. This curious looking perennial tree-like shrub grows up to 10 feet (3 m) tall and is named for its resemblance to a hooded monk. Its succulent and hairy leaves, arranged in dense spirals, have evolved to protect the marcescent plant against cold; when the leaves die, they wrap the trunk like a warm blanket.

Paipa's neoclassical Iglesia Catedral San Miguel Arcángel boasts an austere beauty.

Playa Blanca, a sugar white beach that melts into jade green waters.

To the west of the lake, the village of **Iza** delights with its quintessential colonial architecture painted a uniform white and bottle green. Set amid lush meadows shaded by willows and yews, this village is wed to the dairy and wool industry; it also has thermal springs (Iza is a Chibcha word for "place of healing").

Iza can be reached from the lovely colonial village of **Tibasosa,** 5 miles (8 km) west of Sogamoso. Tibasosa enjoys a thriving tourist trade and is rivaled in beauty by **Mongüí,** 7 miles (11 km) east of Sogamoso. Voted the most beautiful village in Boyacá, this sleepy mountain village is improbably known as a major producer of soccer balls, which are for sale in town.

Parque Nacional Natural El Cocuy

Twenty-five snowcapped peaks sparkle amid this 1,180-square-mile (3,060 sq km) national park, a trekker's dream that is a high-mountain refuge of pristine and rugged splendor. An alpine wonder on a par with the Alps, Cocuy is about as pristine as any Andean destination in South America. Despite its remoteness, Colombia's premier

Iza
🏔 91 B1

Tibasosa
🏔 91 B1

Mongüí
🏔 91 B1

Parque Nacional Natural El Cocuy
🏔 91 B2–C2
✉ Cra. 10A #20-30, Bogota
☎ 57-1/353-2400 or 7/890-0359
💲 $$
parquesnacionales.gov.co

trekking destination has only recently been safe to visit. In 2003, an elite Colombian army brigade drove out the ELN and FARC guerrillas who had used Cocuy as a base.

Today, the park remains a sanctum of a different sort: Endangered spectacled bears, Colombia, although the snowcap is retreating at a frightening rate. The high sierra peaks—15 of which top 16,400 feet (5,000 m)— compose only a tiny fraction of the park, which extends east downhill through thick montane forest to the *llanuras* (plains) of **Arauca.** The park overlaps the

Every house in El Cocuy is whitewashed, with mint green trim.

mountain tapirs, and all the known species of Colombian felines live here. Andean condors soar overhead. And the park shelters more than 700 species of endemic flora, including valleys of *frailejón*-studded *páramo.*

The park spans an elevation range of 17,487 feet (5,330 m) and covers more than 1,180 square miles (3,060 sq km). The ice-tipped Sierra Nevada constitutes the largest glacial mass in

U'Wa indigenous reservation and four other indigenous *resguardos* (reservations).

Several summits require technical know-how and gear, and should not be attempted by the inexperienced climber. Even one-day hikes are physically demanding. And a complete 44-mile (71 km) circuit takes up to a week, stitching together snowcapped peaks and lagoons via high-altitude passes and deep cirque valleys. Hikers must register at the park headquarters or ranger station before departing and after completing the trek. December through March is the best time to visit, with sunny skies; most other months, rain (often torrential and enduring) can be expected. You'll need to be self-sufficient.

Arriving at the park requires a full-day drive from Tunja as you scale three mountain passes and drop into a series of Andean-scale valleys. The scenery is kaleidoscopic, causing double takes that conjure images of England's Lake District and the Scottish Highlands. Prepare for washouts that can halt your progress en route to the sleepy gateway villages of El Cocuy and Güicán. The two communities are connected by paved road and by a 27-mile (43 km) high-mountain dirt road via Alto de la Cueva. Three access routes to the park branch off this dirt road: Ritacu'wa (north), Hacienda La Esperanza (center), and Valle de Lagunillas (south).

El Cocuy: This charming village is prettier than the nearby community of Güicán, thanks to its cobbled streets and whitewashed colonial-era houses painted with mint green trim—uniform by local decree. El Cocuy has several budget hotels plus the park headquarters. As much as anywhere in the nation of Colombia, Cocuyanos (people from El Cocuy) dress in fedoras and woolen ponchos, adding sartorial elegance to the town's charm. The plaza's **Iglesia de Nuestra Señora de la Paz** stands over a scale model of Parque Nacional Natural El Cocuy.

Güicán: This mountain village, 6 miles (10 km) northeast of El Cocuy, lacks its neighbor's colonial charm. Although founded in 1756, much of the original colonial architecture was ravaged by a fire in 1860 (and, later, civil war) and replaced with a mishmash of modern styles. Güicán is closer to the national park, a five-hour hike away. Its beautiful **Iglesia de Nuestra Señora de la Candelaria** faces onto the town's tiered main plaza. Pilgrims flock here to pray to an effigy of the Virgen Morenita de Güicán, an indigenous U'Wa figure whose apparition is said to have miraculously appeared on a cloth—a Spanish trick to convert the indigenous people to Christianity. ■

El Cocuy
Ⓜ 91 B2

Güicán
Ⓜ 91 B2

EXPERIENCE: Hike to El Púlpito del Diablo

The most popular one-day hike in PNN El Cocuy is to the **Devil's Pulpit,** a mesa atop which the devil is said, according to popular legend, to appear on New Year's Eve. It's best to acclimatize overnight at **Sisuma,** a hostel run by CoopSerguías beside **Laguna la Pintada.** From here, it's a one-hour hike through a vale framed by lateral moraines to the foot of the main moraine. A climb up a boulder field delivers you atop a cliff, where you're offered jaw-dropping views. Allow another hour to ascend a granite slope scoured into a slick glaze by the receded glacier. Finally, you reach the pulpit. Allow at least six hours round-trip.

Cocuy Circuit Trek

Parque Nacional Natural El Cocuy lures intrepid hikers seeking the satisfaction of trekking amid some of South America's most stunning peaks. Day hikes are possible; the week-long circuit demands stamina, determination, good hiking shoes, rain-resistant clothing, and a warm sleeping bag to guard against the cold nights spent at the snow-clad heights.

A hiker on the Cocuy Circuit trek looks up at the distant Púlpito del Diablo, covered in snow.

The *vuelta,* or circuit, covers 5,742 feet (1,750 m) in elevation range and can be started from either of the mountain villages of El Cocuy or Güicán. Most trekkers choose a clockwise route from Güicán.

Before setting off, stop by park headquarters *(tel 57-7/890-0359)* in El Cocuy or Güicán to pay your entrance fee *($$$)*. Beforehand, make sure to purchase a copy of the 1:200,000 trail map at one of the mountain tourism stores in the area. Also inquire about hiring a guide or porter *($$$)* from the **ASEGUICOC** *(tel 57/311-236-4275)* guide association. The trails are well marked, but a guide is strongly recommended. Pack high-mountain camping gear (including tent, stove, and compass), sufficient food, and proper clothing to foil the weather. Don't forget sunscreen and sunglasses.

The Trek

Begin your six-day loop trek at **Güicán** (9,678 feet/2,950 m). From here, hike six hours uphill to **Cabañas Kanwara** ➊ *(tel 57/311-231-6004)*

NOT TO BE MISSED:

Paso El Castillo • Laguna de la Plaza
• El Púlpito del Diablo

to acclimatize overnight. Next morning, walk up through fields of *frailejónes* (see sidebar p. 104) as you follow the trail north via **Parada de Romero,** to **Paso Cardenillo** ➋ (14,433 feet/4,399 m), the first mountain pass. Stay to the east side of the valley as you descend to the first night camping site beside **Laguna Grande de los Verdes** ➌ (13,432 feet/4,094 m).

Next day, ascend to **Alto de los Frailes** (13,934 feet/4,247 m) and turn south, beyond which the spectacular scenery soars. After a brief, steep descent, snowcapped sentinels guide you through the vale of the Río Frailes. Passing above **Lago de la Isla,** to your east, ascend the **Paso de la Sierra** ➍ (15,381 feet/4,688 m). It's often snow covered, but the path is well marked by cairns. Sparkling like a sapphire below, **Laguna de Avellana** ➎ (14,534 feet/4,430 m) lures you downhill to camp.

The trail then descends to the marshy **Valle de los Cojines** cushioned with mossy plants–an emerald green counterpoint to the vertical scarp of glacier-tipped **Ritacuba Blanco** ➏ (17,497 feet/5,333 m), the tallest summit in PNN El Cocuy. Follow the path as it detours downhill, east to the **Cascada del Río Ratoncito** waterfall, tumbling to the plains of Arauca. Returning to the valley, cross the creek and continue south, along the western side of the valley. Passing the east side of **Lago del Rincón,** it's an hour-long clamber to **Paso El**

Castillo (15,092 feet/4,600 m). Until recently glacier-clad, the pass now poses no technical challenge. Take time to savor the sensational vistas before descending the rock-strewn trail to camp at **Laguna del Pañuelo** ❼ (14,272 feet/4,350 m).

After a chilly night, start at dawn to ascend **Paso Balcones** (14,600 feet/4,450m). The pass requires care for its scree-covered northern slope glissades to a cliff. You're now in the remotest part of the park. The relatively unmarked path (watch for cairns) follows the west side of a gorgeous vale squeezed between peaks glistening with snow of fast-receding glaciers. Magnificent views open up to the east as you approach to camp at **Laguna de la Plaza** ❽, beneath jagged peaks including to the west **El Púlpito del Diablo** (see sidebar p. 107).

From here, a gradual ascent leads to **Paso Patio Bolas** (14,370 feet/4,380 m). Eastward, the land drops precipitously to the Casanare Basin, often hidden beneath a blanket of cloud far below you. You are now amid a barren landscape, the trail marked by large cairns as you ascend to **Paso Cusiri** (14,632 feet/4,460 m), an exposed region often whipped by high winds. The well-signed trail drops through the Río Lagunillas ravine to **Los Lagunillas**–your final camp at **Sisuma** ❾. Beyond **Paso La Cueva** (11,155 feet/3,400 m), it is an 8-mile (13 km) downhill hike to **El Cocuy** (9,022 feet/2,750 m).

🅜	See also map p. 91 B2
▶	Güicán
🕑	5–7 days
⬌	44 miles (71 km)
▶	El Cocuy

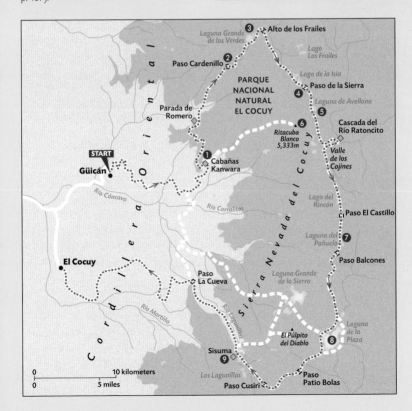

Santander

To the northwest of Boyacá, the department of Santander is named for independence hero Francisco de Paula Santander. One of the most mountainous of Colombian regions, Santander is known for its rugged medley of soaring mountains and deep river gorges, most famously the Cañón del Chicamocha.

El Monumento a la Santandereanidad recognizes the popular revolt against Spanish rule.

Santander
🅰 91 A2–B2

Visitor Information
✉ Visita Santander, Cra. 19 #31-65, Bucaramanga
☎ 57-7/633-9666
turismo@santander .gov.co

Socorro
🅰 91 B2

Voted Colombia's most beautiful colonial town and blessed with some of the loveliest boutique hotels in the country, the hillside town of Barichara is the most rewarding of many typical Santanderano villages tucked into the folds of the Cordillera Oriental. Nearby San Gil is a center for a burgeoning adventure-sports business—from white-water rafting to paragliding and mountain biking. Another colonial charmer, Girón, lies within a 20-minute drive of Bucaramanga—a modern, pulsing city of more than

1.2 million people. The journey between San Gil and Bucaramanga leads through the Cañón del Chicamocha—Colombia's equivalent of the Grand Canyon— via a major highway that links Tunja to the Caribbean lowlands.

Socorro

This charming and historically important hillside town has been called the "Cradle of Latin American Independence," as it was here on March 16, 1781, that the Revolución Comunera (Revolution of the Commoners)—the first spontaneous revolt against Spanish rule—occurred. The seismic event is recalled in palm-shaded **Plaza de la Independencia,** where a statue honors heroine Manuela Beltrán, who sparked the revolt by shouting "Long live the King and death to bad government." To learn more, visit the **Casa de la Cultura** *(Calle 14 #12-31),* which has exhibits in rooms that open to a moss-covered weathered stone patio. Dominating the square, the sandstone **Catedral del Nuestra Señora de Socorro** has an imposing neoclassical facade with twin bell towers and an unadorned, barrel-vaulted roof.

Socorro sits at 4,265 feet (1,300 m) at the northern end of a broad northwest trending valley farmed in sugarcane. Founded in 1681, its historic core is preserved more or less in entirety. Walk uphill along Calle 14 to view the **Convento de San Juan Buatista,** the oldest Capuchin monastery in Colombia.

San Gil

Visitors with adrenaline-charged adventure in their plans head for San Gil, 12 miles (20 km) north of Socorro. Founded in 1689 by Don Gil Cabrera y Dávalos in a deep valley on the north bank of the Río Fonce, San Gil has evolved into Colombia's main center for white-water rafting, kayaking, paragliding, and other extreme sports. A tight-packed and bustling city, its traffic-thronged colonial core of narrow streets is laid out in a grid around **Parque La Libertad.** Looming over the square, the **Catedral de la Santa Cruz** is unusual for its octagonal twin campaniles. Off of the park's southeast corner, the

San Gil

 91 B2

Visitor Information

✉ Instituto de Cultura y Turismo de San Gil, Calle 12 #10-31

☎ 57-7/724-4617

turismoensangil .gov.co

EXPERIENCE: Down the Rapids

The Cordillera Oriental's steep terrain and plentiful rainfall produce the perfect conditions for white-water rafting. And rafting provides the ultimate combination of natural beauty and thrills as you plunge like a log down a flume through the valleys of the Ríos Chicamocha, Fonce, Magdalena, and Suárez.

Pick a river that gives you the level of challenge you're looking for. Rivers are rated from Class I (flat water, considered a float trip) to Class V (high waves, deemed suitable for experts only). San Gil is Colombia's capital of rafting, and Rio Suárez is the Dom Perignon of white water, with Class IV and V rapids guaranteed to have you laughing with sheer delight. San Agustín is a base for

Class II–V trips on the Río Magdalena.

Trips last from two hours to half a day. Bring a swimsuit, a T-shirt, and river sandals or sneakers that you don't mind getting wet. Expect to get drenched: That's half the fun. Remember to take plenty of sunscreen (you'll be in the sun all day) as well as a set of dry clothes and shoes to change into at the float's end. Tour companies supply mandatory life vests and helmets.

Colombia Rafting Expeditions
Carrera 10 #7-83, San Gil, tel 57/311-283-8647, colombiarafting.com
Magdalena Rafting
Calle 5 #16-4, San Agustín, tel 57/311-271-5333, magdalenarafting.com

Barichara

🗺 91 B2

Visitor Information

✉ Oficina de Turismo, Cultura y Deportes, Calle 5 #6-39, 2nd fl.

☎ 57-7/726-7052

🕐 Closed Sat.–Sun.

Casa de la Cultura *(Calle 12 #10-31, tel 57-7/724-4617, closed Sun.)* has a small museum dedicated to local indigenous culture; the city's official tourist bureau is also here.

The other in-town site not to miss is **Parque El Gaillineral** *(Calle 6 & Malecón)*—a 10-acre (4 ha) nature reserve at the confluence of the Quebrada Curití and Río Fonce. Walk among the

The Río Fonce is one of Colombia's most popular white-water rivers, drawing adventure seekers from near and far.

dense-packed *chimimango* trees festooned with tendrils of tilland-sia—old-man's beard moss. The watery environment teems with birds and butterflies, and offers a dreamlike escape from the city hubbub.

San Gil's **Malecón,** the river-front promenade, is lined with adventure-sports companies offering a cocktail of activities, including white-water trips on the Río Fonce (Class II–III), the Río Chicamocha (Class III–IV), and the challenging Río Suárez (Class IV+).

A one-hour drive south of town is **Charalá,** a colonial-era town that is a center for rappel-ling down waterfalls. The most popular site is **Cascadas de Juan Curri,** a 590-foot (180 m) cas-cade in three stages, with a pool for swimming at the base. **Curití,** another colonial pueblo off the main highway 4 miles (7 km) northeast of San Gil, is a center for paragliding.

Barichara

Officially named Colombia's most beautiful colonial town, Barichara is truly enchanting. Founded in 1714 and perfectly preserved, it was declared a national monument in 1978. Its hillside setting 14 miles (22.5 km) northwest of San Gil resembles a Hollywood stage set. Its streets are paved with flagstones and lined with whitewashed traditional homes made of *tapia pisada* (mud and straw), with *zócalos* (the bulging lower third of exterior walls) painted in a colorful trim. Many homes have received thoughtful

EXPERIENCE: Fun for the Family

If you're traveling with children, here are three venues to keep them happy:

Parque Nacional del Chicamocha
Chicamocha, 31 miles (50 km) from the city of Bucaramanga, is an activity park set high on a mountainside with spectacular views over the Cañón del Chicamocha. A 4-mile-long (6.3 km) aerial tram—one of the longest cable cars in the world—spans the canyon. The park has something for every age, from a goat-petting zoo, ostrich park, and waterslides for youngsters to dune buggies, paragliding, and a zip line ride for mom and dad. *(Map 91 B2, Vía Bucaramanga–San Gil km 54, Aratoca, tel 57-4/656-9006, parquenacionaldelchica mocha.com, closed Mon.–Tues., $$–$$$$).*

Maloka
An underground Interactive Science and Technology Center in Bogotá, Maloka seeks to educate with its nine galleries and 300 interactive displays on subjects such as the human body, movement and thought, marine monsters and biodiversity, and the universe. Fascinating documentaries (in Spanish) are screened in a cinedome. *(Cra. 68 D #24A-51, Bogotá, tel 57-1/427-2707, maloka.org, $$).*

PANACA
Popular with Colombian families, the National Park of Agriculture and Livestock is designed to connect urban dwellers to nature. The sprawling farm-focused park exhibits more than 4,500 animals displayed in ten themed stations (cattle, horses, hogs, etc.), displaying worldwide exotic species—from the French Percheron draft horse to African Watusi cattle. Kids from 7 to 70 will enjoy days full of nature and fun. *(Quimbaya, tel 01-8000-123-999, panaca.com.co, $$$).*

---

conversions as boutique hotels and restaurants.

Combine this with fine churches, lofty views, and a perfect climate. No wonder Barichara is favored for filming telenovelas. Barichara is also the setting for several cultural festivals, including the **Festival de Cine Verde** *(Calle 5 #8-80, info@festiver.org, festiver .org),* in mid-September, dedicated to documentaries and films that foster environmental awareness.

Begin a walking tour in spacious **Parque Principal.** Reached by a broad flight of stairs, the sandstone **Catedral de la Inmaculada Concepción** is especially graceful when illuminated at night. Catty-corner, the **Casa de la Cultura** *(Calle 5*

INSIDER TIP:

Barichara is one of the most beautiful small towns in Colombia, a center for artisans and vacationing Bogotaños.

—THOMAS CLYNES
National Geographic
magazine writer

#6-29, tel 57-7/726-7002) houses a museum that regales the town's history. The adjoining town hall hosts the tourism office. Other sites not to miss include the simple **Capilla de San Antonio** *(Cra. 4 & Calle 5)* and **Capilla de Jesús Resucitado** *(Cra. 7 & Calle 3),* beside the fascinating

Guane
⚠ 91 B2

**Parque Nacional
Natural Serranía
de los Yarigüíes**
⚠ 91 B2
✉ Calle 11 #9-39,
San Vicente de
Chucurí
☎ 57-7/625-6858

cemetery. Dawn is a good time to visit, when the tombstones are enshrouded in ghostly mist. Now walk uphill to the **Capilla de Santa Bárbara** (*Cra. 11 & Calle 6*), atop the hill beside **Parque para las Artes Jorge Delgado Sierra.** Barichara is famous for its stone masons and sculptors; the park displays 27 contemporary stone statues. A bonus is the fabulous view over the **Río Suárez canyon** to the Cordillera de los Cobardes, the westernmost chain of the Andean Cordillera Oriental.

Reserva de las Aves Reinita Cielo Azul

San Vicente de Chucurí is the main gateway to this bird reserve, which adjoins Parque Nacional Natural Serranía de los Yariüíes. This tiny (545 acres/221 ha) reserve protects a patch of remnant Colombian oak forest, which is a rare habitat for many threatened species, including the recurve-billed bushbird and Santander poison dart frog. An old coffee farm provides lodging in the park headquarters, and the park has excellent trails. Serious birders may also want to watch for the helmeted curassow in Reserva de las Aves Pauxi, 2.5 miles (4 km) north of Reinita Cielo Azul. Both reserves are run by Pro-Aves. Guided tours are offered by **EcoTurs** (*tel 57-1/287-6592, ecoturs.org*).

Guane: A treat is to follow **El Camino Real**—a rocky path built by the pre-Columbian Guane people that leads 3 miles (5 km) downhill from Barichara to the hamlet of Guane. Both the path and village are national monuments. The path originally extended from Girón to

Barancabermeja and was rebuilt in 1864. Take plenty of water and wear hiking shoes, as the rocks are uneven. (The path begins in Barichara at the junction of Calle 4 and Carrera 10, where the Piedra de Bolívar honors the Liberator's visits to Barichara.)

The walk is its own reward. But Guane repays your effort with the **Iglesia de Santa Bárbara.** Built in 1720, it has a side chapel dedicated to Santa Lucia, the patron saint of sight. She holds in her hands a gold chalice with two eyes (resembling the face of the Muppet Kermit the frog).

You may need to ring the doorbell or otherwise summon the curator to enter the **Museo Paleotológico y Anthropológico de Guane,** stuffed with fossils of ammonites, fish, eels, squids, and corals found locally. Tracing the history of the region, its displays range from a petrified mummy of a pre-Columbian Guane to a 19th-century tobacco press. The statue in the plaza honors *cacique* Guaneuta, who preferred suicide by drowning rather than submit to the Spanish. Before returning to Barichara, sample *sabajón,* a creamy nonalcoholic drink made of goat's milk.

Parque Nacional Natural Serranía de los Yariüíes

Extending down the western flank of the Cordillera Oriental, this 304-square-mile (787 sq km) national park offers sensational hiking and birding. It protects ecosystems from tropical premontane rain forest

Barichara's sun-filled Catedral de la Inmaculada Concepción sits in the spacious Parque Principal.

to high-altitude *páramo,* and is a habitat for woolly monkey, jaguar, spectacled bear, and at least nine endemic bird species, including the saffron-headed parrot and white-mantled barbet. Its gateway is **San Vicente de Chucurí,** 30 miles (50 km) northwest of Barichara along rough unpaved roads via Zapatoca.

Parque Nacional del Chicamocha

Dramatically positioned on a ridgetop overlooking the Río Chicamocha canyon, this theme park is popular with Colombian families (see sidebar p. 113). The cliff-hugging road between San Gil and Bucaramanga is one of Colombia's most scenic drives and snakes to the depths of the canyon. One of the deepest canyons in the world, it plunges more than 3,940 feet (1,200 m). You can also cross the gorge via a 4-mile-long (6.3 km) aerial tram, but be prepared for long lines on weekends. The facility includes a small re-creation of a traditional Santander village, plus a toboggan ride, skating ring, and an unusual zip line. The most unusual feature is **El Monumento a la Santandere-anidad,** a metaphoric explosion that represents the Revolución Comunera in 1781, which eventually led to independence from Spain. The 35 patinated figures shown include Archbishop Antonio Caballero y Góngora (1723–1796)—the "Traitor of

Parque Nacional del Chicamocha

🅰 91 B2
✉ Vía Bucara-manga–San Gil km 54, Aratoca
☎ 57-4/656-9006
🕐 Closed Mon.–Tues.
💲 $$–$$$$

parquenacional delchicamocha.com

Bucaramanga

91 B2

Visitor Information

✉ Instituto
Municipal
de Cultura y
Turismo, Calle
30 #26-117

☎ 57-7/634-1132

Museo Casa
de Bolívar

✉ Calle 37
#12-15C,
Bucaramanga

☎ 57-7/630-4258

🕐 Closed Sun.

💲 $

the Revolution"—shown holding an ax in one hand and in the other a "liar's mask" in the manner of a Greek dramatis persona.

Bucaramanga

Bucaramanga is a metropolis of more than one million people packed into a valley surrounded by mountains. Founded in 1622, its colonial core has been engulfed by modernity. Although not considered a destination in its own right, this energetic, convoluted, traffic-thronged city 261 miles (420 km) north of Bogotá does have its draws.

The historic heart of the "ciudad de los parques" ("city of parks") is **Parque Custodio García Rovira,** on the city's west side. The main Santander government buildings surround the square,

which also hosts the **Iglesia de San Laureano,** started in 1865 and crowned by one of the oldest clocks in the country. Cross to the west side to admire the **Monument of Conquistadores** catty-corner to the tiny **Capilla de los Dolores** *(Calle 36 & Cra. 10),* the city's oldest church. The **Museo Casa de Bolívar,** one block east of the square, displays weapons, uniforms, mummies, and textiles of the Guane indigenous culture. Now cross the street to the **Casa de la Cultura** *(closed Sun.),* exhibiting works by Santandereano artists. Bucaramanga even has a **Museo de Arte Moderno,** with a fine collection of Colombian modern artworks.

Eight blocks east along Calle 36 is **Parque Santander,** laid out in the 19th century with a statue

The towers of Iglesia de San Laureano in Bucaramanga feature one of the country's oldest clocks.

of the hero of independence. Its main draw is the **Catedral de la Sagrada Familia** (*Calle 36 #19-56*), completed in 1887 with a white facade crowned by a sculpture of the Sagrada Familia between sextagonal bell towers. Nature lovers might appreciate **Parque de Agua** (*Cra. 34 & Calle 20, $*), a secure tree-shaded, water-themed park with cascades and boardwalks and lakes filled with hyacinths and fish. More so, the **Jardín Botánico Eloy Valenzuela** (*Cra. 9 & Calle 3, tel 57-7/648-0729, closed Mon.–Fri., $*), on the banks of the Río Frío in the southern suburb of Floridablanca, is a tranquil showcase of more than 400 plant species. It has an Asian garden and bamboo glen, and is dotted with lakes.

Girón: The colonial town of Girón lies 2.5 miles (4 km) to Bucaramanga's northwest—only a 15-minute drive, yet a world away. Founded in 1638, the entire town is a national monument made up of 48 blocks of predominantly 18th-century homes and mansions lining cobbled streets frozen in time. Every building has a whitewashed facade, red-tile roof, and dark chocolate trim. The town's main site is the **Basilica Menor San Juan Bautista,** completed in 1711 on the main plaza. It is flanked by twin bell towers containing eight bells brought from Toledo.

Piedecuesta: Bucaramanga's hotels fill during Easter week, when thousands of visitors flock for the Semana Santa celebrations

---

EXPERIENCE:
Playing *Tejo*

Who says beer and gunpowder don't mix? In Colombia they're essential ingredients for *tejo*, a local pastime and passion. Games are played at *canchas de tejo* (tejo courts), usually associated with bars. Teams compete by hurling underarm a 4-pound (2 kg) metal disc (tejo) at a clay-filled box 65 feet (20 m) away: The bull's-eye is a *bosín* (metal ring) containing a triangular *mecha* (wax-paper fuse) stuffed with gunpowder. Players imbibe copious amounts of beer (beer companies sponsor professional teams) to aid their aim.

Most towns in the highlands have canchas de tejo. Try the following:

Cancha de Tejo Gómez Niño, Calle 57 #16-17, Bucaramanga, Santander, tel 57-7/644-5209

Cancha de Tejo Los Amigos, Cra. 4A #3-32, Salento, Quindió, tel 57/312-792-8486.

Peperepe, Calle 7 S #8-20, La Candelaría, Bogotá, tel 57-1/289-1541

---

in Piedecuesta, a colonial town on the main highway 10 miles (17 km) south of the city. The processions are marked by Christians dressed in red-and-white and purple-and-black costumes, which are eerily reminiscent of those worn by the Ku Klux Klan.

You can learn about coffee production at **Hacienda El Roble,** an old hacienda that doubles as a deluxe boutique hotel. It offers guided coffee tours of the 740-acre (300 ha) estate, which grows more than 60 varieties of shade-grown organic coffee. Mountain biking and horseback rides are offered. ■

Girón
🗺 91 B2

Piedecuesta
🗺 91 B2

Hacienda El Roble
✉ Mesa de Los Santos, 19 miles (30 km) SW of Piedecuesta
☎ 57/310-273-3495

Norte de Santander

Extending along the Venezuelan border north of Santander and Boyacá, this off-the-beaten-path region is a transition zone that merges with Venezuela's Lake Maracaibo basin. A stunning mountain drive, the eerie geologic formations of Los Estaroques, and one of Colombia's most important historic sites are among its attractions.

A high-school band marches through Pamplona on Colombia's Independence Day.

Norte de Santander
91 B3

This department is named for military and political leader Francisco de Paula Santander. The region is intimately linked with the battle for independence from Spain; the new federation of Gran Colombia was birthed when the first congress convened at Francisco de Paula Santander's estate in Villa del Rosario. During the 1980s, Norte de Santander became a major base for FARC and ELN. (The Colombian Army guards the main highways and has an ongoing effort to clear the rural zones of guerrillas. Check current conditions with local police before venturing along Highway 66.)

The Bucaramanga–Cúcuta highway climbs over the northern extent of the Cordillera Oriental, passing through some of the most rugged mountain scenery in Colombia. East of the university town of Pamplona, you'll wind down the flank of the Cordillera Oriental to emerge on the semiarid plains upon which the border city of Cúcuta sprawls. The highway peaks at a windswept altiplano amid a landscape that resembles the Welsh highlands. Locals bundle up in woollen clothes and balaclavas against the icy winds. Allow six hours each way and make sure to fill up with gas before setting out.

Pamplona

This city of 100,000 people, midway between Bucaramanga and Cúcuta, comes as a pleasant surprise after such a huge swathe of mountain wilderness. The town is sheltered in the Valle del Espíritu Santo and enjoys an agreeable climate. It was founded in 1549 and despite its isolation became an important political and religious center. It played an important role in the independence movement, and in 1857 became the first capital of Santander Department. Today, Pamplona is a cultural hub lent vigor by the Universidad de Pamplona.

Much of the colonial core was wiped out by an earthquake in 1875. Nonetheless, several notable colonial buildings still stand on the main square, **Plaza Aguela Gallardo.** To the east, the **Catedral de Santa Clara** dates back to 1584 but has been extensively remodeled after being damaged by earthquakes. Pamplona boasts a fistful of small museums. The most significant is the **Museo de Arte Moderno Ramírez Villamizar** in a 16th-century mansion on the east side of the plaza. It celebrates local artist Eduardo Ramírez Villamizar (1923–2004),

known for his geometric abstract sculptures. The **Museo Arquidiocesano de Arte Religioso** (Calle 5 #4-87, tel 57-7/568-2816, closed Sun.) displays a fine collection of religious antiquities.

Parque Nacional Natural Tamá

The 185-square-mile (479 sq km) national park occupies the southeast corner of Norte de Santander and is near a Venezuelan counterpart with a similar name. It extends down the eastern slopes of the Cordillera Oriental, spanning ecosystems from humid premontane rain forest to mist-shrouded cloud forest and high-mountain *páramo*. The southern half of the park abuts Parque Nacional Natural El Cocuy. Its many impressive waterfalls include the recently discovered **Tamá waterfall** (2,690 feet/820 m),

Pamplona

🅰 91 B3

Visitor Information

✉ Instituto de Cultura y Turismo Pamplona, Calle 5 #6-45

☎ 57-7/568-2043

Museo de Arte Moderno Ramírez Villamizar

✉ Calle 5 #5-75, Pamplona

☎ 57-7/568-2999

🕐 Closed Mon.

mamramirez villamizar.com

Parque Nacional Natural Tamá

✉ Cra. 6 #14-52, Toledo

☎ 57-7/567-0316 or 1-800-012-9722

Cúcuta

Visitor Information

 Secretaría
de Cultura
y Turismo,
Edificio, Rosetal,
Calle 10 #0-10

☎ 57-7/578-4949

cucuta-nortede
santander.gov.co

Casa Natal Museo General Santander

 Autopista
Internacional
km 6 via San
Antonio, Villa
del Rosario

☎ 57-7/570-0265

🕐 Closed Mon.

💲 $

---

one of the world's tallest falls. The park provides habitats for many mammals, including mountain tapir and spectacled bear.

The visitor center at **Orocué** has cabins. The park can be reached by four-wheel drive from Pamplona to Chinácota and the hamlet of Herrán. Check with officials about security before taking this route or visiting this park.

Cúcuta

Despite its forlorn setting in a sizzling basin of thorn scrub and cacti, Cúcuta is a wealthy and modern commercial city that thrives on its free-trade zone and with contraband from nearby Venezuela. Cúcuta's downtown is

Ant Snacks

Santandereanas proclaim a lowly protein-rich ant as their favorite regional dish. The *hormiga culona* (big-butt ant) is a springtime delicacy in the municipalities of San Gil and Barichara, where the inch-long (2.5 cm) queens of the *Atta laevigata* species are harvested during the March to June rainy season; this is when they make their nuptial flights. The wings are removed and the plump, juicy bodies soaked in salt water, then roasted and chomped whole as snacks. They're given as wedding gifts—a tradition inherited from pre-Columbian days when the ants were cultivated by the Guane Indians for use in mating rituals.

a trove of ritzy shopping malls and fashion boutiques, while the suburban roads are lined with scores of gas stations and hundreds of vendors selling pilfered gasoline at bargain prices from plastic bottles.

The first battle in Simón

Bolívar's campaign that led to Venezuelan independence was fought here on February 28, 1813. In 1875, a great earthquake destroyed much of the town, which was founded in 1733. It has been thoughtfully rebuilt with tree-lined streets. Spacious **Parque Santander** hosts a bronze statue of Cúcuta-born General Santander, plus the neoclassical **Catedral de San José de Cúcuta** (*Cra. 5 & Calle 10*). Two blocks southeast, leafy brick-lined **Parque Colón** is worth browsing for the charming Capilla del Carmen chapel; monuments to independence and to explorers Cristóbal Colón (Christopher Columbus) and Amerigo Vespucio; and the **Casa de la Cultura** (*Calle 13 #3-67, tel 57-7/571-6689, closed Sat.–Sun.*).

El Parque Gran Colombiano: Located beside the Cúcuta–Venezuela highway in the colonial village of **Villa del Rosario,** the Great Colombia Park preserves the site where on August 30, 1821, Simón Bolívar, Francisco de Paula Santander, and other independence leaders convened the Congress of Cúcuta to establish Gran Colombia, write the constitution, and elect a president.

The hallowed venue includes **Casa Natal Museo General Santander,** where Francisco de Paula Santander was born on April 2, 1792. Today a national monument, its displays include Santander and Bolívar's uniforms. South of the casa, a narrow park shaded by towering royal palms runs 229 yards (200 m) to the **Templo Histórico,** the church where the congress convened and

INSIDER TIP:

You can buy the regional speciality— sweet, salty, or spicy fried ants—by the bagful from local markets.

—AARON RETTIG
Colombia Whitewater *co-author*

Bolívar was sworn in as president on October 3, 1821. Built in 1821, it was almost totally destroyed by the 1875 earthquake. A marble statue of Bolívar occupies the ruin.

Ocaña

The off-the-beaten-track mountain town of Ocaña is second in size to Cúcuta and has many fine colonial buildings that recall its importance as the setting for the Gran Convención of 1828, intended to resolve the constitutional crisis between supporters of Simón Bolívar and Francisco de Paula Santander. Its historic core includes the **Convento y Templo de San Francisco,** the religious complex that hosted the congress. Ocaña is linked to Cúcuta by Highway 70. Sinuous as a snake, it winds over the Cordillera Oriental and connects with the Bucaramanga–Valledupar highway at Aguachica. The route is superbly scenic but subject to landslides. Do not travel this route at night.

Área Natural Única Los Estoraques: Ocaña is the gateway to Los Estoraques Unique Natural Area. The protected area spans 1,580 acres (640 ha) of sandstone cliffs sculpted by the elements into fantastical geologic formations. Watch out for deadly snakes underfoot.

Trails lead from the ranger station, 0.6 mile (1 km) west of **La Playa de Belén.** One of the best preserved colonial villages in Colombia, this exquisite hamlet is virtually devoid of tourists. Every house is whitewashed and trimmed in chocolate, with a rust red base. ∎

Ocaña
🅜 91 B3

Área Natural Única Los Estoraques
🅜 91 B3
✉ 0.6 miles (1 km) W of La Playa de Belén, Norte de Santander
☎ 57-7/563-2289

The city of Pamplona occupies an Andean basin, surrounded by mountains.

From palm-fringed coastline, snowcapped mountains, and windblown desert to the colonial gem of Cartagena

Caribbean Lowlands

A *palenquera,* an Afro-Caribbean woman, sells fruit in Cartagena.

Caribbean Lowlands

Swashbuckling Cartagena de Indias is Colombia's best known and second most-visited destination, after Bogotá. Its narrow streets lined with meticulously renovated colonial buildings pull you gleefully into the past. Beyond the spotlight are white-sand beaches, snowcapped mountains, and even the Sahara-like Desierto de la Guajira.

Plaza San Pedro Claver exemplifies the colonial beauty of the city of Cartagena.

A favorite stopover for cruise ships, Cartagena became one of Spain's most important New World ports four centuries ago, with massive fortifications to guard against pirates and privateers. In 1984, UNESCO declared the city a World Heritage site. Enclosed within fortress walls, the city is a mosaic of cobbled plazas, bougainvillea-festooned mansions, and centuries-old cathedrals and castles. Today, the restored city hums with a hip spirit and teems with trendy restaurants and hotels hidden behind antique facades.

Farther east, the port city of Barranquilla hosts a superb museum, plus the country's biggest Carnaval—a five-day bender second in size only to that of Rio de Janeiro. The perfect antidote to this feast is a detox dip in the oozy thermal mud of Volcán de Lodo El Totumo.

Nearby, the city of Santa Marta explodes with festivities for the annual Fiesta del Mar. Simón Bolívar died here: The site of his death—Quinta de San Pedro Alejandrino—is a national shrine.

National Parks

Santa Marta is also a base for exploring the lovely beaches that extend along the shores of Parque Nacional Natural Tayrona, a backpacker favorite. Inland, the Sierra Nevada de Santa Marta bursts from the jungle floor to reach 18,700 feet (5,700 m), just 25 miles (40 km) from the shore. The mountains are a haven for birders, and for hikers seeking Ciudad Perdida—Lost City—a mini-Machu Picchu that requires several days to reach. Descendants of the indigenous Tairona people who built Ciudad Perdida still inhabit the rugged mountains and cling to their ancient ways. Visitation is strictly controlled.

Remarkably, the Sierra Nevada lies within a two-hour drive of Colombia's driest region—Península de la Guajira, a desert zone in the northeast of Colombia. You can overnight in traditional *rancherías* (family ranches) of the Wayúu indigenous people and hike massive sand dunes that rise from the turquoise sea.

Watery World

Much of the Caribbean hinterland is laced by waterways unspooling through coastal lowlands filled with brackish swamps. The flatland forms the floodplain of the Río Magdalena, Colombia's longest river. Annually flooded, this labyrinth of braided channels and seasonal sloughs is a birder's haven. The colonial-era city of Mompox sits in the midst of this watery world.

To the southwest, the mangrove-lined Golfo de Urabá is a destination now being promoted for its beaches. Turbo, the funky main city, is a gateway by water taxi to the fine sands, coral reefs, and Kuna indigenous communities around Capurganá. ■

Cartagena

With its breathtaking colonial architecture, horse-drawn carriages, and cobbled, tree-shaded plazas, the city of Cartagena de Indias—once one of the most important trading ports in the New World—is one of the most exciting destinations in Colombia today. You'll probably fall in love with the city's fairy-tale charms, tempting you to linger and explore for days.

Historic El Centro, part of the UNESCO World Heritage site, abounds with both color and energy from early morning through late evening.

Cartagena
🗺 125 B2
Visitor Information
✉ Muelle Turístico la Bodeguita, Piso 2
☎ 67-5/655-0211
cartagenadeindias .travel

The colonial city was founded by Pedro de Heredia (1520–1554) on June 1, 1533, and named for Cartagena, Spain. (Locals claim that beneath Calle Santa Teresa is a cemetery where the native Calamari people—brutally murdered by Spanish conquistadores—are buried.)

Cartagena had a deep bay protected by man-made bulwarks and commanding hills. It was one of the three main ports of the Spanish treasure fleet and flourished as a center of trade. The city was pillaged several times, including in 1568 by Sir Francis Drake, who held the city ransom. Vast fortifications were built, including a perimeter wall (completed in 1756) that helped repel a major attack by British forces in 1741; the wall still stands. Cartagena was one of the three seats of the

Inquisition, which operated here from 1610 to 1821.

The city had its golden age of commerce in the 18th century, when wealthy merchants and nobles added many of the fine mansions and public edifices seen today. The wars of independence, which began in 1811, marked the beginning of Cartagena's decline. Although the city weathered Colombia's civil strife, during the 20th century, the city sank into decay. The poor filled the vacuum created by an exodus of wealthy families.

World Heritage Site

In 1984, UNESCO named the city a World Heritage site, while the hit movie *Romancing the Stone* spotlighted Cartagena (the "Cartagena" scenes were actually filmed in Veracruz, Mexico), prompting a tourism boom. The colonial core has since been restored and reinvigorated with boutique hotels, fine-dining restaurants, and chic stores. Teeming with energy, this lived-in antique quarter today draws more tourists than anywhere else in Colombia.

Allow at least three days to fully explore the old city, which is adjacent to a modern zone of oceanfront high-rise condominiums and hotels resembling Miami's South Beach. The old quarter is laid out in a rough grid with several sun-washed plazas. To get your bearings, board a horse-drawn carriage for a guided tour.

Have some small bills handy to tip the *palenqueras*—Afro-Caribbean women clad in traditional garb and carrying baskets of fruits on their heads—who demand payment to pose for your camera. Cartagena can be so hot and humid as to resemble a sauna. Except for a few overly pushy money changers and wily pickpockets, that's about the extent of the city's dangers.

Beyond the historic core, the ungainly metropolitan area sprawls southward. Leaving (or entering) on the Medellín road is an extended exercise in frustration: It can take well over one hour to negotiate the traffic congestion.

INSIDER TIP:

Don't miss watching the sunset from the walls of the old city. Try Café del Mar (*Baluarte de Santo Domingo*) for a cocktail at dusk.

—ALISON INCE
National Geographic contributor

El Centro

The colonial city was built in two walled sections divided by a channel now occupied by Avenida Venezuela. The "inner" town contains most historic sites of interest, concentrated in El Centro, where the colonial upper class lived. Streets retain their colonial names, which change virtually with every block.

A *palenquera* walks past Fernando Botero's "Reclining Nude" in Plaza de Santo Domingo.

Museo Histórico

✉ Calle de la Inquisición, Plaza de Bolívar

☎ 57-5/664-4570

💲 $$

muhca.gov.co

Museo del Oro Zenú

✉ Calle 33 #3-123, Plaza de Bolívar

☎ 57-5/660-0778

🕐 Closed Mon.

banrepcultural
.org/cartagena

The main square is **Plaza de Bolívar** *(Calle de la Inquisición & Calle San Pedro Claver)*. Thick with palm and shade trees, it displays a life-size statue of the hero atop his charger. The square was originally used for military parades; after 1610 it echoed to the screams of suspected heretics being tortured beyond the magnificent baroque stone entrance of the Palacio de la Inquisición, on the west side. Today, it houses the **Museo Histórico**, displaying instruments of faith-based sadism, including a rack and a witch-weighing contraption. Upstairs, the broader history of Cartagena is regaled in dioramas occupying the old halls of the dreaded Audience of the Tribunal.

On the plaza's east side, the must-see **Museo del Oro Zenú** is agleam with pre-Columbian gold, including delicate gold felines, fish, frogs, and other anthropomorphic pendants. Another gem, the recently restored **Catedral Santa Catalina de la Alejandría,** dating from 1577, rises over the northeast side of the square. Lit at night, its bell tower is one of the most recognizable landmarks in the city.

One block to the northwest, mimes and palenqueras add vibrant color to **Plaza de Santo Domingo,** an intimate and lively social setting for open-air restaurants. The square is also home to a voluptuous reclining nude statue by Fernando Botero, attracting a constant stream of admirers. Note the crooked bell tower of the 17th-century **Iglesia Santo Domingo.** According to legend, it's the result of the devil's failed attempt to demolish the sanctuary.

Another of Cartagena's major churches—the baroque **Iglesia de San Pedro Claver**—can be found in **Plaza de San Pedro Claver** (*Cra. 4 & Calle 31*). The church is named for a Jesuit priest, Pedro Claver (1580–1652), who worked to improve the lot of slaves as a down payment on future sainthood. He was canonized in 1850. His bones are displayed in a glass case beneath the altar, and the cloister has a museum of religious art. The square is filled with abstract sculptures that belong to the **Museo de Arte Moderno,** displaying contemporary art.

Horse-drawn *coches* (carriages) await customers on **Plaza de los Coches** (*Cra. 7 & Calle 34*). The triangular plaza is pinned by a statue of Pedro de Heredia, the city's founder. It is framed to the south by **La Muralla** (the old city wall) and to the north by balconied houses above a portico arcade known as **El Portal de los Dulces**—Door of Sweets–due to the confectionery stalls beneath. The octagonal **Torre de Reloj** (Clock Tower) was built in 1888 atop what was the main entrance to the city: **Boca del Puente.**

The Boca del Puente opens to the **Camellón de los Mártires**—Walkway of the Martyrs. The broad rectangular plaza was laid out in 1911 for the city's centenary of independence from Spanish rule. At its heart stands a monument in Carrera marble of a woman holding her hand palm up toward the sea. It bears the Latin inscription *Noli me tangere* (Don't touch me), an allusion to warn would-be invaders. The plaza runs perpendicular to the harbor, where two huge bronze statues of Pegasus front the city's Convention Center.

Tour boats to Playa Blanca and Isla del Rosario depart from the dock that runs parallel to La Muralla.

Plaza de los Noches opens west to triangular Plaza de la Aduana, the largest of the city's colonial plazas. It is named for the customs offices that during the 20th century occupied the Antigua Real Contaduria, the 18th-century

royal offices of the Kingdom of Spain, on the west side. The building's portal once served as the city's Muslim market. Since 1970, the building has operated as the town hall. A white marble statue of Christopher Columbus alongside an indigenous woman, erected in 1894, studs the plaza; the tall pedestal is engraved with bas-reliefs of Columbus's three caravels.

San Diego

North of El Centro, this area has some of the prettiest colonial (continued on p. 133)

Museo de Arte Moderno

✉ Calle 30 #4-08
☎ 57-5/664-6770
🕐 Closed Sun.
💲 $

Fernando Botero

Sculptor Fernando Botero was born in Medellín in 1932. Colombians consider him a living national treasure. Many of his works parody priests, presidents, and soldiers, portrayed mockingly as inflated and infantile. His pleasingly plump figures are instantly recognizable trademarks of Colombia's most famous artist. After leaving school at 14, he trained as a matador before studying art in Madrid, where he copied Velázquez and Goya. In 1953, he went to Italy where he studied art history. He was heavily influenced by muralist Diego Rivera while traveling in Mexico in 1956 and 1957. In 1958, he won the prestigious Salón de Artistas Colombianos.

In the Footsteps of Gabriel García Márquez

This walk takes in the Cartagena of Nobel Prize–winning novelist Gabriel García Márquez, for whom the surreal city was inspirational. Connecting places that appear in his novels, the tour allows you to feel as if "Gabo's" novels and characters come alive through the soles of your feet.

The old city of Cartagena has changed little since Gabriel García Márquez lived here in the 1940s.

García Márquez worked here as a journalist in the late 1940s. Although he arrived in 1948 and stayed only one year, he portrayed Cartagena's charms and complexities—a place of "amethyst afternoons and nights of antic breezes"—in many of his novels. "All of my books have loose threads of Cartagena in them," he once remarked. "When I have to call up memories, I always bring back an incident from Cartagena, a place in Cartagena, a character in Cartagena."

Start your walk in **Plaza de San Diego,** at the **Hotel Sofitel Santa Clara ❶**—the former Santa Clara convent that was an inspiration for

NOT TO BE MISSED:

Hotel Sofitel Santa Clara • Plaza Fernández de Madrid • Portal de los Dulces • Plaza de Bolívar

García Márquez's beguiling 1995 novella, *Of Love and Other Demons;* here the maid, Mary ("Servant of all the Angels"), was taken to be exorcised after she was bitten by a rabid dog. When in town, the novelist was known to

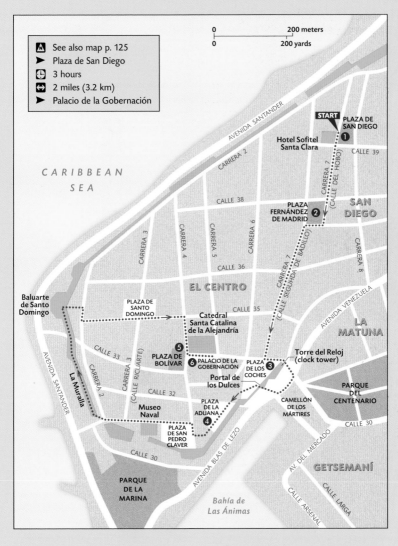

See also map p. 125
► Plaza de San Diego
🕒 3 hours
↔ 2 miles (3.2 km)
► Palacio de la Gobernación

0   200 meters
0   200 yards

CARIBBEAN
SEA

AVENIDA SANTANDER

START   PLAZA DE
SAN DIEGO
❶

Hotel Sofitel
Santa Clara

CALLE 39

CARRERA 2

CARRERA 7
(CALLE DEL HOBO)

CALLE 38

PLAZA
FERNÁNDEZ   ❷
DE MADRID

SAN
DIEGO

CARRERA 3

CARRERA 4

CARRERA 5

CARRERA 6

CARRERA 7

(CALLE SEGUNDA DE BÁDILLO)

CARRERA 8

CALLE 36

EL CENTRO

CALLE 35

AVENIDA VENEZUELA

LA
MATUNA

Baluarte
de Santo
Domingo

PLAZA DE
SANTO
DOMINGO

Catedral
Santa Catalina
de la Alejandría

AVENIDA SANTANDER

La Muralla

CALLE 33

CARRERA 2

CARRERA 3
(CALLE RICUARTE)

PLAZA DE
BOLÍVAR   ❺

❻ PALACIO DE LA
GOBERNACIÓN

PLAZA
DE LOS
COCHES

❸

Torre del Reloj
(clock tower)

PARQUE
DEL
CENTENARIO

CALLE 32

Portal de
los Dulces

Museo
Naval

PLAZA
DE LA
ADUANA
❹

CAMELLÓN
DE LOS
MÁRTIRES

CALLE 30

GETSEMANÍ

PLAZA
DE SAN
PEDRO
CLAVER

AVENIDA BLAS DE LEZO

AV. DEL MERCADO

CALLE 30

PARQUE
DE LA
MARINA

Bahía de
Las Ánimas

CALLE ARSENAL

CALLE LARGA

frequent the hotel bar. His modernist home (*Calle Zerrezuela & Calle del Curato*), enclosed behind orange walls immediately west of the hotel, served as the fictional home of Fermina Daza and her nouveau riche father in *Love in the Time of Cholera*. (*For a self-guided "Gabriel García Márquez–Gabo's Cartagena" audio tour, contact Tierra Magna Tours, tel 57-5/655-1916, tierramagna.com.*)

From here, walk down Carrera 7 (Calle del Hobo) one block to **Plaza Fernández de Madrid ❷**, which García Márquez recast as Park of the Evangels in *Love in the Time of Cholera*. On the east side of the square, the white house with a parrot-shaped door knocker and vine-covered second-floor balcony was the fictional home of Fermina. Join the old men at one of the benches where lovelorn Florentino Arizo might have sat, "pretending to read a book of verse in the shade of the almond trees," while spying on Fermina's comings and goings.

Now follow Carrera 7 (Calle Seguhda de Badillo) south to **Plaza de los Coches** ❸ (see p. 129), used as the setting where aristocratic child rebel Sierva Maria is bitten by a rabid dog in *Of Love and Other Demons*. Here, too, García Márquez opens *Love in the Time of Cholera* beneath the **Portal de los Dulces**, where Dr. Juvenal Urbino rushes to examine the corpse of his friend Jeremiah, who has poisoned himself to escape old age.

turn left and follow the pedestrian walk beneath **La Muralla** (see sidebar p. 139).

Turn right in front of the **Museo Naval** onto Carrera 3 (Calle Ricuarte) and head for **Plaza de Santo Domingo** (see p. 128); the cathedral's warped tower played a key part in Gabo's literary magic realism. From here, it's a few minutes' walk to **Plaza de Bolívar** ❺. Having arrived penniless in 1948, Márquez slept on a bench on his first night in Cartagena. On the north side, the **Museo Histórico** (see p. 128) was the inspiration for the school to

Many of Gabriel García Márquez's novels and short stories were inspired by his time in Cartagena.

Beyond the clock tower, the **Camellón de los Mártires** (see p. 129) is where the future Nobel laureate allegedly told his father he was quitting studying law to devote himself to writing, to which his father replied, "You will eat paper!"

The Portal de los Dulces opens west onto **Plaza de la Aduana** ❹, setting for the gypsy fair in the opening of *One Hundred Years of Solitude*. Next, walk across the plaza, with its lovely balconied buildings housing the town hall and statue of Christopher Columbus. You'll emerge on **Plaza de San Pedro Claver** (see pp. 128–129);

which Fermina Daza walked every day in *Love in the Time of Cholera*. Here, visit the **Catedral Santa Catalina de la Alejandría** (see p. 128), where three bishops officiate the marriage of Fermina—Florentino's lifelong love obsession—to Juvenal Urbino. The broad cobbled plaza on the cathedral's south side is lined by a colonnaded arcade, that of the **Palacio de la Gobernación** ❻. It served as the Portal de los Escribanos (Arcade of Scribes) in *Love in the Time of Cholera*, where protagonist Florentino penned love letters on behalf of others.

streets in Cartagena. Stop to admire the antique door knockers, tall shutters, and bougainvillea spilling over wood-beamed balconies. Many of the colonial mansions have been made into boutique hotels offering deluxe modern comforts behind time-worn facades.

On Cartagena's most intimate plaza, **Plaza de San Diego,** pop inside the **Hotel Sofitel Santa Clara** (Calle del Torno #39-29)—a former convent—to admire the courtyard and former crypt below the bar. The plaza is usually bustling with students from the Colegio Salesiano, located on the east side. Visit at night to dine at one of its lively restaurants.

Three blocks to the west, the **Teatro Heredia** (Cra. 4 & Calle 38, tel 57-5/664-6023, closed Sat.–Sun., $), on Plaza de la Merced, was completed in 1911 in republican style. Its four-tier, horseshoe-shaped auditorium features a beautiful ceiling mural and can be viewed on a guided tour.

Forming the far northeast corner of the Centro Histórico are **Las Bóvedas.** This row of 23 storerooms built into the city walls in the late 18th century now serves as a crafts market. The Baluarte de Santa Catalina military bastion, above Las Bóvedas, protected the old city against attack from the north. Its bunker is today a small museum—the **Museo de las Fortificaciones** (cnr. Playa del Tejadillo & Playa del San Carlos, $) depicting the city's early defenses. The bastion is a good place to start a walk west

atop La Muralla, the thick salt-bleached stone fortress walls.

Getsemaní

Getsemaní is a working-class extension of the Centro Histórico and is separated from El Centro and San Diego by the broad, modern thoroughfare of

INSIDER TIP:

Getting lost in the old city amid the colorful mansions, the city wall along the Caribbean, and the street performers will make finding your way back a pleasure.

—RACHAEL JACKSON
National Geographic Channels researcher

Avenida Venezuela (the market areas to either side of the boulevard require caution). Getsemaní was also enclosed within the old city walls. Still somewhat seedy, it is rapidly being upgraded by entrepreneurs with an eye on the gentrification that has graced El Centro and San Diego.

The streets pulse after dark with mainly salsa and some *vallenato*. In the evening, Avenida del Mercado and its harbor-front extension (Calle Arsenal) resemble one big block party typified by **Quiebra Canto** (Cra. 8 #25-119, tel 57-5/664-1372, quiebracanto.com), the city's hottest salsa joint.

A trumpeter welcomes visitors to the Castillo de San Felipe de Barajas.

Castillo de San Felipe de Barajas

✉ Cra. 17 & Calle 30

☎ 57-5/656-0590

💲 $$

Beyond El Centro

Beyond the walled city are many places worth exploring, including the third largest castle in the New World.

Castillo de San Felipe de Barajas:

Largest of the various forts that ringed the city, this massive castle stands atop San Lázaro hill, a ten-minute walk east from Getsemaní along Calle 30. It served to guard the city's landward side. Initiated in 1536 and built by slaves, it was added to several times and finally completed in 1657 (the impregnable bastion would be exceeded in size only by Havana's Fortaleza San Carlos de la Cabaña and San Juan's Castillo de San Cristóbal).

Lit at night, its sloping ramparts are bathed in a golden glow, like a movie set. You can explore the Almacén de Pólvora (Gunpowder Store) and warren of tunnels, but hire a guide to make sense of the fortress. English-speaking guides tout their services (*$$*).

Below the castle stands a statue of Don Blas de Lezo, the Spanish admiral who successfully defended the city against British forces in March 1741. Some 220 yards (200 m) east is **Las Botas Viejas** (Old Boots Monument), a huge pair of bronze boots that record the poem by Cartagena-born poet Luis Carlos López (1883–1950), who declared that he loved the city "as much as my shoes."

Cerro de la Popa:

For a sweeping perspective of Cartagena, take a taxi (walking is unwise) to the city's highest point, which spreads the city

INSIDER TIP:

Hire a guide at the Castillo de San Felipe de Barajas. You'll want an expert to lead you through the fort's elaborate system of dark, narrow tunnels.

—RACHAEL JACKSON
National Geographic Channels researcher

at your feet. The 486-foot-tall (148 m) **Stern Hill,** which rises to the east of San Felipe castle, is named for its resemblance to the poop of a Spanish galleon. It's topped by an imposing 17th-century fortress-convent, resembling (thought Gabriel García Márquez, in *Autumn of the Patriarchs*) "an ocean liner aground on top of the roofs."

The **Convento de Nuestra Señora de la Candelaria** *(tel 57-5/666-2331, $)* was founded by Augustine monks in 1607. It no longer serves as a convent, but it does remain a pilgrimage site for those who come to pray at an effigy of the Virgen de la Candelaria.

Bocagrande: Stretching along the shore south of the Centro Histórico like a shepherd's crook is a wide sandy spit—Bocagrande—studded with towering 21st-century condos. This bent finger of land resembles Miami's South Beach. Many of the city's ritziest hotels are here, lining a drab gray-sand beach. Each November, the shorefront **Avenida San Martín** is the hottest ticket in town as Colombia's most beautiful women strut the boulevard in hopes of being crowned Miss Colombia (see sidebar below). The day after Miss Colombia is chosen, she poses on the beach with a palenquera—a tradition said to ensure good luck. The finale of the Concurso Nacional de

Miss Colombia

Colombians are obsessed with beauty pageants. The Concurso Nacional de Belleza (National Beauty Contest), held annually in Cartagena to crown Miss Colombia, is a national holiday. Magazines devote entire issues to the event, when Cartagena erupts with parades and parties. Local governments sponsor contestants. In the 1990s, drug barons also funded contestants; Maribel Gutiérrez Tinoco (Miss Colombia 1990) gave up her title to marry cartel boss Jairo "El Mico" Duran. Even Colombia's prisons hold pageants, inspiring Gabriel García Márquez to write in *The Funerals*

of Mama Grande: "There is a queen for mango, for pumpkin, for the green pumpkin, for the green banana, for the yellow banana, for the cassava just to mention a few."

When Luz Marina Zuluaga won the Miss Colombia title in 1958, she was awarded a mansion and tax exemption for life. Vanessa Mendoza, the first black woman to win Miss Colombia (2001), got a postage stamp in her honor. Former beauty queens have become a culture minister and even a defense minister. Paulina Vega, Miss Colombia 2013, won the Miss Universe 2014 title.

Simón Bolívar

Adored throughout South America as El Libertador, Simón Bolívar (1783–1830) is considered the George Washington of Colombia. Born in Caracas, he was bequeathed a fortune when his parents died while he was still a child. Bolívar joined the independence cause in 1810 and, in 1813, captured Caracas as head of a nationalist army: the start of a chain of victories that led to the first union of independent nations—Gran Colombia—in Latin America in 1819. Bolívar drew up the constitution and became Gran Colombia's first president.

On April 27, 1830, he resigned as president and died on December 7, in Quinta de San Pedro Alejandrina in Santa Marta, where he was buried in the cathedral. In 1842, his body was moved to Caracas, where he slumbers in the National Pantheon of Venezuela.

Parque Nacional Natural Corales del Rosario y de San Bernardo

🗺 125 A2
☎ 57-1/353-2400 ext. 138

E-mail: atencion usuario@parques nacionales.gov.co

Belleza (National Beauty Contest) coincides with Cartagena's Independence Day, when the entire city explodes with street parades and fiestas.

Excursions From the City

To explore beyond the city, consider a day trip to nearby sites.

Parque Nacional Natural Corales del Rosario y de San Bernardo: Excursion boats depart Cartagena for Isla Barú (a peninsula separated by a canal from the mainland) and the 27 offshore coral islands that make up the **Islas del Rosario archipelago,** some 30 miles (50 km) southwest of Cartagena. The islands are protected within a marine park that covers 463 square miles

(1,199 sq km) south to the Archipelago de San Bernardo.

The park is a major nesting site for marine turtles and protects four-fifths of the coral reefs along Colombia's Caribbean coast, plus mangrove forests, coastal marshlands, and marine waters. The largest island—**Isla Grand** (part of the archipelago but not part of the park)—is dotted with hotels and villas, many of them built with *dinero sucio* (drug money) and now going to ruin. On tiny **Isla de San Martín de Pajarales,** west of Isla Grande, fish,

INSIDER TIP:

Take a midday private taxi instead of a morning tour bus to visit the mud baths at Volcán de Lodo El Totumo. The price is about the same, and you'll avoid the crowds.

—ALISON INCE
National Geographic contributor

dolphins, and marine turtles swim around in wire pens at the **Acuario Ceiner,** which has dolphin shows.

Tour boats fast and slow operate from the Muelle (dock) Turístico la Bodeguita in Cartagena (*$$$–$$$$; buy tickets at the dock*). They typically combine visits to Isla Rosario and Isla San Martín with a visit to **Playa Blanca,** midway along the oceanfront shore of **Isla Barú** (*$*). Isla Barú is the nicest beach in the area—its sugar white sands melting into pale green shallows. A outlying barrier reef stems the waves, but hawkers are numerous and persistent.

Volcán de Lodo El Totumo:
An absolute must-do experience when visiting Cartagena

After paying your entry fee (*$*) to the local Asociación de Trabajadores del Volcán del Totumo cooperative, you climb a wooden staircase and slip into the 10-foot-wide (3 m) pool, boxed by a wooden frame surrounded by rails. The 49-foot-tall (15 m) volcano has no discernible bottom. You float in mud the consistency of molasses. Giant bubbles—the

Volcán de Lodo El Totumo
📍 125 B2

Isla Rosario is the perfect place to sunbathe.

or Barranquilla is to steep in the thermal mud at this minivolcanic cone, which spews lukewarm liquid clay instead of lava. The highest mud volcano in Colombia is located midway between Cartagena and Barranquilla. There's a sign on the coast road about 31 miles (50 km) northeast of Cartagena.

result of gases from decaying materials—belch up every minute or so, splashing bathers in dark mud. When you're finished, you walk downhill about 55 yards (50 m) to the Cienaga de Totumo to rinse off in the grungy waters, where local women are on hand to help you with your bath for a fee. ■

Pirates

Pirates color Colombia's chromatic past. Swashbuckling a blazing trail through the Indies, cutthroat buccaneers, privateers, and pirates were the terrorists of their day, entirely lacking in compassion and scruples. For almost two centuries, these wild and ruthless sea rovers plundered the Spanish Main, the Spanish-controlled Caribbean coastline from Mexico to the Orinoco River. No Spanish stronghold was as tempting as the port of Cartagena, one of the New World's three main gateways for great galleons laden with treasure en route to Spain.

A Samuel Scott painting of the 1708 battle between the British and Spanish off Cartagena's shores

From the earliest days of Spain's discovery of the Americas, Cartagena served with Panama's Portobelo and Cuba's Havana as the chief conduit for South America's unsurpassed wealth. From Colombian emeralds to silver and gold pillaged from the Inca of Peru, treasure in mind-boggling quantity was transported to Cartagena to await shipment to Spain with the twice-yearly treasure fleets. The city was a plump plum ripe for picking and was first plundered in the early 1540s by French pirate Robert Baal. Daring foreigners seized Spanish galleons at random, often with the sanction of Spain's sworn enemies.

England, France, and Holland licensed individual captains as privateers to attack Spanish ships and cities in the New World.

The most notorious privateer was Sir Frances Drake (ca 1540–1596), who first sailed to the New World in 1567, with his cousin John Hawkins and a cargo of African slaves. Their fleet was attacked by the Spanish, searing Drake–a devout Protestant–with anti-papist hatred. In 1568, Hawkins returned and besieged Cartagena; in 1572, Drake ransacked Nombre de Díos in Panama, captured several Spanish vessels, and sailed for England with the ships' holds groaning with treasure.

Sanctioned by Queen Elizabeth I, in 1577, he set out again with five vessels and the purpose of plunder. After pillaging the Pacific coast of South America, Drake captured the *Nuestra Señora de la Concepción* treasure ship and returned to England in 1580 having circumnavigated the world. Drake returned to Colombia in 1586, captured Cartagena, and destroyed the cathedral and much of the city, which he ransomed for a fortune in treasure.

The Buccaneers

In the mid-17th century, a new breed of cut-throats appeared. The buccaneers began life as a motley group of seafaring miscreants who had coalesced off Hispaniola, where they hunted wild boar and raised livestock. The

Spanish resented their presence, however, and drove them to sea. They formed the Brethren of the Coast and turned to piracy against the Spanish. Success swelled their numbers as they captured ships, grew more powerful, and eventually were welcomed to Port Royal, Jamaica.

Chief among them was Henry Morgan (1635–1688), a ruthless Welshman who led the brotherhood to unsurpassed heights of success and depravity. When Morgan sacked Portobelo in 1668, he used Catholic nuns and monks as human shields against Spanish fire. Morgan narrowly escaped with his life in March 1669, when his flagship, H.M.S. *Oxford,* exploded while en route to attack Cartagena. His ruinous rape of the Spanish Main was crowned in 1671 by the sacking of Panama City. Although Morgan was recalled to England to stand trial, he was exonerated, knighted, and named governor of Jamaica.

In 1697, Spain and England made peace and embarked on a crusade to suppress piracy.

La Muralla

Initiated in 1586, Cartagena's city wall—La Muralla—was designed to protect the city against attack. Constructed in stages, the protective perimeter complex we know today was not completed until 1796, under the direction of Spanish engineer Antonio de Arévalo (1715–1800). Enclosing the Ciudad Amurallada (walled city) entirely, it measured 2.5 miles (4 km) in length, of which 2.25 miles (3.5 km) remain standing today.

Measuring up to 26 feet (8 m) tall, the coralstone fortification is one of the best-preserved colonial walls in the New World. It featured a moat, plus 16 *baluartes* (bastions)—protruding pentagonal elements armed with cannons, with sentry boxes jutting out at each corner—connected by 14 curtain walls with seven main entry gates. A breakwater erected in 1761–1771 protected the northwestern walls from wave action.

South & West of Cartagena

The flat and fertile hinterland south of Cartagena is off the beaten tourist path, largely because much of it floods seasonally for eight months a year. Yet this watery world has helped preserve the UNESCO World Heritage city of Mompox as a colonial gem that time has passed by. The Caribbean shore sidles south to the Golfo de Urabá—an up-and-coming destination known for its Kuna indigenous people and for its superb white-sand beaches and coral reefs.

A campesino (peasant farmer) on his bicycle carries palm fronds to be used for thatch.

Visitors are rewarded with fabulous bird-watching, mud volcanoes, dolphins in the Golfo de Morrosquillo, the other-worldly charms of Mompox, and gorgeous beaches and col-orful indigenous culture in the Golfo de Urabá—a beach-and-mangrove-fringed gulf next to the border with Panama.

Until recently, much of the region far south of Cartagena was relatively risky to visit. The Cartagena–Medellín and

Medellín–Turbo highways were the scene of frequent kidnappings. Much of the territory was also a feuding ground between left-wing guerrillas and equally ruthless paramilitaries, who as recently as a decade ago controlled Turbo and other regional communities. The Colombian Army has since secured the main highways. How-ever, avoid driving at night and consider towns such as Cacucasia and Montería as places to pass through, not linger.

San Basilio de Palenque

This small, isolated, and iconic
Afro-Colombian community
in the Montes de María chain,
southeast of Cartagena, has for
centuries been home to the
descendants of runaway slaves,
who founded it as a *palenque—*
stockaded settlement—in 1603.
The community preserves the
customs of its African forebears
(especially music and dance),
and even speak a unique Creole
language—*palenquero*. It flairs with
riotous color and sound each
mid-October for the Festival de
Tambores (Festival of Drums).
Cartagena's flamboyantly dressed
palenqueras come from here.

Mompox

Santa Cruz de Mompox was
founded in 1537 on the banks
of the Río Magdalena in the
days when the river was a major
highway of commerce. The
bayou town became a wealthy
trading port, graced by churches
and beautiful colonial houses
displaying elaborate wrought-
iron grills atop pedestals. Then
the river shifted course and

Mompox lost much of its
import. Steeping in the midst
of a swampy floodplain, the
time-warp town (it was named
a UNESCO World Heritage site
in 1995) evokes Gabriel García
Márquez's fictional town of
Macondo—the isolated magic-
realist setting for *One Hundred
Years of Solitude*. In fact, Mompox was the setting for García
Márquez's *Chronicles of a Death
Foretold*. Be prepared for stifling
heat and humidity.

Of Mompox's many churches
(open for Mass only), the most
intriguing is **Iglesia de Santa
Barbara** *(Calle de la Albarrada &
Calle 14)*, with exquisite stucco
adornments and a baroque
octagonal bell tower. Be sure to
visit the **Museo Cultural de Arte
Religioso,** displaying parts of
the original wall murals exposed

**San Basilio de
Palenque**

🇦 125 B2

✉ 35 miles (56 km)
SE of Cartagena

Mompox

🇦 125 B1

Visitor Information

✉ Carrera 2da,
Palacio de San
Carlos

☎ 57-5/685-5039

santacruzdemom
pos-bolivar.gov.co

**Museo Cultural
de Arte Religioso**

✉ Calle Real del
Medio #17-07

☎ 57-5/685-6074

🕐 Closed Sun.–
Mon.

💲 $

Harpy Eagles

With a wingspan of 7 feet (2.1 m)—the largest of any bird in the world—the endangered *Harpia harpyja* is also the largest bird of prey in the Americas. It soars above the lowland rain forests of Chocó and Amazonas while looking for monkeys, sloths, and other tree-dwelling prey, which it seizes on the wing with huge talons. This charcoal gray bird is made strikingly handsome by a feathery ruff and by a crown of long feathers atop its light gray head. Once common throughout Central and South America, its range has diminished.

Golfo de Urabá
🅰 125 A1

beneath modern stucco; and the **Alcaldia** (*Calle 19 & Cra. 2a*), or town hall, occupying the former Convento de San Carlos. It's fronted by a life-size bronze statue of the "Liberty maiden," inscribed with Simón Bolívar's words: *"Si a Caracas debo la vida, a Mompos debo la gloria"* ("If to Caracas I owe my life, I owe my glory to Mompox").

At the east end of town, the main street—**Calle Real del Medio**—is lined with family workshops that produce furniture and *talleres de filagría*—silversmith workshops—such as Joyería Villa Real, where Alejandro Villa Real crafts bracelets and earrings in a room filled with caged songbirds. Rise at dawn to visit the informal **riverfront market** (*Calle de la Albarrada*).

Jacanas, herons, grebes, and black ibises feed in the ink black lagoons that surround Mompox.

Getting to Mompox: Surrounded by seasonally flooded lagoons and braided channels, it requires careful planning to reach. From the west, a ferry departs from 5 miles (8 km) north of Magangué (*tel 57/311-412-3693, daily at 5 a.m., 8 a.m., 10 a.m., 1 p.m., 3 p.m., & 5 p.m., leaves when full, $*). To the east, Mompox is linked to the main Bucaramanga–Bosconia highway, but the route from Pelaya via El Banco is a muddy crawl (high-ground-clearance four-wheel drive is a must) and passage is tenuous; the preferred route is via El Paso (*accessed from the Curumaní–Bosconia highway at Cuatro Vientos*), then Astrea and El Banco.

Golfo de Urabá

Tucked into the far northwest corner of Colombia, this oblong-shaped gulf is a booming resort destination.

On the western side of the gulf, in Chocó Department, rain forest extends up the Serranía de Darién mountain range, whose crest forms the border with Panama. The calls of howler monkeys and screech of macaws broadcast the richness of local fauna of the **Darién,** an unconquered region that divides the Americas north and south. The area surrounding the gulf has witnessed some of the worst violence in Colombia in recent decades. Fortunately, the guerrillas and paramilitaries are now gone from the coastal zone. But inland jungle hikes are out of the question without a guide.

The gateway to the gulf by boat is **Turbo,** a port town that steeps in soporific heat. Turbo is reached by paved road from

Medellín (170 miles/275 km), and by muddy country roads from Montería *(allow 6 hours)*. For safety, travel the roads only by day.

Capurganá, a landlocked Afro-Colombian fishing village just 3 miles (5 km) south of the Panamanian border, has evolved as a laid-back resort. Backed by rugged mountains, Capurganá enjoys a magnificent setting and fulfills the image of a Caribbean idyll. Coconut palms hover over whiter-than-white sands dissolving into turquoise waters speckled with lush isles and tiny cays protected by coral reefs. It has a wide choice of hotels. You can fly here from Medellín, or arrive by early morning water-taxi from Turbo *(2.5 hours, $$$$$)*.

A multitude of beaches include the golden sands of reef-protected **Playa La Caleta,** where crystal-clear waters tempt snorkelers. For the best beach, take a *lancha* (boat) or hike *(1 hour)* to **Bahía El Aguacate** (it can get crowded with excursion tours), or the charmingly funky border hamlet of **Sapzurro** in a horseshoe bay speckled with coral reefs.

Local outfitters offer scuba diving, and hotels can arrange half-day rain forest hikes or horseback rides to **El Cielo waterfall,** or excursions to **Parque Nacional Acondi Playona,** created in 2013 as a sanctuary for hawksbill and leatherback turtles. The beauty of the sand-fringed bays and turquoise waters around Capurganá is exceeded only by that of the Kuna, who cling to an indigenous culture that is one of the most colorful and intact in the world. ∎

Capurganá
▲ 125 A1

Seasonally flooded lagoons and water channels surround the 16th-century town of Mompox.

North Central

Stretching along 100 miles (160 km) of shoreline, this region packs a huge punch, from the Carnaval-crazy port city of Barranquilla to the pre-Columbian Lost City high in the Sierra Nevada de Santa Marta. These snowcapped mountains soar above the palm-fringed beaches of Parque Nacional Natural Tayrona.

El Rodadero is one of Colombia's most popular beach resorts, where you can swim with dolphins.

Barranquilla

125 B2

Visitor Information

✉ Secretaría de Cultura, Patrimonio y Turismo, Calle 34 #43-31, Barranquilla

☎ 57-5/339-9450

Barranquilla

The frenetic port city (pop. 1.2 million) at the mouth of the Magdalena River is given short shrift by vacationers focused on Cartagena and Santa Marta. Yet Barranquilla, midway between both, has much to offer. The upscale modern city to the north contrasts with the cha-otic, trash-strewn barrios to the south. The latter includes the city's historic core, dating from its founding in 1629. Almost all

sites of interest are in, or on the edge of, the modern city.

A fertile fiesta of Spanish, Afri-can, and indigenous celebration, Barranquilla is a perfect storm of color, culture, and cacophony. Never more so than during mid-February, when the city goes wild for its Carnaval, a five-day bacchanal that is Colombia's fore-most folk celebration. The city announces itself on the highway with a billboard that reads "37°C *de calidad humana*"—a reference to its average temperature of 98.6°F, that of the human body.

El Prado & Barrio Abajo:
The heart of the city, the monied and modern El Prado district was laid out in 1921 with palm-shaded boulevards and beautiful mansions in republican style. One now houses the **Museo Romántico,** the city's small history museum. More interesting are the sculptures along **El Prado Boulevard,** such as **Monumento al Heroe Caido** (Calle 59 & Cra. 54). This levitated figure wrapped in a shroud and encased in glass honors victims of Colombia's Violencia (see pp. 29–30).

Nearby, art enthusiasts will appreciate the **Museo de Arte Moderno** (MAMB), displaying works from throughout Latin America. Carrera 54 leads east

past the **Teatro Amira de la Rosa** (Cra. 54 #52-258, tel 57-5/349-1210), a fine example of modernist architecture from 1982, with a striking exterior mural by Colombian painter Alejandro Obregón (1920–1992) measuring 197 feet (60 m) long. Continue two blocks east to Barrio Abajo, a working-class district enlivened by homes painted in colorful tropical fruit pastels.

Housed in a classic colonial-style building, the **Casa del Carnaval** is the headquarters of the Carnaval de Barranquilla Foundation. Opened in 2011, its superb interactive museum—the Sala del Carnaval Elsa Caridi—displays costumes and masks.

Plaza de la Paz: One of Barranquilla's two must-see sights is the **Catedral Metropolitano** (cnr. of Calle 53 & Cra. 46), on

Museo Romántico
✉ Cra. 54 #59-199
☎ 57-5/339-9000
🕐 Closed Sun.
💲 $

Museo de Arte Moderno
✉ Cra. 56 #74-22
☎ 57-5/369-0101
🕐 Closed Sun.
mambq.org

Casa del Carnaval
✉ Cra. 54 #49B-39
☎ 57-5/319-7616
🕐 Closed Mon.
carnavaldebarran quilla.org

EXPERIENCE: Local Music & Dance

Champeta, cumbia, and *vallenato* may be distinct musical forms, but all three evolved around Cartagena and were spawned in the same cultural crucible from African, Spanish, and indigenous elements.

Cumbia, oldest of the three, began as a courtship dance among African slaves. Infused with West African rhythms, the patterns of this complex folk dance invoke ankles weighted with shackles. By the 1940s, cumbia had reached an urbane middle-class audience and was refined with mambo-style brass band sounds.

Champeta sprang up in the 1970s in the poorer barrios of Cartagena as a hybrid fusion of cumbia, soca, calypso, and reggae that was blended with purer African sounds.

Vallenato is also a hodgepodge that evolved from cumbia, and is an accordion- and bass guitar–based music that gained popularity throughout Colombia in the 1980s.

Take a class at one of the following dance schools so that you can keep up with the locals:

Crazy Salsa (Calle 38 #8-55, Cartagena, tel 57-5/660-1809, crazysalsa.net). This school also teaches other Latin dance forms, from *bachata* to salsa.

Learn More Than Spanish (Cra. 9A #61-51, Bogotá, tel 57/310-775-0768, learnmorethanspanish.com). This British-run Spanish-language school combines language lessons with dance instruction.

Museo del Caribe

✉ Calle 36 #46-66, Barranquilla

☎ 57-5/372-0582

$ $$

culturacaribe.org

Santa Marta

🄰 125 B2

Visitor Information

✉ Secretaría de Tourism, Calle 17 #3-120

☎ 57-5/438-2587

santamarta.gov.co

Avenida Olaya Herrera on the west side of the Peace Plaza, which was remodeled in 2011. The modernist cathedral was designed by Italian architect Angelo Mazzoni (1894–1979) and completed in 1982, after 27 years, with a stunning interior. A massive bronze sculpture of Christ by Rodrigo Arenas Betancourt soars over the simple marble altar. The vaulted concrete ceiling is open to the elements. You may even see vultures roosting on the upper reaches, peering down eerily on congregants during Mass.

Around Parque Cultural del Caribe: Farther east on Avenida Olaya Herrera is the world-class **Museo del Caribe,** which opened in 2009 in a sensational modern structure with walls of slate and glass. Its central theme is Colombia's Caribbean culture, organized into five main themes on six levels. Particularly fascinating is the third floor dedicated to audiovisual interviews of Colombians speaking on nationality and identity.

Next, head north two blocks to the **Edificio La Aduana** (Vía 40 #36-135, tel 57-5/369-3700), the old customs building built in 1919. Restored, it now serves as an archival and cultural center. On its northern end is the old **Estación Montoya** railway station displaying *Doña Helena,* a steam locomotive manufactured in England in 1904.

Four blocks south of the Museo del Caribe, the city's

littered colonial quarter is centered on **Plaza San Nicolás** (Calle 33 & Cra. 41), dominated by the Gothic **Iglesia de San Nicolás de Tolentino,** with twin octagonal bell towers.

Santa Marta

A popular resort destination for middle-income Colombians, this coastal town is one of Colombia's oldest cities. Founded in 1525, almost a decade before Cartagena, it was from here that Gonzalo Jiménez de Quesada set out to explore and colonize the interior. Despite its antiquity, Santa Marta's relatively humble colonial core has little of the picture-perfect beauty of Cartagena, which eclipsed it as a port at an early stage.

INSIDER TIP:

Bring food to share with others in the *palcos* **(Carnaval bleachers). You'll be there most of the day, and it's a perfect chance to make friends in Barranquilla.**

—ALISON INCE
National Geographic contributor

Out-of-town vacationers flock to Quinta de San Pedro Alejandrino, the hallowed national shrine to Simón Bolívar; and to the resort of **El Rodadero,** 3 miles (5 km) south of Santa Marta, where the **Acuario y Museo del Mar de Rodadero** (tel 57-5/422-7222, acuario rodadero.com, $$$) displays 100 marine species, from sea horses to sharks, in netted ocean pens and tanks. You can even swim with dolphins.

The town explodes in revelry each July during the five-day **Fiesta del Mar** (tel 57-5/438-2107 or 438-2777 ext. 260), with water-themed activities, street parades, and beauty pageants to elect the local Sirena del Mar and national Reina Fiesta del Mar.

Santa Marta has gone chic in recent years. Several boutique hotels have opened. And the city's renaissance has been crowned by a new marina (marina santamarta.com.co).

Casco Histórico: The colonial quarter (bet. Paseo de Bastidas & Cra. 5, & Calles 11 & 22) extends three blocks inland from the malecón. Officially the Paseo de Bastidas, the seafront boulevard is named for city founder Rodrigo de Bastidas (1460–1527), whose monument at Calle 15 faces onto **Plaza de Bolívar** (Calle 15 & Cra. 14), the main plaza. After admiring the bronze Monumento Simón Bolívar, cross to the park's north side and the Casa de la Aduana (Customshouse), the city's oldest building, housing the remodeled **Museo del Oro Tairona**—the town's pre-Columbian gold museum.

Follow Calle 15 east one block and turn right for Plaza de la Catedral, where the whitewashed **Catedral de Santa Marta** contains an elaborate marble sarcophagus wherein slumbers

Rodrigo de Bastidas. The most intimate square, and a setting for many of Santa Marta's liveliest bars, is **Parque Santander** (Calle 19 & Cra. 3). Colloquially called Parque de los Novios (Couples Park), as in colonial days it was used for chaperoned encounters, it features a statue

Museo del Oro Tairona

✉ Calle 14 #1C-37, Santa Marta

☎ 57-5/421-0251

🕐 Closed Sun.

proyectos
.banrepcultural.org
/museo-del-oro
-tairona

Shakira

Singer-songwriter Shakira is the highest-selling Colombian artist of all time, having sold more than 70 million albums worldwide. She is particularly known for her belly-dancing routines while performing Latin rock-and-roll. Shakira Isabel Mebarak Ripoll was born in Barranquilla in 1977 and is of Italian, Lebanese, and Spanish descent. She wrote her first song at the age of eight. In 1996, her *Pies Descalzos* album launched her to fame in Latin America and Spain. She broke into the English-speaking world in 2001, with the release of *Laundry Service,* which has sold more than 13 million copies. Shakira has her own cosmetic brand and has starred in several telenovelas. She often performs at benefit concerts, and in 1995 she founded the Pies Descalzos Foundation—a charity that operates special schools for poor children.

---

of Francisco Paula de Santander. Two blocks to the southwest, the former Hospital San Juan de Díos, dating from 1690, now hosts the **Museo Antropológico y Etnográfico** (Anthropological and Ethnographic Museum), with galleries dedicated to the history of the Caribbean, Santa Marta, and the Sierra Nevada and its indigenous communities.

**Quinta de
San Pedro
Alejandrina**

✉ Cra. 32 & Calle
29, Santa Marta

☎ 57-5/433-1021

💲 $

museobolivariano
.org.co

Taganga

🅰 125 B2

Aracataca

🅰 125 B2

**Quinta de San Pedro
Alejandrina:** An obligatory
stop for South American visitors
to Santa Marta is the former
sugarcane hacienda where
independence hero Simón
Bolívar died on December 17,
1830—a place that reduces
many visitors to tears. Period
pieces include the bed in which
the Liberator died and even
a life-size marble effigy of his
corpse. A palm-lined esplanade
flanked by flags of the American
nations leads to a pantheon
containing the Altar de la Patria
monument. The garden to the
left of the mausoleum contains
a 164-foot-long (50 m) mural
of Bolívar's life by Peruvian artist Mauro Rodríguez Cárdenas.
To its north, a 19th-century
addition houses the **Museo
Bolivariano de Arte Contem-
poráneo,** displaying art from
the past century.

Beyond Santa Marta

Taganga: This fishing village
2 miles (3 km) northeast of
Santa Marta is popular with
foreign backpackers, despite its
detritus-strewn beach. The setting in a sweeping bay clasped
by steep headlands is almost
Mediterranean, aided by weathered fishing boats and nets
piled on the beach. The ocean
and reefs teem with marine life.
Taganga has many dive shops.

Aracataca: Fans of novelist Gabriel García Márquez
shouldn't miss a pilgrimage
to this small town, 50 miles
(80 km) south of Santa Marta.
García Márquez, often referred
to as "Gabo," was born and
raised in Aracataca. A part of
the steamy banana zone, Aracataca is a mini-Macondo—the
magic-realistic village brought
to vivid life in García Márquez's

A visitor pays homage to liberator Simón Bolívar at Quinta de San Pedro Alejandrina.

One Hundred Years of Solitude. The somnolent town seems afflicted by arrested drowsiness.

Start your visit at the **Museo Telegrafo** *(Calle 9 #5-30)*, tucked behind the quaint village church where Gabo was baptized. The former Casa del Telegrafista, where Gabo's father worked, is now a museum stuffed with period dusty miscellany re-creating Gabo's life. Don't miss the **library** *(Calle 5 #4A-32)*, where yellow butterflies dance around "Remedios the Beauty" lying supine atop an open book as she ascends to heaven.

Ground zero is the **Casa Museo Gabriel García Márquez,** which opened in March 2010 as a reproduction of the small farmstead house where Gabo was born and raised by his grandparents. The 14-room museum is furnished with wrought-iron beds and similar domestic accoutrements typical of the era. The various rooms are themed from his biographical novels, such as the porch with the begonias and the *taller de filagriá* (silversmith's workshop) displaying the "gold fish" that he mentions in *One Hundred Years of Solitude;* and the Cuarto de los Trastos (Room of Trunks), full of old chests, which young Gabo was forbidden to enter. In *One Hundred Years of Solitude,* the room served as the Room of Oblivion, where bad memories, family tragedies, and episodes not worth airing were left.

Ciénaga Grande de Santa Marta:
The marshland of Santa Marta is one of South

America's largest coastal wetlands and was designated a biosphere reserve in 2000. This mosaic of lagoons, mangroves, and seasonally dry forest surrounds the largest lagoon in the country and spans 40 miles (65 km) of coast between Barranquilla and the town of **Ciénaga** 18 miles (30 km) south of Santa Marta). The **reserve** is closed to ecotourism, but you can easily spot neotropic

---

Shutterbug Etiquette

Colorfully dressed Guambiano indigenous people in Silvia will have you reaching for your camera. However, many Guambiano adults don't like being photographed. Taking pictures without asking is considered offensive by most indigenous groups in Colombia. The Kogi of the Sierra Nevada de Santa Marta often refuse to be photographed because they believe a photograph captures a person's soul or can be used to cast magic spells. Be respectful of such feelings and of local customs. Many nonindigenous Colombians also refuse to be photographed. The general rule: Ask permission. If a person refuses your request for a photo, honor their wishes.

---

cormorants, wattled jacanas, jabiru storks, and roseate spoonbills alongside the coast highway. The highway passes several impoverished *pueblos palafiticos* (stilt villages) that rise above the lagoons.

Minca

To escape the stupefying lowland heat, head inland to Minca, a peaceful mountain village 9 miles (14 km) southeast of

---

Casa Museo Gabriel García Márquez
- Cra. 5 #6-35, Aracataca
- 57-5/425-6588
- Closed Mon. & 1 p.m.–2 p.m. Tues.–Sat.
- Donation

Ciénaga Grande de Santa Marta
- 125 B2
- 57-5/421-3089

Minca
- 125 B2

Sunrise in Parque Nacional Natural Tayrona

Reserva de las Aves El Dorado

🏔 125 B2

☎ 57-1/340-3229 (c/o ProAves)

💲 $$

proaves.org

Santa Marta. The Zona Cafetera (coffee zone) begins at this tiny hamlet nestled at about 2,100 feet (640 m) in elevation in a fold of the Sierra Nevada de Santa Marta. It's a great place to relax at hotels of all price ranges. If you are driving, a four-wheel drive is recommended.

The badly deteriorated road continues uphill 2.5 miles (4 km) to **Pozo Azul,** a series of cascades and pools (a 20-minute hike from the road) that sparkle jade in dry season; after rains, ferocious currents make bathing unsafe. Nearby, you can tour **Hacienda La Victoria** *(tel 57/315-733-1744, 4 miles/6 km above Minca, facebook .com/LaVictoria1892),* an organic coffee farm.

Reserva de las Aves El Dorado:

Birders strike aviary gold at the El Dorado Bird Reserve, 14 miles (22 km) above Minca. Created in 2006, ProAves' flagship reserve extends upward from 2,950 to 8,530 feet (900–2,600 m) elevation, protecting subtropical and montane rain forest that resounds with birdsong. The checklist includes 410 bird species, including 19 endemic to these mountains. The 2,175-acre (880 ha) reserve also shelters such endemic amphibians as the San Lorenzo harlequin frog, and endemic mammals include the Santa Marta tree rat.

Five short trails begin at the visitor center and lodge. One leads to a lookout with sensational views of snow-clad peaks. The **Condor Observation Tower** offers an occasional sighting of Andean condors. The rugged access road requires high-ground-clearance four-wheel drive; it continues uphill to the **San Lorenzo Forest**

Reserve, protecting the habitat of the Santa Marta parakeet. Reservations are recommended for overnight stays.

Parque Nacional Natural Tayrona

Beginning immediately east of Taganga (see p. 148), Tayrona National Natural Park extends along 20 miles (30 km) of rugged shore and rises inland to 2,950 feet (900 m) in elevation atop the foothills of the Sierra Nevada de Santa Marta. Nowhere else in Colombia offers such a winning combination of accessibility, palm-fringed beaches, rain forest

INSIDER TIP:

Tayrona National Natural Park is the closest thing to the dream of a lost paradise. An endless path of white pebbles leads you to an important indigenous tribe. And guess what—they sell a delicious chocolate bread.

—OLIVER EHMIG VELEZ
National Geographic photographer

teeming with wildlife, and a major archaeological site.

The western **Palangana sector** (8 miles/12 km E of Santa Marta) draws locals from Santa Marta for the silvery beach at **Playa Neguanje.** The main

eastern entrance is at **El Zaíno** (15 miles/24 km E of Santa Marta), from where a hilly trail winds through rain forest full of agoutis, white-faced monkeys, and scarlet macaws. The trail spills onto **Playa Cañaveral,** a beach that merges west into **Playa Arrecifes.** Surf pounds ashore, making swimming dangerous. To bathe, follow the trail west to **Playita Arenia,** a palm-fringed cove with calm waters; and, beyond, **Cabo San Juan,** where a tombolo connects a rocky headland to the shore. Allow eight hours for a round-trip hike from El Zaíno, where horses can be rented at the trailhead 1 mile (2 km) from El Zaíno Ranger Station.

From Cabo San Juan, a challenging 2-mile (3 km) trail follows a pre-Columbian track to **Pueblito,** an archaeological site deep in the jungle. Don't hike alone, as problems have been reported. An easier route is to drive from the highway at Carabaso (13 miles/20 km E of Santa Marta).

Parque Nacional Natural Sierra Nevada de Santa Marta

Rising in great tidal waves to the southeast of Santa Marta, the rugged Sierra Nevada is the planet's largest coastal massif. Reaching an altitude of 18,946 feet (5,775 m) just 29 miles (46 km) from the sea, this free-standing vertical wilderness is also one of the highest ranges in the world from base to summit. Sunlight glints on the glacier-capped peaks of

**Parque Nacional
Natural Tayrona**

◪ 125 B2

☎ 57-1/587-5181

⑤ $$$

**aviaturecoturismo
.com**

**Parque Nacional
Natural Sierra
Nevada de Santa
Marta**

◪ 125 B2–C2

✉ Calle 17 #4-06

☎ 57-5/423-0752

**E-mail: sierra
nevada@parque
nacionales.gov.co**

EXPERIENCE: Trek to Ciudad Perdida

Founded high in the Sierra Nevada around A.D. 800, the mountain city of Teyuna was abandoned following the Spanish conquest. Shrouded in jungle, its fabled location thereafter inspired legends, drawing treasure hunters who stumbled upon it in 1972. Today, grueling and not without hazards, the six-day round-trip trek to Ciudad Perdida (Lost City; see p. 154) is the ultimate Indiana Jones–style adventure.

The 32-mile (52 km) trek through jungle is physically challenging, but the reward is enormous. By day, you hike in ferocious heat; by night, you shiver while sleeping in hammocks. The trail is extremely muddy and involves river fordings and a cliff-face climb. Be prepared to brave torrential midafternoon rains, plus biting insects and possible encounters with deadly *rabo amarillos* (fer-de-lance) snakes.

Day 1: Transfer by four-wheel drive to the mountain hamlet of Mamey via a steep, pot-holed dirt road (bring your passport to present at a military checkpoint) that ascends the Buritaca Valley. From the trailhead, it's a three-hour hike. The first 30 minutes is flat; be prepared for a steep, muddy 2.5-hour climb to the campsite, where showers and a cooked dinner await. By 9 p.m. you'll be in bed.

Day 2: After breakfast, you set out about 9 a.m. for a relatively easy three-hour downhill hike to a riverside camp. En route, you pass through an open valley, thick bright green montane forest, and the Kogi village of Muthanzi, arriving in time for lunch and a swim.

Day 3: Set out around 8 a.m. for the six-hour ascent to Ciudad Perdida. Steep ascents and descents are punctuated by eight waist-deep river crossings of the Río Buritaca—you wade across with your backpack atop your head. After the final fording,

INSIDER TIP:

Along the way to Ciudad Perdida, you climb to 3,609 feet (1,100 m), passing villages of Kogi Indians, and descendants of the Tayrona.

—SIBYLLA BRODZINSKY
Freelance journalist, Colombia

you scramble up a slippery embankment and begin to climb a mist-shrouded ancient staircase, whose 1,200 steps— a breathtaking 30-minute ascent—deliver you at Ciudad Perdida and a basic campsite.

Day 4: You have a full day to explore the city's 169 terraces and grassy plazas linked by rock-paved paths guarded by the Colombian Army. From on high, there are jaw-dropping views in every direction.

Days 5 & 6: After an early morning breakfast, set out for the eight-hour descent to Camp 1. The following day, it's a relatively steep three-hour descent to the trailhead, where a vehicle returns you to Santa Marta.

What to Take

Take two sets of clothes: one for hiking and one for night. Essentials include a flashlight and batteries, fleece sweater and long pants, hiking shoes (and sandals for wading), water bottle and water purification tablets (don't believe tour guides who say they'll be provided), waterproof jacket, wash kit, and insect repellent.

Getting There

Tours (US$250) depart Santa Marta most days. The area is under Colombian military control. You must join a guided tour from an authorized operator:

Magic Tour: Calle 16 #4-41, Santa Marta, tel 57-5/421-5820, magictourcolombia .com

Turcol Turismo: Carrera 13 #313, Centro Comercial San Francisco, Local 115, Santa Marta, tel 57-5/421-2256, turcoltravel.com

Wiwa Tour: Cra. 3 #18-49, Santa Marta, tel 57-5/420-3413, wiwatour.com

Cabins at Ecohabs rise above Playa Cañaveral, a popular beach with a pounding surf.

Pico Cristóbal Colón and **Pico Simón Bolívar,** which together form Cerro Horqueta—one of Colombia's tallest mountains.

The park extends inland from the shore immediately east of the Río Don Diego and climbs to the Colón glacier. Spanning 1,478 square miles (3,828 sq km), the region—declared a UNESCO biosphere reserve in 1979—encompasses almost all the climatic zones and ecosystems of the neotropics, from sea level to snow level. The Sierra Nevada is home to the world's largest number of endemic bird species. Jaguars, pumas, and ocelots prowl the forests. The higher slopes shelter spectacled bears and tapirs, and Andean condors soar high overhead.

Some 53,000 indigenous people consider these heights sacred and guard them jealously from outsiders. The Arhuaco, Kogi, Kankuamo, and Wiwa ethnic groups are closely related descendants of the ancient Tayrona civilization—an advanced people who built sophisticated cities linked by stone pathways. The conquistadores enslaved the Tayrona and looted their cities, which were abandoned. The survivors fled into the high mountains, where their descendants live today as inheritors of their ancestors' view of the world and traditions. The shamans are instantly recognizable in their all-white serapes, tall coned skullcaps, and beautifully stitched shoulder bags.

Access: Most of the region is autonomous indigenous territory and off-limits. Access to

Ciudad Perdida
 125 B2

Pueblo Bello
 195 B2
☎ 57-5/579-3217
**pueblobello-cesar
.gov.co**

the park is limited to two official entry points: From the west via Minca to San Lorenzo Forest Reserve (see pp. 150–151), outside of the park; and from the north via the Buritaca Valley, leading to Ciudad Perdida. You can also visit the **Arhuaco territory** by invitation from Pueblo Bello, on the south side of the Sierra Nevada. Contact the National Parks

jungle of the **Buritaca Valley.** It was founded by the Tayrona more than 1,000 years ago, predating its more famous Peruvian cousin, Machu Picchu, by some 650 years. The hilltop settlement sheltered a population exceeding 3,000 people. Their homes stood atop circular stone foundations laid out on tiered terraces along a central axis. Teyuna was abandoned after the Spanish

Camera-shy Arhuaco children tender smiles in Nabusimake.

Office in Santa Marta (see p. 151) for information on visiting San Lorenzo ($$$). This is no place to explore unguided.

Ciudad Perdida: More than 250 pre-Columbian settlements have been identified in the Sierra Nevada de Santa Marta. By far the most impressive is **Teyuna,** far up the roadless

conquest and consumed by jungle. Studied by archaeologists since 1975, the site is protected as the **Teyuna–Ciudad Perdida (Lost City) Archaeological Park** (see sidebar p. 152).

Pueblo Bello

Gateway to the southern Sierra Nevada de Santa Marta, this mountain town (3,940 feet/

1,200 m elevation) 22 miles (35 km) west of Valledupar abuts the **Arhuaco autonomous territory.** Arhuaco mingle with Hispanics in Pueblo Bello—a place to gain an awareness of the Arhuaco people's struggle to maintain their culture.

Arhuaco *mamo* (community leader) Luis Guillermo Izquierdo *(tel 57/315-750-1585, fundamarin .org)* will educate you on Arhuaco philosophy, traditional agricultural practices, and efforts to establish a livelihood raising and selling organic produce at the **Jardín Botánico Busintana,** a sacred botanic garden.

Nabusimake: Nabusimake is the principal village and spiritual center of the Arhuaco, who live in 36 villages dispersed throughout the mountains *(visits only by invitation).* The access road, 1.2 miles (2 km) north of Pueblo Bello, is barred by a walled gate and Arhuaco gatekeeper. The two-hour drive up the mountain is an arduous challenge: A high-ground-clearance four-wheel drive is essential. A *colectivo* runs daily from Pueblo Bello, conditions permitting.

The village, in a broad vale cusped by pine-clad mountains, is considered sacred and remains off-limits to most visitors, who must content themselves with staring over the stone perimeter wall. Founded in 1750, it consists of about 75 thatched homes made of river stones and adobe. (Photography is forbidden.) You

can rent a room with community leader José Camillo and Cha Cha Hipolita *(tel 57/317-233-1427).*

Valledupar

Capital of Cesar Department and the scratchy music called *vallenato,* Valledupar is the gateway to La Guajira Peninsula from Bucaramanga and Bogotá. Founded in 1550 on the west bank of the Río Guatapurí, Valledupar is famous for its April **Vallenato Music Festival**

INSIDER TIP:

You can stay at the Ecohabs resort (see Travelwise p. 289)—a set of secluded huts built into a hill east of Tayrona—or rent hammocks or tent sites for US$6–US$9 per night at El Cabo beach.

—THOMAS CLYNES
National Geographic
magazine writer

(festivalvallenato.com). The main architectural draws are the 17th-century **Iglesia de la Inmaculada Concepción** *(Calle 15 #4-85),* on the charming Plaza Alfonso López, and a series of traffic circles studded with monuments. The city occupies a stifling semiarid plain. To escape the heat, head north on Carrera 4 to **Parque Leyenda Vallenata,** where locals picnic along the bank of the boulder-strewn river. ■

Nabusimake
▲ 125 B2

Valledupar
✉ 125 C2

Visitor Information
✉ Officia de Cultura y Turismo, Calle 16 #12-120
☎ 57-5/574-8230

cesar.gov.co

La Guajira

South America's northernmost tip at the far northeast of Colombia is a desert region populated by the fiercely independent Wayúu. Materially poor but rich in spirit, this indigenous group of people welcomes visitors to their sparsely inhabited yet starkly fascinating world of sand dunes, salt pans, and flamingo-filled turquoise lagoons.

Wayúu women, skilled at weaving colorful crafts, paint their faces during ritual celebrations.

Península de la Guajira

✉ 125 C2–C3

Visitor Information

✉ Dirección de Turismo de la Guajira, Cra. 1 #6-5, Ríohacha

☎ 57-5/727-1015 or 278-9080

laguajira.gov.co

This is true desert of the cactus-studded plains and sand dune belts that spill down to the Caribbean Sea. In the far northeast corner, clouds condense around the Serranía de Macuira mountains, feeding a unique dwarf cloud forest. Flamingos are the name of the game at Santuario de Fauna y Flora Los Flamencos, west of the city of Ríohacha; and in Bahía Hondita—a jade-colored lagoon at Punta Gallinas, the peninsula's tip.

La Guajira appeals to adventurers, including those who kite and windsurf at Cabo de la Vela. The region is a focus of cultural-based ecotourism where visitors are hosted at simple Wayúu *rancherías* (communities) providing an opportunity to appreciate their culture. The Wayúu Culture Festival is held in Uribia each May or June.

Península de la Guajira forms a pincer around the Golfo de Venezuela; a 3-mile-wide (5 km) eastern sliver of the peninsula is Venezuelan territory, although the Wayúu recognize no such border.

Baja & Media Guajira

The relatively moist Baja (Low) Guajira at the base of the peninsula extends west and south of Ríohacha, the departmental city. Media (Middle) Guajira, a low-desert transition zone to the north and east of Ríohacha, is bisected east–west by Highway 90 (linking Ríohacha to Maicao and Venezuela) and Highway 88, which leads north to the Wayúu town of Uribia and south to Valledupar (see p. 155). The two highways intersect at Cuatro Vías.

Midway between Valledupar and Maicao is **El Cerrejón** (map 125 C2, tel 57-5/350-2441, cerrejon.com), one of the world's largest open-pit coal mines. The mine employs 7,800 people and extracts 32 million tons (29 million tonnes) a year. You can visit the site on guided tours.

Ríohacha: This sprawling capital city (pop. 170,000) of La Guajira Department is the gateway to the peninsula. About 105 miles (170 km) east of Santa Marta, it was founded in 1535 by German explorer Nikolaus de Federman and evolved as a port and pearling city. Today, the beach-fringed resort town draws working-class families and also thrives on the smuggling trade from Venezuela. Most visitors to La Guajira Peninsula overnight here before joining a guided tour. The coast road (Hwy. 90, or Troncal del Caribe) from Santa Marta turns inland here and runs ruler straight to Maicao (the only other town in the region) and the Venezuelan frontier.

The Wayúu

This Amerindian group speaks Wayuunaiki, part of the Arawak linguistic family, and they exist frugally as goatherds and fishermen. Never subjugated by the Spanish, they are divided into matriarchal castes. Extended families live alone in widely dispersed *pichis* (huts) of *bareque* (wattle and daub) and *yotojoro* (dried cactus stem), comprising *rancherías* of five or six houses. Wayúu women are skilled at weaving colorful hammocks, handbags, and bracelets. They paint their faces black with a mixture of goat fat, mushroom juice, and dust as a kind of sunblock. Wayúu traditions include polygamy. At first menstruation, girls are educated separately for a month on how to attend to their future husbands.

The town's sites can be explored in a few hours, beginning with the beachfront **Paseo de la Marina** boulevard and boardwalk pier (Calle 1 & Cra. 6). A patinated bronze life-size statue of Nikolaus de Federman stands in a triangular plaza two blocks east (Cra. 3). After watching fishermen tending their nets on the beach, head inland one block to **Parque José Prudencio Padilla** (Calle 2 & Cra. 8), the colonial plaza. The 16th-century **Catedral de Nuestra Señora de los Remedios** has been remodeled several times.

Santuario de Fauna y Flora Los Flamencos: The Flamingos Wildlife Sanctuary, 13 miles (20 km) west of Ríohacha, lies north of the coast highway. High concentrations of brine shrimp sustain a resident population of West Indian flamingos. The

---

Ríohacha
125 C2–C3

Santuario de Fauna y Flora Los Flamencos
125 C2
Regional Office, Calle 17 #4-06, Santa Marta
57-5/423-0752
ecoturismosantuario.weebly.com

17,300-acre (7,000 ha) reserve of marshes, lagoons, and dry forest is also habitat to 185 other bird species (80 percent are migrants), including fishing eagles and roseate spoonbills. Four species of marine turtles crawl ashore to nest in the sands.

The road leads via the village of Camarones to Laguna Navio Quebrado and the funky fishing village of **Los Cocos,** beside a palm-shaded beach. Local fishermen will punt you across the estuary mouth (you can wade across September through December) to sign in at the **Centro de Visitantes Los Mangles** *(tel 57/301-675-3862),* which has trails, basic accommodations, birding tours, and a marine turtle conservation program. Take a *panga* (ferry boat) from here to see the flamingos. Guides can be hired in the village from the Asociación de Guias *(tel 57/311-680-7140)* or the Grupo de Guias Wayúu *(tel 57/312-694-0773).*

Sainn Wayúu: One of several indigenous rancherías within a one-hour drive of Ríohacha, Sainn Wayúu *(Vía Ríohacha–Maicao km 12, tel 57/312-650-3942)* is a good place to learn about Wayúu culture. Surrounded by thick forest, this single-family community gives demonstrations of dance and music, such as *majayura,*

EXPERIENCE: Helping Save Marine Turtles

Seven species of marine turtles roam the world's oceans, from the diminutive ridley to the Cadillac-size leatherback. Populations are endangered worldwide, and several species are nearly extinct.

Volunteer your time and talents to help increase marine turtle numbers. Five species of turtles nest on Colombia's pristine beaches, and they can be seen at any time of year.

Leatherback turtles, called *tortuga caná* or *tortuga de cuero* in Colombia, come ashore February to July at Acandí and Playona, in the Gulf of Urabá. Green turtles can be seen at Playa Blanca and Isla Rosario near Cartagena, and the beaches of La Guajira from June to October. Hawksbill turtles nest in far smaller numbers at Santa Marta, and loggerheads are also found on the Caribbean shore, notably on the beaches of La Guajira. The olive ridley is the most common nesting species in Colombia, coming ashore July to December principally at Playas El Valle, Amarales, Mulatos, and Vigía, plus Isla Gorgona. In Colombia, female ridleys are individualists and do not exhibit mass nesting of tens of thousands of individuals together during full moons, as in Costa Rica and Nicaragua.

The following organizations welcome volunteers for turtle conservation:

El Almejal Ecolodge & Rainforest Reserve, Bahía Solano, tel 57-4/412-5050, almejal.com.co

Fundación Hidrobiológica George Dahl, Punta Gallinas, La Guajira, tel 57-5/370-4765, fundaciongeorgedahl.com

Research Center for Environmental Management and Development (CIMAD), Vía Panamericana La Morada Casa 143, Jamundi, tel/fax 57-2/519-1341

World Wildlife Fund Colombia, Cra. 35 #4A-25, Cali, tel 57-2/558-2577, panda.org.

The tangerine-colored Playa del Pilón, near Cabo de la Vela, is enhanced by multihued rocks.

the ritual of the young Wayúu virgin. Visitors can try weaving and sample local dishes, such as *friche* (sheep's entrails) and *mazamoora* (a corn-based drink). The community also operates as a hostel; you sleep in hammocks and are awakened by the reveille call of howler monkeys. Bring insect repellent. It's best to come with a group, such as organized by Kaishi Travel *(tel 57-5/717-7306, kaishitravel.com).*

INSIDER TIP:

La Guajira is the area where those who want to escape the crowds of Tayrona come. The beaches are empty, but inland just a few miles is true desert.

—LARRY PORGES
National Geographic Travel Books author

Manuare
125 C3

Manuare: This small seafront town 11 miles (18 km) west of Uribia is known as La Novia Blanca (White Bride) for the salt flats west of town. Salt has been the town's raison d'être since it was founded in 1723. The *salinas* (salt flats) spread over 9,884 acres (4,000 ha) and include tiny artisanal plots tended by Wayúu. At the east end of town, huge salt mountains rise beside a ship-loading dock; guided tours are offered from the entrance gate, where impoverished children tout themselves as guides.

With a four-wheel drive (or a *moto*-taxi), you can reach **Playa El Pájaro,** a lovely white-sand beach backed by the shallow **Musichi lagoon**—a sanctuary for West Indian flamingos, which parade

Punta Gallinas

🏛 125 C3

around in hot pink. It's about 13 miles (20 km) west of Manuare. **Coopmur** (tel 57/313-502-6496, e-mail: coopmur@hotmail.com), a women's cooperative, offers tours.

Alta Guajira

The "real" La Guajira Alta (High) lies north of **Uribia** (the last settlement with provisions), where goats and donkeys nibble at cactus and thorn scrub poking up through the shimmering haze. Swept by dry trade winds, the **Desierto de Ahuyama**—the

---

EXPERIENCE:
The Fun of Four-wheel-drive Touring

Colombia's often arduous driving conditions make a four-wheel-drive vehicle a must for exploring, particularly in the north. Even on major highways, landslides and subsidence are common, while paved roads can often wash out in the rainy season. Farther afield, rock-strewn roads can deteriorate in muddy bouillabaisses in the wet season, and dusty tracks in the dry season. A four-wheel-drive vehicle will help allay such obstacles, while adding an Indiana Jones–style sense of adventure. **Big Willys Jeep Safaris** (tel 57/320-720-7961, facebook.com/BigWillysJeep Safaris) offers tours by Willys Jeeps.

---

heartland of the Wayúu—is searingly hot year-round. In wet season, the labyrinthine tracks that link remote rancherías become muddy mires. Don't travel alone. Travel with a guide or join an organized tour from Ríohacha, mostly because bandit groups still operate in the region.

Unpaved Highway 88 continues north from Uribia alongside the railroad track that connects El Cerrejón coal mine to the coal-loading port of Puerto Bolívar. En route, it passes the Parque Eólico wind turbines at the turnoff for Cabo de la Vela, 10 miles (17 km) west of Highway 88.

Cabo de la Vela: The most developed "tourist" enclave of La Guajira, Cabo de la Vela draws the majority of visitors to the region. Off-beat and off the beaten path, what was once a remote Wayúu fishing village is today an ecotourism hot spot, with restaurants and several dozen rancherías to lay your head. They're sprinkled along a narrow 1.2-mile-long (2 km) sliver of gray sand lining a bay where winds whip up the excitement for kite- and windsurfing.

The real beauty lies 2 miles (3.2 km) north of the village at **Playa del Pilón,** where tangerine sands are found in a cove beneath **Pilón de Azucar,** a headland of blue-gray shales. Hike a trail to the top for stunning views of the coast and Alta Guajira.

Punta Gallinas: Punta Gallinas is the northernmost point in South America. Scorched beneath cloudless skies, and scoured by searing winds, the point is marked by a derelict light station. Lizards with impossibly iridescent green-blue tails scurry about underfoot. The point tips a peninsula that hooks around **Bahía Hondita,** a jade-colored bay with flamingos.

Driving to Punta Gallinas has risks. Hence, most people arrive on motorized boats from isolated beaches west of Puerto Bolívar. Kaishi Travel (see p. 159), in Ríohacha, can arrange the three-hour boat ride as part of an all-in-one package that includes an overnight stay at Hospedaje Alexandra, a Wayúu ranchería; plus a four-wheel-drive tour to **Playa Caroba,** where 80-foot-tall (24 m) sand dunes curve up from the Caribbean. The tangerine sands are an important nesting site for marine turtles. The Fundación Hidrobiológica George Dahl (see sidebar p. 158) has a tiny biological station at **Playa Kijoru,** where turtle eggs are hatched and the hatchlings are released to the sea.

Parque Nacional Natural Serranía de Macuira: This remote park in the extreme northeast of the peninsula is a biogeographical island encompassing the Macuira mountain range, which rises to 2,834 feet (864 m) atop Cerro Palúa. The upland oasis captures much of the moisture that seeps into the water table of La Guajira.

The ecosystems range from dry tropical forest on the western slopes to dwarf cloud forest on the eastern slopes. The 61,776-acre (25,000 ha) park is good for wildlife viewing—17 of the 140 bird species are endemic. Access is from Nazareth, 71 miles (115 km) northeast of Uribia. Don't hike alone; hire a Wayúu guide. ■

Parque Nacional Natural Serranía de Macuira

🗺 125 C3

Visitor Information

☎ 57-1/353-2400 ext. 138

parquesnacionales .gov.co

NOTE: One tour operator for Parque Nacional Serranía de Macuira is Kaishi Travel, tel 57/311-429-6315.

The Wayúu, an Amerindian group that speaks Wayuunaiki, keep goats and donkeys.

From stylish, cosmopolitan Medellín to majestic mountain peaks and fertile valleys studded with coffee plantations

Western Highlands

"Hombre a caballo," one of the 23 bronze statues by Fernando Botero in Medellín's Plaza Botero

Western Highlands

Medellín—once know for drug trafficking and violence—is today Colombia's most dynamic and exciting city. When coupled with the lush Coffee Triangle of Juan Valdez fame and the snowcapped mountains of Los Nevados, the appeal of the Western Highlands is uniquely rewarding.

Salento is a good place to buy hammocks and colorful *ruanas* (ponchos).

This region is finally being discovered by travelers. Medellín, once synonymous with *narcotraficante* Pablo Escobar, has transcended that image. The nation's most visually appealing major city, Medellín—Colombia's second largest city—is an industrial giant that combines its magnificent setting with an efficient mass-transportation network, world-class hotels, and avant-garde museums.

The Western Highlands region was relatively isolated from the rest of Colombia throughout most of the colonial past and evolved its own personality. Residents of Antioquia—a northern department—are known as *paisas* and pride themselves as hardworking, strong-willed achievers who represent the best elements of the national psyche. This is much owed to the many 16th-century Basques who settled

Antioquia and whose influence defined the conservative, close-knit Antioquieño culture.

Zona Cafetera

To the south of Antioquia is Colombia's principal coffee-growing zone. Called the Eje Cafetero (Coffee Axis), or Triángulo de Café (Coffee Triangle), the region is shaped like an inverted triangle, with the cities of Manizales, Pereira, and Armenia for its north–south axis. The steep hillsides are quilted with *fincas* (large farms) where you can learn about coffee production and sample fresh-ground gourmet coffees.

Immensely popular with Colombian families, Parque Nacional del Café is a kind of Disneyland themed around coffee. The Jardín Botánico del Quindío shouldn't be missed for its botanical collection. And a journey to the well-preserved colonial town of Salento can be combined with visits to the exquisite Valle de Cocora.

Mountain Highs

The region is also rich in biodiversity and natural wonders. The Cordillera Occidental is the least populated of the three Andean cordilleras; its slopes are shaded by mist-shrouded forests. The Cordillera Central possesses some of Colombia's highest peaks, sheltering endangered mammals and endemic bird species. Several birding venues are here: Reserva Forestal Nacional Protectora Río Blanco is considered one of the world's top birding sites.

The Río Blanco reserve is within minutes of the university town of Manizales, a great base for exploring the region. The snowcapped volcanic peaks of Parque Nacional Natural Los Nevados appear within fingertip reach. Few visitors take advantage of the lodges, or well-maintained trails that lead through valleys and glaciers, jewel-like lakes and conical summits.

Much of the more remote terrain remains guerrilla territory. Exploring remote country trails on your own is foolhardy. ∎

NOT TO BE MISSED:

Fernando Botero's sculptures in Medellín   **170**

The floral displays at Medellín's Feria de las Flores   **171**

Taking a stroll back in time in Santa Fé de Antioquia   **174–175**

The view from atop El Peñol de Guatape   **175–176**

Spotting rare endemic birds at the Río Blanco reserve   **184–185**

The snow line in Parque Nacional Natural Los Nevados   **185, 187**

Touring a coffee plantation in the Zona Cafetera   **186**

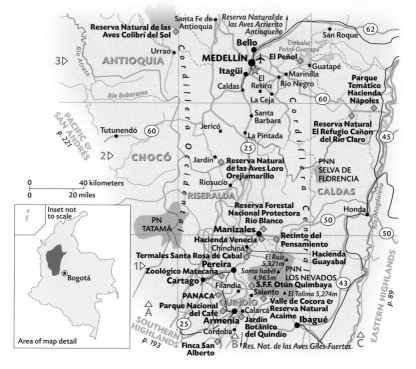

Medellín

A well-managed, world-class modern city with stunning architecture, Medellín delights visitors with its sophistication and wealth of attractions. Wedged in the narrow Aburrá Valley, the capital of Antioquia is a major commercial, cultural, and industrial hub with self-assured style.

The efficient and easily navigated Metro de Medellín links most major sites of interest in the city, including Plaza Botero, where 23 of Fernando Botero's statues are on display.

Medellín (pop. 2.3 million) occupies a narrow valley edged by sharp-angled mountains. Nestled at almost 5,000 feet (1,524 m) in elevation, the City of Eternal Spring enjoys a perfect combination of warm days and cool nights. Surrounded by flower farms, it is the second largest supplier of flowers in the world—after the Netherlands. Its annual Feria de las Flores (Flower Festival) in July and August includes parades,

equestrian events, concerts, and even a classic car rally.

The city was founded in 1616 (centered on El Poblado, it was reestablished in 1646 around Parque Berrío), but grew slowly. Hence the city has a relatively insignificant colonial core. Creation of the University of Antioquia in 1803 established Medellín as a leading educational center, while the 19th-century coffee boom and arrival of a railway in 1875 fostered a commercial explosion. A textile industry established in the early 20th century set the stage for Medellín's current status as one of the world's leading fashion centers.

Decades of Challenge

The political violence sparked by Jorge Eliécer Gaitán's assassination in 1948 flooded Medellín with refugees from the countryside, overwhelming the city's infrastructure. In the 1980s, the city evolved as the planet's cocaine capital, with the highest city murder rate in the world. The late *narcotraficante* king, Pablo Escobar (see sidebar p. 176), ruled Medellín.

(see sidebar p. 176)

INSIDER TIP:

Due to city-planning rules requiring that public art be part of any new construction, central Medellín has become a fantastic open-air art gallery.

—THOMAS CLYNES
National Geographic
magazine writer

He won over much of the poor with largesse, while his terrorists murdered policemen, businessmen, and politicians. His death in 1993 marked a beginning of the end to the mayhem.

As a counterpoint to the violence, a Metro rail network was conceived to connect disenfranchised and angry sectors of society with city life. The system was completed in 1996 at a cost of US$1.9 billion. Three MetroCable aerial tram lines have since been added. A source of city pride, the Metro system carries more than 300,000 people daily and is now a tourist attraction, whisking visitors safely over the shantytowns.

Since 2003, aggressive security and social policies (such as megaschools and libraries in the city's poorest neighborhoods) have transformed Medellín into a city of relative peace and tranquillity. Murders have dropped some 80 percent since a peak in 1991. As a result, foreign tourism has blossomed. Most violence is between criminal bands and relegated to impoverished barrios (about 40 percent of the population live in marginal communities). The army has been deployed in the more

Medellín

🅰 165 B3

Visitor Information

✉ Convention & Visitors Bureau, Calle 41#55-80, Office 302

☎ 57-4/261-6060

medellinconvention bureau.com

✉ Subsecretaría de Turismo, Calle 41# 55-35

☎ 57-4/385-6966

medellin.gov.co

EXPERIENCE:
Using the Metro de Medellín

If you want to explore the city, use the Metro de Medellín (*tel 57-4/444-9598, metrodemedellin.gov.co, $*). **An axis linking north and south, east and west, and rich and poor, it is Colombia's only rail-based Metro system. The trains run with Swiss-clock precision on an every-three-minutes schedule at peak hours. With huge windows, the cars provide an excellent means of seeing and exploring the city. The Metro stations are also well policed; every platform is patrolled and has a *puesto de policía*—a police bureau. They're perfectly safe for tourists, but leaving the stations to wander through such barrios as Comuna 13 isn't wise.**

Museo História del Ferrocarril

✉ Cra. 52 #43-31
☎ 57-4/381-0733
🕐 Closed Sat.–Sun.

violent neighborhoods, such as the notorious Comuna 13. The **Casa de la Memoria** *(Calle 51 #36-66, tel 57-4/383-4001, www .museocasadelamemoria.org)* keeps alive the memory of those killed in Colombia's violence.

Getting Your Bearings

The city sprawls north–south along the valley floor to either side of the canalized Río Medellín. Most sites of interest are in the downtown Zona Centro, in a ten-block belt between Plaza Botero and the Centro Administrativo La Alpujarra. The city's hip social center is Parque de Lleras, to the south in El Poblado, with a Latin-flavored nightlife hot enough to sizzle. Lack of directional road signs are a bane if you're driving, but the Metro connects El Poblado with downtown and most touristic sites beyond.

The **Turibus Cultural** *(tel 57-4/371-5054 ext. 213 or 214, turibuscolombia.com)* sightseeing

bus departs Parque El Poblado *(9 a.m. & 1 p.m. daily)* on four-hour tours, with brief stops at major cultural sites in the city.

The Medellín Convention & Visitors Bureau arranges bilingual guides through the Asociación de Guías de Turismo de Antioquia *(tel 57-4/206-6149, e-mail: asoguian@ gmail.com)* and has tourist bureaus called Punto de Información Turísticas (PITs) at strategic points. **SiClas** *(tel 57/310-835-8134, siclas .org)* offers city bicycling tours.

Zona Centro

The lion's share of visit-worthy sites concentrates in the city's downtown Central Zone, east of the river and west of Carrera 46.

Centro Administrativo La Alpujarra: A good place to begin your exploration is with La Alpujarra Administrative Center *(Calle 44 #52-165)*, the seat of the Antioquia and Medellín governments. The **Gobernación de Antioquia** *(Calle 44 #52-165, tel 57-4/444-4144, medellin.gov .co, closed Sat.–Sun.)* can be toured by appointment. Identical buildings face each other to either side of a concrete plaza marked by the **Monumento a la Raza.** Rodrigo Arenas Betancourt's 125-foot-tall (38 m) dramatically twisted metal sculpture tells the history of Antioquia. To the south is the **Estación Antigua Ferrocarril.** The French Renaissance–style train station built in 1914 now houses the **Museo História del Ferrocarril,** a railway museum that displays an antique Baldwin steam train.

ColombiaModa

Couture-conscious Colombians look to Medellín to set *la moda*—the trend. The city is a kind of South American Paris, with one of the most active and avant-garde fashion industries in the world. The textile industry accounts for almost one-third of Medellín's employment. Labels from Brooks Brothers to Oscar de la Renta are manufactured here. And the city's ColombiaModa *(colombiamoda.com),* held each July, is South America's most prestigious fashion event, drawing an international A-list of elite stylists and slinky models, who show off the latest lingerie and other fashions during a four-day catwalk event.

Sculptor Fernando Botero's voluptuous nude figures grace many of Medellín's plazas.

Immediately west of La Alpu-jarra, across Carrera 57, are the ultramodern Plaza Mayor Convention Center and the landmark Empresa Públicas de Medellín (EPM), headquarters of the regional public utilities company. Between the two buildings, the tranquil **Plaza de los Pies Descalzos** (Barefoot Plaza) invites you to take off your shoes and socks and experience the sensory pleasure of its Zen garden, bamboo labyrinth, and sandpit.

To the north of La Alpujarra, across Calle 44, **Plaza de las Luces** is remarkable for its 300 lit-from-within metal masts, floodlit at night; and for the Biblioteca EPM, a strikingly contemporary library. Standing four-square on the east side of Plaza de las Luces is **Edificio Carré** (*Calle 44B #52-17, tel 57-4/514-8200, closed Sun.*). Named for French architect Emile Charles

Carré (1869–1909), this redbrick architectural gem today houses the Ministry of Education.

Parque San Antonio: This ungainly concrete plaza (*Calle 45 #46-92*), two blocks east of Plaza de las Luces, is a venue for concerts. It is flanked by Botero sculptures including on the east side the twin **"Pájaros de Paz"** ("Birds of Peace"). One of the bronze statues, which stand side by side, is torn and shredded—the result of a bomb placed beneath the original in 1995, killing 22 concertgoers. Botero donated the copy in 2000.

Parque Berrío: The epicenter of the city, Parque Berrío is a gathering spot for lottery sellers, trouba-dours, and parishioners attending the **Basilica Nuestra Señora de la Candelaria** (*Cra. 50 & Calle 51*), Medellín's most important church. Dating from 1776, the cathedral's

Museo de Antioqua

✉ Cra. 52 #52-43

☎ 57-4/251-3636

museodeantioquia.co

Palacio de la Cultura Rafael Uribe Uribe

✉ Cra. 51 #52-03

☎ 57-4/320-9780

$ Closed Sun.

culturantioquia .gov.co

antiquity is magnified by its setting in the midst of skyscrapers and the elevated Parque Berrío Metro station. A Botero statue stands in front of the Banco de Colombia building on the south side.

Plaza Botero: Carrera 51 leads north from Parque Berrío one block to **Plaza Botero,** a huge L-shaped plaza studded with 23 bronze sculptures donated by Fernando Botero, hence its nickname: Plaza de las Esculturas (Plaza of the Sculptures). More

The remarkable gray-and-white-banded Gothic Renaissance structure on the plaza's east side is the **Palacio de la Cultura Rafael Uribe Uribe.** Initiated in 1925 as the Antigua government building, today it houses a library, art gallery, and city archives.

Parque Bolívar: Two blocks northeast of Plaza Botero, the Zona Centro's fourth major square (*Cra. 49 & Calle 54*) is dedicated to the Liberator. At its core is a life-size bronze statue

Visitors are enthralled by Parque Explora's aquarium, an interactive fun-filled experience.

Jardín Botánico

✉ Calle 73 #51D-14

☎ 57-4/444-5500

$ $

botanicomedellin.org

works by Botero are displayed in the **Museo de Antioquia,** on the plaza's west side. The ground floor has interactive exhibits dedicated to Colombia's diverse cultures; the second floor displays works by leading Colombian artists; the third floor is devoted to Botero, but also has works by Picasso, Rodin, and Wilfredo Lam.

of Simón Bolívar mounted on a steed. On the southeast corner stands the art deco **Teatro Lido** (*Cra. 48 #54-20, tel 57-4/251-5334*), opened in 1945. Dominating the skyline to the north is the huge, austere, neo-Romanesque **Catedral Metropolitana** (*Cra. 48 #56-81*), the world's largest church made of fired brick and completed in 1931. Time your visit for the first Saturday of the month, when the park hosts the city's major *mercado de pulgas* (flea market). Avoid the park at night.

Zona Norte

North of the city center you'll find a half dozen key sites served by the Universidad Metro station *(Cra. 53 & Calle 73),* named for the **Universidad de Antioquia** *(Calle 67 #53-108, tel 57-4/219-8332, www.udea.edu.co),* Medellín's main university, immediately southwest of the station. Its **Museo Universitario** *(tel 57-4/219-5180)* is devoted to natural sciences and pre-Columbian culture.

The main draw is the **Jardín Botánico,** the city's botanical garden. It covers 40 acres (16 ha), including a desert garden, tropical moist forest, *humedal* (wetland), and lake. The garden is the principal venue for the week-long flower festival **Feria de las Flores** *(54-4/444-4144, feriadelasflores medellin.gov.co)* held beneath the Orquideorama, a huge hexagonal, beehive-shaped lattice rooftop.

Combine the garden with the adjacent, must-see **Parque Explora** in futuristic red buildings. Youngsters in particular will enjoy the fun and fascinating interactive experiences that teach about biology, geography, media, physics, and technology. The upper level includes a world-class aquarium. Its 25 tanks exhibit many of the most representative species that inhabit Colombia's rivers and oceans, including piranhas, electric eels, sea horses, and a panchromatic kaleidoscope of fish. And don't miss the small vivarium, displaying snakes and poison dart frogs.

To the station's south side, the **Parque de los Deseos** (Park of Wishes) plaza is also dedicated to learning. Its various contemporary monuments are themed to the plaza's **Planetario de Medellín,** the planetarium. Medellín's remarkable **Museo Cementerio de San Pedro** *(Cra. 51 #68-68, tel 507-4/212-0951, free guided tours Sun. 2 p.m.–5:30 p.m.),* five blocks to the east, is worth seeking out. The cemetery, established in 1842 and declared a national monument, is a haven of tranquillity and flamboyant marble ornamentation.

Another of the city's most important cultural sites—the **Casa Museo Pedro Nel Gómez**—is a short distance

Pico y Placa

To reduce traffic congestion, Medellín bans private vehicles on certain days of the week, Monday–Friday 6:30 a.m.–8:30 a.m. and 5:30 p.m.–7:30 p.m., according to the last digit of the license plate. The following *pico y placa* (peak hour and license plate) restrictions applied for August 3, 2015, through February 3, 2016: Monday 2-3-4-5; Tuesday 6-7-8-9; Wednesday 0-1-2-3; Thursday 4-5-6-7; Friday 8-9-0-1. The groups rotate to the following day each six months *(for detailed information, visit picoyplaca.info).* Bogotá's pico y placa bans private vehicles Monday–Friday 6 a.m.–8 p.m. The groups rotate to the following day each June 1. Other cities have similar rules. Tourists are not exempt.

Parque Explora

✉ Cra. 52 #73-75
☎ 57-4/516-8300
🕐 Closed Mon.
💲 $$

parqueexplora.org

Planetario de Medellín

✉ Cra. 52 # 71-117
☎ 57-4/516-8300
🕐 Closed Mon.
💲 $

planetariomedellin .org

Casa Museo Pedro Nel Gómez

✉ Cra. 51B #85-24, Barrio Aranjuez
☎ 57-4/223-2633
🕐 Closed Sun.
💲 $

facebook.com /casamuseo pedronelgomez

Biblioteca España

 Parque Biblioteca España, Cra. 33B #107A-100, Barrio Santo Domingo

☎ 57-4/385-6717

🕓 Closed Sun.

INSIDER TIP:

There are a lot of great hostels in the city of Medellín. And one of the best is Casa Kiwi (casakiwi.net). Of course the Medellín nightlife is like no other on the planet.

—JESSE COOMBS
National Geographic adventurer

north, in the hills of the working-class barrio of Aranjuez. The refurbished hillside residence preserves the former home of Colombia's leading humanist artist (1899–1984). The museum maintains his furnished bedroom in its original condition, and displays many of his original paintings, sculptures, and illustrations, including walls covered with murals of nudes (his favorite theme). The highlight is his black-and-white preparation for "La República," displayed in the library. Take a taxi, and don't wander the surrounding area.

The hills that rise behind the museum ascend to **Barrio Santo Domingo.** Just over a decade ago Santo Domingo was a total no-go zone, where even the police did not dare venture. The slum is now policed and relatively safe. It's also an unlikely tourist attraction, easily reached via the MetroCable from the Acevedo Metro station. A ten-minute ride takes you up via three stations to Santo Domingo. The landscape is completely dominated by the **Biblioteca España,** a dramatic black cubist library perched on the hillside amid many makeshift brick homes.

South of La Alpujarra

West of the river are two sites of modest interest. For a bird's-eye view of the city, head to **Pueblito Paisa** (*Calle 30A #55-64, tel 57-4/235-8370*). This miniature reconstruction of a traditional Antioquian village is laid out atop Cerro Nutibara, a 262-foot-tall (80 m) hill, 0.6 mile (1 km) southwest of La Alpujarra. Popular with local families, the touristy contrivance appeals

Good Love & Good Luck

Fernando Botero is known for his voluptuous figures in sculpture. They are scattered about in public places around Colombia as well as displayed in museums. Many Colombians believe that the artist's sculptures bring good fortune and good luck, so visitors—natives and non-natives—have taken to fondling and caressing his curvaceous statues of naked figures. For example, Botero's "Soldado Romano" ("Roman Soldier")

sculpture—one of 23 Botero bronzes in Medellín's Plaza de las Esculturas (also known as Plaza Botero; see p. 170)—is said to bring love, or at least good sex, to anyone who touches its genitals.

So many Colombians and tourists have now touched the breasts of the "Reclining Nude" in Plaza Santo Domingo, Cartagena, they have turned her nipples shiny as they seek some good love and good luck to rub off on them.

The buildings of the Poblado District reflect Medellín's modernity and sophistication.

mainly for the views of Medellín spread out below. To the south of Cerro Nutibara, Medellín's **Zoológico Santa Fe** displays Colombia's own creatures, such as tapirs, peccaries, and monkeys. However, the restrictive cages are dispiriting for visitors who appreciate the natural habitat of such wildlife. The zoo's African creatures fare better.

The best works by Medellín's contemporary artists are displayed at the **Museo de Arte Moderno,** in a former steel factory. Stylishly remodeled, the museum features permanent and temporary exhibits, all appropriate to this avant-garde space, which has a splendid café. Avant-garde is also a fitting description for **Parque Lleras** (Calle 9 & Cra. 40), the epicenter of the city's club scene. More than two dozen bars, nightclubs, and restaurants rub shoulder to shoulder, drawing Medellín's most

stylish young adults. The square lies at the heart of **El Poblado,** the original Spanish settlement of 1616, centered back then on **Parque Poblado** (Cra. 43 & Calle 9), on Medellín's busy and broad main north–south boulevard.

In recent decades El Poblado has evolved as the city's ritziest area. The Golden Mile—a Miami-style boulevard lined with high-rise banks, hotels, and deluxe condo towers—unfurls south from Plaza El Poblado and features striking avant-garde architecture. The slopes to the east are studded with handsome high-rises scratching the sky. The most remarkable site, not to be missed, is the French-style Gothic castle uphill from Parque Lleras. Inspired by a Loire Valley château, it was built in 1930 by a wealthy landowner who filled it with antiques and artwork from around the world. It's now the **Museo El Castillo**. ∎

Zoológico Santa Fe
✉ Cra. 52 #20-63
☎ 57-4/444-7787
$ $
zoologicosantafe .com

Museo de Arte Moderno
✉ Cra. 44 #19A-100, Ciudad del Río
☎ 57-4/444-2622
🕐 Closed Mon.
$ $
elmamm.org

Museo El Castillo
✉ Calle 9 Sur #32-269
☎ 57-4/266-0900
$ $
museoelcastillo.org

Antioquia

Medellín is surrounded by the mountain terrain of Antioquia, dotted with sleepy *paisa* villages, such as Santa Fé de Antioquia, one of Colombia's most striking and well-preserved colonial towns. Exploring the scenic highlands is a good way to spend a few days.

Motos ratónes (trishaw taxis) are a fun way to reach—and cross—the Puente Colgante de Occidente.

Santa Fé de Antioquia

🗺 165 B3

Visitor Information

✉ Calle 42B #52-106, Medellín

☎ 57-4/409-9000

antioquia.gov.co

Much of this rugged terrain is relatively isolated and rarely explored. Don't stray too far off the beaten path, where security could become an issue.

Santa Fé de Antioquia

About 50 miles (80 km) northwest of Medellín, this colorful and well-preserved colonial town is a popular weekend destination for city dwellers escaping the cool highlands for a balmier climate. Founded in 1541, it blossomed as the early capital of Antioquia until eclipsed by Medellín in 1826. Since then, time seems to have passed the town by.

Start at **Plaza Mayor,** the

tree-rimmed main square. Here, the neoclassical **Catedral Basilica de la Inmaculada Concepción** dates from 1837 and is notable for its sculpture of the "Last Supper." Another church not to miss is **Iglesia Santa Bárbara** (*Cra. 8 & Calle 11*), completed in 1728 with a simple redbrick facade topped by scrolls. The adjoining seminary displays religious icons in the **Museo de Arte Religioso** (*Calle 11 #8-12, tel 57-4/853-2345, closed Mon.–Fri., $*). The town's other ecclesiastical gems are the tiny yet charming neoclassical **Iglesia de Jesús Nazareno** (*Cra. 5 & Calle 10*) and the **Iglesia de Nuestra Señora de Chiquinquirá** on

Plazuela de la Chincha, the center of Santa Fé's nightlife.

Next, hop aboard a *moto ratón* (trishaw taxi) for the **Puente Colgante de Occidente** (2.2 miles/ 5 km NE of Santa Fé), a narrow suspension bridge flanked by peaked towers at each end. The 954-foot-long (291 m) bridge over the Río Cauca dates from 1895 and is a national monument.

Nature Reserves

Birders and hikers will thrill to the opportunities in Antioquia, where ProAves' 771-acre (312 ha) **Reserva Natural de las Aves Arrierito Antioqueño** draws birders keen to spot the chestnut-capped piha. Located at **El Roble,** about 109 miles (175 km) northeast of Medellín, it has well-maintained trails and a colonial-era lodge.

ProAves' **Reserva Natural de las Aves Colibrí del Sol,** some 10 miles (17 km) north of **Urrao** (43 miles/70 km SW of Santa Fé), protects cloud forest that is a habitat for the critically endangered dusky star-frontlet hummingbird. The visitor center has accommodations.

Circuito de Oriente

Perfect for a daylong excursion, the Eastern Circuit is a tourist route linking half a dozen sites of interest in the highlands east of Medellín. The Vía Las Palmas Autopista (freeway) climbs from downtown Medellín to **El Retiro,** a colonial village known for its small *talleres* (workshops) selling rustic furniture and crafts.

La Ceja, a cultivation center for flowers, enjoys a crisp alpine climate to El Retiro's southeast. Standing on the northwest corner of the main square, the **Iglesia de Nuestra Señora de Chiquinquirá** has a magnificent gilt-carved cedar altar that belies the chapel's small size. To the north is **Río Negro** *(map 165 B3),* a center for *viveros* (flower farms) and the setting for Medellín's international airport.

North of Río Negro, the road to **Marinilla** is lined with Antioquian country homes. This market town is a hub for *chivas,* or buses.

INSIDER TIP:

La Ceja is a beautiful town with tremendous character and wonderful restaurants. Try a *chiva* (bus) ride for a firsthand sense of local life.

—JESSE COOMBS
National Geographic adventurer

Embalse Peñol-Guatapé: A 30-minute drive from Marinilla through rolling farmland leads to the agricultural town of El Peñol, gateway to the Embalse Peñol-Guatapé, a beautiful reservoir created in 1978 by a dam that provides one-third of Colombia's electricity. Studded with isles, it has evolved as a major resort area. Rising over the lake is **El Peñol**—a 656-foot-high (200 m) granite monolith resembling the Sugarloaf of Rio de Janeiro. This enormous geological marvel can be scaled

Reserva Natural de las Aves Arrierito Antioqueño

⛰ 165 B3

Visitor Information

✉ c/o EcoTurs Colombia, Cra. 20 #36-61, Bogotá

☎ 57-1/245-5134

ecoturs.org

proaves.org

Reserva Natural de las Aves Colibrí del Sol

⛰ 165 A3

Visitor Information

✉ c/o EcoTurs Colombia, Cra. 20 #36-61, Bogotá

☎ 57-1/245-5134

ecoturs.org

proaves.org

La Ceja

⛰ 165 B3

Embalse Peñol-Guatapé

⛰ 165 B3

Pablo Escobar

Pablo Emilio Escobar Gaviria (1949–1993) was born impoverished in Río Negro, Antioquia. In the early 1970s, he began smuggling drugs and eventually controlled the Medellín cartel. In 1989, *Forbes* magazine named him the seventh richest man in the world. He dealt with authorities by bribing or killing them—he offered *plata o plomo* ("silver or lead"). He funded the storming in 1985 of the Supreme Court by M-19 guerrillas, and he attempted to kill presidential candidate César Gaviria Trujillo by bombing Avianca Flight 203, which resulted in 110 deaths.

After ordering the assassination of presidential candidate Luis Carlos Galán, he was confined in a luxurious private prison, where he continued to operate his cartel. He later escaped and was gunned down on the rooftops of Medellín. **Paisa Road** *(tel 57/317-489-2629, paisaroad .com)* offers an Escobar-themed tour.

Reserva Natural El Refugio Cañon del Río Claro

 165 C2

✉ Autopista Medellín–Bogotá km 152, 12 miles (20 km) W of Doradal

☎ 57-4/268-8855

rioclaroelrefugio .com

Parque Temático Hacienda Nápoles

 165 C2

✉ 0.6 mile (1 km) E of Doradal, Puerto Triunfo

☎ 57/314-892-2307

$ $$$–$$$$

haciendanapoles.com

for the spectacular view by a 649-step staircase built into a fissure.

The nearby quaint colonial village of **Guatapé** is painted in Crayola colors. Many homes feature *zócalos* (the extended lower third of exterior walls) adorned with three-dimensional depictions of village life. Turibus Guatapé *(tel 57-4/371-5054 ext. 213, turibus colombia.com)* runs a daylong excursion to the village Sundays at 7 a.m. from Medellín.

Magdalena Medio

Highway 60—the Autopista Medellín–Bogotá—cuts across the Cordillera Central, transcending the scenic canyon of the Río Claro, in an area known as Magdalena Medio (Middle Magdalena). The breathtaking setting of **Reserva Natural El Refugio Cañon del Río Claro** is a bonus for visitors who flock to enjoy calm Class I rafting and kayaking, and a zip line canopy tour. The private reserve also has trails, plus a cave—**Cueva de los Guácharos**—with dripstone formations and flocks of *guacharos,* the endemic and nocturnal oilbird.

Parque Temático Hacienda Nápoles: The former country estate of Pablo Escobar (see sidebar above) is today a theme park owned by the municipality. Spanning 8 square miles (20 sq km), the ranch centers on Escobar's mansion. The rotting carcass of a building is now the **Museo Memorial,** showing in gory detail his campaign of narco-terrorism. The small Piper aircraft that he used to fly his first shipments of cocaine is mounted above the entrance gate. His rusted car collection is also here.

Escobar's estate was stocked with African game. Hippos still inhabit a lake, and zebras, rhinos, and other animals can be seen. The life-size concrete dinosaurs he had built have been rehabilitated in **Parque Jurásico.** Hacienda Nápoles includes a wild river water park, three hotels, plus camping in safari-style tents.

Jardín

This small town, about a four-hour drive southwest of Medellín, is one of the most beautiful of Antioquian colonial pueblos. A lovely mountain setting adds to its charm. Its cobbled main square is presided over by the neo-Gothic **Iglesia de la Inmaculada Concepción Basilica Menor,** which is a national monument. A five-minute ride by *teleférico* (aerial tram) ascends to a mountain peak for a view of the

town and valley. Don your hiking shoes, or rent horses, to visit the **Cueva del Esplendor** (Cave of Splendor), where a waterfall cascades from above.

Reserva Natural de las Aves Loro Orejiamarillo: Just a 45-minute drive (four-wheel drive required) southeast of Jardín, the 465-acre (188 ha), rain-soaked Yellow-eared Parrot Reserve was created in 2006 to protect the habitat of this critically endangered bird and the wax palm (see sidebar p. 189) upon which it depends for nesting. Destruction of the wax palm for use in candles and for religious ceremonies almost wiped out the parrot population. Fortunately, education programs and implementation of nest boxes has increased the population from 81 to about 1,000 individuals. ■

Jardín
165 B2

Reserva Natural de las Aves Loro Orejiamarillo
165 B2
Visitor Information
☎ 57-1/245-5134
ecoturs.org

proaves.org

An ice-cream seller greets some children in front of the 1728 facade of Iglesia Santa Bárbara.

A Drive Into Coffee Country

The superbly scenic mountains southeast of Medellín are a gateway to the Eje Cafetero—the coffee axis. Much of the route described here is officially designated a UNESCO World Heritage site, dotted with picturesque colonial towns.

The main route is paved; however secondary roads are mostly not. A four-wheel-drive vehicle is recommended but not essential. You want an early start to arrive in Manizales by nightfall.

Exit **Medellín** on the Pan-American Highway (Hwy. 25), which soon narrows to one lane in each direction as it climbs out of the valley. Beyond the town of **Caldas ❶**, you snake up through pine forest on the switchback road, accompanied by heavy truck traffic. After about 3 miles (5 km), you emerge on a ridgetop

NOT TO BE MISSED:

Los Farallones • Museo Nacional de Sombreros • Plaza Bolívar • Templo de la Inmaculada Concepción

studded with villages set amid dark green coffee fields, with vast views to valleys on either side. From the cloud-shrouded village of **Santa Barbara,** the highway snakes downhill into a broad valley of emerald pastures. Glimpses of twin craggy pitons ahead—**Los Farallones**—draw you on to **La Pintada ❷**, a village nestling on the west bank of the Río Armas.

One hundred twenty feet (36.5 m) south of La Pintada, turn left off the highway at the sign for Aguadas; you cross the river again via an old suspension bridge. The partially paved road winds alongside the river before veering uphill to the hamlet of **La Lorena** (16 miles/25 km from Aguadas), where you get a fine view of a valley to the left. Passing through the quaint colonial village of **Armas,** note the gold-painted bust of Simón Bolívar in the tiny plaza. From here, the road clings to a precipitous mountainside corduroyed with coffee bushes as it climbs to the delightful hillside town of **Aguadas ❸**. The townsfolk are known for weaving iraca palm fronds into broad-rimmed *aguadeño* hats.

A highlight is the **Casa de Cultura** (*Cra. 3 & Calle 6, tel 57-6/851-5170, closed Sun.*), where the **Museo Nacional de Sombreros** displays more than 300 traditional hats from throughout Colombia. The town's whitewashed church with red, green, and gold trim is fronted by a life-size, copper-colored statue of Bolívar atop a

Age-old haciendas tucked into sheltered vales line the route.

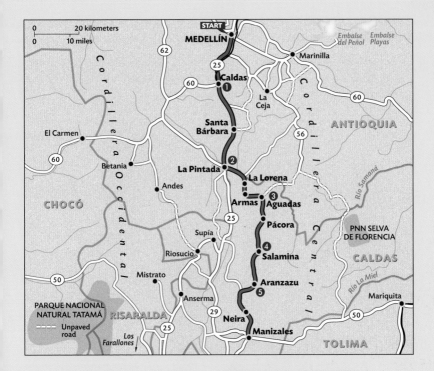

plinth; and the plaza boasts a fanciful fountain adorned with cherubs.

Another 7 miles (12 km) brings you to **Pácora.** This delightful colonial town is worth a quick stroll around **Plaza Bolívar** (it too has a copper-colored statue of Bolívar), where *chivas* (buses) gather in front of the ocher church. Continuing south from Pácora, the road is intermittently paved and subject to landslides. Your reward is a sensational vista across a deep valley to Salamina (21 miles/34 km from Pácora), hung by a thread on the mountainside. Descending steeply to the valley bottom, you will find yourself amid thick tropical foliage and fields of sugarcane before clawing your way up the far side.

Salamina ❹—declared a site of cultural interest and tourism in 1982—delights with its quintessential Colombian colonial architecture, including its beautiful church—**Templo de la Inmaculada Concepción**—unusual for its flat ceiling with carved wooden ceiling.

🅰	See also map p. 165
▶	Medellín
🕐	8 hours
↔	145 miles (233 km)
▶	Manizales

The exit for Manizales is behind the police station (*Cra. 11 & Calle 6*). Leaving town, look back for a dramatic vista of Salamina. Road conditions improve as you approach the town of **Aranzazu** ❺. A gorgeous vista of distant high mountain peaks to your left is a bonus to your trip.

Beyond Aranzazu, the paved road winds down through a narrow, steep-sided valley shaded by tall stands of bamboo, green as limes. Beyond, pass through the ungainly town of **Neira** without stopping; its sole saving grace is the magnificent view toward Manizales that the town offers from its mountainside perch. After another 15 miles (24 km), you'll arrive in **Manizales** in time for sunset.

Zona Cafetera

The Coffee Triangle is an apt name for the Zona Cafetera, Colombia's principal coffee-growing area. Shaped like an inverted triangle, this region of lush green valleys is dotted with old haciendas offering tours of their coffee fields.

The region, which spans the departments of Caldas, Quindío, and Risaralda, is considered the heart of *paisa*—a tranquil and traditional Colombia where *chivas* (buses) still link agricultural towns, operating alongside World War II–era Willys Jeeps that bounce along the country lanes, hauling heavy sacks of coffee and loads of bananas. The towns of Manizales, Pereira, and Armenia make for a vertical axis down the center, hence the region's other nickname: Eje Cafetero (Coffee Axis).

Manizales

A delightful large city in Colombia, easygoing Manizales, 157 miles (254 km) south of Medellín, owes its modern vibe to its late blooming. Founded only in 1849, and rebuilt after a disastrous fire in 1925, it is perched atop the razor's edge of a ridge at 7,054 feet (2,150 m) in elevation, offering views of the snowcapped Los Nevados mountains.

A university town with a cool student vibe, Manizales (pop. 400,000) is renowned for its **Festival Internacional de Teatro** *(tel 57-6/885-0165, festivalde manizales.com)*, the Zona Cafetera's principal cultural festival. The historical core is laid out in a grid to the northwest end of town. Carrera 23 (Avenida Santander) bisects the center.

Plaza de Bolívar: This paved and treeless main square *(Calle 23 & Cra. 22)* boasts a controversial bronze sculpture of Simón Bolívar—"Bolívar Condor"—by

Catedral Basilica Nuestra Señora del Rosario in Manizales

EXPERIENCE: Bullfighting

Many Colombians enjoy bullfighting and pack the *plaza del toros* in season, when the world's top matadors come to show off their skills. Introduced to Colombia in the 16th century, the highly ritualized *corridas de toros* (running of bulls) honors classic Spanish ceremony and tradition. Three *toreros*, or *matadores*, each fight two adult bulls and are assisted by two mounted *picadores* (lancers), three *banderilleros* (flagmen), and a *mozo de espada* (sword servant). Many Colombians oppose the bloody sport for its cruelty. In 2012 Bogotá mayor Gustavo Petro banned bullfighting; he was overruled in 2015 by the Constitutional Court, which ruled it "an artistic expression." The legal tussle is ongoing.

The bullfighting season varies depending on the city (*Nov.–Feb.*), but displays are held throughout the year. Most major cities have a plaza del toros. The four most important sites are:

Plaza de Toros de Manizales, Cra. 27 #10A-04, Manizales, tel 57-6/883-8124, cormanizales.com

Plaza de Toros La Macarena, Cra. 63 #44 A-65, Medellín, tel 57-4/260-7193, cormacarena.com.co

Plaza de Toros de Cañaveralejo, Calle 5 #55-00, Cali, tel 57-2/518-1818, plaza toros.com

Plaza de Toros Santamaría, Cra. 6 #26-50, Bogotá, tel 57-1/334-1628.

Rodrigo Arenas Betancourt, who depicted him as a naked semi-human with a condor head and wings. The statue is almost lost in the shadow of the **Catedral Basilica Nuestra Señora del Rosario.** Its spired steeple soars 371 feet (113 m); you can even ascend the stairs to the Polish Corridor lookout (*closed Tues.–Wed.*). The Gothic cathedral, completed in 1939, is made of unfinished concrete. Facing the cathedral on the plaza's east side, the republican-style Palacio del Gobierno, dating from 1928, has a somber facade and effusive interior moldings.

Three blocks northwest brings you to **Plaza Alfonso López Pumarejo** (*Cra. 19 & Calle 21*), hosting the **Iglesia Sagrado Corazón de Jesús,** a Gothic church fronted by a bronze statue depicting three Augustine friars. Pre-Columbian gold glitters in the **Museo del Oro,** in the Banco

República building, 55 yards (50 m) southeast of Plaza de Bolívar.

Other Sites: Architects on a busman's holiday will find much to admire, including the beautiful neoclassical **Estación del Ferro-carril** (*Cra. 21 & Calle 45*), the old railway station that today houses the Autonomous University of Manizales and displays the 1915 *Pichinga* steam locomotive.

The redbrick **Plaza de Toros** (*Cra. 27 #10 A-04, tel 57-6/883-8124, cormanizales.com*), built in the 1950s as a copy of that of Córdoba, Spain, resounds with cheers during bullfighting season (*Jan.–Feb.*). Two blocks north, note the impressive bronze **Monumento a "Pepe" Cáceres** (*Cra. 23 & Calle 10*) showing Manizales's most famous torero, José Humberto Eslava Cáceres (1935–1987), giving a pass to a bull.

(continued on p. 184)

Zona Cafetera
Visitor Information
paisajecultural
cafetero.org.co

Manizales
🅰 165 B2
Visitor Information
✉ Punto de Información Turística, Cra. 22 & Calle 31
☎ 57-6/874-9712
culturayturismo
manizales.gov.co

Museo del Oro
✉ Cra. 23 #23-06
☎ 57-6/884-8515
🕐 Closed Sat.–Sun.
banrepcultural.org
/manizales

Parrots & Macaws

Colombia boasts 51 of the world's 330-plus species of parrots, including 7 of the 18 macaws. The quintessential birds of the neotropics, these gregarious creatures (flocks of several hundred birds are common) are characterized by their uncanny intelligence and loquacious gift for the gab.

Chestnut-fronted macaws are the smallest of Colombia's seven macaw species.

Parrots possess four toes on each foot, with two facing forward and two backward, providing the dexterity to grasp fruits and nuts as if the birds had opposable thumbs. Their hooked and immensely strong beaks have evolved to slice through nuts and seeds like metal cutters, while rasplike ridges inside the upper bill can grind even the hardest pits to dust.

Most parrots are lime green, with varying colored markings that separate the species and subspecies apart. The most common genus includes the more than 50 species of so-called Amazon parrots—medium-size, stocky birds with heavy bills and slightly rounded, truncated tails. Savvy beyond their size, they have the intelligence and temperament of a two-year-old child. Most birds waterproof their feathers using a special gland in the middle of their lower back with secretions that act as both an antibacterial and antifungal agent. The Amazon parrots lack this gland and instead employ a powder from their down feathers.

The gaily colored macaws—the giants of the parrot kingdom—are as haughty and elaborately plumed as emperors, with authoritative voices to match. Two of Colombia's seven species of macaws are endangered due to deforestation, poaching for their long tail feathers plucked for use in folkloric ceremonies, and the despicable yet booming exotic pet trade.

The great green macaw, or Buffon's macaw, has all but vanished in much of its former range and is found only in Chocó Department; these bright green birds blush when excited, their white featherless cheeks turning rose-petal pink. Although not yet considered endangered, the bloodred green-winged macaw *(Ara chloroptera)* has diminished greatly in numbers in recent years due to loss of habitat and poaching. Measuring more than 3 feet (1 m) to the tip of its tail feathers, it's also the largest of Colombia's macaws. Although the scarlet macaw *(Ara macao)* has the largest range of any macaw and is numerous in Colombia's Amazon Basin, its population is now fragmented. Named for its bloodred plumage, the scarlet macaw has wings of bold royal blue and yellow. The amiable blue-and-gold macaw *(Ara ararauna)* is instantly recognizable by its dazzling coat of teal blue and yellow chest. It too occupies the Colombian lowlands, however in diminishing numbers.

The blue-and-yellow macaw, which has a wavering squawk, favors swampy areas of Colombia's lowlands.

Birds Under Threat

Parrots and macaws make their nests in hollowed-out tree trunks. Logging of mature trees has reduced available nest cavities, with devastating effect on parrot populations. Two Colombian species—Fuertes's parrot and the yellow-eared parrot—are critically endangered. The Fuertes's parrot (also known as the indigo-winged parrot) was rediscovered in the central Andes in 2002, after being considered extinct since 1911. Fundación ProAves *(proaves.org)* has an Adopt a Nest Box program. By protecting the wax palms on which the yellow-eared parrot depends, the program has helped the population recover from a low of 81 to more than 1,000 individuals today.

Males feed their partners by regurgitating food, while females incubate the eggs and feed the young. Monogamous for life, most parrots are often seen flying in pairs, the male and female squawking endearing love notes as they sail overhead like double rainbows with their wings almost touching.

EXPERIENCE: Wildlife Venues Not to Miss

Colombia is a veritable Noah's Ark of tropical fauna, yet most of the wildlife isn't necessarily easy to see in the wild. Sighting a spectacled bear in its high-Andean terrain is cause for celebration, as is spotting a jaguar prowling the lowland jungle. Visit one of these venues where spotting fauna is easy:

Lagos de Menegua (see pp. 249–250; *tel 57/315-326-6068, lagosdemenegua.com*) guarantees superb birding and a likelihood of encountering monkeys and giant anteaters.

Parque Temático Hacienda Nápoles (see pp. 176–177; *tel 57-4/444-2975, haciendanapoles.com*) displays tapirs, wild cats, and monkeys.

Zoológico de Cali (see p. 199; *tel 57-2/488-0888, zoologicodecali.com.co*) is Colombia's finest zoo. Andean condor, spectacled bear, and giant anteater are among the almost 200 native Colombian species.

Zoológico Santacruz (see pp. 86–87; *tel 57/310-329-8880, zoosantacruz.org*) is good for seeing endangered Andean species, such as the spectacled bear and Andean condor.

Hacienda Venecia

🅐 165 B1

✉ 2.2 miles (3.5 km) E of Chinchiná

☎ 57/320-636-5719

haciendavenecia.com

Recinto del Pensamiento

🅐 165 B1

✉ Vía al Magdalena km 11, E of Manizales

☎ 57-6/889-7073

🕐 Closed Mon.

💲 $$

recintodelpensamiento.com

Reserva Forestal Nacional Protectora Río Blanco

🅐 165 B2

✉ FUNDEGAR, Av. Kevin Ángel #59-181, 3 miles (5 km) E of Manizales

☎ 57-6/887-9770

culturayturismomanizales.gov.co/attraction/parque-tematico

E-mail: **sergiofundegar@gmail.com**

Beyond Manizales

West of Manizales, the mountains fall abruptly to the town of **Chinchiná,** 2,624 feet (800 m) below. Between the two cities lie some of the Eje Cafetero's premier coffee farms. One of the most rewarding is **Hacienda Venecia,** a beautiful paisa mansion built in 1910 in lush gardens full of birdsong. It offers one of the best coffee-estate tours in the region and has riverside forest trails. The white-and-bloodred farmhouse also serves as a romantic boutique hotel (see Travelwise p. 291). It's hidden in a valley bottom off the Manizales–Chinchiná Autopista and is a devil to find, as the narrow dirt access road isn't marked.

A quick immersion in coffee cultivation is also included in a guided tour at **Recinto del Pensamiento,** a nature-themed park and research center of the Coffee Growers of Caldas' association. Sprawling over 434 acres (176 ha), the site extends uphill into cloud forest. You can hike a steep trail through a bamboo grove and

INSIDER TIP:

A must-see is the Rió Samana near Cocorná. Its crystal green waters are a real jewel as they run through the middle of a huge jungle.

—JESSE COOMBS
National Geographic adventurer

forest, or take a ski lift–style tram to reach the main sights, which include a hummingbird station, walk-through butterfly enclosure, and an orchid garden.

Reserva Forestal Nacional Protectora Río Blanco:

Known as the site of the antpitta, this forest reserve is considered Colombia's premier birding site. Above **Barrio Toscana,** 3 miles (5 km) northeast of Manizales, the reserve is owned by the municipal water company and managed by the Fundación Ecológica Gabriel Arango Restrepo (FUNDEGAR). It ranges from 7,349 to 12,140 feet (2,240–3,700 m) in elevation, and thus represents several ecosystems. A guide is obligatory and should be arranged through FUNDEGAR.

The **Casa de Colibrís** visitor center (which offers simple lodging) is named for the 23 species of hummingbirds (*colibrís*) that whir about feeders around the balcony. Barely a ten-minute hike up the trail delivers an encyclopedia's worth of rare birds. Many birders visit simply to spot the endemic and endangered brown-banded

---

Nevado del Ruiz Eruption

Nevado del Ruiz, northernmost of the Andean volcanoes, erupted suddenly on November 13, 1985, spraying red-hot lava, ash, and rocks over its glacier-clad summit. The pyroclastic flows that poured downhill were hastened by melting glaciers, creating massive lahars—superfast avalanches of hot debris-filled mud—that struck the town of Armero like a runaway train, wiping it off the map and killing more than 23,000 people. The eruption was the world's deadliest lahar to date.

Frailejónes stud the landscape beneath the Nevado del Ruiz volcano.

antpitta, the endemic bicolored antpitta, and the chestnut-crowned antpitta. Other avian gems to cross off your list include the endemic rufous-fronted parakeet and golden-headed quetzal.

Parque Nacional Natural Los Nevados

The snowy peaks of Los Nevados are only a 90-minute drive east of Manizales. The park covers 207,668 square miles (537,858 sq km), spanning ecosystems from cloud forest and *páramo* to permanent snows.

This wild realm of hot springs, jade-colored lakes, plunging gorges, and basins studded with *frailejónes* is also a trove of precious wildlife, including Andean condor, spectacled bear, and mountain tapir. An overnight is advisable, but the park can be visited on a day trip from Manizales. January and February are the best months.

The three tallest volcanoes— **El Ruiz** (17,457 feet/5,321 m), **Santa Isabel** (16,289 feet/ 4,965 m), and **El Tolima** (17,303 feet /5,274 m)—are snowcapped year-round. All three are climbable, although they're off-limits when showing signs of activity. El Ruiz has been intermittently active since 2012.

The northernmost volcano, **Nevado del Ruiz** is the easiest to access. Turn off Manizales–Ibagué highway at Restaurant La Esperanza (17 miles/27 km E of Manizales) for **Las Brisas,** the park entrance, where you can hire an obligatory guide. **Agencia de Viajes y Turismo Confamiliares** (*tel 57-6/878-3111, mercadeo nevados@gmail.com, $$$$ including park entrance & guide*) offers a daily minibus shuttle from Manizales.

A dirt road leads from Las Brisas to El Cisne Visitor Center and Lodge, 15 miles (24 km)

Parque Nacional Natural Los Nevados

🅰 165 B1

✉ Cra. 26A #68-44, Manizales

☎ 57-6/887-1611 or 886-4104 in Manizales

🕑 Last park access 2:30 p.m.

💲 $$$$

parquesnacionales .gov.co

E-mail: nevados@ parquesnacionales .gov.co

EXPERIENCE: Learn About Coffee & Coffee Culture

Colombia is world renowned as a major producer of coffee that rivals the best in the world. The highlands are patterned in endless rows of dark green corduroy. Coffee's importance to the historical evolution of the modern nation is such that Juan Valdez, the iconic fictional coffee farmer (represented currently in real life by Carlos Castañeda) who represents the National Federation of Coffee Growers, is synonymous with Colombia itself (see sidebar opposite).

A worker husks coffee cherries in a traditional *trapiche*.

Colombia has some 565,000 coffee farmers, who together produce about 12 percent of the world's coffee (second only to Brazil). The *Coffea arabica* coffee plant grows best in well-drained soils at elevations of 2,500 to 4,000 feet (760– 1,200 m), with nearly constant temperatures between 59°F and 82°F (15°C–28°C), and a wet and dry season. In Colombia, the combinations of slope, aspect, rich volcanic soils, and climatic conditions produce a coffee that connoisseurs acclaim as one of the world's best.

Seedlings are planted in rows that follow the contours of the mountain slopes under shade trees or tousled banana plants, which fix nitrogen in the soil. The bushes begin fruiting by their fourth year. The beans are surrounded by lush green berries that turn bloodred, signifying time for the seasonal harvest *(Sept.– Dec. in the north and east; March–June in the south)*.

The fleshy outer layers of the handpicked cherries are removed to expose the beans, which are blow-dried or spread out in the sun. The leathery skins are stripped away; the beans are roasted, sorted, vacuum sealed, and shipped to market.

These venues will help you appreciate coffee's hallowed place in the Colombian psyche:

Finca San Alberto *(tel 57/316-827-1421, cafe sanalberto.com),* above Buenavista, south of Armenia, has a sensational setting and the most in-depth tour.

Hacienda Venecia *(tel 57/320-636-5719, hacienda venecia.com, $$$$; see p. 184),* a prize-winning coffee estate at Chinchiná near Manizales, has tours in English.

Parque Nacional del Café (Vía Montnegro km 6, tel 57-6/741-7417, *parquedel cafearmenia.com, $$$,* see p. 191), west of Armenia, is a Disneyland-style theme park that will delight kids while providing an education on coffee culture.

You can also stay at *fincas* (large farms). Contact **Haciendas del Café** *(club haciendasdelcafe.com).*

away, in a basin with magnificent views. You pass through the **Valle Lunar,** a barren moonlike landscape; and **Valle de las Tumbas,** a sacred pre-Columbian sacred site where you can peer into the **Cañon del Río Molinos**—a canyon in which Andean condors can often be seen. Passing the extinct La Olleta crater, the dirt road switchbacks up to **El Refugio,** a cabin and café at 15,800 feet (4,816 m). During dormancy you can ascend the glacier (with a permit) to **Nevado del Ruiz** crater. At El Cisne, a 2-mile-long (3 km) hike leads uphill through *páramo* to **Laguna Verde,** green as a Colombian emerald under a sunny spotlight.

Pereira & Around

This ungainly city (pop. 576,000) might be a disappointment to visitors expecting colonial quaint, as earthquakes have taken their toll. But be sure and visit the **Plaza de Bolívar** (*Cra. 7 & Calle 19*). The tree-shaded main square, bustles with shoe shiners and hawkers. On the park's east side, the massive bronze **Bolívar Desnudo** monument by Rodrigo Arenas Betancourt shows the national hero naked on horseback, urging it on with ferocious passion. The redbrick **Catedral de Nuestra Señora de la Pobreza** is impressive for its unusual timber-frame ceiling.

The city's dynamic **Viaducto César Gavira Trujillo**—a 1,443-foot-long (440 m) cable-stay bridge spanning the Río Otún—makes for an impressive entrance or exit.

Juan Valdez

Juan Valdez, the fictional Colombian coffee farmer, has been the iconic representative of Colombia since he first appeared in advertisements for the Federación Nacional de Cafeteros (National Federation of Coffee Growers) in 1959. He was "born" at the Doyle Dane Bernbach ad agency to promote Colombian coffee as the richest coffee in the world. Ever since, he has appeared dressed in sombrero and sash, accompanied by his mule Conchita, bearing sacks of fresh-picked coffee beans. Juan Valdez's trademark appearance and greeting—"¡Bueeenos Dias!"—are integral to his mission: To symbolize the proudly kept traditions of Colombia's 560,000-plus *cafeteros* (coffee growers).

Beyond Pereira

The area around Pereira is a cornucopia of sites, from orchid farms and hot springs to well-preserved colonial towns. To the west of Pereira, horticultural centers are tucked off the Pereira–Cartago highway (Hwy. 25). Orchid lovers will delight at **Orquídeas Eva**, which produces more than 30 species of orchids for sale. Nearby, **Agrícola Las Cascadas** cultivates anthuriums.

Cartago: Founded in 1540 at the northern end of the sultry **Valle de Cauca,** Cartago (18 miles/29 km SW of Pereira) is Colombia's capital of embroidery. Its star attraction is the neoclassical **Catedral de Nuestra Señora del Carmen** (*Cra. 12 & Calle 10, tel 57-2/213-3770*), modeled on St. Peter's Basilica in the Vatican, but with a freestanding campanile.

Pereira

▲ 165 B1

Visitor Information

✉ Instituto Municipal de Cultura y Fomento al Turismo, Calle 19 #5-48

☎ 57-6/311-6544 ext. 752

pereiracultura yturismo.gov.co

Orquídeas Eva

✉ Vía Cerritos km 14, entrada 8

☎ 57-6/337-9029

orquideaseva.com

Agrícola Las Cascadas

✉ Vía Cerritos km 7, entrada 4

☎ 57-6/337-9190

anturiosdepereira.com

Cartago

▲ 165 B1

Cooling off beneath the waterfalls at Termales San Vicente

Termales Santa Rosa de Cabal

🗺 165 B1

✉ 6 miles (9.5 km) E of Santa Rosa de Cabal

☎ 57-6/364-5500

💲 $$

termales.com.co

Santuario de Fauna y Flora Otún Quimbaya

🗺 165 B1

✉ c/o Asociación Comunitaria Yarumo Blanco

☎ 57/314-674-9248 or 310-379-7719

yarumoblanco.co

Nearby is **Casa del Virrey** (*Calle 13 #4-53, tel 57-2/212-8557*), the former viceroy's mansion, preserved with period furnishings.

Hot Springs: Pack your swimwear to steep in the hot springs that seep from the mountains east of Santa Rosa de Cabal. Well-marked to the northeast of Pereira, the road from Santa Rosa leads 6 miles (9.5 km) to the **Termales Santa Rosa de Cabal** hot springs. A stone path leads uphill through landscaped gardens and cascades to thermal pools at the base of a 100-foot-tall (30 m) waterfall.

Termales San Vicente Grand Spa (*tel 57-6/333-6157, sanvicente.com.co*), signed off the road to Santa Elena, offers a similar

alternative. It offers thermal mud treatments, plus it has waterfall rappelling, a zip line, and trails for guided birding trips.

Santuario de Fauna y Flora Otún Quimbaya: Just 8 miles (14 km) southeast of Pereira by dirt road via the community of El Cedral, this 1,208-acre (489 ha) wildlife reserve on the western foothills of the Cordillera Central delights nature lovers with its wealth of flora and fauna, scenic beauty, easy access, and well-maintained interpretive trails. Rising from 5,905 feet to 7,874 feet (1,800–2,400 m), its sub-Andean rain forests include elegant stands of wax palms, plus mysterious cloud forests shrouded in mists. Trails lead from the visitor center at

La Suiza. The reserve adjoins Parque Nacional Natural Los Nevados (see pp. 185, 187).

Filandia: South from Pereira, the Circuito Turístico Sur Oriente (Southwest Tourist Circuit) dual carriageway is well named for its spectacular scenery as it unfurls along a ridge of the

INSIDER TIP:

You may be dreaming of a fresh cup of coffee, but the real secret is to have the hot chocolate. Perfect for a cool morning.

—JEFF JUNG
National Geographic contributor

Cordillera Central. Although established only in 1878, the lovely hilltop village of Filandia, 4 miles (7 km) west of the highway, is worth the detour to sample life in a traditional, tight-knit pueblo paisa famous as the setting for *Café con Aroma de Mujer (Coffee With the Scent of a Woman),* a popular Colombia telenovela (soap opera). Mules laden with sacks of coffee beans trot by, led by cowboys with machetes at their side. Dignified elders with sun-creased faces idle the time chatting in the town plaza, surrounded by venerable Willys Jeeps. And womenfolk weave straw hats and baskets on the doorsteps of whitewashed houses with wooden balconies and trims ablaze with a wide range of Crayola colors.

The route to Filandia runs alongside the **Refugio Ecológico Los Colibrís,** a forested ecological corridor signed with symbols of various animals and birds.

Salento & Valle de Cocora

Founded in 1842, the typical paisa town of **Salento** has the most complete Antioquian architecture of any small town in the region.

Quindío Wax Palm

The Quindío wax palm *(Ceroxylon quindiuense),* Colombia's national tree, is endemic to the country and grows primarily in Quindío in Zona Cafetera at elevations above 6,560 feet (2,000 m). The tallest palm tree in the world, the *palma de cera* soars to a height of up to 213 feet (65 m). It grows extremely slowly and can live up to 100 years. Since 1985, the palm—the exclusive nesting tree of the endangered yellow-eared parrot—has been a legally protected species. Nonetheless, it is threatened due to its popularity for use in Palm Sunday celebrations.

Salento's centenary buildings are awash in harmonious color, especially along Calle Real (Calle 6), the main street lined end to end with *fondas* (restaurant-bars) and souvenir stores.

Its setting is best appreciated from the **Mirador de la Cruz,** which has views east to the peaks of Los Nevados. It's reached by a 240-step staircase at the north end of Calle Real, or by car east along Calle 4.

After strolling Salento, follow the Río Quindío into the **Valle de Cocora** *(map 165 B1).* The valley's

Filandia
165 B1

Salento
165 B1

Armenia
🅰 165 B1

Museo del Oro Quimbaya
✉ Av. Bolívar #40 Norte, 3 miles (5 km) NE of downtown
☎ 57-6/749-8169
🕐 Closed Mon.

banrepcultural.org /armenia

PANACA
🅰 165 B1
✉ Vía Vereda Kerman km 7, Quimbaya
☎ 57-6/758-2830
🕐 Closed Mon.
💲 $

panaca.com.co

beauty is owed to the native wax palms *(palmas de cera)* rising from the emerald hills like slender Corinthian columns.

The dirt road climbs to the hamlet of **Cocora,** set amid alpine meadows at 9,383 feet (2,860 m). Beyond, the rocky track ends at **Finca La Montaña,** a wax palm nursery from where you can set out on foot or horseback through the upper valley. The most popular hike (a 6-hour loop) ascends into cloud forest and the **Reserva Natural Acaime** *(map 165 B1)*. The trail is muddy and requires multiple river crossings.

Armenia & Around

Armenia, the sprawling capital (pop. 290, 000) of Quindío, is limited in aesthetic appeal. Like most towns in the region, it was founded late in the day—as recently as 1889. The most

recent of several earthquakes to devastate Armenia ripped the city apart in 1999, flattening its historic buildings and killing more than 1,000 people. Nonetheless, it buzzes with energy as a student town and commercial center.

The not-to-miss attraction is the **Museo del Oro Quimbaya,** the Gold Museum, housed in an impressive redbrick building designed by Rogelio Salmona (see sidebar p. 71). In **Plaza de Bolívar** *(Cra. 13 & Calle 20)*, a classical life-size bronze statue of the Liberator is overshadowed by Rodrigo Arenas Betancourt's massive **Monumento al Esfuerzo** (Monument to Effort) and the **Catedral de la Inmaculada Concepción,** a refreshingly modern church with a triangular ceiling and lovely stained glass.

Want to milk a cow? Or ride a water buffalo? Or see a zebroid

EXPERIENCE: Learn Spanish in Colombia

Colombia has plenty of Spanish language schools to choose from, even in the Western Highlands, offering from a one-week quickie immersion class to month-long (or longer) intensives. Spanish language courses are also a tremendous way for an immersion in local culture, not least because most schools room their students with local families. And many combine tuition with dance classes and/ or excursions. Rarely do classes take up more than 20 hours a week; 4 hours daily, Monday through Friday, is the norm. Here are a few reputable schools:

Amazon Spanish College *(Calle 12 #9-30, Leticia, tel 57-8/592-4981, amazon spanishcollege.com)* offers a rare opportunity to combine Spanish study with exploring

the Amazon rain forest. Visitors have a choice of accommodations, with local families or in the school's own bungalows.

Nueva Lengua *(Calle 69 #11A-09, Bogotá, tel 57-1/813-8674, nuevalengua .com)* has schools in Bogotá, Cartagena, and Medellín, with courses from 1 to 24 weeks. It has options to combine language study with learning to surf, kite surf, or scuba dive.

Universidad del Norte Instituto de Idiomas *(Vía Puerto km 5, Barranquilla, tel 57-5/350-9509, uninorte.edu.co/es /web/spanish)* offers a multidisciplinary Spanish for Foreigners Program at elementary, intermediate, and advanced levels. Courses weave in social and cultural activities.

Sombreros vueltiaos—traditional straw hats—can be found in the town of Salento.

(half zebra, half horse)? The farm-focused **Parque Nacional de la Cultura Agropecuaria (PAN-ACA)** exhibits more than 2,000 horses and other farm animals. And everyone loves the themed equestrian and dog shows. A kind of tropical Disneyland, **Parque Nacional del Café** (map 165 B1; see sidebar p. 186) also aims at Colombian families. The theme park is laid out over 133 acres (52 ha), re-creating a traditional coffee plantation. The **Museo del Café** (Coffee Museum) has excellent motion-activated exhibits. The highlight is a folkloric show that tells the tale of coffee in Colombia.

To the southeast of Armenia, the **Jardín Botánico del Quindío** is one of Colombia's finest botanical gardens, noteworthy for its many bamboos and palms. A guided walk leads through 37 acres (15 ha) of tropical woodland rich with the trilling of birds. Almost 50 species of butterflies flit about inside a walk-through enclosure.

Farther south, a snaking road leads uphill to **Finca San Alberto**, a not-to-be-missed premium coffee estate perched above the hill town of Buenavista. The fascinating guided tour here includes an education in coffee tasting.

Reserva Natural de las Aves Giles-Fuertes: For many birders, the holy grail can be found in this 909-acre (368 ha) reserve, which protects the only known habitat of the critically endangered Fuertes's parrot. The bird had not been seen in 90 years until ProAves' ornithologists rediscovered it in 2002. A two-hour drive south from Armenia, and one hour by dirt track from the village of Génova, the reserve is shrouded in clouds, which nourish the mistletoe the bird feeds on. Lodging is not available at this reserve. Contact EcoTurs *(tel 57-1/287-6592, ecoturs.org)*. ∎

Jardín Botánico del Quindío

⬛ 165 B1

✉ Av. Centenario #15-190, Calarcá, 4.3 miles (7 km) SE of Armenia

☏ 57-6/742-7254

🕐 $$

jardinbotanico quindio.org

Finca San Alberto

⬛ 165 B1

✉ Buenavista, 21 miles (33 km) SE of Armenia

☏ 57/316-827-1421

💲 $$$

cafesanalberto.com

Reserva Natural de las Aves Giles-Fuertes

⬛ 165 B1

The irrepressible rhythmic pulse of Cali set amid a dizzying array of topography—from mountains to *páramo* to desert

Southern Highlands

A Guambiano man rests on a hillside
near his home in Silvia.

Southern Highlands

Cali, Colombia's third largest city, is synonymous with salsa. The sultry dance-crazy city is an exciting mélange of cultures and of sites old and new. Beyond the city limits, Colombia's southwest quarter has mesmerizing pre-Columbian ruins not to be missed. And the scenery shifts as if on a hinge—from the Desierto de Tatacoa to the *páramo* of the Andean Cordillera Central.

A side altar adorns the inside of Iglesia de San Francisco, Popayán's largest church.

North of the Ecuadorian frontier, the great Andean massif separates into three distinct chains: the narrow Cordillera Oriental, the Cordillera Central, and to the west the rain-soaked Cordillera Occidental. Between them run two great valleys. Cali spreads out upon the Valle de Cauca, a deep rift as flat and as green as a billiard table, west of the Cordillera Central. To the east, the valley of the Río Magdalena is parched and sparsely settled.

You don't have to be an archaeology buff to marvel at the statues at San Agustín or the tombs in the Cordillera Central at Tierradentro. Together, these mementos of an advanced northern Andean culture that flourished from the first to the eighth centuries make up the largest group of religious monuments and megalithic sculptures in South America.

Another highlight is Popayán. One of the nation's best preserved colonial cities, this white-washed city is almost entirely intact, boasting lovely churches and boutique hotels. The town makes a good base for exploring the region, especially Parque Nacional Natural Nevado del Huila, named for a highly active volcano. Hot springs and the second largest glacier in Colombia are among its attractions. Popayán is also a gateway to the homeland of the Guambiano indigenous people in the communities east of the town of Silvia. The Guambiano are known for their distinct costumes: Males wear royal blue skirts and black shawls, while women wear black skirts and blue shawls. Both adopt black bowlers.

Though Cali may be best known for salsa nightclubs, it has a colonial core full of surprises, including splendid museums. A high-energy city with a youthful edge, Cali is considered the place to learn to dance salsa like a pro: Its many dance schools are a major tourist draw. Cali also has superb restaurants and hotels.

To the far south, Nariño Department has as much in common with neighboring Ecuador as with the rest of Colombia, including the ruddy windswept cheeks and sharp facial features of its inhabitants. Nowhere is the Ecuadorian influence more strongly felt than in Pasto, a tight-packed border town that's the gateway to Santuario de Las Lajas—a Gothic shrine with a stunning setting over a river gorge.

FARC (see sidebar p. 30) was founded here in 1964, and the region has long been considered an epicenter of fighting between guerrillas, paramilitaries, and the army. Since 2008, FARC has attacked several towns in the region and held up traffic on the Cali–Buenaventura highway; the ELN has been blamed for a car bomb explosion in June 2011 in Popayán. Several foreign governments have

NOT TO BE MISSED:

Learning to dance salsa in Cali   198

A visit to Zoológico de Cali   199

A traditional meal at Cali's La Galería de Alameda market   199

Wandering the colonial streets of Popayán   203–204

The shrine at Santuario de Las Lajas   209

Marveling at the statues in Parque Arqueológico Nacional de San Agustín   213–214

The pre-Columbian tombs of Parque Arqueológico Nacional Tierradentro   215, 218–219

issued warnings against all travel in the south, although the vast majority of travelers thrill to their visits without incident. ■

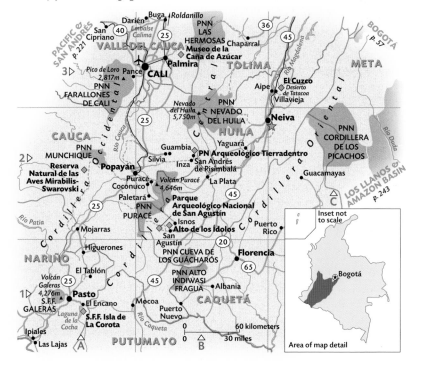

Cali & Around

With its delightful colonial core, splendid modern architecture, superb zoo, and a sexy salsa vibe, the city of Cali is one of the most exciting destinations in Colombia today. If you can cope with the city's frenetic pace, even a short stay here will be time well spent.

The Tango Vivo y Salsa Viva dance troupe performs on stage. Throughout Cali, fast-footed salsa dancers show off their footwork.

Cali

⚑ 195 B3

Visitor Information

✉ Oficina de Cultura y Turismo, cnr. Cra. 4 & Calle 6

☎ 57-2/885-6173

www.cali.gov.co /cultura

✉ Valle del Cauca Chamber of Commerce

☎ 57-2/866-0000

www.valledelcauca .gov.co

Santiago de Cali

Colombia's third largest city was founded in 1536 by conquistador Sebastián de Belalcázar (1479–1551) at an elevation of 3,540 feet (1,079 m). The valley floor, with its fertile soils and steamy climate, was perfect for growing sugarcane, and Cali's hinterland evolved as Colombia's principal sugar-growing region—a role it assumes to this day. African slaves were brought in to toil under the equatorial sun. Today, this city of 2.3 million people has one of the highest populations of African descendants in Colombia.

In the mid-1970s, Cali developed a reputation as a dangerous place to visit. For two decades, citizens lived through a narco-terror nightmare as FARC, paramilitaries, and the immensely powerful Cali drug cartel warred against each other and the government. Though the cartel was eventually destroyed, Cali still has a sobering homicide rate.

Nonetheless, Caleños—local residents—are friendly. Cali has

one of the largest zoos in South America. Its fanatical salsa aficionados set the pace for the rest of the country to follow. Its Feria de Cali (Cali Fair) cultural festival, in December, is legendary. The city has wonderful gastronomy. And juxtaposed against Cali's vibrant contemporary city center, the overlooked colonial core is a trove of historic churches, museums, and bohemian life.

The farsighted Secretaria de Cultura y Turismo, charged with developing tourism, has introduced a double-decker tourist bus (tel 57-2/551-1111, facebook.com/ Coomoepal, $), plus the Guardia Civîl, whose duties include leading tours.

INSIDER TIP:

Spend an afternoon taking salsa lessons at a top-level academy in the world's salsa capital. Then show off your moves at night in Juanchito, a suburb where locals strut their stuff.

—SIBYLLA BRODZINSKY
Freelance journalist, Colombia

Centro Histórico: Most sites of interest concentrate in the historic core. Begin your exploration at the PIT Tourism Bureau in the Centro Cultural Santiago de Cali, a modernist redbrick interpretation of Mudejar style.

Across the street, **La Merced** complex dates back to the city's

founding in 1536. Occupying Sebastián de Belalcázar's former home, the **Museo de Arte Colonial y Religioso La Merced** is a must-see for its impressive collection of religious art and iconography dating back to the 16th century. Ask to see the private chapel of La Virgen de la Merced.

The museum adjoins the **Museo Arqueológico La Merced** (Archaeological Museum), in the former Convento de la Merced, which dates to 1536. Its exposed foundations and walls offer a fine example of colonial construction. The highlight is a superb collection of pre-Columbian ceramics and curled up mummies, encased in glass.

The pre-Hispanic theme is echoed one block southeast at the **Museo del Oro Calima del Banco de La República,** which displays gold artifacts of the local pre-Columbian cultures. Though few in number, the exhibits astound. Catty-corner, the eye-pleasing **Teatro Municipal** (Cra. 5 & Calle 7, tel 57-2/881-3131, teatromunicipal.gov.co), in French neoclassical style, is embellished with lovely frescoes.

One block east, turn south for the 18th-century **Complejo Religioso de San Francisco.** On the southwest corner, the **Torre Mudéjar** (Calle 9 & Cra. 6) bell tower stands over the Templo de la Virgen de la Inmaculada— a lovely ice-blue chapel.

To the south of La Merced, colonial-era San Antonio is laid out like a mantilla fan at the base of a hill topped by the quaint Iglesia San Antonio. Dating from

Museo de Arte Colonial y Religioso La Merced

✉ Cra. 4 #6-117, Plazoleta La Merced

☎ 57-2/888-0646

🕐 Closed Sun.

💲 $

Museo Arqueológico La Merced

✉ Cra. 4 #6-59

☎ 57-2/889-3434

🕐 Closed Sun.

💲 $

Museo del Oro Calima del Banco de La República

✉ Calle 7 #4-49

☎ 57-2/883-6945 or 684-7754

🕐 Closed Sun.– Mon.

banrepcultural.org /cali

Museo de Arte Moderno La Tertulia

- ✉ Av. Colombia #5-105 Oeste, Santa Teresita
- ☎ 57-2/893-2939
- 🕐 Closed Mon.
- 💲 $

museolatertulia.com

1757, the church contains valuable 17th-century *tallas quiteñas*—carved statues of the saints.

Plaza Caicedo: Stately royal palms tower over Cali's clamorous main square *(Car. 5 & Calle 11)* at the heart of the city. To its southwest rises the neoclassical **Catedral Metropolitana,** which was completed in 1841 with marble columns and a humbling gilt altar. The French-inspired masterpiece running the length of the plaza's east side is the 1933 **Palacio Nacional,** the city government headquarters.

Now follow Calle 12 north one block to **Parque de las Poetas,** laid out in 1995 and named for its green-painted sculptures of local poets. Real-life composers clack away on old typewriters. The men type up legal documents or romantic poems for anyone so in need. Passing the elaborately spired Gothic **Iglesia la Ermita,** cross over the Cali River by the footbridge to enter **Paseo de Bolívar,** a tree-shaded plaza studded by a statue of Simón Bolívar.

Santa Rita & Santa Teresita: The twin upscale areas northwest of San Antonio follow the tree-lined Río Cali. Here, at Calle 30, **Parque de los Gatos** (Cats Park) is named for the city's emblematic "El Gato del Río," a huge bronze monument of a cat by local artist Hernando Tejada. About a dozen artsy tiger-size cat sculptures also prowl the park along the river's north bank. Now cross to the south bank for the **Museo de Arte Moderno La Tertulia** on Avenida Colombia. A triptych, its three distinctive

---

EXPERIENCE: Dance Salsa Like a Native

Cali is renowned as the capital of sizzling salsa and is considered ground zero for aficionados who want to learn to dance like a pro. Locals, known as Caleños, are famous for their fast footwork. The classic Cali style is characterized by skill and lightning speed in moving the feet, marking time with synchronous body gestures. This style contrasts with that of other salsa-dancing countries, which are more expressive in using the upper body, waist, and hips. In fact, Cali has numerous dance styles, from the relatively slow *cañadanga* to fast-paced *shindig*.

Take some salsa classes before heading out to a dance club. Cali has more than 200 salsa schools and as many dance clubs. Top schools include the following: **Fundación Escuela de Baile**

Acrosalsa Latina *(Cra. 31 #44-55, tel 57-2/392-3842, e-mail: carlosacrosalsa latina@gmail.com).* The school offers private lessons in your hotel, as well as private and group instruction in its studio in Barrio El Poblado and in the Roosevelt sector.

Son de Luz Escuela y Academía de Baile *(Calle 7 #27-32, tel 57-2/557-0851, sondeluz.co).* This school also has outlets in Popayán.

Tango Vivo y Salsa Viva *(Calle 5 B5 #36-94, tel 57-2/557-0618, tangovivoy salsaviva.com).* The city's foremost dance school has classes for all ages and also puts on *espectáculos* (shows). The owners' foundation offers tuition to children from impoverished districts. The school has produced several national champions.

Cali's Museo de Arte Moderno La Tertulia exhibits works by local and international artists.

modernist buildings focus on exhibits by Colombian and international artists.

It's a pleasant stroll 1.2 miles (2 km) west to the **Zoológico de Cali,** the nation's best zoo. The zoo displays more than 1,200 animals and almost 200 species (80 percent are native to Colombia), including a giant anteater, spectacled bear, and Andean condor. Other highlights include a large aquarium and a walk-through aviary.

Around Town: A rainy day in Cali and you're wondering what to do? Then check out the animals at the **Museo de Ciencias Naturales Federico Carlos Lehmann Valencia** *(Av. Roosevelt #24-80, tel 57-2/514-6848, inciva .org, $),* near the junction with Calle 5. No stuffy closet, this superb natural science museum features lively interactive displays. **La Galería de Alameda** *(Calle 8 & Cra. 24)* is another hidden gem not to miss. This traditional covered market occupies an entire city block and has sections devoted to fruit and veggies, meats, fish, flowers, and artisanal products. Take a taxi.

Take a cab also to **Cerro los Cristales** to see the Cristo Rey, a mountain topped by an 85-foot-tall (26 m) statue of Christ with arms spread to embrace the city below. Pilgrims trek the snaking road during Easter. Stop en route to admire the **sculptures of the biblical Golgotha scene** carved into the hillside sandstone, below the statue. The astonishing figures are the work of local artist Carlos Andres Gómez *(facebook .com/geoglifos).*

Zoológico de Cali
- ✉ Cra. 2 Oeste & Calle 14, Santa Teresita
- ☎ 57-2/488-0888
- 💲 $

zoologicodecali .com.co

Buga

195 B3

Valle del Cauca

The **Río Cauca** is birthed in the Cordillera Central and flows north through some of the best farmland in the country to eventually spill onto the Caribbean lowlands far to the north. Valle del Cauca is also the name of a department that extends west to the Pacific coast,

centered on the port city of Buenaventura (see p. 227).

The valley is thinly populated and is planted in sugarcane. The valley produces 95 percent of the nation's sugar, the region's largest employer. Venturing through undulating cane fields—dusted in summer with delicate white blossoms—to visit old haciendas lets you breathe in the atmosphere of the past.

The most genuine experience can be enjoyed at **Hacienda Piedechinche,** set amid lovely gardens and just 26 miles (42 km) northeast of Cali, via the town of Palmira. Dating from 1715, the adobe *casa colonial* is today the **Museo de la Caña de Azúcar** (Museum of Sugarcane, *(tel 57-2/667-0196, museocana deazucar.com)*, furnished with an assortment of period pieces. Other attractions include a functioning waterwheel and *trapiche* (sugarcane press), plus 18th-century carriages.

Casa Museo Hacienda El Paraíso *(tel 57-2/514-6848, inciva.gov.co $)*, 2.5 miles (4 km) north of Piedechinche, is beloved by Colombian literary fans. Surrounded by roses, this exquisite farmhouse built in 1828 is the setting for Jorge Isaacs's (1837–1895) romantic novel *María*—a classic of Latin American literature.

Buga: Founded in 1555, this small, recently beautified town is an unsung gem, with a splendid colonial core—a national monument. Pilgrims are drawn to the **Basilica del Señor de los Milagros** *(Cra. 14 & Cra. 3,*

A colorful mural adorns the cupola of Buga's Basilica del Señor de los Milagros, home to a gold-plated statue of Christ.

Parque Nacional Natural Farallones de Cali

A huge chunk of the Cordillera Occidental due west of Cali is protected within Parque Nacional Farallones de Cali. One of the most diverse parks in the country, only a portion of the 792-square-mile (2,050 sq km) reserve is open, after years in which guerrillas controlled the area. It ranges from an elevation of 656 feet (200 m) on the Pacific side to 13,451 feet (4,100 m)—a huge span encompassing a variety of ecosystems from lowland rain forest to *páramo*. The one sector open to visitors is **El Topacio,** just a 40-minute drive west from Cali. The visitor center at El Topacio is accessed from the mountain resort town of Pance, popular on weekends with Caleños escaping the heat. From here, you can take a day hike to and from **Pico de Loro,** the park's most accessible peak. It's a muddy scramble in places. Sloths, tamanduas, and five species of monkeys are easily spotted for the patient hiker. But birds rule the roost. An astonishing 700 species have been recorded here.

milagrosodebuga.org). This red stone church has a gorgeous interior. Mendicants focus their sights on a gold-plated 5-foot-7-inch-tall (1.7 m) figure of Christ, to which miracles are ascribed. Shops that surround the church sell religious icons to visiting pilgrims.

Carrera 3 leads north two blocks to Buga's graceful and leafy main plaza, where the 18th-century **Catedral de San Pedro** has a Baroque gilt cedar altar.

Embalse Calima: This beautiful man-made lake, in the mountains about 20 miles (32 km) west of Buga, is reminiscent of England's Lake District. The cool climate and lovely views tempt Caleños on weekends. The lake narrows at its west end to a dam overlooking a narrow canyon. Wind whips up through the defile, thrilling the kite- and windsurfers skimming across the lake, especially from July to September; **Kite Colombia** *(tel 57/317-821-4889, kitecolombia.com)* offers lessons.

The only settlement, **Darién,** in the far northeast, resounds to the mechanical coughing of Willys Jeeps and the *clip-clop* of horses' hooves.

The Cordilleras

The **Cordillera Occidental** runs ruler straight along the Valle del Cauca's western edge. The chain's rain-drenched western slopes drop sharply to the Pacific lowlands. East of the valley, the rugged **Cordillera Central** rises to 17,602 feet (5,750 m) atop **Nevado del Huila.** The tallest volcano in Colombia also has the country's second largest glacier, after El Cocuy. In 2007, the volcano awoke from a 400-year slumber and has been rumbling menacingly ever since. Hence, **Parque Nacional Natural Nevado del Huila** is currently closed to visitors.

Parque Nacional Natural Las Hermosas protects a vast realm of cloud forest and *páramo,* a high-altitude Andean grassland. However, since FARC is still active in the area, the park is closed for ecotourism. ■

Parque Nacional Natural Farallones de Cali

🗺 195 A3

Visitor Information

☎ 57-1/353-2400

parquesnacionales.gov.co

Embalse Calima

🗺 195 B3

Parque Nacional Natural Nevado del Huila

🗺 195 B2–B3

Visitor Information

☎ 57-1/353-2400

parquesnacionales.gov.co

Cauca & Nariño

South of the Valle de Cauca, the Pan-American Highway climbs into a rugged zone where the Cordilleras Central and Occidental converge. The delightful colonial city of Popayán is a star attraction, while the Santuario de Las Lajas and off-the-beaten-path Laguna de la Cocha richly reward visits to the far south.

Floodlights add a romantic note to Popayán's cathedral, one of many churches in the capital city.

The region has something for everyone, including a chance to interact with the Guambiano indigenous group in the town of Silvia, northeast of Popayán. Outdoor enthusiasts can take to the trails in Parque Nacional Natural de Puracé.

The region was inhabited in pre-Hispanic days by the advanced Tumaco culture. It was settled at an early stage in the Spanish conquest when conquistador Sebastián de Belalcázar founded the cities of Pasto and Popayán.

The region was ruled by the Real Audiencia de Quito and ever since has had close affinities with Ecuador and Peru. Many among the local populace have aquiline noses, reflecting a strong Andean indigenous influence.

More recently, the region has been a traditional stronghold of FARC, which was founded here. The Colombian Army maintains checkpoints at regular interviews along major highways. However, FARC has increased its attacks significantly in recent years, and wandering off on your own isn't wise. Try to avoid driving at night.

Popayán

Known as the White City for its chalk white buildings, this city at the southern end of the Valle de Cauca was founded in 1537. It became an important administrative and religious capital, aided by its position as the natural gateway between Quito and Bogotá.

Popayán, the capital of Cauca Department, is notable for its many churches dating from the 17th and 18th centuries. It suffered several earthquakes (most recently in March 1983). Several buildings are now atmospheric hotels. A large student population adds vitality to this otherwise relatively somnolent town, whose core is laid out in a compact grid.

The Sights: The logical place to begin is peaceful **Parque Caldas** (Calle 5 & Cra. 6). A likeness of scientist and nationalist hero Francisco José de Caldas (1768–1816) gazes over the tree-shaded square. Dominating the plaza on its south side, the **Catedral Basílica Nuestra Señora de la Asunción** (Calle 5) was completed in 1906 in neoclassical style (four progenitors were all destroyed by earthquakes). Adjoining it to the north side is a four-square clock tower—the **Torre de Reloj**—built in 1682 and fitted with a clock in 1737. Other important buildings include the town hall, taking up an entire block to the east side.

Art lovers can head west down Calle 5 to the **Casa Museo Negret y MIAMP.** The city's

modern art museum is dedicated to local artist Edgar Negret (1920–2012). To the right of the entrance is Casa Museo Negret, with colonial-era uniforms and other relics displayed in rooms framing a gallery of Negret's modernist sculptures. To the left, the Museo Iberoamericano de Arte Moderno de Popayán (MIAMP) exhibits abstract art.

Walk one block north on Carrera 10 and turn right to enter the **Iglesia de San Francisco** (Calle 4 & Cra. 9). Completed around 1795, the city's largest church is also its most architecturally stunning. East from Plaza Caldas, Calle 4 leads one block to the city's quaintest church, notable for its exquisite facade. Completed in 1741, the **Templo Santo**

INSIDER TIP:

Plan to visit Popayán during Easter week. Some of the processions, celebrations, and traditions trace back to the 1500s.

—LARRY PORGES
National Geographic Travel Books
author

Domingo (Calle 4 & Cra. 5) fuses baroque, Renaissance, and Spanish churriguersco styles. The tourism bureau is 165 feet (50 m) south of the church.

Teeming with religious art, the **Museo Arquidiocesano de Arte Religioso** richly rewards a visit. The most spectacular exhibit is a figure of the Virgen Inmaculada

Popayán
▲ 195 A2

Visitor Information
✉ Oficina Departmental Turismo Gobernación del Cauca, Calle 6 #4-21
☎ 57-2/833-3033
popayan.gov.co/turistas

Casa Museo Negret y MIAMP
✉ Calle 5 #10-23
☎ 57-2/824-4546
🕐 Closed Tues.
💲 $
museonegret.wordpress.com

Museo Arquidiocesano de Arte Religioso
✉ Calle 4 #4-56
☎ 57-2/824-2759
🕐 Closed Sun.
💲 $

Reserva Natural de las Aves Mirabilis-Swarovski

🗺 195 A2

Visitor Information

☎ 57-1/340-3229
& c/o Ecoturs
57-1/245-5134

proaves.org

ecoturs.org

Silvia

🗺 195 B2

de la Apocolipso by Bernardo de Legarda (1700–1773). It depicts an angel standing atop a serpent coiled around a huge globe of pure silver.

Two architectural standouts await along Calle 7, one block north of Plaza Caldas. The first is the **Panteón de los Próceres** (Cra. 7 #3-55, closed Mon.–Fri.), a slender neoclassical edifice dating from the 1930s. Here, 12 marble urns contain the remains of 14 national heroes from Popayán,

---

Guambiano

The Guambiano indigenous people number about 20,000. They occupy the high, cold moorlands between Puracé and Nevado del Huila volcanoes. They eke out an existence in the Páramo de las Delicias, growing potatoes, raising tilapia, and harvesting endemic plants for use in traditional medicine and religious rituals, based on worship of Mother Earth. The Guambiano proudly cling to their original language–Wam. Most still dress in traditional garb: the men in blue skirts and black shawls fringed in pink, the women in black skirts and blue shawls and pageboy hairdos. Both genders wear trilby hats.

---

plus a bust of Simón Bolívar. The pantheon adjoins the impressive **Teatro Guillermo Valencia** (Calle 3 #6-81, tel 57-2/824-1106, teatroguillermovalencia.com), built in eclectic style in 1927, with a roofline adorned with life-size figures of the Muses. Continue north one block to view the **Puente del Humilladero** (Cra. 6 & Calle 2), an arched bridge built in 1873.

Twilight is a good time to visit the hilltop **El Morro de Tulcán**

for a sunset view over the city. Immediately northeast of the colonial core, it's topped by a life-size statue of Sebastián de Belalcázar atop a steed. The same holds true for **Capilla de Belén,** a hilltop chapel built in 1681 (rebuilt in 1885 after an earthquake) and containing an effigy of St. Ecce Homo, the city's patron saint. It's reached by a stone-lined path that begins at the east end of Calle 4 and switchbacks uphill; it is lined with religious statues. Don't go unaccompanied at sunrise or sunset, or after dark. At the base of Belén hill stands **La Ermita** (Calle 5 & Cra. 2) chapel, which dates back to the city's foundation. It is the city's oldest church.

Around Popayán

In the mountains surrounding Popayán, birds abound, particularly in the **Reserva Natural de las Aves Mirabilis-Swarovski,** 37 miles (60 km) west of Popayán. ProAves established the 2,700-acre (1,093 ha) reserve in 2004 to protect the critically endangered colorful puffleg, discovered here in 1967. The bird, which is endemic to the Pacific slopes of the Cordillera Occidental, is often seen at feeders around the visitor center, which boasts a wonderful view over the Tambito Valley. Some 280 bird species inhabit the montane cloud forest.

Security remains a concern in this area; thus, at press time visitors are not encouraged.

Silvia: This mountain market town, 33 miles (50 km) northeast of Popayán, is home for the

Guambiano women dress in identical fashion and wear pageboy hairstyles.

Guambiano people (see sidebar opposite), one of the most traditional of Colombia's indigenous groups. The heart of Guambiano territory is the vale immediately north of town that leads to the hamlet of **Guambia,** high amid cold mountain terrain. Try to visit Silvia on Tuesday, when the Guambiano flock to town to sell crafts such as *ruanas* (ponchos) in the market. The Guambiano have a ready smile for a friendly face and are usually happy to pose for your camera after you've shown the courtesy of either asking or engaging in conversation.

Parque Nacional Natural de Puracé

On weekends, many residents of Popayán lace up their boots to hike **Volcán Puracé** (15,243 feet/4,646 m), which rises east of the city. It's the westernmost of seven contiguous volcanic cones that form the Coconucos chain—the core of the 320-square-mile (829 sq km) Puracé national park. Four of Colombia's greatest rivers—the Magdalena, Cauca, Caquetá, and Patía—rise here.

A century ago the two main peaks were glacier-covered; these days the permanent cap is gone and you can hike to the summit (check before setting out, as the park has been sporadically closed in recent years for security reasons). It takes about three hours from the ranger station at **Pilimbalá** (10,988 feet/3,349 m), from where it's 4 miles (7 km) to the crater via a well-defined trail. Set out in early morning for views. Be cautious near the plunging

Guambia
- 195 B2

Parque Nacional Natural de Puracé
- 195 B2

Visitor Information
- ✉ PNN Surandina, Cra. 9 #25N-06, Popayán
- ☎ 57-2/823-1212 or 8/521-2578
- $ $$

parquesnacionales .gov.co

E-mail: purace@ parquesnacionales .gov.co

Pasto

Visitor Information

✉ Oficina
Departmental
de Turismo de
Nariño, Calle 18
#25-25

☎ 57-2/723-5003

**turismo.narino
.gov.co**

Pre-Columbian gold, Museo del Oro Banco
de La República, Pasto

crater edge: Fumaroles belch out
sulfurous and acidic smoke. Dress
appropriately for the cold, fickle
weather. The ranger station has
lodging and serves meals.

Northern Route: The road
from Popayán to the north is
breathtakingly scenic as you climb
through a gorge to reach a fork
at 11 miles (18 km). The unpaved
road to the left leads along the
northern base of the volcano
to **La Plata** via Puracé and (after
12 miles/19 km)
El Cruce,
where another turn leads south
and passes sulfur mines en route
to **Pilimbalá.** The road to La Plata
continues east before dropping to
the village of **Inza.** En route, you'll
pass an Andean condor view-
point, **Laguna de San Rafael,**
and the **Huancayo Visitor Center,** a main ranger station. Trails
lead from here to the **Termales**

San Juan hot springs and the
spectacular **Bedón waterfall.**

Southern Route: The main
road from Popayán continues past
the La Plata fork to Coconuco,
and ultimately to Isnos and San
Agustín (see p. 213). The hamlet
of **Coconuco** has nearby hot
springs plus access to the volcano.
The road climbs south from Coconuco via a wind-whipped alpine
pass to the **Valle de Paletará—**an
altiplano basin framed by a mountain meniscus. At its eastern end
sits the hamlet of **Paletará,** from
where a side road leads to **Laguna
del Buey** (a tapir habitat) and the
volcano. Immediately beyond, you
pass through a *páramo* studded
with *frailejónes*—a prelude to a vast
swathe of montane cloud forest
that smothers the continental
divide. Frequent military posts
attest to the presence of guerrillas
in the remote vastness, but the
road is considered safe.

Pasto & Around

This chaotic Andean city of more
than 400,000 is Ecuadorian in
look and spirit. **San Juan de
Pasto** was first laid out in a grid
in 1537 at a brisk altitude of 8,290
feet (2,527 m) in the Atriz Valley.
During the wars of independence,
Pasto sided with Spain and was
ravaged by Simón Bolívar's forces.
Earthquakes have since destroyed
much of the colonial core.

Looming to the west of the
city, **Volcán Galeras** is quilted
with cattle pastures and arable
fields. The volcano (14,029 feet/
4,276 m) entered an active phase
in 2005, and several modest

EXPERIENCE: Hiking in Colombia

One of the great draws to Colombia is its fantastic opportunities for hiking. Blessed with nature reserves and vast swathes of Andean wilderness, the country is nirvana to trekkers.

While the tall hills that rise immediately east of Bogotá are a good starting point for day hikes, longer and more demanding adventures await throughout the country in rugged mountain zones acclaimed among the best in South America. For a special experience, take one of the following five hikes.

Parque Nacional Natural de Puracé

The relatively straightforward and nonchallenging hike to the active summit crater of **Volcán Puracé** is a walk in the park, and it can be done round-trip in one day from the Pilimbalá Ranger Station (see p. 205). Being able to stare down into the bowels of this slumbering giant will get your adrenaline pumping. And what spectacular views from on high.

Parque Nacional Natural El Cocuy

Considered by many hikers as the crème de la crème of Colombia's trekking environments, this park (see pp. 105–107) combines spectacular Andean terrain and glacial peaks with crystalline lakes, valleys studded with *frailejónes*, and a rare opportunity to spot spectacled bears and Andean condors. For a great one-day hike from the village of El Cocuy,

A hiker rests while taking in the view in Parque Nacional Natural El Cocuy.

rise before dawn to ascend to **El Púlpito del Diablo**— a mesa at the snow line. Suitably equipped devotees of high-altitude adventure should consider taking the six-day trans-Cocuy trek (see pp. 108–109).

Parque Nacional Natural Los Nevados

This stunning national park (see pp. 185–187), barely a one-hour drive from Manizales, grants access to the snowcapped volcanoes of the Cordillera Central. Opt for a relatively easy three-hour round-trip hike to **Laguna Verde** from the El Cisne Visitor Center, or a more challenging ascent of **Nevado del Ruiz,** the northernmost volcano of the Andes.

Cerros Orientales, Bogotá

The eastern hills that flank the capital city are laced with signposted trails through forests that are a watershed for Bogotá. A popular option is the policed **Sendero Quebrada La Vieja** trail, accessible from a Bogotá Waterworks entry at the junction of *circunvalar* ring and Calle 72. It leads to an overlook of the city. Check security with police beforehand, and don't hike alone.

Ciudad Perdida

The challenging trek to Colombia's mini equivalent of Machu Picchu in the Sierra Nevada de Santa Marta takes six days through rain forest and cloud forest (see p. 152).

Museo del Oro del Banco de La República

✉ Calle 19 #21-27

☎ 57-2/721-9100

🕐 Closed Sun.–Mon.

banrepcultural.org/pasto

Laguna de la Cocha

🅰 195 A1

explosions have since occurred. Hence, the **Santuario de Fauna y Flora Galeras** has been closed to visitors since 2006.

The mountainous route south from Popayán to Pasto features some of the most dramatic scenery in all Colombia. The road is washed out in places and subject to subsidence. About 19 miles (30 km) south of Popayán, you'll drop through a sparsely inhabited

---

EXPERIENCE:
Make It a *Moto*

Colombia has many motorcycle enthusiasts; two of every five vehicles is a *moto*. And lots of foreign bikers tour the Southern Highlands every year. Take a moto tour with **Motolombia** *(tel 57-2/396-3849, motolombia.com)*, in Cali, which rents bikes and arranges shipment for bikers bringing their own wheels. Adventures 57 *(Carrera 13 #35, Bogotá, tel 57-1/610-9439, www.adventures57.com)* rents BMW enduro motorcycles, has 9- to 16-day guided tours, and even has an off-road academy at Tenjo. Tourists are exempt from the requirement that motorcyclists display their license plate number on the back of their helmets.

---

valley where the mercury rises and cacti stud the parched earth.

Pasto's half a dozen sites of interest revolve around the main square, **Plaza de Nariño** *(Calle 18 & Cra. 24)*, paved with pink brick. Looking over affairs from atop a plinth is a likeness of nationalist hero Antonio Nariño. On the park's northwest side, don't miss the Moorish-inspired **Templo de San Juan Bautista**. Its amazing interior dates from 1669. Ticking

off ecclesiastical sites, step north and west one block to the somber redbrick **Catedral de San Ezequial** *(Calle 17 & Cra. 26)*, then return via the plaza for the **Templo de la Merced** *(Calle 18 & Cra. 22)*, with a richly adorned Gothic interior.

Departing from the church, your eye is drawn south to the modernist **Centro Cultural Leopoldo López Álvarez.** The complex includes the **Museo del Oro del Banco de La República.** Although tiny, the Nariño gold museum showcases stunning pre-Columbian gold adornments relating to communities of the Nariño highlands and Pacific coast.

Laguna de la Cocha: This beautiful lake is a favored weekend getaway for Colombians. Set in a lush alpine valley, the lake measures 8 miles (14 km) long by 3 miles (5 km) wide. Its marshy perimeter—a Ramsar-designated wetland—is a birding haven.

Access is via the village of El Encano, at the east end of the lake, about 17 miles (27 km) east of Pasto. Passing through the village, follow the signs for **El Puerto,** a hamlet built atop the floodplain (a four-wheel drive is required to negotiate the muddy road). This remarkable one-street hamlet is composed of Swiss-style houses built on stilts alongside a serpentine canal. Every structure is garlanded with geraniums.

Sharp-nosed *lanchas* (motorboats; $$) await to run visitors on lake tours or the short distance to **Santuario de Flora y Fauna Isla de La Corota.** Trails lead around this tiny island wildlife sanctuary, carpeted with ferns and orchids.

Ipiales

This agricultural and textile manufacturing town only 4 miles (7 km) from the Ecuadorian border wins no beauty contests. Ipiales's treeless paved central **Parque de la Independencia** features the redbrick, classical **Catedral Bodas de Plata** and a modernist-style town hall. The reason most people visit is the nearby Santuario de Las Lajas, southeast of town.

Las Lajas: To reach Las Lajas, you'll pass through the barrio of **El Charco.** It's renowned for its restaurants serving *cuy*—guinea pig—roasted on open-air street-front grills.

A colorful hillside hamlet, 4 miles (7 km) east of Ipiales, sits above the Río Guáitara and clings to a cliffside perch by a thread. Its stone-paved streets are traffic free and lined with souvenir stores. The village thrives on the visitor traffic that throngs to the **Santuario de Las Lajas,** a Gothic confection built atop a bridge spanning a gorge below the village. According to superstition, an apparition of the Virgin Mary emerged from the rock more than a century ago. Ever since, it has been designated a place of pilgrimage.

The national monument is built up against the sheer cliff. Completed in 1949, it was declared a minor basilica in 1954. A long staircase to the church is lined on its cliff-face side by hundreds of plaques giving thanks for believed miracles. Its exterior features murals above wooden doors carved with biblical bas-reliefs. The interior is a jaw-dropper. The altar, built into the rock face, is painted with Virgin Mary's image. Downstairs is the crypt, which hosts a small museum (*$*). ∎

Santuario de Flora y Fauna Isla de La Corota
🅰 195 A1

Ipiales
🅰 195 A1
ipiales-narino.gov
.co/turismo.shtml

Las Lajas
🅰 195 A1

A llama perches on a bluff overlooking Las Lajas. The animals are a big attraction in the area.

Volcanoes

Volcanoes are the primary vents in the Earth's crust through which hot molten rock—magma—wells up from the mantle of liquid rock beneath the crust. Colombia has six active volcanoes (another six are dormant or extinct), making it one of the most volcanically active areas of the world.

Smoke pours from Nevado del Ruiz, one of Colombia's deadliest volcanoes.

Volcanoes are associated with the movement of rigid pieces of the Earth's crust that ride atop the asthenosphere made of hot, plastic rock—a process called plate tectonics. The major and minor plates pull apart or push against one another. Convection currents rise from deep within the Earth's interior, bringing molten material to the surface and forming necklaces of fire along the fractured joint lines.

There are two types of volcanoes. Colombia's volcanoes are andesitic types, taking their name for the Andes mountains and typical of coastal ranges worldwide. They occur where two or more plates are thrust together, forcing the thicker continental plate to ride over the ocean plate. The friction created as one plate grinds beneath the other under enormous

pressure produces molten magma. Silica-rich magma is stiff and viscous and results in high, steep-sided, cone-shaped volcanoes that typically rise 100 miles (160 km) more or so inland from the subduction trench.

Basaltic formations, such as those of Hawaii and Iceland, are normally associated with mid-ocean ridges, where the plates are pulled apart.

Deadly Explosions & Lahars

Andesitic volcanoes are highly explosive. Once a volcano has been primed, the violence of an explosion depends on the relative content of water and silica, and the shape of the conduit. Water, which seeps into magma chambers, provides the explosive potential of steam. When a dome is plugged by solidified lava, the magma

Victims displaced by the 1985 eruption of volcano Nevado del Ruiz await relief supplies.

becomes supersaturated with pressurized steam until the volcano is at a breaking point; it ruptures explosively at its weakest spot. When blasted laterally from the volcano, the lava appears as a *nouée ardente* (glowing cloud), a superheated avalanche that can roar downhill with the force of a thermonuclear explosion. The vast quantities of dust and energy released sometimes spawn above the volcano great clouds charged with lightning and triggering tremendous storms that dump torrential rain.

At other times, the walls protecting a crater lake may rupture and the water cascades downhill, turning into a lahar—a massive avalanche of mud up to 100 feet (30 m) deep and as destructive as a runaway train. In 1985, a small eruption of Colombia's Nevado del Ruiz melted glaciers at the volcano's summit; the resulting lahar swept through the town of Armero, killing 23,000 people. Fourteen municipalities around Nevado del Huila remain

on alert after an increase in volcanic activity since 2007. Volcán Galeras is the most volatile and active of Colombia's volcanoes..

Volcanoes can lie dormant for centuries, before awakening with a series of mutterings that grow gradually stronger and more ominous. Then—*BOOM!* The mountain detonates either all at once or in an ongoing series of thunderous explosions. In lush tropical settings such as Colombia, such eruptions often set off stampedes of wildlife, so that settlements in their path of flight become overrun with ants, centipedes, and venomous snakes.

Several volcanoes, such as Volcán de Lodo El Totumo (see p. 137), near Cartagena, are associated with features such as the fumaroles and boiling mud pools that occur where rainwater seeps into the porous ground above the volcano's magma chambers. Rising back to the surface, the water begins to boil as pressure is released, emerging in great vents of steam.

Andean Condor

Soaring majestically over the Andes, the Andean condor—Colombia's national bird—is one of the world's largest flying birds, with a wingspan up to 10 feet (3 m). Riding on thermals, the bird ranges vast distances while spying for carrion. Its featherless head is an adaptation for feeding inside a carcass. It also exposes the blood-soaked skin to the sterilizing effects of ultraviolet light and dehydration. Condors have been hunted in the mistaken belief that they kill livestock. By the 1980s, the Colombian population had plummeted to a mere 15 individuals. A breed-and-release program has since increased their number tenfold.

Huila

The department of Huila is located on the cusp of the Río Magdalena Valley and the mountains—peaking with snowcapped Nevado del Huila—that flank it. The vale is a rain shadow, the setting for the Desierto de Tatacoa. In the highlands, surreal pre-Columbian statues and underground tombs are enigmatic attractions not to miss.

Pre-Columbian statuary, tombs, and sarcophagi stud the landscape around San Agustín.

The Río Magdalena, Colombia's longest river, is birthed in the Cordillera Central and spills into a narrow valley that broadens northward and eventually opens onto the Caribbean plain. The mighty Magdalena was the main "highway" for early Spanish conquistadores such as Gonzalo Jiménez de Quesada. The valley is cut north–south by a well-maintained and little-trafficked highway.

The entire upper Magdalena Valley is semiarid and infertile. The sun beats down hard as a nail upon the eerily stark Tatacoa Desert north of the city of Neiva. Sprinkled throughout these mountains are archaeological sites—centered on San Agustín and Tierradentro—that astound. Huge stone statues lying half-buried in the luxurious undergrowth and elaborate tombs carved into the

INSIDER TIP:

San Agustín is famous for its archaeological findings. Many travelers have been captivated by its beauty and decided to stay.

--OLIVER EHMIG VELEZ
National Geographic photographer

granite earth add up to the largest trove of pre-Columbian sites in South America.

San Agustín

This lovely hill town occupies a sloping *meseta* (highland plateau) at about 5,577 feet (1,700 m)—an intermediate step in the Río Magdalena's steep, wild descent to the main valley floor. Founded in 1552 by Alejo Astudillo, the town retains its calm colonial ambience. Reason enough to visit if not for

the remarkable pre-Columbian tombs and stone statues dispersed in several sites to either side of the river gorge, which divides the meseta in two.

More than 500 monolithic colossuses, caryatids, and totems stud the landscape between San Agustín, on the southwest side of the gorge, and San José de Isnos, to the northeast. Scattered over an area of approximately 772 square miles (2,000 sq km), the collection of statuary is named a UNESCO World Heritage site.

Parque Arqueológico Nacional de San Agustín:

The San Agustín Archaeological Park, 1.2 miles (2 km) west of San Agustín, is the main site. Guides are available at the entrance, which has a museum *(closed Mon., $)* and from where a 1.2-mile-long (2 km) loop trail leads through forest to four concentrations of monumental

San Agustín
🅰 195 B2
Visitor Information
✉ Calle 3 esq. Cra. 12
☎ 57-8/837-3062 ext. 15
E-mail: turismo@ sanagustin-huila .gov.co

Parque Arqueológico Nacional de San Agustín
🅰 195 B2
💲 $
sanagustin-huila .gov.co

Stone Gods

Little is known about the culture that flourished and disappeared between the 6th century B.C. and 14th century A.D., leaving a legacy of giant stone statues and underground tombs in the upper Magdalena Valley of the Colombian Andes. Although excavations began in the 1930s, archaeologists are still at a loss to explain who the people were who settled the region, where they came from, and where they went.

The monolithic statues, sarcophagi, and tombs were made to serve as a link between the living, the dead, and their deities. Hewn of volcanic rock, the statues range in size from barely 12 inches

(30.5 cm) to 25 feet (8 m). Most are rectangular or oval, and carved with anthropomorphic or zoomorphic figures representing a pantheon of gods and creatures frightening and benign.

Some depict snakes, frogs, and birds of prey—symbols of creation, wealth, and power in pre-Columbian culture. Others are warrior figures with jaguar-type fangs and fierce expressions—perhaps an allusion to a shaman, or spiritual leader, who was thought capable of transforming himself into a jaguar. Many statues guard monumental tombs that were looted decades or centuries ago for their precious relics.

Isnos
195 B2

stone statues and tombs. The figures were originally painted with red, blue, and yellow dyes; much of the paint job is still faintly visible.

At the **Alto de Lavapatas** meseta, note the warrior figures with swollen cheeks. The well-named **Bosque de las Estatuas** (Forest of Statues) features 40 statues displayed along a 1,968-foot-long (600 m) trail in a forest setting. The trail next leads downhill to **Fuente de Lavapatas,** a complex maze of pools and water channels hewn from bedrock carved with figures of animals and humans. It was used for religious ceremonies and ritual baths.

Alto de los Ídolos: This hilltop site at **Isnos,** 15.5 miles (25 km) northeast of San Agustín, occupies two plateaus reached via a trail that winds uphill through the clammy jungle. Tumuli contour the meseta like a basket of eggs: Most of these man-made mounds have been cut away to expose massive stone sarcophagi topped by huge slabs. Each is guarded by fearsome figures poised at the portals. Here, you'll find the tallest statue discovered, measuring 19 feet (6 m) tall.

Alto de las Piedras: This site ($), about 4 miles (7 km) west of Isnos (24 miles/40 km NE of San Agustín), is most famous for "Doble Yo" ("Double Self"), a statue of a guardian with two bodies and two heads, which combine to form a single feline head; and for a 13-foot-tall (4 m) hilltop figure showing a woman giving birth.

Other Sites: A guided horse-back ride is a fine way to arrive at **El Tablón,** 4 miles (6 km) west of Obando. Here, five anthropo-morphic statues rise from a field. Rides continue to **La Chaquira,** where steps lead down to a rocky perch overhanging the Magdalena canyon. The boulders that seem at any moment about to roll off the precipice are etched with petroglyphs; some show monkeys.

At **Estrecho de Magdalena** (Magdalena Narrows) the river narrows down to a 7.2-foot-wide (2.2 m) defile that slices through a sheer rock meseta. The cascades give a sense of the fun to be had while white-water rafting on the river. **Magdalena Rafting** (Calle 5A #16-04, San Agustín, tel 57/311-271-5333, viajes-colombia.com) offers trips.

EXPERIENCE: How to Make *Bandeja Paisa*

The national dish, *bandeja paisa* (see p. 34) is a giant's feast—it means, appropriately, "paisa platter"—of multiple meats. It's popular in Huila and the Southern Highlands as well as in the rest of the country. Here's a version you can make: Marinate steak with salt, pepper, and garlic for a few hours; then chop into tiny pieces and sauté with more garlic, onions, and bell peppers; add beef stock and simmer. Stew red kidney beans with steak in meat stock; add tomato paste and cook until creamy. Serve with a grilled chorizo sausage, *chiccarón* (pork rind), boiled white rice topped with two fried eggs, plus fried plantains and half an avocado.

Parque Nacional Natural Cuevas de los Guácharos

Caves of the Oilbirds National Natural Park is named for the oilbird *(Steatornis caripensis)*, which dwells in caves on the western slope of the Cordillera Oriental. The park was created in 1960 as the nation's first ecological reserve, encompassing cloud forest to *páramo*. The rust-colored

from San Agustín. Deep in the Cordillera Central, Tierradentro National Archaeological Park protects more than 200 subterranean funerary tombs carved into solid bedrock. Centered on the mountain hamlet of San Andrés de Pisimbalá, in Cauca Department, the collection of tombs was named a UNESCO World Heritage site in 1995. San Andrés has

Parque Nacional Natural Cuevas de los Guácharos

🅰 195 B1

Visitor Information

✉ Cra. 4 #9-25, Acevedo, Huila

☎ 57-8/831-7487

E-mail: guacharos@ parquesnacionales .gov.co

The tombs at Segovia are etched with linear and anthropomorphic motifs.

nocturnal relative of the nightjar feeds on the fruits of laurel trees and oil palms, and forms nesting colonies atop mounds of guano inside caves. The bird is so-named because the squabs, or hatchlings, fatten rapidly and in times past were harvested commercially to be rendered for oil.

Parque Arqueológico Nacional Tierradentro

Colombia's second most important archaeological site is distinct

simple hotels and is reached from La Plata, in Huila Department (see p. 206), via Highway 26, just north of Popayán via Inza; or in a four-wheel drive with high-ground clearance from Silvia via Guambia.

San Andrés, on the western foothills of Nevado del Huila volcano, is fascinating for its tiny, whitewashed, thatched church—the **Iglesia Doctrinera,** overlooking the hamlet. This beautiful 16th-century structure could have *(continued on p. 218)*

Parque Arqueológico Nacional Tierradentro

🅰 195 B2 & 217

San Andrés de Pisimbalá

🅰 195 B2 & 217

Neiva to San Andrés de Pisimbalá Drive

This scenic adventure into the Cordillera Central leads to the reclusive hamlet of San Andrés de Pisimbalá, where you can immerse yourself in traditional mountain life and explore the pre-Columbian tombs of Tierradentro. A four-wheel-drive vehicle is recommended (but not essential) for this excursion.

Begin your journey at the junction of Highway 45 and Highway 43, on the west bank of the Río Magdalena outside **Neiva** (see p. 219). After 2 miles (3 km), turn left at the sign for Yaguará. The paved road hems the west side of the broad, semiarid valley and occasionally runs alongside the river.

After 16 miles (25 km) you get your first view of **Embalse Betania ❶**—a large man-made reservoir—spread out ahead. The lake is a popular venue for water sports; its shores are lined with resort hotels. Skirting the lake's north shore, you pass the largest dam in Colombia—its HEP station generates 15 percent of the nation's electricity—to enter the small town of **Yaguará ❷**. This pleasant agricultural town with a twin-spired Gothic church at its core is surrounded by rice fields and cattle pasture.

Beyond Yaguará, the road climbs to a mountain ridge that offers vistas west toward snowcapped **Nevado del Huila** (see p. 201) and a broad valley framed by a ragged scarp-faced mountain range to the south. You now drop downhill to a Y-fork: Keep left to ascend to the hilltop village of **Iguirá ❸**, 1 mile (1.5 km) away. Stop to admire its lovely plaza and church with a redbrick bell tower. Here the paving gives way to dirt.

The relatively smooth dirt road to the hamlet of **Pacarrí** dips and rises through a broad vale and mountain pass, with picture-perfect vistas around every bend. At Pacarrí, you pick up the paving again. The road leads through pastures to the agricultural service town of **Tesalia**. Keep straight through Tesalia

NOT TO BE MISSED:

Embalse Betania • Iguirá • Puerto Valencia • Nevado del Huila • Parque Arqueológico Nacional Tierradentro

and follow the signs for La Plata, to the right, at the junction with Highway 24 (2.5 miles/ 4 km) beyond town. The **Río Paéz** (on your right) guides you through a deep intermontane valley in which the regional agricultural town of **La Plata ❹** lies. Turn right in town on Calle 7, then right again on Carrera 4 for the mountain village of Inza.

Parque Arqueológico Nacional Tierradentro

This road to Inza is paved for the first 5 miles (8 km). Beyond, asphalt gives way to rock, dust, and potholes as you follow a riverside ridge through a gorge subject to landslides (a two-lane concrete surface was being laid in 2011, with plans to eventually link La Plata to Popayán). The pretty village of **Puerto Valencia ❺** is nestled on a shelf above the river about 13 miles (20 km) north of La Plata. Keep straight to reach **Puente Juntas,** a bridge that spans the Río Paéz.

Another 1.5 miles (2 km) brings you to the hamlet of **Guadalejo ❻**, where the road splits for Belalcázar and Parque Nacional Natural Nevado del Huila (the road to the right, however, is currently impassable to vehicles beyond Belalcázar). Take the hairpin bend to the left by the soccer field for Inza.

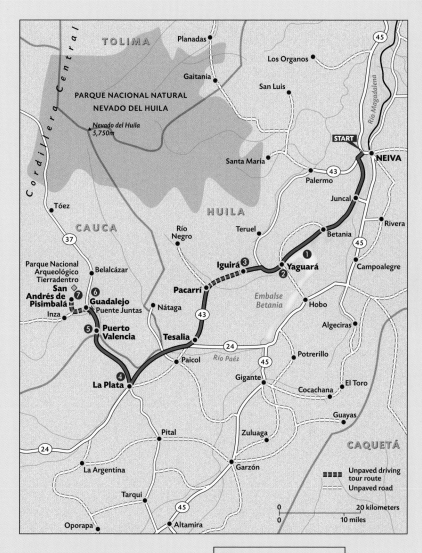

TOLIMA

Planadas

Los Organos

Gaitania

San Luis

PARQUE NACIONAL NATURAL
NEVADO DEL HUILA

Nevado del Huila
5,750m

Santa Maria

START

NEIVA

Río Magdalena

Palermo

Juncal

Rivera

Tóez

HUILA

Río
Negro

Teruel

Betania

45

CAUCA

37

Parque Nacional
Arqueológico
Tierradentro

Belalcázar

Iguirá ❸

Yaguará ❶
❷

Campoalegre

**San
Andrés de
Pisimbalá** ❼ ❻ **Guadalejo**

Pacarrí

Embalse
Betania

Hobo

Inza Puente Juntas Nátaga

43

Algeciras

❺ **Puerto
Valencia** **Tesalia**

24

Río Paéz

Potrerillo

45

Paicol

Gigante

El Toro

La Plata ❹

Cocachana

Guayas

24

Pital

Zuluaga

CAQUETÁ

La Argentina

Garzón

▪▪▪▪ Unpaved driving
tour route

Tarqui

- - - Unpaved road

45

0   20 kilometers

Oporapa Altamira

0   10 miles

You begin to climb the mountainside, leaving the river behind. About 1.5 miles (2 km) uphill you round a bend to enter a valley with astonishing views of mountains beyond.

The abrupt change in landscape is jolting. Prepare to stop at the army checkpoint, beyond which signs that read "Pisimbalá Tierradentro" let you know you're on the right road. Follow the signs as the road splits for Inza (left) and Tierradentro (right). The

⛰	See also map p. 195
▶	Neiva
🕐	1 day
↔	120 miles (193 km)
▶	San Andrés de Pisimbalá

road rises steeply to **Parque Arqueológico Nacional Tierradentro** (see pp. 215, 218) and 1 mile (1.5 km) beyond, the hamlet of **San Andrés de Pisimbalá** ❼ (see p. 215).

Cacti finger the sky in the Desierto de Tatacoa.

inspired French architect Le Corbusier's Ronchamp.

Nasa indigenous people inhabit the mountains above San Andrés and pass through on Saturday en route to the weekly market in Inza. (FARC has a long history of indiscriminately targeting the Nasa, who speak their own language, *paéz.*) San Andrés is protected by the Colombian Army.

Caciques and priests were laid to rest in the tombs, carved between 900–600 B.C. and A.D. 900. Dug into the bedrock, each is accessed by a short but steep staircase twining around a vertical shaft. Averaging about 10 feet (3 m) high by 16 feet (5 m) wide, most are supported by twin pillars carved with linear and anthropomorphic designs in red and black on a white background.

Begin your exploration at the **Museo Etnográfico,** about 0.6 mile (1 km) below San Andrés. It focuses on colonial culture and history. Across the street, the single-room **Museo Arqueológico** focuses on pre-Columbian culture. A trail behind the Ethnographic Museum leads steeply uphill *(15 mins.)* to **Segovia,** where you will find the greatest concentration of tombs. You can continue uphill *(10 mins.)* to **El Duende,** a smaller site.

A third site, **El Tablón,** located 0.6 mile (1 km) east of San Andrés, features freestanding statues representing human figures with arms placed on their chests. It can be reached by road.

A modestly demanding trail that begins beside La Posada hotel winds up through the forest to **Alto de San Andrés,** offering spectacular views.

Neiva & Around

The capital of Huila Department and its center of cultural, economic, and social life, this city on the east bank of the Río Magdalena is only 1,450 feet (442 m) above sea level. Founded on May 24, 1612, by conquistador Diego de Ospina y Medinilla, the city is worth a quick exploration in passing. The must-see sites include **Parque Santander,** with its courthouse, government buildings, and the **Catedral de la Inmaculada Concepción.** The most dramatic of the city's monuments is **Son-eto Los Potros,** rising over the Río Magdalena.

INSIDER TIP:

White-water rafting on the upper Río Magdalena is possible, and visits deep into the southern cordillera may be arranged by local companies.

—MARK HENTZE
Colombia Whitewater co-author

Desierto de Tatacoa: Northeast of Neiva, temperatures soar to 104°F (40°C) and giant cacti dot the rust red Tatacoa Desert. The 127-square-mile (330 sq km) desert is made more surreal by the proximity of the Río Magdalena and the snowcapped peaks of Nevado del Huila on the western horizon. Remains of large mammals and reptiles from the antediluvian dawn are embedded in the tangerine cliffs and mesas.

Neiva
⚐ 195 C2 & 217

Desierto de Tatacoa
⚐ 195 C3

El Cuzco
⚐ 195 C3

Cockfights

Colombian men are fanatical about cockfighting, a legal spectator sport introduced by the Spanish centuries ago. Bloody affairs, fights are held in *clubes gallísticos* or *galleras*—circular cockfight pits found in many rural communities and towns, and in cities like Cartagena. Here, frenzied crowds gather to wager large sums and indulge the nation's sense of machismo. The combatants are matched by weight and size. Owners dote over their prized *gallos,* whose feathers are oiled and thighs shaved before combat. Roosters fight to the death with fake razor-sharp spurs, or even razors, used to claw at their opponents.

The most interesting section is **El Cuzco,** where a small astronomical observatory overlooks dramatic formations. Linger for a demonstration of the night sky, by arrangement with astronomer Javier Fernando Rua Restrepo *(tel 57/310-465-6765, facebook.com /Tatacoa.Astronomia).* The desert can be accessed from Highway 45 at Aipe and Pala, north of Neiva. Public transportation runs the 11 miles (18 km) to El Cuzco via the small colonial pueblo of Villavieja. Check out its **Capilla de Santa Barbara,** built in 1748. Also visit the **Museo Paleontológico de Villa-vieja,** which displays fossils. ■

One of the wettest regions on Earth, featuring resplendent flora and fauna, beautiful beaches, and Afro-Colombian culture

Pacific &
San Andrés

The rugged Pacific surf along
Chocó's shoreline

Pacific & San Andrés

Colombia's sultry Pacific littoral west of the Cordillera Occidental is a wet, lush wonderland tailor-made for nature lovers. Far to the north, the Caribbean isles of San Andrés and Providencia are ringed by some of Colombia's most beautiful beaches. Together, they tempt with scuba diving, whale-watching, and colorful Afro-Colombian communities.

Sitting and texting on the pier in Buenaventura

Extending from the Panamanian to the Ecuadorian border, the mainland region of Chocó (in the north) and Nariño (in the south) is smothered in rain forest that merges into mangrove forest along the shore. The lion's share of visitors to Chocó fly to Bahía Solano for beach vacations centered on the funky coastal village of El Valle and nearby Parque Nacional Natural Utría. Humpback whales play in these Pacific waters in summer months and can be seen during whale-watching trips and even from shore. Marine turtles haul ashore to nest on Chocó beaches. And toucans and monkeys screech in the rain forests.

Pack waterproofs! Rains lash the region. In fact, the area around Quibdó, Chocó's main

city, is one of the wettest places on Earth. Merging north into the world-famous Darién region of Panama, the nearly impenetrable jungle of northern Chocó Department is a last frontier for machete-requiring exploration. No road penetrates the area. Plus, the area is notorious as an active zone for bandits and deadly serious narco-terrorists.

Farther south, the port city of Buenaventura is a gateway to Parque Nacional Natural Gorgona and, far out to sea, the Santuario de Fauna y Flora de Malpelo—two island national parks. Both environments are fabulous venues for whale-watching and scuba diving. Vast mangrove forests protected in Parque Nacional Natural Sanquianga offer sensational birding and can be reached by boat from the coastal communities of Guapí and the southernmost city, Tumaco. Quibdó, Buenaventura, and Tumaco can be reached by highways that scale the mountains and probe to the coast, but check the security situation before setting out.

The region is primarily populated by Afro-Colombians—descendants principally of *cimarrones* (escaped slaves). Small indigenous communities are sprinkled along the river-banks or deep in the jungle.

The beautiful islands of San Andrés and Providencia (Old Providence to locals) are the yin to the yang of Gorgona and Malpelo. These gems stud the Caribbean, 370 miles (595 km) northwest of Cartagena. San Andrés is a major resort destination lined by seamless white sands. Providencia's barrier reef, at 20 miles (32 km) long, is the second longest in the Caribbean and forms the nucleus of the UNESCO Seaflower Biosphere Reserve.

The isles are populated by the Raizal—a Protestant Afro-Caribbean ethnic group, speaking a quasi-English Creole language and eating Jamaican dishes such as *rondón* (fish stew with cassava and yams). ■

NOT TO BE MISSED:

Hiking the trails at Parque Nacional Natural Utría 226–227

Riding the rails to San Cipriano 228–229

Whale-watching at Parque Nacional Natural Gorgona 229–230

Sampling Raizal life on Providencia 238–240

Scuba diving at Parque Nacional Natural Old Providence & McBean Lagoon 240–241

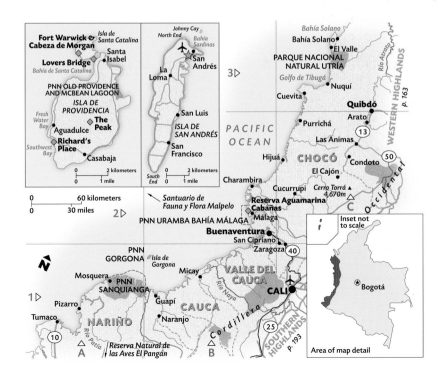

Chocó & Nariño

Humpback whales pay seasonal visits to the warm waters around Bahía Solano, drawing many visitors for eyeball-to-eyeball encounters. Nature lovers can explore dense rain forests and mangroves teeming with wildlife, while Afro-Colombian and indigenous Emberá communities provide opportunities for fascinating cultural encounters.

Rain forest vegetation teems down to the sands at El Valle. The beach is perfect for walks, and humpback whales can sometimes be seen from shore.

Chocó

⚑ 223 C2

Visitor Information

✉ Corporación
   de Turismo de
   Buenaventura,
   Calle 1 #1A-88,
   Conmutador
   Buenaventura

☎ 57-2/242-4508

ccbun.org

Chocó Department takes up Colombia's far northwest corner, extending south of the Panamanian border. Swaddled almost entirely in rain forest, this mostly low-lying region is drained by the Río Arato, which flows north to the Golfo de Urabá.

Tourism to the region is limited to the coastal region around Bahía Solano, where dense jungle fringes dozens of gorgeous beaches

separated by tangled mangroves. The coastal zones of Valle del Cauca Department, Cauca Department, and Nariño Department, to the extreme southwest, are a virtual copy of Chocó, centered on the port city of Buenaventura and the smaller port town of Tumaco, respectively.

Together, the region's full potential as a hothouse of biodiversity and a fascinating venue of cultural intrigue is waiting to be tapped. In Utría—within Chocó—an Afro-Colombian community organization, Mano Cambiada, is working to change that by sponsoring cultural and ecotourist services. Still, beyond the Bahía Solano area and the port towns, the security situation continues to hamper major tourism expansion.

Nonetheless, wherever you travel in Chocó and Nariño you are greeted with a smile by warm-hearted, intelligent Afro-Colombian people. Beyond the few urban centers, these marginalized and impoverished people live mostly in isolated communities scattered along the coast, or inland along the rivers, where hamlets of indigenous Emberá are found. Traditionally neglected by Bogotá, three-quarters of Chocó's populace lack basic services, and the region has the highest mortality rate in Latin America.

The region is also subject to immensely corrupt local politics and to the predations of FARC and armed bandit groups battling for control of lucrative trafficking routes, among other reasons. Until recently, the entire region was considered a *zona roja* (red zone), where the risk of kidnapping and violence was extreme. The Awá indigenous people of Nariño have been especially brutalized and suffer the highest rate of forced displacement in the country.

Today, the Colombian Army's presence is considerable, and the areas described below are considered safe. However, venturing into the *selva* (forest) is a recipe for potential problems.

Bahía Solano & Around

The largest of the many communities speckling the Pacific shore, the small landlocked town of Bahía Solano (pop. 10,000) is about 90 miles (145 km) south of the Panamanian border. The town is served by an airstrip, with daily flights from Medellín; and by boats from Buenaventura. The approach from the sea offers an excellent view of the bay. Bahía Solano—a center for deep-sea sportfishing (May is the best month)—also has several hotels.

INSIDER TIP:

Colombia has many fruits (and fruit juices) you've never heard of. Don't miss out on trying as many as you can. Taste a new one every day.

—JEFF JUNG
National Geographic contributor

A scuttled former Colombian navy boat, *Sebastián de Belalcázar,* lies on the seabed 110 feet (35 m) down, enticing advanced-level divers. The former U.S. Navy vessel is a Pearl Harbor survivor. After World War II, it was donated to Colombia and renamed for the Spanish conquistador. Today, it's a haven for marine life, including grouper and snapper.

El Valle: The main center of tourism is El Valle, a funky Afro-Colombian fishing village linked by road to Bahía Solano, 11 miles

Bahía Solano
🗺 223 C3

Visitor Information
✉ Palacio Municipal, Bahía Solano
☎ 57-2/682-7418
bahiasolano-choco .gov.co

El Valle
🗺 223 C3

Parque Nacional Natural Utría

◮ 223 C3

✉ Centro de Visitantes Jaibaná

☎ 57/310-348-6055 or 313-759-6270

$ $$$$$

parquesnacionales.gov.co

(18 km) to the north; it's a 45-minute road by beaten-up *chiva* or *moto*-taxi. Brown-sand beaches unfurl along the shore—a great place to chill out in a hammock while watching surfers tackling the beach breaks. Colorful fish wriggle in rocky tide pools known as *acuarios naturales*. And olive ridley turtles (colloquially called *golfinas*) come ashore from the beginning of August to the end

of November to deposit their eggs. **El Almejal Ecolodge & Rainforest Reserve** (see Travelwise p. 299) welcomes volunteers for its golfina conservation project, which educates locals and extracts eggs from nests for incubation. Guests at El Almejal are offered nighttime nesting tours, plus the opportunity to release hatchlings to the sea. The lodge also has its own nature reserve and offers predawn canoe trips up the

Río Tundo—perfect for appreciating the mangrove forests as they awaken with birdsong. Don't be surprised if river otters pop their heads up beside your canoe. Time your visit for the week before Christmas and the Festival de la Virgen del Carmen, when a raft festooned with flowers carries an effigy of the virgin downriver, with locals paddling their canoes alongside.

In summer months, visitors fly in for the great whale parade. Beginning in June, as many as 2,000 humpback whales migrate up to 5,300 miles (8,500 km) from their southern summer habitat off Patagonia and Antarctica (July–Aug. is best; by the end of Oct., they are gone). Several companies offer whale-watching trips. On occasion, you can even spot whales breaching while you stand on the shore.

Parque Nacional Natural Utría: A 30-minute boat ride south from Bahía Solano or El Valle, this coastal national park can also be reached by the **Sendero El Valle**—a six-hour trail. A tropical menagerie slithers, slides, and swings through the dense forest—from Geoffrey's tamarin, tamanduas, and sloths to toucans and blue-and-yellow macaws. Jaguars, tapirs, and harpy eagles are among the rarer species you may see.

Humpback whales sometimes enter the Ensenada de Utría, a large finger of a bay framed by thick forested hills. The park headquarters—Centro de Visitantes Jaibaná—displays an entire

Emberá

The Emberá are hunter-gatherers who speak a Chibcha language and are related to Amazonian tribes. They live off fishing and subsistence farming, and hunt by using blow darts tipped with the deadly skin secretions of *Phyllobates terribilis*—one of the deadliest of all poison dart frogs and found only on Colombia's Pacific coast. Though traditionally nomadic and lacking tribal organization, in recent years they have coalesced to form permanent villages, encouraged by the Colombian government. They have suffered severely from attacks by FARC, ELN, and paramilitaries. Also, the intrusion of Christian missionaries and other Western influences continue to dilute their traditional practices.

skeleton of a young humpback whale. Bring your snorkel gear: The waters immediately in front of the headquarters shelter a sunken ship that draws myriad fish. You can overnight in bunk cabins run by a local cooperative, Mano Cambiada *(tel 507/310-348-6055, facebook.com/Mano Cambiada, $$$),* and meals are served to visitors with reservations.

All three Emberá *resguardos* (reservations) in the area are within Parque Nacional Natural Utría.

Nuquí: Embedded in a shoreline jungle about 37 miles (60 km) south of Bahía Solano, this small village abuts a lovely beach lined with small eco-hotels, such as El Cantil Ecolodge (see Travelwise p. 299). Nuquí is reached by boat from Bahía Solano. A carbon copy of El Valle, it's a base for whale-watching, scuba diving, and excursions to PNN Utría, although many folks visit simply to laze in a hammock and forget the cares of the world. Hire a fisherman and his boat for a trip out to sea by dugout canoe to watch him cast his nets and pull in his catch—the best time is between April and June, when huge schools of *agallada* sardines arrive.

Buenaventura

One-third of all Colombia's legal exports—and many of its illegal ones too—pass through Buenaventura, the country's major port city, 78 miles (125 km) west of Cali. A major port expansion and construction of a free-trade zone is now underway. Nonetheless, the lasting impression is not one of wealth. Many among the overwhelmingly black population are impoverished and live in mosquito-plagued wooden shanties built on stilts atop the mudflats. Exceedingly violent criminal gangs roam these slums; exploring is foolhardy.

Buenaventura is used as a base for adventures farther afield. It is a major launching point for Parque Nacional Natural Gorgona and for whale-watching excursions, which depart from the Muelle Turístico—the tourist dock *(Calle 2 & Cra. 1ra).*

Parque Nacional Natural Uramba Bahía Málaga:

Created in 2009 as Colombia's 56th national park, this newcomer

Nuquí
🗺 223 C3

Buenaventura
🗺 223 B2

Parque Nacional Natural Uramba Bahía Málaga
🗺 223 B2
☎ 57-2/667-6041 ext. 134
parquesnacionales .gov.co

Emberá girls are tattooed with *tagua* juice for decoration and to keep pesky mosquitoes away.

San Cipriano
🅰 223 C2

spans 185 square miles (479 sq km) of marine waters and tropical rain forest. This jewel of tropical biota is a mini-Amazon whose appeals are worth the discomforts of sodden humidity and rains.

In the tropics, water spells life. From crocodiles in the marshy wetlands to sleek jaguars on the prowl, Uramba Bahía Málaga park is earning a reputation for some of the nation's best wildlife viewing, not the least for its 360 bird species. Only a 45-minute boat ride from Buenaventura, its draws include boat trips through mangrove ecosystems, where river otters, sloths, and tree boas are easily seen while navigating the narrow channels.

Reserva Aguamarina Cabañas *(tel 57-2/246-0285, reserva aguamarina.com)*, in Ladrilleros, makes a good base for exploring the park. A 20-minute walk leads

INSIDER TIP:

If you choose to sleep in a hammock, the secret to getting a good rest is lying on your side. After that, you'll likely be a convert to the curious weightlessness of the experience.

—ALISON INCE
National Geographic contributor

to a Wounaan indigenous community. Kayaking excursions go to **Isla Palma** and to beaches along **Bahía Malaga** such as **Playa Dorada** and **Playa Chucheros,** where a waterfall cascades onto the beach. Hikes lead to the **Sierpes waterfalls,** with pools that invite a cooling dip. At **La Manigua Botanic Garden** *(e-mail: jardinbotanicolamanigua@hotmail .com)*, owners Pilar Quintana and Conor McShannon conserve the region's plants.

San Cipriano: The Cali–Buenaventura road via Lobo Guerrero is immensely scenic as you cross and descend the relatively low Cordillera Occidental. A dual highway is currently being built to ease the flow of heavy truck traffic. The current route is subject to frequent landslides (and infrequent attacks by FARC).

The road is paralleled by a railroad track used by freight trains and by *moto-brujas* taxis that connect local communities, such as

---

What to Know About Riptides

Ferocious ocean currents called riptides are a constant danger along much of Colombia's shoreline. They occur when the volume of incoming water is so great that the waves form a dam preventing the water's retreat. Any weak point in the waves is sufficient to form a fast-moving channel for egress, drawing excess water from up and down the beach. Waders caught in the current will be dragged out to sea. The natural instinct is to strike for shore—a big mistake. Riptides are so powerful that even the strongest swimmer can quickly tire and drown. Since the channel is usually relatively narrow, the key to escaping is to swim parallel to shore (that is, perpendicular to the current).

San Cipriano. These ingenious rail carts consist of a wooden platform with basic seats, driven by a motorcycle whose rear wheel rides the rail while the raised front wheel is affixed on top of the cart. En route from Cali, you will find the easiest access is at the hamlet of **Zaragoza,** reached by a pedestrian suspension bridge over the river. Moto-brujas await customers on the far bank. It's an 18-minute ride to San Cipriano, or 40 minutes to Córdoba.

Guapí

This gritty, landlocked Afro-Colombian coastal town 99 miles (160 km) southwest of Buenaventura is the main gateway to Parque Nacional Natural Gorgona, hovering on the horizon offshore. Embedded in the rain forest and mangroves, Guapí is connected to Cali by air. Fishing is the town's lifeblood. A must is to stroll the riverfront fish market, where women wear broad-rimmed straw hats and a common frown. Warming only slowly to strangers, they shun being photographed like the plague.

The town is known for marimba music and hosts an end-of-year festival, the **Festival de Música del Pacifico.** Look for near-toothless but ever grinning marimba player Don Dioselino Rodríguez, who sets up his rustic homemade marimba on the streets. Every December 8, locals adorn their *lanchas* (motorlaunches) with flowers and lights and form a nighttime floating parade for the Día de la Inmaculada Concepción.

Parque Nacional Natural Sanquianga: Sanquianga National Natural Park, about 18 miles (30 km) southwest of Guapí, protects a sizable piece of the mangroves along Colombia's Pacific coast. Brown-sand beaches unspool along more than 37 miles

A nonvenomous boa constrictor slithers on Isla Gorgona.

(60 km) of shore backed by mangrove forest. Prevalent wildlife includes sloths, caiman, river otter, and four species of monkeys, plus an entire menagerie of birds. And marine turtles plod ashore to nest above the high-water mark. Inquire at Guapí's waterfront for boat excursions. The park is currently closed to visitors.

Parque Nacional Natural Gorgona: A "devil's island" of the Pacific, Isla Gorgona served between 1960 and 1984 as a prison mostly for Colombian political criminals. Today, creepers and mosses have reclaimed the ruins, and the former administrative

Guapí
🅰 223 B1
Visitor Information
✉ Guapí Cauca, Carrera 2a #5–73, Guapí
☎ 57-9/840-0488
guapi-cauca.gov.co

Parque Nacional Natural Sanquianga
🅰 223 A1

Parque Nacional Natural Gorgona
🅰 223 B1
☎ 57-2/667-6041 ext. 128
💲 $$$

parquesnacionales .gov.co

E-mail: gorgona@ parquesnacionales .gov.co

Malpelo

223 B2

Visitor Information

✉ Fundación Malpelo y Otros Ecosistemas Marinos, Cra. 7 #32-33, Piso 27, Bogotá

☎ 57-1/587-5545

fundacionmalpelo .org

parquesnacionales .gov.co

quarters have metamorphosed as an eco-hotel.

The isle—22 miles (35 km) offshore—is named for its large number of venomous snakes that slither about the jungle and hotel grounds. For this reason rubber boots (provided) are a necessity on trails and anywhere after dark. Measuring some 5 miles (8 km) long by 1.5 miles (2.5 km) wide, the densely forested island takes up only 3 percent of the park; the rest (an archipelago formed by Isla Gorgona and Isla Gorgonilla) is a marine reserve. Humpback whales frequent the warm waters that surround the isle. Most visitors come for encounters with whales, to view marine turtles nesting, or to dive the superb coral reefs.

Barcos Asturias (tel 57-2/242-4620 or 767-4078, e-mail: barco asturias@yahoo.com) offers boat service from Buenaventura, and lanchas can be chartered from Guapí—a bumpy 90-minute ride. There's no dock: You must wade ashore (or be carried)—a major problem for visitors with disabilities. National Park guards will search your bags upon arrival and departure. Day visits only are permitted following an attack by FARC in November 2014, but **Pacific Diving** (tel 57-2/554-2619, pacificdivingcompany.com) has dive trips to Gorgona aboard the live-aboard Sea Wolf.

Santuario de Fauna y Flora de Malpelo

The island of **Malpelo** pokes up 1,234 feet (376 m) above the ocean, 304 miles (490 km) west of Buenaventura. It forms part of the underwater volcanic chain stretching from the Galápagos Islands of Ecuador to Costa Rica's Isla del Coco. The isle covers 1.3 square miles (3.5 sq km), but the sanctuary, which was declared a UNESCO World Natural Heritage site in 2006, also encompasses marine waters measuring 3,384 square miles (8,765 sq km).

EXPERIENCE: Explore the Mangroves

The redolent world of the mangrove forests teems with wildlife. Exploring silently by canoe or boat provides a fascinating insight into this coastal ecosystem of vital importance (see sidebar p. 42). Mangrove systems fringe almost the entire Pacific coast and Golfo de Urabá, plus much of the Caribbean shoreline. One-third of Colombia's mangroves are protected within Parque Nacional Natural Sanquianga, south of Guapí, but these are currently off-limits to visitors.

Consider these options:

El Almejal Ecolodge & Rainforest Reserve (tel 57-4/412-5050, almejal.com.co) offers canoe trips on the Río Tundo from El Valle, in Chocó.

Nueva Lengua Tours (tel 57/315-855-9551, visitcartagena.com) can arrange canoe trips of Ciénaga de la Virgen, a mangrove ecosystem near Cartagena.

Reserva Aguamarina (tel 57-2/246-0285, reservaaguamarina.com) specializes in canoe trips of the mangroves around Buenaventura (see p. 227).

The waters around Isla Malpelo are known for large schools of fish.

Although virtually bare of vegetation, Malpelo is a veritable tropical ocean ark. Its endemic species include a land crab *(Gecarcinus malpilensis)*, a gecko *(Phyllodactylus transversalis)*, and various lizards, and the fabulous birdlife includes the world's largest colony of masked boobies. Advanced divers rank Malpelo as one of the world's best diving spots. Whale sharks, devil manta rays, and schools of giant pelagics are major draws, alongside hammerhead, yellow, silky, and Galápagos sharks, plus various species of whales.

The journey aboard local dive boats from Buenaventura takes 36 hours. **Pura Colombia** *(pacific-diving.com)* and **Pacific Diving** *(pacificdivingcompany.com)* also have diving at Malpelo aboard dive vessels that depart from Costa Rica.

Reserva Natural de las Aves El Pangán

ProAves' 9,800-acre (3,966 ha) El Pangán bird reserve is an ornithologist's delight. Located in the picturesque **Río Ñambi Valley** midway between Pasto and Tumaco, this rain-drenched reserve takes the local name for the long-wattled umbrella bird. It rises from lowland wet forest to subtropical mountain cloud forest. Keen-eyed birders can spot 49 of 65 Chocó endemics, among them the banded ground-cuckoo, the Baudó guan, and the endangered Chocó vireo. ◾

Reserva Natural de las Aves El Pangán

🅜 223 A1

☎ 57-1/340-3229 (c/o ProAves)

💲 $$

proaves.org /rna-el-pangan

Whales Ahoy!

Colombia's offshore waters have enough whale excitement to outdo Marine World. The warm tropical oceans and shallows draw dozens of species of dolphins and larger cetaceans. Some are seasonal visitors that can dependably be seen at predictable times of the year. Others are year-round dwellers.

Humpbacks can be seen up and down the Pacific coast, often traveling in pairs.

Although humpback whales and occasionally other whale species can be seen off the Caribbean seaboard, the prime Colombian habitats for cetaceans are the waters surrounding Isla Gorgona and in Bahía Solano and the Golfo de Tribugá. The sweeping action of nearby Pacific equatorial currents scoops up oceanic nutrients from the deep, resulting in a supply of planktonic soup and shoaling fish of unsurpassed richness. The warm, clear waters off Colombia, Panama, and Costa Rica are also perfect for breeding and calving.

Humpbacks from the southeast Pacific summer in the cold oceans off the south coast of Chile, where they gorge themselves on Antarctic krill. As the southern winter approaches, they migrate north to their tropical breeding and birthing grounds in the waters off Chocó and the Golfo de Panamá. The first animals

begin arriving in June, their slow progress betrayed by explosive exhalations of breath. By October they begin heading back to southern Pacific waters. Humpback whales—identified by their elongated jaws, white underbellies, and long pectoral fins—are felicitous lovers. Promiscuous, too, males push and shove each other to mate with a female in heat, while the female commonly mates with several males in succession. Nonetheless, during copulation, much tender touching takes place. The subsequent year, pregnant females return to the same waters to give birth to their 2,500-pound (1,150 kg) offspring and about one month later are in estrus again.

Bryde's whale, fin whale, pilot whale, four species of beaked whale, and even blue whale—at up to 300,000 pounds (136,078 kg), the largest creature that has ever lived on Earth—

are also seen in Colombian waters. While they prefer deeper oceanic waters, North Atlantic blue whales have even been reported off Colombia's Caribbean coast and San Andrés and Providencia. Pods of orcas can be seen at certain times of the year around Isla Gorgona. Like humpbacks, orcas (the largest members of the dolphin family) visit during annual feeding and breeding migrations. Almost always traveling in groups related by birth, these "wolves of the sea" come into Colombian waters to hunt prey, such as smaller dolphins but also larger whales. They are easily distinguished by their tall, sharply pointed dorsal fins and their black bodies streamlined for speedy attacks, with a distinctive white saddle patch and eye patch.

Firsthand Sightings

Humpback whales can sometimes be seen frolicking as close as 1,300 feet (400 m) from the shore, especially off the coast of Chocó and the beaches of Isla Gorgona. Close encounters of the first kind are virtually guaranteed on whale-watching trips, especially during summer months, when male humpbacks' songs resonate through the hull of your boat. A special thrill is the sight of a massive whale surging out of the water. Most whale species make Herculean leaps, sometimes repeatedly, before crashing down with an explosive splash that echoes across the water. Experts are baffled by this spectacular behavior, called breaching. Patience is a prerequisite; you may spend hours without sighting a whale,

INSIDER TIP:

From July to August, humpback whales come to give birth and mate in the waters surrounding the unpopulated island of Gorgona, once used as a prison and now a secluded national park.

—SIBYLLA BRODZINSKY
Freelance journalist,
Colombia

but whales aren't shy when they do come into view, often passing within a short distance of boats.

Whale-watching trips are offered seasonally *(typically June–Oct.)* by **El Almejal Ecolodge & Rainforest Reserve** *(tel 57-4/412-5050, almejal.com.co)* in El Valle; **El Cantil Ecolodge** *(tel 57-4/448-0767, elcantil.com)* and **Ecolodge Nautilos** *(tel 57-4/322-3625, nuquinautilos.com)* in Nuquí; **Aviatur** *(tel 57-1/587-5181, aviatur ecoturismo.com)* in Bahía Solano; and **Bahía Mar Lanchas** *(tel 57-2/242-6041, bahiamarlanchas .com)* on the Muelle Turístico Buenaventura. In 2008, Colombia's environmental authorities partnered with MarViva *(marviva.net)* to patrol and protect the Bahía Málaga Sanctuary and the national natural parks of Isla Gorgona, Sanquianga, and Utría.

Hammerhead Sharks

There's no mistaking a hammerhead shark, with its flattened head extended to each side of its body, like a rectangular foil or thin hammer, with eyes to each margin. These fish inhabit Colombia's warm tropical and subtropical waters close to shore or above nutrient-rich marine shelves, such as off Isla de Malpelo. They frequently form schools of 100 or more individuals. The nine species include the great hammerhead, which grows to 20 feet (6 m) and is potentially dangerous to humans—it is even cannibalistic. The unusual head shape enhances the shark's 360-degree vision and electroreceptory and olfactory senses.

San Andrés & Providencia

These isles are an anomaly for their location off the coast of Nicaragua, far to the north of Colombia. They beckon with sugar white beaches that dissolve into the turquoise Caribbean. Divers delight to discover one of the largest barrier reefs on the planet. And the Raizal—English-speaking descendants of African slaves—who populate the isles add an enigmatic twist to Colombia's cultural potpourri.

Walking along the pristine beach of Southwest Bay, on the island of Providencia

San Andrés and Providencia are the largest isles of an archipelago that covers 115,831 square miles (300,000 sq km) of the western Caribbean. They were formed during the Miocene epoch by volcanic eruptions. They're only 96 miles (154 km) east of Nicaragua, which has claimed the archipelago in a bitter territorial dispute. In 2007, the International Court of Justice ruled that Colombia's claim to the islands was valid.

The isles are a core part of the 25,097-square-mile (65,000 sq km) Reserva de Biosfera Seaflower,

created in 2000 and named in honor of the vessel that brought the first English, who colonized the isles in 1631, along with their Jamaican slaves. The isles later became a base for pirates and privateers. The cutthroat pirate Henry Morgan is said to have set out from here to sack Panama. The islands were ceded to Spain in 1782 and came under Colombia's control after independence in the 1820s.

About one-third of the population is Raizal. They pledge allegiance to the Colombian flag, but feel stronger affinity to Jamaica and Nicaragua's English-speaking Mosquito Coast. Raizal are Protestant to the core (Baptists and Adventists predominate), sing hymns in English, and are served by the English-language *Caribbean Post*. And *mento* (Jamaican folk music), reggae, and calypso blare alongside *vallenato*. Many Raizal are Rastafarians and sport impressive dreadlocks. Since the 1950s the Colombian government promoted mass migration of Spanish-speaking mainland Colombians, resulting in Raizal discontent. In the late 1960s, a separatist movement evolved.

For beaches, visit San Andrés. For immersion in Raizal culture, choose Providencia. The former is served by direct flights from Colombia, Nicaragua, Costa Rica, and Panama. Providencia is linked by air to San Andrés. Strict baggage limits apply for domestic flights. Visitors must buy a *tarjeta de turismo* (tourist visa; $$$$) upon check-in or arrival. You need your passport. The isles are best visited in the dry season *(Dec.–June),* when trade winds take the heat off the sun.

(continued on p. 238)

EXPERIENCE: Dive! Dive! Dive!

With long coastlines and numerous offshore islands, Colombia is one of the best scuba-diving destinations in South America and the Caribbean. Pristine coral reefs combine with huge swarms of pelagics and shipwrecks to give divers metaphoric raptures of the deep.

In the Caribbean, there's excellent diving off the islands of San Andrés and Providencia; and on the mainland off Santa Marta and Taganga, and at Capurganá in the Golfo de Urabá. Many resort hotels have scuba facilities, while small outfitters have shops at key beaches.

On the Pacific coast, the two principal dive centers are **Bahía Solano** (see p. 225) and **Parque Nacional Natural Gorgona** (see pp. 229–230). Colombia's Pacific waters are known for fast currents and extreme tides; the water is colder than the Caribbean, but aquatic species are more abundant.

Standout dive sites include:

The *Blue Diamond* **freighter**—surrounded by coral at depths of 35 feet (11 m) off the shore of San Andrés—has swim-through sections of the wreck.

Santuario de Fauna y Flora de Malpelo, 300 miles (490 km) west of Buenaventura, is world renowned for whale and hammerhead sharks. It is Colombia's top-ranked site, a destination chosen by experienced divers.

Sebastián de Belalcázar, a scuttled Colombian Navy ship, lies 110 feet (34 m) down off Bahía Solano. It's now a condominium for huge grouper, snapper, and morays. For advanced-level divers.

The following full-service diving companies come highly recommended:

Diving Planet (*Calle Estanco de Aguardiente #5-09, Cartagena, tel 57/ 300-815-7169, divingplanet.org*)

Karibik Diver (*Av. Newball 1-248, San Andrés, tel 57-8/512-0101, karibikdiver.com, $$$$$*)

Poseidon Dive Center (*Taganga, tel 57-5/421-9224, poseidondivecenter.com, $$$$$*)

Pura Colombia (*pacific-diving.com*) and **Pacific Diving** (*pacificdivingcompany.com*) offer dive trips at Santuario de Fauna y Flora de Malpelo aboard live-aboards that depart Buenaventura.

A Drive Around San Andrés

This 19-mile-long (30 km) scenic circuit follows the *circunvalar*—the coast road—that encircles the isle. You can travel around the isle in about three hours, but it's best to add time for lingering on beaches and mingling with local Raizal in churches or who are slapping down dominoes in the shade of the coconut palms.

Guides in colorful sarongs welcome visitors to 19th-century Casa Museo Isleña.

Start in San Andrés town by renting a scooter, golf cart, or even a Jeep from Rent-a-Car Esmeralda (*Av. Colombia #1, tel 57-8/512-8116, e-mail: rentacaresmeralda@yahoo.com*). If you rent a scooter, lather on the sunscreen and wear a hat, as you'll be exposed the entire time to the sun beating down as hard as nails.

Leave **San Andrés** by heading west along Avenida Colombia to Avenida Providencia. Turn left, as the seafront is closed to traffic. Providencia becomes Avenida Las Américas, which leads to Avenida 20 de Julio. Turn right to return to the shore, and then turn left to rejoin Avenida Colombia. You have a lovely view across **Bahía Sardinas** toward Johnny Cay. Passing the airstrip on your left, the beach to your right is lined with small fishing boats. Fishermen can sometimes be seen mending their nets or painting their boats.

NOT TO BE MISSED:

Casa Museo Isleña • San Luis • La Loma Baptist church

After 1.2 miles (2 km), stop at **Casa Museo Isleña ❶** (*Circunvalar km 5, tel 57/8-512-3419, $*), a vernacular two-story home maintained as it would have looked in the late 19th century, including rooms furnished in period antiques as if the owners were still at home. Ladies in colorful skirts lead tours that end with a lesson in various dance styles.

According to local legend, pirate Henry Morgan buried his treasure in **Cueva de Morgan** (*tel 57-8/513-2946*). Stop to visit the cave (1.2 miles/2 km from Casa Museo) in a gated compound where an admission fee ($) also includes a *mento* (Jamaican folk music) and calypso dance show. The cave is often packed with tourists who arrive on *chiva* bus tours.

A little more than a mile (2 km) south, the road curls around **El Cove ②**—a cove with good snorkeling that extends south along a beach and shallows called **La Piscinita**. The **Restaurant West View** (*Km 11, tel 57-8/513-0341*) offers good seafood and great views.

The Last Stretch

Reaching the southern tip of the isle, watch for **Hoyo Soplador ③,** a blowhole that blasts a vertical jet. Beyond, the road curls north along a sandy shore overgrown with sea grape. Stop at **Begue's Beach** and drink refreshing coconut water from a nut husked by Begue, a Raizal with a smile to melt ice.

This southeast shore has the nicest sands on the island—the **Playas de San Luis.** The sands dissolve into electric blue waters. Midway up

the eastern seaboard you arrive at **San Luis ④,** a low-key, exclusively Raizal hamlet of weathered clapboard homes strung along a 2-mile (3 km) stretch of coast road. On Sunday, its many Protestant churches burst with congregations dressed in their finest clothes, and rousing hymnals compete with reggae riffs. Don't miss the cemetery, full of graves dating back more than a century.

Another 0.6 mile (1 km) brings you to **Rocky Cay**—a lively beach resort community. Immediately beyond, turn left and power up the steep hill to the charming ridgetop Raizal community of **La Loma.** Turn left at the top of the hill. Look on your right for the lovely clapboard **Baptist church,** established in 1847 with a needle-sharp spire. You'll exclaim at the fabulous views east over the turquoise shallows called the **Acuario,** studded by **Haynes Cay** and other islands. Retrace your route through La Loma, keeping straight as the narrow lane snakes downhill to San Andrés town, completing your tour.

San Andrés

Visitor Information

✉ Secretaría de
Turismo,
Av. Newball,
at commercial
dock

✉ Av. Colombia &
Av. 20 de Julio

☎ 57-8/513-0801
ext. 104

🕐 Closed Sat.–Sun.

sanandres.gov.co

Jardín Botánico

✉ San Luis, 3 miles
(5 km) S of San
Andrés

☎ 57-8/513-3390

💲 $

San Andrés

Shaped remarkably like a seahorse and measuring 7 miles (12 km) long by 1.2 miles (2 km) wide, San Andrés is a favorite resort destination for mainland Colombians, and for scuba divers from around the world. Touristy, predominantly Spanish **San Andrés town,** at the far north, contrasts with the Raizal-dominated rest of the isle.

Called El Centro by Spanish-blood Colombians, and North End by the Raizal, the town curves around a peninsula at the northeastern tip of the isle. It draws the bulk of visitors to the hotels, bars, and restaurants that line beach-fringed **Bahía Sardinas. Avenida Colombia**—the *malecón,* or seafront boulevard—runs along the shore. Inland, the town holds somewhat less appeal. Even this idyllic isle suffers from crime; avoid wandering away from San Andrés' main streets and walking around at night.

Johnny Cay hovers on the horizon 0.6 miles (1 km) from shore. Boats for the cay leave at 9:30 a.m. *($),* but can be hired for private runs *($$$);* return boats depart the cay at 1:30 and 3:30 p.m. Buy your ticket at the Cooperativa de Lancheros hut, on the east end of Bahía Sardinas.

You can play the part of Captain Nemo aboard the **Semisubmarino** *Manatí (tel 57-8/512-3349, semisubmarino manati.webnode.com.co),* a 40-passenger semisubmersible that runs underwater-viewing trips from the beach.

The waters around San Andrés offer dozens of dive sites, from beds of sea grass to coral-strewn vertical walls. The most dramatic sites concentrate on the southeast side of the island, although getting there can be a bone-jarring boat ride. To the northeast, a barrier reef protects turquoise shallows with isolated coral formations.

A key attraction is the *Blue Diamond,* a medium-size freighter impounded in the 1990s for running drugs and later scuttled on the east side of the island. Its innards—accessed by an open bow hatch and a hole in the side—make for fascinating exploration. If you tire of sun, sand, and sea, seek out the **Jardín Botánico**—the isle's botanic garden, with trails and a lookout tower offering lovely views over the garden and coral reefs; hour-long guided tours are offered.

RaizalSpeak

The native-born Afro-Caribbean islanders—the Raizal—of San Andrés and Providencia speak a form of Creole language called Bende that is closely related to that of the Anglophone Caribbean and Central America's Caribbean populations, from Belize to Panama's Bocas del Toro. Though its origins are English—the Colombian Constitution recognizes English alongside Spanish as an official language of the archipelago—it is barely intelligible to most other English speakers. Bende has its own grammar, phonetics, and syntax, and it marries Spanish words and expressions and elements of West African tongues.

Providencia

Tiny teardrop-shaped Old Providence, as locals call it, is a

A vendor offers fresh-husked coconut at Begue's Beach on San Andrés.

Providencia

223 Inset

Visitor Information

57/8-514-8054

20-minute flight from San Andrés, 56 miles (90 km) to the south. You can circle the isle by scooter in two hours. This craggy volcanic island is a peaceful throwback to the Caribbean of yesteryear, free of mass tourism and all-inclusive megaresorts. The laid-back population numbers barely 5,000 people, almost all of them Raizal who cling tightly to their patois tongue (see sidebar opposite).

Despite its magnificent coral formations and barrier reef, Providence has few beaches. Tourism to the isle is minimal.

The **Folkloric, Cultural & Sport Festival, Horse Race, & Regatta** is a must-experience. Held at Southwest Bay throughout June, it features horse races on the beach, a sailboat regatta, beauty contest, plus plenty of festival revelry and crabs to eat.

The **Festival del Chub**, a festival seafood in early January, features fisher boat races.

Around Southwest Bay: Most visitors stay at small hotels on Southwest Bay, where calm waters are washed over by a coral reef offering exciting snorkeling. Time your visit for Saturday afternoons, when locals race down the narrow 0.6-mile-long (1 km) beach on their horses. At any time, walk the sands to **Richard's Place**, a colorful beach bar and restaurant run by an ever smiling Rasta. Crabs scurry among the mangrove roots to the rear. Loggerhead, hawksbill, and green turtles nest on these sands.

To explore the mountainous interior, follow a trail that begins in the hamlet of **Casabaja,** just 1.2 miles (2 km) east of Southwest Bay. It leads to **The Peak—**a three-hour one-way hike ending with a 360-degree view.

Around Santa Isabel: The little port town of **Santa Isabel,** the administrative capital, is set

At the end of the rainbow lies San Andrés Island and Providencia, a place where the seven colors are melted in the ocean and you can eat the world's most delicious five-buck lobster.

—OLIVER EHMIG VELEZ
National Geographic photographer

beneath dramatic mountains on the northeast of the isle. For the best perspective, cross **Lovers Bridge**—a 328-foot-long (100 m) boardwalk—to **Santa Catalina,** a hilly speck of an isle across the Canal Aury channel. A paved footpath runs along the shore and leads uphill to **Fort Warwick,** today nothing more than a rock wall topped by two cannon. From here, steps lead down to the rocky shore and the **Cabeza de Morgan,** an outcrop that resembles a human head and is named for Henry Morgan.

The hamlet of **Freshwater Bay,** on the island's southwest, enjoys a gorgeous setting over multihued waters, and there are several lovely cafés and quaint hotels to choose from.

Diving & Snorkeling: The isle is surrounded by some of the most pristine coral reefs in the Caribbean, including a 20-mile-long (32 km) barrier reef. The vast

The Raizal—an Afro-Caribbean ethnic people—cling to their Jamaican roots.

EXPERIENCE: *Posadas Nativas—Local Inns*

Colombia's equivalent of a bed-and-breakfast program, the *posadas nativas* (native inns) program is an initiative of the Ministry of Tourism. Most of these quaint, no-frills tourist inns are run by Raizal and offer the chance to experience local culture, customs, and hospitality, first-hand.

The family-run properties also offer tremendous value for money, although facilities are usually simple. Most are air-conditioned, but some may lack hot water. Check to see if meals are included, or can be prepared.

Here are three of the best:

Coconut Paradise Lodge (*Calle Claymount #50-05, La Loma, San Andrés,*

tel 57-8/513-3926, $$, e-mail: oldm26 @hotmail.com) exemplifies typical island architecture and enjoys a lofty perch high atop the somnolent village of La Loma. This restful lodge offers plenty of comfort.

Posada Betito's Place (*Santa Isabel, Providencia, tel 57/314-471-5574, facebook.com/PosadaBetitosPlace, $$*) is decorated with shipwreck miscellany and offers lovely views toward Crab Cay. Betito, the owner, offers boat and fishing trips for guests.

Posada Nativa Miss Trinie (*Cra. San Luis #4-16, San Andrés, tel 57/315-593-0455, posadanativa.com*) is one of the nicest options, run with loving care.

---

complex comprises 78 percent of Colombia's coral reefs and is one of the Caribbean's premier destinations for scuba.

The east side of the island, with shallow lagoons protected by the barrier reef, is for snorkeling only. The west side is for diving and has 50-plus sites. Most are within a ten-minute boat ride of the shore. One of the most revered sites is *El Planchon,* a coral-encrusted German U-boat that sank during World War II. **Felipe's Place** features a vast soft coral garden studded with rigid pillar corals and sponges. Expert divers can descend the **Stairway to Heaven,** which begins some 80 feet (24 m) down and features a gorge and a grotto with great tube sponges at 170 feet (52 m) in length.

The tourism office sells the *Old Providence & Santa Catalina Island Diving Guide.* The **Sirius Hotel &**

Dive Center (*tel 57-8/514-8213, siriushotel.net*), at Southwest Bay, specializes in diving. **Sonny Dive Shop** (*tel 57/318-274-4524, sonnydiveshop.com*) specializes in Nitrox and night dives.

Parque Nacional Natural Old Providence & McBean Lagoon:

The regional mangrove park covers 2,459 acres (995 ha) of turquoise shallow, coral reefs, and coastal mangroves within two calm bays—**Hooker** and **Haine.** The park is accessed either by a 20-minute flight from San Andrés or an eight-hour boat ride from there. From the hamlet of **Maracaibo** a 0.6-mile (1 km) interpretive trail grants access to the redolent world of the mangroves. The best way to explore is to rent a kayak from Posada Coco Bay (*tel 57/311-804-0373*), in Maracaibo, or join a snorkeling or dive trip. ■

Parque Nacional Natural Old Providence & McBean Lagoon

🅰 223 inset
✉ Vía San Luis km 26, Bight
☎ 57-8/514-8552

coralina.gov.co

From vast grasslands and cowboy country to the untamed
and wild rain forest of the Amazon Basin

Los Llanos &
Amazon Basin

Poison dart frogs inhabit the moist habitats
of Colombia's rain forests.

Los Llanos & Amazon Basin

The lowlands east of the Cordillera Oriental take up fully half of Colombia. The bottle green tropical plains stretch out as far as the eye can see, with the rolling, seasonally flooded grasslands of Los Llanos and the Orinoco River Basin merging into the vast swathe of lush Amazonian rain forest. A fascinating cowboy culture, Amazonian Indian tribes, and sensational wildlife viewing are prime draws.

Boys play on the banks of the Amazon River at Leticia, gateway to the rain forest in Amazonas.

The region slopes gradually east from the Andean highlands, drained by countless rivers that snake through the plains and merge into the Orinoco and Amazon Rivers. To the north and west is Los Llanos (the Plains)—a mosaic of grassland, forest, and swamp habitats extending into Venezuela. The area is a wildlife wonderland, where creatures great and small are easily seen. Giant anteaters. Llanos long-nosed armadillos. Endemic freshwater turtles. Scarlet ibises. Sighting these and more is virtually guaranteed.

The *llaneros* (plains cowboys) are a sine qua non of Los Llanos, adding a lyrical note to the landscape. *Joropo*, a distinct expression of traditional dance and music, expresses pride in the

bravery and tenacity of the *vaquero* lifestyle.

A well-paved and well-guarded road links Bogotá with Villavicencio, Puerto López, and Puerto Gaitán—the main towns of Meta Department. Another secure road parallels the base of the cordillera, linking the departments of Meta and Casanare. Otherwise, only the barest tendrils of tarmac infiltrate this vast region. Roving paramilitary bandits and general lawlessness make travel into the Los Llanos heartland a dodgy business. The far north departments of Arauca and Vichada and, to the southwest, Caquetá and Putumayo are best avoided, as they are major fronts in the battle between the Colombian Army and FARC. Despite several notable defeats in recent years, FARC still controls much of Arauca and Caquetá, where cocaine base is used as common currency.

To the southeast, the land is carpeted by throttling rain forest of the Amazon Basin, encompassed by the rain-soaked department of Amazonas. All but a handful of visitors arrive by air to Leticia, Colombia's southeastern apex at its junction with Brazil and Peru. The area is called Tres Fronteras (Three Frontiers). Amazonas is rich in indigenous tribes living in harmony with their surroundings: The region has 120 *resguardos indígenas* totaling more than 100,000 square miles (260,000 sq km). The area, which extends north into sparsely inhabited and little-visited Vaupés Department, is even richer in animal species. The lushest environment on Earth, Amazonian rain forests teem with animal life. Of the world's estimated five million plant and animal species, as many as two-thirds inhabit this sodden world of green. Freshwater Amazon dolphin sightings are more or less guaranteed while traveling the rivers, and other exotic creatures await encounters in such national parks as Amacayacu and various private nature reserves. ■

NOT TO BE MISSED:

Watching a *coleo* (rodeo) at Parque Temático las Malocas **247–248**

Bird-watching and hiking at Lagos de Menegua **249–250**

The richly colored Caño Cristales in Parque Nacional Natural La Macarena **250**

Immersing in Yucuna indigenous lifestyle at Maloka Yucuna **253**

An Amazon rain forest hike at Reserva Natural Tanimboca **256**

Taking a boat trip on the Amazon River in search of pink dolphins **258**

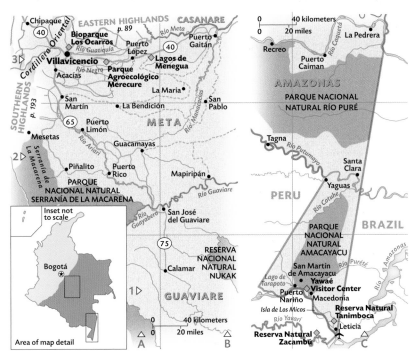

Meta

At the geographic center of Colombia, Meta Department is overlooked by most visitors. Unfairly so, for the huge department—one of Colombia's largest—is the heartland of the plains, and the focus of its distinct *joropo* (traditional dance and music) and *coleo* (rodeo) culture.

A cowboy surveys the weather at Lagos de Menegua. The *llanuras*—flatlands—are cowboy country, and several ranches offer a chance to experience the cowboy lifestyle.

Meta

🗺 245 A2–B2

Visitor Information

✉ Instituto de Turismo del Meta, Cra. 33 #40-2, Edificio Comité de Ganaderos, Villavicencio

☎ 57-8/683-0848

turismometa.gov.co

Meta is the heartland of *música llanera* (see sidebar p. 248) and of the cattle ranching that inspires the cowboy lifestyle. You don't need to probe far to get a full immersion in Los Llanos culture. The region is easily accessed via the Bogotá–Villavicencio highway (Hwy. 40), which drops 7,218 feet (2,200 m) down the eastern slopes of the Cordillera Oriental to deposit you at Villavicencio, the department's capital at a mere 1,532 feet (467 m) elevation. The highway follows the course of the Río Negro as it cuts a deep notch

through the mountains en route to the plains. It's heavily guarded, with armored vehicles at major bridges. Gas tankers thunder along in long convoys, slowing traffic to a crawl on the steepest and most sinuous sections.

The lovely colonial town of **Chipaque** (17 miles/27 km from downtown Bogotá) is worth a stop for its delightful stone-paved square shadowed by a Gothic church. From here, you drop through a deep gorge reminiscent of England's Lake District and pass into a sultrier

Green Anaconda

Los Llanos is one of the homes to the world's largest snake. The green anaconda can reach a length of 30 feet (9 m) and weigh 500 pounds (227 kg). It lives in swamps, marshes, and the riparian habitat of rivers. Nostrils atop its snout permit the hunter to breathe while almost entirely submerged. It ambushes its prey, including crocodiles and jaguars. After grabbing its victim with its teeth, it wraps itself around the animal and squeezes until it stops breathing.

clime. Adding drama to the route are the **Viaducto de Chirajara,** a 950-foot-long (290 m) curling bridge; and the 1.2-mile-long (2 km) **Tunel de Buenavista,** the second longest tunnel in Latin America. Beyond, you emerge to a view of the sprawling city of Villavicencio and the *llanuras* (flatlands) unfurling east like an endless green carpet.

Villavicencio

This city of 421,000 people is La Puerta del Llano—"Gateway to the Plains." Villavicencio, 54 miles (86 km) east of Bogotá, was formally founded in 1840 and named for independence hero Antonio Villavicencio y Verástegui, but it has its antecedents in a cattle ranch on the banks of the Río Guatiquía. It boomed in the late 19th century, when the government sponsored settlement of the plains.

An important agricultural center, it isn't exactly a tourist magnet. It serves the cattle ranches, rice fields, and palm oil plantations that unfold north, east, and south of Villavicencio like a mantilla fan. It's also a center for the petroleum and biofuels industry: Colombia's Ecopetrol corporation pumps oil from the ground east of town.

Each July, the streets of Villavicencio are converted into a giant *joropódromo* for the five-day **Torneo Internacional de Joropo.** This is the time to see locals dressed in the regional costume. The men wear collarless, colorful buttoned shirts, matching baggy half-leg pants, broad-rimmed felt hats, and thin toeless slippers; women wear frilled shoulderless blouses and broad knee-length floral skirts.

INSIDER TIP:

Head to Villavicencio, "Gateway to the Plains" and the best place to launch an adventure by boat, horse, or foot.

—AARON RETTIG
Colombia Whitewater
co-author

For an immersion in cowboy culture, visit in January for the **Feria Exposición Equina, Bovina y Turística de Catama**—an agricultural fair with rodeo and *manga de coleo* (cow roping). Women demonstrate their cowgirl skills,

Villavicencio

🅰 245 A3

Visitor Information

✉ Turismo Villavicencio, Transversal 29 #41-110, Barrio La Grama

☎ 57-8/670-3975

🕐 Closed Sat.–Sun.

turismovillavicencio .gov.co

Parque Temático las Malocas

✉ Camino Ganadero, 5.6 miles (9 km) E of Villavicencio

☎ 57/310-286-5945

🕓 Closed Mon.

💲 $$

parquetematicolas malocas.blogspot .com

too, at the **Concurso Mundial de la Mujer Vaquera** (tel 57-8/684-9724, mundialmujervaquera.com), in late March every year. Llaneros (plains cowboys) kick up the dust year-round at **Parque Temático las Malocas,** a manga de coleo arena on the southeast side of town. Cowboys demonstrate their skills with daily displays of bull riding and manga de coleo. The park also teaches about the cultura llanera (plains culture) with a re-creation of a traditional cattle farm.

Music of the Plains

Melodic, plaintive refrains echo across los llaneros. They're the notes of música llanera, a campesino (peasant farmer) music and dance synonymous with the cattle- and horse-raising plains. The distinctive folkloric genre fuses Spanish and Native American musical influences and evolved in the early 19th century. Singers at local establishments typically belt out proclamations of love and croon about broken hearts, betrayal, and life on the open range. Música llanera is usually played with an arpa (harp), bandola (mandolin), cuatro (four-stringed guitar), and capachos (maracas).

Bioparque Los Ocarros

🗺 245 A3

✉ 1.9 miles (3 km) NE of Villavicencio–Restrepo

☎ 57/320-849-6916

💲 $

bioparque losocarros.com.co

City Sites: Villavicencio's downtown preserves a few colonial-era buildings with bahareque (adobe) walls, but it is known more for its many monuments. Begin at **Plaza Los Libertadores,** the main plaza, and its **Monumento a los Libertadores** featuring busts of liberators Francisco de Paula Santander and Simón Bolívar. Here, too, is the Gothic-style **Catedral de Nuestra Señora del Carmen** erected in 1894

to replace one that been destroyed by fire.

On the western side of the city, **Parque de los Fundadores** (Founders Park) combines several interlinked, grassy plazuelas (squares) filled with interactive games, drawing families on weekends. The massive **Monumento a los Fundadores**—the last work of renowned Colombian sculptor Rodrigo Arenas Betancourt (1919–1995)—stands 72 feet (22 m) and depicts two horses ridden by the city's founder. Two other monuments not to miss are the **Monumento Folclórico Llanero** (Av. Llano & Av. Catama), showing a trio playing harp, maracas, and cuatro guitar; and the **Monumento al Coleo** (Av. Llano & Hwy. 65 to Restrepo), showing a vaquero (cowboy) pulling a running bull's tail.

For a preview of native animal species you might see while exploring Los Llanos, head to **Bioparque Los Ocarros,** a zoo covering 14 acres (5.7 ha). Its almost 1,200 animals include jaguars, tapirs, anacondas, giant armadillos, and anteaters.

Beyond Villavicencio

You can cool off high above Villavicencio on the Antigua Vía (Old Road) to Bogotá, where the restaurant at **Monumento Piedra del Amor** (Antigua Vía a Bogotá km 7, tel 57/314-247-4333) offers sensational views over Villavicencio and the llanuras, unfolding to the distant horizon. The owner has crafted animals of stone at this restaurant. The "Stone of Love"

A musician plays a harp, a key instrument used in *joropo*—traditional dance and music.

is named for the pre-Columbian people who gathered here to celebrate fertility.

Some 5 miles (8 km) east of the city of Villavicencio, the roadside **Monumento a los Caidos en Acción** (Fallen in Action Monument) honors Colombian soldiers assassinated or killed in combat. A wall of honor is carved with their names. It consists of twin monuments, including a giant bust of Gen. Julio Gil Coronado, who was assassinated by FARC at this spot by a bomb on July 19, 1994.

Puerto López & Around

Colloquially promoted as the "Plains Sunrise Route," the route from Villavicencio to Puerto Gaitán is flat as a billiard table. It's lined with emerald green pastures studded with termite hills. Several of the *fincas* (farms)

have metamorphosed into eco-tourist projects.

Passing through the Apiay oil field, you'll reach Puerto López, alongside the Río Meta, 53 miles (85 km) east of Villavicencio. The town is hot and dusty. Four miles (6 km) east of Puerto López, the road climbs an escarpment to **Alto de Menegua,** where a 69-foot-tall (21 m) obelisk marks the exact geographic center of Colombia.

The most exciting destination in the region is **Lagos de Menegua,** 10 miles (17 km) east of Puerto López. This agro-tourism complex is an ecological paradise. The birding here is fantastic. Amazonian motmots . . . kingfishers . . . oropendolas . . . screech-owls . . . cobalt-winged parakeets. It's a long checklist, including green macaws that live in the palm trees that rise from the waters of Lago

Puerto López
🗺 245 A3

Lagos de Menegua
🗺 245 A3
✉ Vía Puerto López–Puerto Gaitán km 17
☎ 57/315-326-6068

lagosdemenegua .com

Puerto Gaitán
▲ 245 B3

Parque Nacional Natural La Macarena
▲ 245 A2
☎ 57-1/3523-2400 ext 138 in Bogotá

E-mail: reservas
.macarenas@
parquesnacionales
.gov.co

de las Palmas. Giant armadillos and anteaters pad through the grasslands, stalked by pumas, while four species of monkeys cavort in the trees. It offers kayaking, fishing, and hiking, and you can saddle up with the cowboys.

It's another 59 miles (95 km) or so to **Puerto Gaitán,** where the paved road gives out beside the wide Río Manacacías. The reason to travel this far is for boat trips in search of pink freshwater dolphins (see sidebar p. 258), best seen in the dry season *(Nov.–March).*

Parque Nacional Natural La Macarena

Named for an isolated low-lying mountain range (90 miles/ 150 km long and 21 miles/ 35 km wide), this remote park was until recent years rebel

infested and a traditional headquarters of FARC. On September 24, 2010, a massive attack by the Colombian military against the headquarters killed FARC's top military leader Jorge Briceño Suárez.

The key allure is the **Caño Cristales**—crystal clear, cold mountain streams that flow over granite bedrock as brilliantly colored as an artist's palette in blue, green, yellow, black, and plum purple. The red is owed to submerged flowers (not algae) in the family Podostemaceae; they bloom June to November. Look closely and you'll see that the yellow is due to crystal-embedded rock glittering in the intense sunlight. The blue, green, and black are due to minerals. Winter is the best time to visit, when river levels increase and the beautiful colors are best revealed.

The park's diverse ecosystems support a high degree of endemism, such as the copper titi monkey. And there are pre-Columbian pictographs, etched perhaps by forebears of the Guayabero people, who inhabit the area.

A guide from the local guide association, **UNIGMA** *(tel 57/320-856-7571, e-mail: guiasunigma@hotmail.com),* is compulsory. Consider taking a package ecotour with a reputable agency such as **Ecoturismo Sierra de La Macarena** *(tel 57-8/664-8405, ecoturismo macarena.com).* Do not explore the park alone. ∎

Ecological Experiment

Los Llanos is the setting for an improbable field experiment in self-sufficiency and ecological sustainability. A 15-hour drive from Bogotá, Gaviotas is a profitmaking community of collective counterculture creativity founded in 1971 by Paolo Lugari, a Colombian visionary, and Belgian millionaire eco-entrepreneur Gunter Pauli. They planted Honduran palms, spawning an ecosystem of more than 200 other plant species as well as resin product, biodiesel, and water-bottling plants. The freewheeling community of 200 refugees, scientists, and tinkerers has since devised dozens of successful inventions. The project will eventually expand to 23,166 square miles (60,000 sq km) and create a clean-tech economy in the region that will support a population of five million people.

Amazonas

The very word itself—Amazonas—conjures up the roar of jaguars and the screech of macaws. Equal to the size of California, or Germany, the Brobdingnagian scale of the Amazonian rain forests is overwhelming, yet all that this region offers—from wildlife galore to indigenous communities—can easily be seen from the main town of Leticia.

Yucuna Amerindians at Maloka Yucuna mark their faces to invoke the spirit of the jaguar.

The vast department of Amazonas is inhabited by barely 67,000 people, most tucked into a pendant—the Amazon trapezoid—at the extreme southeast of the nation. The region is defined by the hydrological basin of the Amazon, Putumayo, and Caquetá Rivers, which drain into the world's largest river basin.

This world of throttling greens is accessed by air to Leticia, then by high-speed *lanchas* or slower paced *peque-peques* (dugout canoes) that head up the tannic rivers. Beyond Leticia, the rain forest is inhabited by a mosaic of 17 distinct indigenous groups, many of whom live much as their forebears did. A few welcome visitors with displays of traditional dancing and other insights into native culture.

Nowhere else does life flourish in such abundance. Moth-ridden sloths moving languidly among the high branches. Sleek jaguars on the prowl. King vultures wheeling and sliding on thermals. And the freshwater *boto*, or pink

Amazonas
Ⓜ 245 C1–C3

amazonas.gov.co
/turismo.shtml

Leticia

⚠ 245 C1

✉ Calle 10 #10-77

☎ 57-8/592-6566

amazonasleticia.co

Amazon dolphin, is commonly seen surfacing, snuffling and snorting to breathe. Much of the wildlife is glimpsed only as shadows, such as the cats. However, with patience (and a good guide), you have a good chance of seeing monkeys galore, as well as iguanas, coatimundis, anteaters, sloths, and birds by the thousands. This mother lode of biodiversity is home to more than 580 species of birds and even more butterflies, plus more than 1,300 species of freshwater fish.

Temperatures average a constant 82°F (28°C) year-round, and the 90-plus percent humidity can leave you drenched in sweat within seconds of even the slightest exertion. February to April are the wettest months. Dry season is July to August, when the river level falls as much as 40 feet (12 m). Year-round, torrential rain can break with cataclysmic force in late afternoon. Night falls dramatically, like a crimson theatrical curtain.

Leticia & Around

Occupying the north bank of the Amazon River, the capital of Amazonas is entirely landlocked at the juncture of Colombia, Brazil, and Peru. You can cross freely to Tabatinga (Brazil) or Santa Rosa (Peru).

Originally part of Peru, Leticia was founded in 1867 by Benigno Bustamante, a Peruvian military commander. It was ceded to Colombia in 1922. Tensions regarding possession erupted in outright war in 1932. The

The riverbank at Leticia, capital of Amazonas, is a hive of commercial activity.

League of Nations brokered a peace that in 1934 recognized Colombia's claim. Colombians from elsewhere in the country were encouraged to settle, boosting Leticia to the status of town. By the 1980s, Leticia was a wild, untamed center for cocaine traffic. Then the Colombian Army moved in, cleaned things up, and set up a base as a foil to the infiltration of Amazonas by leftist guerrillas. A heavily armed presence keeps Leticia and the immediate region safe.

This border town of 40,000 people feels very much the small, and vaguely sinister frontier town that it is. Almost everyone gets around by tricycle *moto*-taxis and motorcycles, which swarm without regard to traffic laws. Contraband trade and tourism keep the town afloat. The waterfront is a hive of activity. Pungent odors of coffee, cacao, and bananas waft up from the muddy banks, where fish large and small are landed still wriggling onto the Muelle Fluvial (river pier).

Otherwise, sites in town are few and can be seen in half a day. Begin with **Parque Santander,** the main square, where giant *Victoria amazonica* water lilies float atop a small lake. At dawn or dusk, thousands of *pericos*—small green parrots—flock, screeching in unison. At the southwest corner, the **Museo Etnográfico del Hombre Amazónico** (*Cra. 11 #9-43, tel 57-8/592-7783, closed Sun.*), in the Biblioteca del Banco de la República, is dedicated to local indigenous tribes, such as the Ticuna.

For an introduction to Amazon ecology visit **Parque Ecológico Mundo Amazónico,** a multidimensional complex where owner Rafael Clavijo teaches about indigenous farming and use of medicinal plants. It also has endemic animals, plus an aquarium with tropical fish.

Parque Ecológico Mundo Amazónico

✉ Vía Tarapacá km 7.7
☎ 57-8/592-6087
🕐 Open Sun. by appointment
💲 $
mundoamazonico.com

Choosing a Wilderness Guide

When it comes to spotting wildlife and learning about Colombia's flora and fauna, a wilderness guide is essential. The amazing interpretive ability of the finest guides includes an eagle-eye ability to spot and identify wildlife that the untrained eye will surely miss. The best guides have had a lifetime of experience in the field and have built solid reputations. Many are specialists in birds, botany, or herpetology, such as **Daniel Uribe** (*tel 57/ 315-585 7937, danieluribe.com),* perhaps the best birding guide in Colombia.

Maloka Yucuna: For a taste of indigenous culture, arrange a guided hike to Maloka Yucuna, 8 miles (13 km) north of town. At this small thatched homestead, Yucuna Amerindians still hunt with poison-tipped blow darts. You'll also be shown the preparation of coca leaves and how to inhale tobacco through the nose. Just getting to the *maloka* is a fun-filled adventure, as your guide slashes through the vines with a machete, adding just the right touch of jungle mystique. Visits can be arranged through local tour operators.

(continued on p. 256)

Poison Dart Frogs

Breathtaking in their beautiful coloration, poison dart frogs inhabit the warm moist forests of the neotropics of Central and South America. Most are no bigger than a thumbnail, though a few grow to 2 inches (5 cm) long. Notwithstanding their diminutive size, these tiny critters produce some of the deadliest toxins known to man.

A yellow-banded poison dart frog perches on a purple orchid.

These vividly colored frogs are members of the Dendrobatidae family. New species are still being discovered, such as the black-and-red *Ranitomeya dorisswansonae*, first identified in Colombia's Cordillera Central in 2006. Of the 170 or so recognized species, only one-third are known to be toxic.

Poison dart frogs produce bitter-tasting alkaloid compounds that are stored in microscopic mucous glands beneath the frog's skin; they cause any hungry predator to instantly gag. The most potent toxin of all is batrachotoxin, produced by the three extraordinarily lethal species of the *Phyllobates* genus. Found only in Colombia's Pacific lowlands and the Darién of Panama, these are the true poison dart frogs.

Chocó-Emberá Indians have traditionally used *Phyllobates'* secretions to coat the tips of blow darts they use to hunt monkeys and other game. The frogs typically secrete their deadly potions when they feel threatened. However, the silvery yellow, 2-inch-long (5 cm) *Phyllobates terribilis* is lethal to the touch for humans—even without being agitated. This frog's neurotoxin, 250 times more potent than strychnine, is so deadly that a toxin-tipped dart can remain lethal for more than a year.

Toxic to the Touch

The frogs derive their specific toxicity from their diets. The *Phyllobates'* batrachotoxin, for example, is ingested from a little-known group of tiny beetles of the *Choresine* genus that contains high concentrations of the neurotoxin. When removed from their natural diets, the amphibians gradually lose their toxicity.

Nature's touch-me-nots advertise their toxicity through brilliant coloration that serves as a warning to potential predators. Although some are uniform in coloration, typically they have a predominant Day-Glo color on top (usually bright red, orange, green, or blue) and a secondary ventral color (usually yellow, red, white, blue, or black) underneath. Individual species are highly endemic. For example, the *Dendrobates auratus* of Capurganá is green and black, *Dendrobates lehmanni* of Valle de Cauca is banded black and orange, and *Dendrobates*

INSIDER TIP:

Visit where Colombia, Peru, and Brazil meet to see the Amazon pink dolphins and journey into small towns that spring from the jungle.

—ERIC KRACHT
National Geographic Channels staff

fulguritus of the Chocó region is striped black and iridescent green.

Most poison dart frogs are ground dwellers, looking like enameled porcelain figures on the moist forest floor. Boldly diurnal, they hop around by day secure from predation. Males defend their territories and can often be seen wrestling chest to chest. Uniquely immune to the frog's toxin, the fire-bellied snake *(Leimadophis epinephelus)* is their only natural predator.

Poison dart frogs lay their eggs among the leaf litter and go to great lengths to safeguard their offspring. Once the eggs hatch, one parent (either female or male, depending on species) loads the tadpoles on its back and carries them one at a time into the trees, where it deposits them in water-filled leafy funnels of bromeliads. Female poison dart frogs visit their babies every few days to feed them by depositing unfertilized eggs in the water.

EXPERIENCE: Slow Boat to Brazil

Travel to Leticia for a trip downriver to Manaus in Brazil *(5 days)* or upriver to Iquitos in Peru *(12 hours)*. These adventurous trips can resemble a journey on the *African Queen,* depending on the vessel. Most boats are cramped and have shared cabins and hammocks (you may need to supply your own). The cost usually includes meals cooked on board. Vessels to Manaus depart Tabatinga, Leticia's Brazilian twin city, on Wednesday and Saturday. High-speed launches depart Tabatinga for Iquitos on Wednesday, Friday, and Sunday. Make arrangements through **Transportes Amazónicos** *(Calle 8 #11-183, Leticia, tel 57-8/592-5999, transportesamazonicos.com)* or **Transtur** *(Rua Marechal Mallet #349, Tabatinga, tel 97/8113-5239, e-mail: iquitostours@ hotmail.com).* You can also buy tickets at the dock in Tabatinga one or two days before departure.

**Reserva Natural
Tanimboca**

🅰 245 C1

✉ Vía Tarapacá
km 11, Cra. 10
#11-69

☎ 57/310-791-
7470 or 321-
207-9909

tanimboca.org

Isla de Los Micos

🅰 245 C1

Puerto Nariño

🅰 245 C1

Reserva Natural Tanimboca:
This private reserve is a great
place to learn about the rain forest ecosystem and spot wildlife,
including poison dart frogs. The
forest roads lead to a canopy tour,
where you can be winched up to a
treetop platform for a zip line ride
between treetops. A serpentarium
exhibits species of native snakes.
Resident guides share lore about
the use of plants for medicines
and practical items. You can overnight here in a hammock under
thatch, or in Indiana Jones–style
cabins high in the trees.

Isla de Los Micos: Named
for the squirrel monkeys that
inhabit this 1,112-acre (450 ha)
island reserve, Isla de Los Micos—
northwest of Leticia—can be visited on a day trip. The island was
once the private property of Mike
Tsalickis, a U.S. poacher who put
Leticia on the map in the 1960s
and was busted in 1989 for smuggling cocaine. The monkeys, which

include capuchins (white-faced)
and pygmy marmosets, are habitu-
ated to humans. Other activities
include trail hikes, canoeing on
lagoons, and an ascent into the
treetop canopy along *puentes col-
gantes*—suspension bridges. Excursions can be arranged through
Decameron (*Cra. 11 #6-11, Leticia,
tel 57-8/592-6600, $$$$$*), which
administers the isle.

Río Yavari: This river extends
west from the Amazon at Leticia
and forms the snaking border with
Peru (north) and Brazil (south).
Boat excursions along the river
and its tributaries do not require
a visa within 60 miles (100 km)
of the port (*a Brazilian visa must
be acquired in Tabatinga or Leticia if
you plan to go to Palmari*). To make
it worthwhile, plan on overnight-
ing at one of the several nature
reserves that flank the river.
The closest, **Reserva Natural
Zacambú,** 40 miles (70 km)
west of Leticia, is administered
by **Amazon Jungle Trips** (*Cra. 6
#6-25, Leticia, tel 57-8/592-7377,
amazonjungletrips.com.co*).

Puerto Nariño & Around

The riverside village of Puerto
Nariño is Amazonas Department's
second largest settlement, yet it
has only a mere 5,400 inhabitants,
mostly various Amerindians. Some
53 miles (85 km) upriver, west
of Leticia, it is reached by water
taxis operated by **Transportes
Amazonicos** (*Calle 8 #11, Leticia,
tel 57-8/592-5999*) and has several
simple lodgings. The community
occupies the north bank of a
madrevieja (oxbow lake)—the

Piranhas & Candirus

Tales of freshwater piranhas with shark-
like teeth stripping a human to the bone in
seconds are mostly myth. Recent research
suggests that these fish are loners. However, there are a few documented cases of
the much feared candiru, or toothpick fish,
darting up human urethras. This slender,
2-inch-long (3.5 cm) parasitic freshwater
catfish does impale itself (using rear-
pointing spines) inside the gills of larger
fish, then gorges itself with saw-action
teeth. Bathers are warned not to urinate
while swimming in Amazonian waters—
locals say the fish is drawn to the stream
and it can be extracted only by surgery.

EXPERIENCE: Appreciating the Indigenous Way of Life

The Spanish occupation proved devastating to indigenous cultures throughout Latin America. Today, Colombia has dozens of tribes, including those that continue to thrive and others that struggle under various contemporary pressures. Many villages have become heavily Westernized, while others cling tightly to their traditional customs. Tourism is now being promoted as a way of fostering a renewed pride in traditional beliefs, crafts, and customs among native communities throughout Colombia.

To experience indigenous culture and lifestyle, visit one of the following local Amazonian communities. Always remember to maintain a respectful understanding of local mores.

Maloka Huitoso (*Colombia Green Travel, tel 57/321-492-6467, colombiagreentravel.com*) is easily accessible and geared to tourism. The Huitotos community is just 6 miles (10 km) north of Leticia, where it keeps traditional practices alive.

La Guajira is home to the Wayúu, Colombia's largest indigenous group. Many Wayúu *rancherías* welcome visitors for overnights in homes of wood and cactus. **Kaishi Travel** (*tel 57-5/311-429-6315, kaishitravel.com*) specializes in ethno-tours of La Guajira Peninsula.

Pueblo Bello (*Unique Colombia, tel 57-1/344-1380, uniquecolombia.com*), in the Sierra Nevada de Santa Marta, is the gateway to the land of the Arhuaco. These indigenous people are distinguished by their wearing of white serapes and conical hats. With luck you may also be allowed to visit the sacred village of Nabusimake.

Dancers perform a traditional dance at Macedonia in Amazonas.

Comunidad Ticuna San Martín de Amacayacu (*Small World Foundation, smallworld foundation.org*) welcomes volunteers through the Small World Foundation to assist in community development.

Some tips to keep in mind throughout your visit:

• Some cultures avoid direct eye contact with strangers, and stares may be interpreted as rude or threatening. A smile can often break the ice.

• Many indigenous cultures have a village elder or leader. Asking advice or permission demonstrates your respect.

• Arrive with a small package of over-the-counter medicines, pens, or similar useful items to offer as a gift to the village leader.

• Cultures such as the Arhuaco and Guambiano are sensitive to being photographed without permission. If you have a digital camera, showing the subject his/her photograph may help.

• Buying local handicrafts or hiring local guides demonstrates you are not simply intent on taking, but that you wish to contribute to the community's welfare. A visit to these indigenous communities will give you an appreciation of traditional lifestyles.

Freshwater Dolphins

The Amazon river dolphin (*Inia geoffrensis*), or *boto* is a bubble gum pink freshwater dolphin endemic to the Amazon and Orinoco Rivers. The boto grows to about 8 feet (2.5 m) long, bigger than its gray saltwater cousin. It has a fat bulbous forehead with beady eyes, and a humped back with a low dorsal fin and huge flippers. Its skinny, elongated, toothy beak is just right for rooting around in mud for crustaceans or snatching at fleeting fish among a tangle of underwater roots. Its neck vertebrae are also unfused, permitting it to curl 90 degrees like a sinuous snake. It is listed as "data deficient" as of 2011 by the International Union for Conservation of Nature.

Centro de Interpretación Natútama

✉ 150 feet (50 m) E of dock

☎ 57/ 312-410-1925

🕐 Closed Tues.

💲 $

natutama.org

Parque Nacional Natural Amacayacu

🗺 245 C2–C3

E-mail: amacayacu@ parquesnacionales .gov.co

Quebrada Menoe—connected by waterway to the Amazon River.

Puerto Nariño is considered a model ecological village, laid out in a grid of concrete paths framed by well-clipped lawns and picket fences, behind which simple wooden homes have gardens bursting with *Fantasia*-like foliage. It makes a great base for exploring this section of the Amazon River. Start walking at the tourist information booth near the *muelle* (pier). Now head to the hilltop **Mirador Naipata II**—a lookout tower (*Calle 4, closed 12 p.m.– 2 p.m., $*) that offers a sweeping view. To learn more about Amerindian Cocama, Ticuna, and Yagua cultures, visit the **Casa Museo Cultural Ya Ipata Ünchi** (*Cra. 7 & Calle 5, closed Sat.–Sun.*), which has exhibits; and the **Casa Artesanal Tachiwagü** (*Cra. 6 bet. Calle 5 & 6, closed Sat.–Sun., $*), a thatched maloka where elders teach about the indigenous lifestyle.

The **Centro de Interpretación Natútama** teaches about conservation issues using life-size reproductions of manatees, river dolphins, and other Amazon aquatic denizens. It's on the north side of Quebrada Menoe, by the muelle. Next door, the **Fundación Omacha** (*Calle 86A #23-38, Bogotá, tel 57-1/256-4682, omacha .org*) serves the same purpose and welcomes volunteers for its conservation project to save the endangered boto (Amazon river dolphin) and manatee.

Lago Tarapoto: To see botos (and perhaps manatees) in the flesh, hire a fisherman to take you in a peque-peque (motorized dugout canoe) to this lake, about 1.2 mile (2 km) west of Puerto Nariño. This natural aquarium is frequented by Amazon river dolphins, which may leap around your canoe. When the river is low, Lago Tarapoto may be inaccessible. Then, your guide can take you to the **Lago San Juan del Socó** or to the **Río Cacao.** Scarlet ibises and stilt-legged egrets patrol the riverbanks, their heads tilted forward, their long bills jabbing for tasty tidbits.

Parque Nacional Natural Amacayacu

Taking up much of the Amazon trapezoid, this national park protects 1,133 square miles (2,934 sq km) of rain forests and swamp forests of the Amazon floodplain. Amacayacu also serves to preserve the indigenous Ticuna culture by integrating the indigenous communities into ecotourism. The park is the best place in the region for viewing a pristine Amazonian landscape and the teeming wildlife that call it home. Six macaw species are among its 470 species of birds. Twelve monkey species leap from branch to branch, among them the world's smallest primate, the pygmy marmoset.

The riverside **Yewaé Visitor Center**, 7 miles (12 km) is east of Puerto Nariño. The half-mile-long (0.8 km) **Sendero de la Selva** (Forest Trail) boardwalk leads through the dense and humid tropical tangle. Stay on the boardwalk, especially around dusk when deadly fer-de-lance snakes become active. In rainy season, the river spills over a large part of the region; then, you can explore by peque-peque, paddling through narrow waterways—a chance to

spot manatees, river otters, plus four crocodilian species. *Lanchas* run daily from Leticia to Amacayacu *(8 a.m., 10 a.m., & 12 p.m.)* en route to Puerto Nariño; return lanchas pass by for Leticia at 7:30 a.m., 11 a.m., and 4 p.m.

The 4-mile-long (7 km) **Sendero Nainekumawa** leads from Yawaé to **San Martín de Amacayacu,** an indigenous village where visitors can participate in basketry, weaving, and wood-carving workshops. The indigenous community of **Macedonia,** a 15-minute boat ride east from Yawaé, also provides an insight into self-sustaining community living, supplemented by sales of handmade crafts and displays of traditional dance. Nearby, the private **Reserva Calanoa** offers birding, hiking, and canoeing, plus art workshops with the local indigenous community. ∎

Reserva Calanoa
- ✉ 0.6 miles (1 km) NW of Macedonia
- ☎ 57/ 350-316-7210
- $ $$$

calanoaamazonas.com

An Amazon river dolphin *(boto)* surfaces in the Río Cacao.

TRAVELWISE

Planning Your Trip 260–262 • Further Reading 262 • How to Get to Colombia 262 • Getting Around 262–264 • Practical Advice 264–267 • Emergencies 267–269 • Health 269 • Hotels & Restaurants 270–303 • Shopping 304–307 • Entertainment 308–309 • Outdoor Activities 310–311

Chivas are often the only form of public transportation serving many remote mountain zones.

PLANNING YOUR TRIP

When to Go

Time your visit according to where you wish to visit, as the country's climate varies by region, divided in the Colombian lexicon into the *tierra caliente* (hot land), *tierra templada* (temperate land), *tierra fría* (cold land), and *tierra helada* (frozen land). Summer is a meaningless term this close to the Equator. Temperatures vary with elevation rather than with latitude.

More than three-quarters of Colombia, including Amazonia and the Pacific and Caribbean lowlands, lie in the hot zone, below 2,953 feet (900 m) in elevation, where temperatures vary between 75°F and 100°F (24°C–38°C). High season on most of the Caribbean coast coincides with the drier winter weather, but delightful weather is the norm throughout the wetter summer months, when rains typically mean afternoon downpours and trade winds help cool things. La Guajira is an exception: Rains rarely fall on this region. Elsewhere, be prepared for stifling humidity, and for year-round rains in Amazonia and Chocó (one of the wettest regions in the world), where torrential rains peak in late winter.

The Andean highlands at elevations between 2,953 and 6,562 feet (900–2,000 m) enjoy a year-round spring-like climate, with warm to temperate weather. Bogotá, for example, averages 59°F (15°C) year-round with only limited variation

month to month. The daily range is more significant: The daily variation in temperature can range from 68°F (20°C) during the day to 37°F (3°C) at night. Medellín and Cali are somewhat warmer, with mean annual temperatures between 66°F and 75°F (19°C–24°C). In typical years, the highlands are marked by two dry seasons (*Jan.–March & July–Sept.*) and two wet seasons (*April–June & Oct.–Dec.*). The wet season usually means clear mornings and afternoon showers, although prolonged heavy rains are possible. There is considerable variation, however, and intermontane valleys display their own microclimates.

Between 6,562 and 11,483 feet (2,000–3,500 m) (tierra fría), mountain slopes have alpine climates, often with frequent fog and high winds. The upper limit of the cold zone marks tree line and the approximate limit of human habitation, above which the tierra helada is often snowbound, with nights below freezing.

With so much variation, including year-round festivals, there is no "correct" or even "best" time to visit. Nonetheless, many of Colombia's most important festivals take place December–March and June–August. Beyond Cartagena, Colombia's tourism infrastructure is geared to the domestic market. Colombia's peak tourism season is December to February, when Colombians vacation en masse (principally at beach resorts) and prices rise significantly. Easter is also busy.

What to Take

Dress according to the climatic zones you'll be visiting. In general, lightweight, loose-fitting cotton and synthetic clothes are best. Loose-fitting shorts and T-shirts prove comfortable and are acceptable everywhere, including Cali, Cartagena, and Medellín. You'll want some more elegant wear for nighttime, especially for ritzier restaurants and nightclubs and for business meetings. Pack a pair of jeans for Bogotá, where a sweater and/or lightweight jacket is also a must for the occasional cold days and at night.

In the hot, humid lowlands avoid tight-fitting clothes, which are uncomfortable and promote fungal growth. A poncho works well against warm-season downpours, and a fold-up umbrella is recommended for city slicking. Bring swimwear if you plan on heading to the beach. Colombians put great stead in cleanliness–both bodily and clothingwise.

Visits to highland areas require cold-weather clothing, including a windproof jacket for hiking the alpine zones.

Waterproof hiking shoes are a must for exploring mountain trails or wilderness areas, where you should expect to get muddy and wet. You'll want a comfortable pair of walking shoes for exploring the cities; sneakers work fine. And dress shoes are de rigueur at many restaurants and nightclubs. Avoid bright colors (which can frighten away wildlife) if you plan on birding or nature hikes.

You'll need insect repellent, particularly for coastal and humid areas and during wet season in lowland cities. Mosquitoes can be ferocious, and there are plenty of other biting insects in the forests. Rarely are mosquitoes a problem in upland or breeze-swept areas.

Sunglasses are a necessity, as the tropical light is intense, and a sun hat or baseball cap and sunscreen are mandatory, even for brief periods outdoor. Do not underestimate the strength of the tropical sun.

Medicines are widely available. However, you should bring a basic first-aid kit that includes aspirins, Lomotil, antiseptic lotions, Band-Aids, and other essential medications. Bring a spare pair of glasses or contact lenses rather than a prescription.

Similarly, bring all the photographic equipment you'll need, as this is in short supply outside the major cities. Birders should also bring binoculars.

Insurance

Travel insurance is a wise investment. Some of the companies that provide coverage for Colombia include **American Express** (tel 1-800-297-2977, american express.com), **World Nomads** (tel 1-844-207-1930, worldnomads .com), and **TravelGuard** (tel 800/ 826-4919, travelguard.com). **Assist-Card** (tel 1-866-477-6741, wsusa.assist-card.com), based in Florida, has regional assistance centers throughout Colombia

(tel 57-1-8000-910684) and offers comprehensive coverage.

Entry Formalities
Passport & Visas

Citizens of the United States, Canada, and most European nations require a valid passport to enter Colombia. Tourists are permitted stays of 60 days; your stay can be extended for increments of 30 days (US$33) up to six months total by applying to the **Departamento Administrativo de Seguridad** (DAS; *Calle 100 #11B-29, Bogotá, tel 57/01-8000-510454, migracioncolombia .gov.co*). There are also immigration offices in most cities. You must present a valid passport showing stamp of entry, your return ticket (plus a photocopy), four color photographs with a white background, and two photocopies of the ID page and the entry stamp page of your passport. You must pay the fee at specific banks.

You must show a Colombian entry stamp in your passport to be permitted to exit the country. Make a photocopy of the page in the event that your passport is stolen while in Colombia.

Proof of yellow fever vaccination is required for travel to Amazonia, and when crossing between Colombia and neighboring countries, plus Costa Rica.

Canadian visitors are charged US$80 upon entry.

Customs

Colombia's customs bureau, DIAN (Dirección de Impuestos y Aduana Nacional), permits visitors to bring in personal items such as cameras and climbing and sporting gear. Colombia law prohibits the trade or exportation of all wildlife species or products, and of important works of art or historic items, including any pre-Columbian items, considered national treasures. Upon departure, you can request a departure tax exemption (normally US$66) for stays of 60 days or less, as well as a refund of the 16 percent IVA (sales tax) for purchases during your stay.

FURTHER READING

No visit to Colombia would be complete without at least one of Gabriel García Márquez's novels in your carry-on luggage. Here are five must-reads:

A Guide to the Birds of Colombia, by Steven L. Hilty & William L. Brown (1986). Beautifully illustrated field guide to the local avian world, including key birding sites.

Emeralds: A Passionate Guide, by Ronald Ringsrud (2010). A lavishly illustrated, passion-filled coffee-table book that fascinates with the lore and allure of this exotic green gemstone.

Love in the Time of Cholera, by Gabriel García Márquez (1989). Florentino, rejected by the pubescent Fermina, indulges in a life of carnal affairs to heal his broken heart. Set in Cartagena.

One Hundred Years of Solitude, by Gabriel García Márquez (1967). Márquez's most celebrated novel, for which he won the Nobel Prize, regales the rise and fall of the fictional village of Macondo. Magic realism at its most masterful.

Out of Captivity: Surviving 1,967 Days in the Colombian Jungle, by Marc Gonsalves, Keith Stansell, & Tom Howes with Gary Brozek (2009). A vivid and haunting personal account of five and a half years as captives of FARC, as told by three U.S. civilian contractors captured in 2003, following a plane crash in the Colombian jungle.

HOW TO GET TO COLOMBIA
By Air

Colombia is served by direct, nonstop flights from major North American cities, such as Atlanta, Miami, New York, and Toronto; and by direct flights from France, Germany, and Spain. However, from Europe it is usually cheaper to fly via Miami. The majority of flights arrive at Bogotá's recently upgraded El Dorado International Airport *(tel 57-1/425-1000, eldorado .aero).* Other international flights arrive in Barranquilla, Cali, Cartagena, and Medellín. In 2015, the government announced plans to build a second international airport in Bogotá by 2021.

The official taxi booth is outside the customs arrival hall at El Dorado airport; you will be given a receipt with the exact fare to pay the driver. The official rate for a tourist taxi between El Dorado International Airport and downtown is about US$15. Never take a private or illegal taxi from the airport; robberies are frequent and you will overpay.

Colombia's main airline, **Avianca** *(tel 1-800/284-2622, avianca .com)* serves more than 40 destinations throughout the Americas, including flights from Fort Lauderdale, Los Angeles, Miami, and New York to Barranquilla, Bogotá, Cali, and Medellín.

The following U.S. airlines offer regular flights to Colombia: **American Airlines** *(tel 800/433-7300, aa.com),* **United** *(tel 800/864-8331, united.com),* **Delta Airlines** *(tel 800/221-1212, delta.com),* **JetBlue** *(tel 800/538-2583, jetblue.com),* and **Spirit Airlines** *(tel 800/772-7117, spiritair.com).*

By Sea

More than a dozen major cruise lines include Cartagena on their itineraries. For information, contact the **Cruise Lines International Association** *(tel 855/444-2542, cruising.org).*

Private sailboats and cargo boats can be chartered from Panama's San Blas Islands (US$350–US$650). The journey between Portobelo or Puerto Olbadía, Panama, to Cartagena, Capurganá, or Turbo typically takes five days. The largest vessel making the journey is the German-skippered *Stahlratte (stahlratte.org).*

Group Tours

Many travelers opt for the added security of a packaged tour to explore Colombia. Relatively few North American companies offer group tours. Check with your local travel agency.

Most tours focus on cultural highlights, such as Villa de Leyva, the Catedral de Sal, and Santa Fé de Antioquia. A few others focus on nature (especially birding).

GETTING AROUND
Around Colombia
By Air

In addition to the international carriers, Colombia has several domestic airlines serving airports throughout the country. Competition keeps fares low.

Avianca, tel 57-800-095-3434, avianca.com. Colombia's principal airline serves more than 20 domestic destinations.

Copa Airlines, tel 57-1/320-9090, copaair.com. This subsidiary of Panama's Copa Airlines serves 11 domestic destinations.

Easyfly, tel 57-1/414-8111, easy fly.com.co. This budget airline has low fares to 15 locations.

LAN, tel 800/094-9490 (US toll free), lan.com. This airline has flights to 22 destinations within Colombia.

SATENA, tel 57-01/800-091-034, satena.com. This government-owned airline has the widest network of flights, with 39 destinations.

By Bus

Buses from Bogotá to destinations throughout Colombia operate from El Terminal de Transporte *(Diagonal 23 #69-55, tel 57-1/423-3630, terminalde transporte.gov.co),* 3 miles (5 km) west of the city center. The terminal is divided into five modules, color-coded by destination (blue/east and west; red/north; yellow/south; green and purple/taxis).

More than 50 private companies provide fast *(directo)* and/or slower *(regular)* service nationwide. One of the largest companies, **Bolivariano** *(tel 57-1/424-9090, bolivariano.com.co)* links Bogotá with some 20 cities nationwide.

Long-distance service is typically by large modern, air-conditioned bus with reclining seats. Similar service is also offered between other major cities. Farther afield, regional buses can mean anything from a former U.S. school bus to *chivas* (trucks with open-air bench seats) or Willys Jeeps.

Buses, *busetas,* and *colectivos* are the staple of transportation within cities; most are slow, crowded, and charge a set fare, payable to the driver or his assistant. Criminal gangs have infiltrated many routes in recent years, especially in Bogotá.

Buses in Colombia are usually crowded; you should avoid travel on weekends if possible, and always guard against pickpockets and luggage theft.

By Rental Car

Renting a car gives you the most flexibility in your sightseeing. However, car rental is extremely expensive and not without risks. City traffic is dense and chaotic, and few Colombian drivers obey road rules; lane discipline, for example, is nonexistent. Driving is unpredictable: "Dog eat dog" and "Devil take the hindmost" are the philosophies. Car theft is a major problem, as is theft of items inside vehicles, and the renter is liable for 20 percent of the car's value if stolen or damaged.

To rent a car you should be over 25 (some agencies permit younger drivers with credit cards) and hold a passport and a valid driver's license (your home country driver's license will suffice). You will also need a credit card and have to leave a hefty deposit (about US$500). Car rental is expensive. Expect to pay a minimum of US$70 a day plus insurance. Scrutinize insurance and liability clauses before signing a rental contract, paying close attention to any theft clause.

Colombia Rent-a-Car, tel 57-1/300-4050, colombiarent acar.co

Hertz, tel 57-1/756-0600, hertzcolombia.com.co

Dollar, tel 57-1/318-9397, dollar.com. Rents the four-wheel-drive Toyota Prado and is reliable.

By Car

Parts of the nation's 70,000-mile (113,000 km) road network are well maintained with U.S.-style markings. However, some major roads are still in fair to poor condition. Almost all major roads are now safe to travel by day or night, with police and army security points at regular intervals. However, landslides and subsidence are common, and many secondary roads are unpaved. A four-wheel-drive vehicle is recommended for more remote areas and for access to many national parks.

Roads are funded by tolls (typically C$3,000–C$12,000/US$1.70–US$6.75), and tollbooths are found at regular distances, sometimes on even minor country roads. Carry plenty of small bills.

Warning: Stick to main roads wherever possible. Nighttime driving should be avoided, especially in more remote areas, where guerrillas, paramilitaries, or bandits may still operate. Keep the car doors locked at all times, and maintain at least a half tank of gas.

Most gas stations don't accept credit cards. In areas close to Venezuela, such as around Cúcuta and La Guajira, gas stations are a dime a dozen and hundreds of roadside vendors sell gas (poured from plastic bottles) at a fraction of the price of elsewhere in Colombia.

In Bogotá and most major cities, a vehicle restriction rule—*pico y placa*—applies to all noncommercial vehicles, which are barred from the city on specific weekdays according to the vehicle license plate's last digit (see sidebar p. 171).

By Taxi

Nationwide, taxis are the mainstay of inner-city travel, and every town is well stocked with small Hyundai Astro taxis. The same rules apply as for taxis in Bogotá. Your hotel can hail a radio cab or provide a list of recommended taxi companies. In Cartagena, the taxis have stickers displaying fares based on zones. Hailing a taxi off the street isn't safe.

Group Tours

Many visitors choose a packaged excursion as a safe and easy way to explore. Colombia has several dozen reputable tour agencies, including the following:

Aventure Colombia, Calle de Santisimo #8-55, Cartagena, tel

57/314-588-2378, aventure colombia.com. Specializes in small-group travel around Cartagena plus programs nationwide.

Aviatur, tel 57-1/587-5222, aviatur.com. Specializes in tours of Colombia's national parks. Has offices in most cities.

Colombia 57, tel 57-6/886-8050, colombia57.com. Specializes in tours of the Zona Cafetera, luxury travel, and personalized itineraries nationwide. Knowledgeable, conscientious, and efficient, its attention to detail and quality service are proven hallmarks.

Gema Tours, tel 57-1/653-5800, gematours.com. One of Colombia's largest and oldest companies.

Kaishi Travel, tel 57-5/717-7306, kaishitravel.com. One of the leading operators specializing in La Guajira Peninsula.

Uncover Colombia, tel 57/310-865-0695, uncovercolombia.com. Array of day trips around Bogotá, plus longer tours.

In Bogotá
By Bus
Bogotá has a comprehensive bus network. Several private companies compete using a variety of buses and colectivos (minivans), which can be flagged down anywhere along their routes. Flat fares are about C$1,400 (US$0.75). The TransMilenio rapid transit system (C$1,500–1,800/US$0.48–US$0.57) operates articulated buses along eight major dedicated busways; smaller buses link major routes with residential areas. The TransMilenio network has been expanded to serve the airport.

By Taxi
Taxis are the staple form of getting around in town. Small and nimble Hyundai taxis, painted yellow, are cheap and numerous.

Most taxi fares are based on meters. Many thefts have been reported by people hailing taxis off the street; whenever possible (and always at night), call a radio-dispatched taxi, such as **Cooptele-taxi** (tel 57-1/611-1111) or **Taxi Express** (tel 57-1/411-1111). The dispatcher will give you the taxi's license plate; double-check that you are getting into the correct cab. White hotel taxis also operate but charge more than yellow taxis. The tourism ministry issues a "Visitors Taxi Transportation Aid Card" for each major city.

PRACTICAL ADVICE
Communications
E-mail & Internet
Most towns have Internet cafés (usually charging bet. US$1–US$2 per hour), and most tourist hotels are wired for Internet use or have business centers. Free Wi-Fi is a norm in hotels nationwide; others charge US$5 or more per day.

Post Offices
Colombia's postal system is dysfunctional and expensive. The state-run 4-72 (4-72.com.co), formally Administración Postal Nacional (ADPOSTAL), competes with a hodgepodge of private courier companies and has offices throughout the country. Its post offices hours are Monday–Friday 8 a.m.–5 p.m. and Saturday 8 a.m.–noon. The cost of mailing a postcard or letter to North America begins at C$6,100 (US$3.35) and at C$6,600 (US$3.62) to Europe, but more if certified. Allow at least one week for mail to the United States or Canada, and at least ten days for mail to Europe.

You cannot simply mail a letter in a streetside mailbox (there are none). You must buy stamps, register the letter, and be fingerprinted at a post office.

However, service is unreliable and many people use private mail and courier services. **DHL** (tel 57-1/746-9696, dhl.com.co) and **FedEx** (tel 57-1/291-0100, fedex.com/co_english) have offices throughout Colombia and offer reliable express international and domestic service.

Never mail anything of value as theft is common.

Telephones
Colombia has a relatively modern and efficient telephone system. **Telecom** (telecomcolombia.com) is one of the companies that operates landline service, including telephone booths. There are very few public telephones. Three companies provide cellular (mobile) service: **Comcel** (comcel.com), the largest provider, **Movistar** (movistar.co), and **Tigo** (tigo.com.co).

Telephone numbers have seven digits, preceded by a single-digit area code (landlines) or a carrier-specific three-digit prefix (mobile phones). Domestic calls require dialing "0" plus an access code specific to each carrier—5 (Comcel), 7 (Movistar), or 9 (Tigo)—before dialing the area code and telephone number. Making calls between different carriers is expensive, for which reason many Colombians have multiple phones (one for each company). Others receive calls (which are free) on their mobile phones and make calls using any of thousands of street vendors who rent use of mobile phones by the minute at discount rates; look for signs advertising "llamadas" or "minutos."

When calling a mobile phone from a landline, dial 03 plus the prefix and phone number. To call a landline from a mobile phone, dial 03 plus the city code and phone number.

You can bring your cell phone from home, but not all will work in Colombia. You can purchase a cheap cell phone and minutes in Colombia at any Comcel, Movistar, or Tigo office, or at some supermarkets and other outlets.

For direct-dial international calls, dial 009, then the country code and area code, then the number. Calling from abroad, dial 00 (from Europe) or 011 (from North America), plus Colombia's country code 57, then the area code and number. When dialing mobile phones, substitute the carrier access code for the area code.

For directory inquiries, dial 113.

Hotels charge a high fee for calls from in-room phones. Some Internet cafés double as call centers and have cheap rates. **Skype** (*skype.com*) offers the cheapest option for international calls, via the Internet.

Conversions

Colombia uses the metric system for measurement. Here are some useful conversions:

1 mile = 1.61 kilometers
1 kilometer = 0.62 mile
1 meter = 39.37 inches
1 liter = 0.264 U.S. gallon
10 liters = 2.64 U.S. gallons
1 U.S. gallon = 3.79 liters
1 kilogram = 2.2 pounds
1 pound = 0.45 kilogram

Weather reports use Celsius. To convert quickly (but roughly) from Fahrenheit to Celsius, subtract 30 and divide by two. From Celsius to Fahrenheit, multiply by two and add 30.

0°C = 32°F
10°C = 50°F
20°C = 68°F
30°C = 86°F
100°C = 212°F

Electricity

Colombia operates on 110-volt AC (60 cycles) nationwide, although a few more remote places use 220 volts. Most outlets use U.S. flat, two-, or three-pin plugs. Many more remote parts of the country, such as much of La Guajira, do not have electricity; here restaurants and hotels rely on generators or solar power, and often service is limited to certain hours of the day.

Etiquette & Local Customs

Colombian society is diverse. Life in Bogotá and other big cities is cosmopolitan and relatively liberal, while smaller towns and rural villages are far more conservative. Society remains extremely class conscious, with campesinos (peasant farmers), the urban working class, and many indigenous people deferring to people considered of higher status. Colombians respect professional titles and use them when addressing titleholders, such as engineers (e.g., *Ingeniero* Arosamena) and architects (*Arquitecto* Garcia).

Adults are addressed as *Señor* (Mr.), *Señora* (Mrs.), or *Señorita* (Miss). The terms *Don* (for men) and *Doña* (for women) are used for high-ranking or respected individuals and senior citizens. Life revolves around the family. Personal contacts are the key to success, particularly in business and politics.

Behavior is often dictated by a desire to leave a good impression. Colombians are courteous and use courtesies more frequently in writing and speech than North Americans. However, verbal commitments are not necessarily meant to be taken at face value, and a Colombian may say "yes" when he/she means "no" simply to maintain harmony. Colombians normally use the formal *usted* form of "you," while the informal *tu* form is reserved for intimates. Women greet each other by kissing the air next to the cheek; there is usually no contact except between family members and close friends. Hugs (*abrazos*) are also generally used only among close friends and family. The normal greeting is *buenos días* (good morning), *buenas tardes* (good afternoon), or *buenas noches* (good evening). A more informal greeting is *hola* (hi).

Colombians are extremely proud of their country and are sensitive to criticism by foreigners, particularly U.S. citizens due to lingering animosities fueled by past U.S.-Colombian relations. Many indigenous communities are extremely sensitive to intrusions or insults to their culture. Many rural and indigenous folk are also shy and do not like having their photographs taken.

Outside the main tourist areas and business centers you may not be understood in English, so it is advisable to learn a few Spanish phrases. Many restaurants in cities have menus in English, although you may have to ask for them.

Bathing suits are frowned on away from the beach.

Holidays

In addition to Christmas, New Year, and Easter, Colombia observes the following national holidays. Some days change year to year, so check the calendar:

January 6, Día de Los Reyes Magos (Epiphany)
March 19, Día de San José (Saint Joseph's Day)
May 1, Día del Trabajo (May Day)
Ascensión (Ascencion) Monday, six weeks and a day after Easter Sunday
Corpus Christi Monday, nine weeks and a day after Easter Sunday
Sagrado Corazón (Sacred Heart) Monday, ten weeks and a day after Easter Sunday

July 2, Día de San Pedro y San Pablo (St. Peter's and St. Paul's Day

July 20, Día de la Independencia (Independence Day)

August 7, Batalla de Boyacá (Battle of Boyacá)

August 20, La Ascunción de Nuestra Señora (Assumption of Mary)

October 15, Día de la Raza (Columbus Day)

November 5, Todos los Santos (All Saints' Day)

November 12, Independencia de Cartagena (Independence of Cartagena)

December 8, Inmaculada Concepción (Immaculate Conception)

Most tourist sites and services stay open for these holidays, but banks and government offices close.

Liquor & Smoking Laws
Driving while under the influence of alcohol is illegal; a conviction of drunk driving will nullify any insurance coverage for rented cars and probably land you in jail. You do not want to see the inside of a Colombian jail.

In 2008, Colombia enacted a sweeping antismoking law banning smoking in all public venues, from hospitals to hotels, restaurants, bars, and all enclosed public places. Nonetheless, a large percentage of Colombians smoke, and smoking in public places is neither frowned upon nor forbidden.

Cigarettes, including rough, locally made brands and popular U.S. brands, are sold at stores and on the street.

Media
Internet Resources
Colombia Reports (colombiareports .com) publishes daily news online in English, as does **Bogota Free Planet** (bogotafreeplanet.com). *The City Paper* (thecitypaperbogota.com)

is a thoughtful English-language monthly published by longtime Colombian expat resident Richard Emblin.

Newspapers & Magazines
Colombia has three major national newspapers, published in Spanish and available at newsstands around the country. The excellent daily *El Tiempo* sets the standard for quality journalism and covers everything from politics to fashion; *El Colombiano* and *El Espectador* are also good. There are also numerous regional newspapers.

Colombians are extremely literate, and there are plenty of newsagents and magazine stores. Major U.S. magazines, such as *Time*, and dailies, are usually available at leading hotel gift stores.

Several upscale news and lifestyle magazines are published locally, including *Semana* and *SoHo*.

Television & Radio
Television reaches everywhere in Colombia, which has more than two dozen TV stations. Most hotels offer cable or satellite TV with U.S. programs. Colombia has dozens of radio stations. All but a few broadcast local news and Latin music. There is no English-language station, however. The BBC World Service and Voice of America offer English-language news.

Money Matters
Colombia's currency is the peso (often denoted as COP$ or C$). Coins are issued in 50, 100, 200, and 500 peso denominations. Banknotes are issued in 1,000, 2,000, 5,000, 10,000, 20,000, and 50,000 peso denominations. U.S. dollars are rarely accepted for direct payment except in major tourist hotels, which will also change dollars into pesos (usually for a significant commission).

Most cities have private exchange bureaus. U.S. dollars are not widely accepted in banks, which can change dollars for pesos.

Visitors may experience trouble cashing traveler's checks anywhere but banks, due to widespread fraud and holds imposed by banks. Many shops will refuse to accept them.

Take all the cash you think you'll need for a stay in La Guajira and other remote regions, such as Chocó and Amazonia. In these out-of-the-way spots, it is best to carry plenty of small denomination bills.

ATMs
Most banks have ATMs that accept debit and credit cards issued outside Colombia; a fee is typically charged for overseas transactions. Most ATMs limit the amount that can be withdrawn to C$300,000 (about US$160), although some branches permit as much as C$500,000. Most banks permit two or three withdrawals per day.

A healthy dose of paranoia is useful when using ATMs. Always be aware of your environment before and after withdrawing money. Never use a street-front ATM; use a secure ATM booth inside a bank, supermarket, or shopping mall. Put your money away before exiting the ATM booth. Attempt to ascertain if you're being followed before exiting to the street.

Advise your banks of your travel plans for Colombia before leaving; otherwise they may assume that your card has been stolen and freeze your account.

Credit Cards
Credit cards (*tarjetas de crédito*) are widely accepted in all major hotels, restaurants, shops, and many gas stations. Visa is the most commonly accepted,

followed by MasterCard and American Express. Know the number to call if you lose your credit card, and be quick to cancel it if it's lost or stolen.

Opening Times

Opening hours for stores vary widely. Stores typically open Monday–Saturday 9 a.m.–5 p.m., but malls, supermarkets, and many souvenir stores have longer hours and also stay open on Sunday. Museums normally close on Monday.

Banks typically open Monday–Thursday 8 a.m.–11:30 a.m. and 2 p.m.–4 p.m., and Friday until 4:30 p.m. Businesses are typically open Monday–Friday 9 a.m.–5 p.m. but might extend until 7 p.m.; travel agencies and tourist-related businesses also open on Saturday 8 a.m.–12 p.m., and they do not close for lunch. Most government offices are open weekdays 8 a.m.–5 p.m.

Places of Worship/ Religion

Most communities have at least one Roman Catholic church and often a Protestant church. Local tourist information offices and leading hotels can usually supply a list of places of worship. Many churches open only for services.

Restrooms

There are very few public restroom facilities (baños). Most bus stations and restaurants have restrooms. Many facilities, including many budget hotels, request that you deposit toilet paper in a receptacle rather than in the toilet bowl, to avoid blocking the drains.

In Amazonia and La Guajira, some accommodations in more remote areas have over-the-water toilets that dump waste directly into the river. Toilet paper is rarely

available in these places; bring your own.

Time Differences

Colombia time is the same as U.S. Eastern Standard Time (EST), five hours behind Greenwich mean time (GMT). Colombia does not observe daylight savings time, so half the year it is on the same time as Central Daylight Savings Time.

Tipping

Tipping is not a fact of life in Colombia except in tourist areas, where many people in service jobs depend on tips to make ends meet. A 10 percent service charge is added onto restaurant bills, where an extra tip should be given for good service. Hotel porters should be given US$1 per bag (airport porters also expect US$1), and room service staff US$2 per day. Taxi drivers do not expect a tip.

In the countryside, park rangers, boat guides, and others often provide services for which a tip is in order, albeit not expected. Consider it good karma. Tour guides should be tipped for personalized services, and a communally collected tip is often the norm on group tours.

Travelers With Disabilities

With the exception of upscale hotels and recent constructions, few buildings have wheelchair access or provide special toilets or suites. Few buses are adapted for wheelchairs, except for newer TransMilenio and Metro systems, and few curbs are dropped at corners. The Colombian government has set a goal for 100 percent of urban buses to be wheelchair accessible, but progress is slow.

Traveling in Amazonas, La Guajira, and by water poses special barriers.

The following agencies provide information on aspects of traveling abroad for visitors with disabilities:

Gimp on the Go, gimponthe go.com. Internet-based newsletter and forum for disabled travelers.

Disability Rights UK, 49-51 East Rd., London N1 6AH, tel 44-020/7250-8181, disabilityrights uk.org.

Society for Accessible Travel & Hospitality, 347 5th Ave. Ste. 605, New York, NY 10016, tel 212/447-7284, sath.org.

Visitor Information

ProColombia (tel 305/374-3144 in the U.S.) maintains a user-friendly website: colombia.travel. ProColombia is headquartered at Calle 28A #13A-15, Bogotá, tel 57-1/307-8028, but has 15 regional tourist information bureaus (PITs) around the country, all with bilingual staff. The locations and hours of each PIT are displayed on the ProColombia website.

The **Bogotá Tourism Institute** (Cra. 24 #40-66, tel 57-1/217-0711, bogotaturismo.gov.co), the tourism board, is headquartered in Chapinero. It publishes an excellent sightseeing map of Bogotá plus themed brochures, and has 16 tourist information offices throughout the city, including at El Dorado International Airport.

The **Ministerio de Cultura** (Cra. 8 #8-43, Bogotá, tel 57-1/342-4100, www.mincultura.gov.co) promotes four cultural routes, with foldout guides in Spanish on each.

The **Instituto Geográfico Agustín Codazzi** (Cra. 30 #48-51, Bogotá, tel 57-1/369-4000, igac.gov .co) sells topographic maps.

EMERGENCIES
Crime & Police

Crime in major cities can be a significant problem; tourists are especially prone to becoming victims. Caution should be exercised at all times, particularly in Bogotá's historic La Candelaria district, in impoverished urban zones, and by night in all downtown areas, where the threat of knife-point robberies and muggings is severe. Generally speaking, if you're the victim of a robbery, do not resist (Bogotá reported 102 people killed in the first six months of 2010 while resisting robberies involving knives). Don't walk alone at night in cities: Take a radio-dispatched taxi, even if only traveling a few blocks. Do not hail taxis off the street day or night; many robberies have been reported.

Secuestro express is a major problem in cities: Victims are kidnapped (often in taxis hailed off the street) for as long as it takes to be driven to sufficient ATMs to empty their bank account and max out their credit card; or for as long as it takes for the victim's travel companion (or family) to do the same.

Everywhere, there is a danger of pickpockets and snatch-and-grab theft, so be especially wary in crowded areas, such as buses and markets. Car break-ins are a problem, even in supposedly "secure" parking lots. Never leave items unattended, including on beaches. Do not carry large quantities of cash (however, it is considered wise to carry at least US$50 to hand over in the event of a robbery), avoid wearing a watch and jewelry, and keep passports and credit cards out of sight. Scams are also common, especially in private street transactions. A common scam involves Colombians pretending to be plainclothes police with false ID demanding to see your documents, then money.

Hire a guide for sightseeing.

Never accept food, drinks, or cigarettes offered by a Colombian unless that person is known to be trustworthy. Many people are victims of robberies and/or rape after being offered such items tainted with *burundanga* (scopolamine), a debilitating drug. Do not leave food or drink unattended at a bar or restaurant.

Never hike alone, particularly in national parks, where robberies have been known to occur.

If anything is stolen, report it immediately to the police and/or your embassy. The fledgling Policía de Turismo (*Calle 28 #13-15, Bogotá, tel 091/606-7676 ext. 1371, @Policia Bogota, policia.gov.co*) has only a limited presence.

A new professionalism to Colombia's national police force (*policia.gov.co*) belies its reputation for corruption. However, dishonest officials still exist and can be reported to tel 1/166-0555.

Embassies

U.S. Embassy, Calle 24 Bis #48-50 (Gate One), Bogotá, tel 57-1/275-2000, bogota .usembassy.gov
Canadian Embassy, Cra. 7 #114-33, Bogotá, tel 57-1/657-9800, canadainternational.gc.ca /colombia-colombie
U.K. Embassy, Cra. 9 #76-49, Bogotá, tel 57-1/326-8300, bit.ly/1hRuqkZ

Emergency Telephone Numbers

Dial 123 nationwide to summon fire (*bomberos*), police (*policía*), and/or ambulance (*ambulancia*).

Lost Property

There are no facilities for locating or retrieving lost property.

Security

Although the security situation has vastly improved in recent years, certain regions of the country remain off-limits due to the presence of ELN and FARC guerrillas (2014/2015 saw a surge in violence), other narco-terrorists, and lawless bandits. Remote areas of Chocó and Nariño, plus Meta and Caquetá Departments, and the Venezuela border zones are especially problematic. Heavily armed police and army units maintain checkpoints at regular intervals on major roads nationwide, and are ubiquitous in urban zones, but cannot guarantee travelers' safety. Stick to main roads whenever possible, and never drive rural roads at night.

Kidnapping for ransom is a problem, but kidnappings of tourists are rare.

Hire a qualified, licensed guide for mountain hiking, not the least because a sprained ankle or broken leg could otherwise prove fatal. Since 2000, more than 7,000 people have been killed or maimed by land mines planted by leftist guerrillas and right-wing paramilitaries on remote rural trails.

Consult the following for more specific warnings:
Canada Ministry of Foreign Affairs, travel.gc.ca/destinations /colombia
U.K. Foreign Office, gov.uk /foreign-travel-advice/colombia
U.S. State Department, 1.usa .gov/1Jf5UCm

What to Do in a Car Accident

If you are involved in a traffic accident, the involved parties must remain at the scene and not move their vehicles until the police arrive. Moving a vehicle or leaving the scene can constitute an admission of guilt under Colombian law. Take down the license plate numbers and *cédulas* (legal identification) of any witnesses. The transit police (*tránsitos*) will fill out a report that you will need for insurance purposes. If you suspect the other driver has been drinking, request that an *alcolemia* (breathalyzer test) be administered. If someone is seriously injured or killed, contact your embassy.

For traffic police, call 123.

HEALTH

Most towns have private physicians and clinics. In major cities, medical service is up to North American standards. Elsewhere, standards vary widely, with only minimal facilities in rural areas. In Bogotá, two of the best facilities are the **Clínica del Country** (Cra. 16 #82-95, Bogotá, tel 57-1/530 0470, clinicadel country.com) and **Fundación Santa Fe de Bogotá** (Calle 119 #7-75, Bogotá, tel 57-1/603-0303, fsfb.org.co). Government-run centros de salud (health centers) serve virtually every town in the country and offer treatment for nominal fees. However, the service is of low standard, and visitors are advised to seek treatment at private facilities.

Full travel insurance should cover all medical costs—hospitalization, nursing services, doctor's fee, and more. A medical evacuation clause is also important in case sufficient care is not available and you need to return home.

If you require medical help, consult your hotel. Most keep up a list of doctors and medical centers, which can save time. Otherwise, consult the Yellow Pages of the telephone book. Keep any receipts or paperwork for insurance claims.

Make a note of the generic name of any prescription medications you take before you leave home. They may be sold by a different trade name in Colombia.

Health Hazards

Colombia's main health hazards— other than traffic accidents— relate to its tropical climate, where bacteria and germs breed profusely. Wash all cuts and scrapes with warm water and rubbing alcohol. The tap water is safe in most cities, but you should avoid drinking water in rural destinations, along the Caribbean shore, and in all other impoverished communities where you should drink (and brush your teeth with) bottled water. Boil water when camping to eliminate giardia, a parasite that thrives in warm water. Avoid uncooked seafood, vegetables, unwashed salads, and unpeeled fruits.

Be liberal with the application of sunscreen and build up your tan slowly, as the tropical sun is intense and severe sunburn or sunstroke can effectively ruin a vacation. Drink plenty of water to guard against dehydration.

Biting insects abound, particularly in the humid lowlands. Malaria is present in lowland areas and can be a problem mainly on the Caribbean coast and Darién. Consult your doctor for a suitable malaria prophylaxis. Dengue fever is also spread by mosquitoes and occasional outbreaks are reported as far afield as Meta, Antioquia, and Santander. There is no preventative medication, so it is wise to try to avoid being bitten. Use insect repellents liberally and wear earth-colored clothing with long sleeves and full-length pants, good for guarding against chiggers (coloradillas) when hiking in grassland areas; these tiny insects burrow into your skin and cause itching for weeks. Chitras (tiny sand flies) are present on beaches and are active around dawn and dusk; their bite—and the resultant itching—belie their size. Apply Avon Skin-so-Soft, a cosmetic that even the U.S. Marine Corps swears by.

Venomous snakes are common in wilderness areas, especially in the lowlands. Wear closed-toed shoes that cover the ankle to reduce the chance of snakebites, and don't put your hand in places you can't see. If you are bitten, get immediate medical help. Give any visible snakes a wide berth.

Although rabies is now rare in Colombia among cats and dogs, be cautious and do not pet or touch any animal, wild or domestic.

Stingrays linger about in the coastal shallows. Shuffle your feet when wading.

Riptides are an extreme danger along much of the coast, particularly where high surf comes ashore. The beaches of Parque Natural Nacional Tayrona and the Pacific coast are particularly dangerous.

Altitude sickness is always a possibility in the highlands above 8,202 feet (2,500 m). The higher you travel, the greater the potential risk. Symptoms include headaches, dizziness, nausea, and loss of appetite. Extreme cases can lead to death due to high-altitude edema (swelling of the lung or brain). To lessen the potential for sickness, ascend gradually in increments. If you suffer symptoms, do not ascend farther; if they persist, descend to a lower altitude.

Hotels & Restaurants

Accommodations and restaurants in Colombia are varied and reasonably priced, although standards vary widely. Remember that large areas of the country are remote, and the availability of accommodations and restaurants can be limited. More desirable accommodations can fill quickly during busy months, especially during festivals such as Carnaval. Eating out can be a great pleasure in Bogotá, Cartagena, and other major cities, which offer a wide variety of possibilities, including many world-class options. Elsewhere, menus are typically restricted to traditional fare and seafood.

There are great differences between the facilities available, and it will help you to understand these difference when deciding where to stay and eat. In remote regions, such as La Guajira, meals are often bland and your options are extremely limited. A 16 percent sales tax is added to hotel and restaurant bills. All hotels and restaurants are 100 percent smoke-free under existing law.

The following hotels and restaurants are organized by chapter; within each chapter, they appear in alphabetical order by city, and then in alphabetical order according to price range.

Accommodations

There are several types of accommodations. Bogotá and other major cities are blessed with top-of-the-line hotels that meet international standards. These range from small, family-run boutique hotels that combine intimacy and charm, to high-rise international chain hotels, usually with business and or convention facilities. Several have casinos. Some of these hotel chains have toll-free numbers:

Radisson, tel 800/967-9033, radisson.com

Sheraton, tel 800/325-3535, starwoodhotels.com.

The colonial towns of Villa de Leyva, Barichara, and Santa Fé de Antioquia have some of the most atmospheric accommodations in the country, including intimate bed-and-breakfast country inns, and lovely one-of-a-kind boutique hotels are scattered throughout the highlands. Cartagena is filled with a score of world-class boutique hotels, and the past few years has blessed Bogotá with the same. Lovers of one-of-a-kind boutique hotels should consult **Pequeños Hoteles con Encanto** (tel 57-1/226-7247, loshotelescon encanto.com).

The beach resorts—such as Santa Marta, San Andrés, and Providencia—offer a wide range of options, from simple beach-front surf camps to large all-inclusive resorts catering mainly to a domestic clientele. Mid-range hotels are widely available, offering a modicum of services; standards vary. However, certain areas of the country, such as Los Llanos, have relatively few hotels. And the options in places that host major festivals, such as Barranquilla during Carnaval, sell out extremely fast and accommodations can be impossible to find. Plan your stays in such places accordingly.

Colombia has relatively few wilderness lodges. The sole exception is in Amazonas, where facilities range from tent camps to cozy no-frills wooden lodges and a couple more sophisticated options with spas and saunas. Camping is available along beaches and in most national parks. A strong suit is backpackers' hostels: Colombia has several dozen world-class options in almost every quarter of the country: **HoLa** (holahostels.com) represents more than a dozen.

PRICES

HOTELS
An indication of the cost of a double room in the high season is given by **$** signs.

$$$$$	Over $200
$$$$	$100–$200
$$$	$50–$100
$$	$25–$50
$	Under $25

RESTAURANTS
An indication of the cost of a three-course meal without drinks is given by **$** signs.

$$$$$	Over $35
$$$$	$20–$35
$$$	$10–$20
$$	$5–$10
$	Under $5

In La Guajira, hotels are few and beyond Ríohacha are basic, even spartan. Expect homespun *cabañas* made of cactus trunks and bamboo reeds, with thatch or tin for a roof. Few have electricity (lighting is provided by generators), and fewer still have flushing toilets.

In true budget hotels, sink plugs may be missing, showers are often cold, and mattresses are thin and usually well past their prime. Warm (tepid) water may be provided by an electric element above the shower. Ensure windows and doors are secure.

🏨 Hotel 🛈 No. of guest rooms 🍴 Restaurant ⊞ No. of seats 🕐 Hours 🅿 Parking 🚭 Nonsmoking

Avoid "motels," found on the outskirts of most towns and cities; they're rented by the hour for sexual trysts and hygiene will be somewhat lacking.

Unless otherwise stated, all hotels listed here have dining rooms and private bathrooms, and are open year-round.

Travelers will find that hotel rates in Colombia are generally about 15–30 percent or more higher in high season.

Restaurants

Restaurants' opening hours vary too widely to generalize. Many close on Monday. Make reservations for the more expensive restaurants, particularly on weekends. In Bogotá and other major cities, service is usually fast, but elsewhere it is often slow. Life moves at a difference pace: Don't expect to receive your bill without asking for it.

Local fare can normally be enjoyed for less than US$5. Look for *comida corriente*—set lunch plates that usually consist of a choice of meat, rice, beans, and vegetables (or salad) at bargain prices.

The Café Oma chain (*cafeoma .com*) is the equivalent of Starbucks in Colombia and has outlets throughout the country selling quality coffees, desserts, sandwiches, and more.

In remote regions of Amazonia and La Guajira, restaurants can be counted on one hand; most are extremely basic. Here, expect to eat rather blandly in your hotel.

A selection of the best quality restaurants for each area is given below. These are both individual and typical, with notable local associations wherever possible.

B = Breakfast
L = Lunch
D = Dinner

Credit Cards

Giving a card number is often the only way to reserve rooms in upscale hotels. Some hotels add a fee for credit card payments. Most higher-end restaurants accept payment by credit cards for no extra charge.

Abbreviations used are AE (American Express), DC (Diner's Club), MC (MasterCard), V (Visa). A few establishments take PayPal.

Making Reservations

Although most hotels in Colombia have websites, they rely on the telephone for communication, and many hotels are lax about replying to e-mail requests for information and/or reservations. Do not rely on booking by mail, fax, or e-mail. You may have to telephone specific hotels for a reservation. Consider using a reputable local tour company, such as **Colombia 57** (*tel 57-6/ 886-8050, colombia57.com*), to handle your reservations. Take your written confirmation (printed from a confirmation e-mail) with you.

If a Colombian tour operator informs you that the hotel of your choice is full, check directly with the hotel; even the most reputable tour operators have been known to intentionally steer clients toward hotels that pay them preferential commissions.

Although we have tried to give comprehensive information, please check details before booking. This applies particularly to the availability of facilities for disabled guests, acceptance of credit cards, and rates.

■ BOGOTÁ

HOTELS

🏨 HOTEL BOGOTÁ
🍴 REGENCY
$$$$$
CRA. 7 #127-21, USAQUÉN
TEL 57-1/592-1777
hotelregency.com.co
Deluxe business-oriented hotel in the striking form of a glass-fronted cylinder. The spacious bedrooms feature avant-garde styling, plus safes, LCD TVs, Wi-Fi, and luxury linens. The hotel has five bars as well as the sophisticated **Restaurante Phoenicia.** Located close to shopping and business district, in the north of the city, and near the trendy Usaquén nightlife.
🛈 92 🔌 🅢 🎽 🎧
🅢 All major credit cards

🏨 HOTEL PORTON
🍴 BOGOTÁ
$$$$$
CALLE 84 #7-55, EL RETIRO
TEL 57-1/616-6611
hotelportonbogota.com.co
A gracious Georgian-style interior exudes comfort and charm for this boutique hotel tucked away on a quiet cul-de-sac in El Retiro district. Guest rooms offer more contemporary style and feature halogen ceiling lights, flat-screen TVs, gleaming wooden floors, luxurious linens, and Wi-Fi. The Porton's **Le Jardin Perdu Restaurant** is acclaimed in the city and offers an extensive wine and liquor list.
🛈 38 🔌 🎧 🅢 All major credit cards

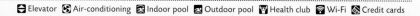

🔌 Elevator 🅢 Air-conditioning 🖼 Indoor pool 🏊 Outdoor pool 🎽 Health club 🎧 Wi-Fi 🅢 Credit cards

🏨 SOFITEL BOGOTÁ
🍴 VICTORIA REGIA
$$$$$
CRA. 13 #85-80,
LA CABRERA
TEL 57-1/646-6390
sofitel.com

Now stylishly contemporary after a recent remake, this hotel in the northern part of the city will suit both business and leisure travelers. Guest rooms have modish and soothing lilac or salmon and white color schemes. The hotel is located close to a lively night scene and designer shopping district. Chef Mauricia Rodriguéz works culinary wonders with fusion dishes in the **Basilic** gourmet restaurant, with its Regency decor.

ⓘ 102 🚫 🔄 🛗 🚰 🅿️

🅰️ All major credit cards

🏨 W BOGOTÁ HOTEL
$$$$$
CARRERA 9 #115-30
TEL 57-1/746-7111
whotels.com/bogota

The very definition of high-tech, this pet-friendly new-comer offers highly original and avant-garde design and decor, including marble floors and a hip lounge.

ⓘ 168, 33 suites 🅿️ 🚫 🛗 📶

🅰️ All major credit cards

🏨 SHERATON BOGOTÁ
HOTEL
$$$$–$$$$$
AV. EL DORADO #69C-80,
SALITRE
TEL 57-1/210-5000
starwoodhotels.com

Situated in a modern commercial district, on the west side of the city close to the airport, this hotel squarely caters to business travelers. The marble-clad lobby sets the tone. Contemporary styling in impeccably clean, comfy, and functional rooms

with king-size beds and Wi-Fi. Its many facilities include a barber shop and indoor heated pool.

ⓘ 247 🔄 🚫 🛗 🚰 🅿️ 📶

🅰️ All major credit cards

🏨 104 ART SUITES
$$$$
CRA. 18A #104-77,
CHICÓ NORTE
TEL 57-1/602-5959
104artsuites.com

This pet-friendly design hotel will awe sophisticates with its hip retro-modernist design and chic decor, including avant-garde art illumined by halogen lighting. Each suite is individually designed by a Colombian artist, but all have free Wi-Fi, oversize flat-screen TVs, king beds, and cool accoutrements. Some have kitchenettes, but there's also a super stylish restaurant serving creative cuisine

ⓘ 27 🚫 🔄 📶 🅰️ All major credit cards

🏨 B.O.G. HOTEL
$$$$
CRA. 11 #86-74,
CHICÓ
TEL 57-1/639-9999
boghotel.com

Its super contemporary exterior hints at the modish furnishings within at this hip design hotel in the heart of trendy Chicó. Classy bronze, gray, and green color schemes (inspired by Colombia's gold and emerald), and über luxury combine in minimalist guest suites. B.O.G. has an elegant fine-dining restaurant and full-service spa.

ⓘ 55 🚫 🔄 🛗 🅰️ All major credit cards

🏨 GHL HOTEL HAMILTON
$$$$

PRICES

HOTELS
An indication of the cost of a double room in the high season is given by **$** signs.

$$$$$	Over $200
$$$$	$100–$200
$$$	$50–$100
$$	$25–$50
$	Under $25

RESTAURANTS
An indication of the cost of a a three-course meal without drinks is given by **$** signs.

$$$$$	Over $35
$$$$	$20–$35
$$$	$10–$20
$$	$5–$10
$	Under $5

CRA. 14 #81-20,
ZONA ROSA
TEL 57-1/621-5455
ghlhoteles.com

Tucked into the heart of Zona Rosa, this charming redbrick hotel is perfect for shopping mavens and night owls, located literally a stone's throw from the core of Bogotá's epicenter of clubs, bars, and clothing boutiques. Although rooms are small, they're stylishly furnished and offer Wi-Fi, cable TV, and other modern amenities, including comfy beds. Limited parking.

ⓘ 41 🅿️ Limited 🚫 📶

🅰️ All major credit cards

🏨 HOTEL DE LA ÓPERA
🍴 $$$$
CALLE 10 #5-72,
LA CANDELARIA
TEL 57-1/336-2066
hotelopera.com.co

Behind the pink colonial facade of this upscale hotel

---

on a pedestrian-only street adjoining the Teatro Colón lurks a thoroughly contemporary gem. Guests rooms in the colonial wing (which envelops two courtyards) are more sedate, with understated yet elegant Italianate furnishings and throw rugs atop wooden floors. A second, newer, wing offers rooms with chic urbane styling that would do IKEA proud. The top-floor **Restaurante Mirador,** one of two in the hotel, offers a panoramic city view. The upscale Thermae Spa offers treatments from acupuncture to massage and mud therapy.

① 42 🖾 🖨 🖾 🖾 🖾 🖾
🖾 All major credit cards

🏨 MORRISON 84
$$$$
CALLE 84 BIS #13-54,
CHICÓ NORTE
TEL 57-1/622-3111
morrisonhotel.com
This six-story redbrick hotel is inspired by contemporary decor and also incorporates up-to-date modern styling and features, including a 24-hour glass-walled business center. Bedrooms offer Wi-Fi, minibars, and flat-screen cable TVs. The restaurant terrace overlooks leafy Parque León de Grieff, a stone's throw from the trendy bars and restaurants of Zona T. Local gym access.

① 62 🖾 🖾 🖾 🖾 🖾 All major credit cards

🏨 PAVILLON ROYAL
$$$$
CALLE 94 #11-45,
CHICÓ
TEL 57-1/657-8787
pavillonroyal.com.co
Aiming for business travelers and urbane sophisticates, this deluxe hotel in the Royal chain has loft-style suites

throughout. It rises over Parque 93—ground zero in the city's trendy restaurant and night scene. Tangerine-and-chocolate color schemes are set against clinical white. Safes, Wi-Fi, and flat-screen TVs in guest rooms. The **Indigo** restaurant is highly rated for its fusion seafood.

① 42 🖾 🖾 🖾 🖾
🖾 All major credit cards

🏨 HOTEL HABITEL
$$$–$$$$$
AV. EL DORADO #100-97,
FONTIBÓN
TEL 57-1/419-9999
www.hotelhabitel.com
Perfectly positioned for late-night arrivals or early-morning departures, this redbrick, low-rise hotel is literally a five-minute drive from the airport. Sophisticated in every regard, it offers divine comforts in chic, totally soundproofed guest suites with king beds, swivel flat-screen TVs, and other state-of-the-art amenities. Dining options include a steak house and **Manduka,** serving fusion cuisine. Free airport transfers 24/7 are a major plus.

① 92 🖾 🖾 🖾 🖾
🖾 All major credit cards

🏨 CROWNE PLAZA TEQUANDAMA
$$$–$$$$
CRA. 10 #26-21,
TEQUANDAMA
TEL 57-1/382-0300
ihg.com
Crowne Plaza's trademark style infuses this huge tower hotel. It possesses a pedigree as the city's top hotel for visiting dignitaries, ranging from Presidents Kennedy and Clinton to Pope John Paul II and Fidel Castro. The Tequendama, as everyone knows it, offers plenty of comfort and services,

including an antiques-filled lobby plus state-of-the-art amenities in contemporary-style guest rooms, including flat-screen TVs and Wi-Fi. Its location is perfect for exploring around Parque de la Independencia and it is 20 minutes' walking distance from La Candelaria. A solid bargain, perfectly located for exploring central Bogotá.

① 571 🖾 🖾 🖾 🖾
🖾 All major credit cards

SOMETHING SPECIAL

🏨 HOTEL CASA DECO
$$$–$$$$
CALLE 12C #2-36,
LA CANDELARIA
TEL 57-1/282-8640
hotelcasadeco.com
One of the most exciting hotels to open in Bogotá in recent years, this Italian/Colombian-owned and -managed boutique option plays on an art deco theme, beginning with the restored 1930s-era structure. Peace, relaxation, and attentive service are the watchwords at this oasis in La Candelaria. Lovely contemporary mosaics in the lobby echo tasteful art throughout the hotel. Each room is color-themed and individually styled; all boast flat-screen TVs, Wi-Fi, safes, and minibars. The restaurant is a delightfully airy space, and the rooftop bar with terrace offers panoramic city views and is a venue for live music.

① 21 🖾 🖾 🖾 AE, MC, V

🏨 THE ORCHIDS
$$$–$$$$
CRA. 5 #10-55,
LA CANDELARIA
TEL 57-1/745-5438
theorchidshotel.com
With its gorgeous period furnishings and decor, this newcomer defines a new level of luxe for small

boutique hotels in the historic core. Individually styled suites combine sensuality with divine comforts. Its excellent restaurant earns raves for delivering gastronomic delights under Chef Harry Sasso, plus there's a library and music room, both honoring literary and music greats of past centuries.

🛈 7 🚭 🛇 All major credit cards

🏨 HOTEL CASA DANN CARLTON
$$$
CALLE 94 #19-71,
CHICÓ
TEL 57-1/635-0100
casadann.com.co

An elegant old-world hotel with modern comforts and conveniences, this hotel in upscale Chicó district serves both business and leisure travelers. Cozy guest rooms have Wi-Fi and choice of queen or king beds. A pleasant restaurant serves nouvelle cuisine and has efficient service. Quiet bar, plus business center, and golf privileges at Club Pueblo Viejo.

🛈 139 🖨 🚭 🛇 All major credit cards

🏨 ABADIA COLONIAL
$$
CALLE 11 #2-32,
LA CANDELARIA
TEL 57-1/341-1884
abadiacolonial.com

A hilly location and historic charm combine in this Italian-run boutique hotel in a restored yet rustic colonial structure. Spacious and tidy guest rooms (to the rear of the building) have gracious furnishings, cable TV, phones, safes, and small bathrooms. A simple restaurant is set in a sun-drenched patio. Perfectly located for exploring La Candelaria.

🛈 12 🛇 All major credit cards

🏨 CASA QUINTA
$$
CRA. 4 #17-59,
LA CANDELARIA
TEL 57-1/337-6500
casaquintahotel.com

A budget option that has plenty of character, this small hotel just off Parque de los Periodistas has pleasant rooms furnished with medieval-style reproduction furnishings and Botero prints. Ceramic floors, refrigerators, ceiling fans. It has a bar, Jacuzzi, and free Wi-Fi, but can be noisy.

🛈 20 🚭 🛇 MC, V

🏨 CASA PLATYPUS
$–$$
CRA. 3 #16-28,
LA CANDELARIA
TEL 57-1/281-1801
casaplatypusbogota.com

Located on the northwest side of La Candelaria, in front of Parque de los Periodistas, this restored colonial home has rooms furnished with wooden floors and antique reproductions. Facilities include Wi-Fi, an Internet lounge, a communal kitchen, and a rooftop terrace. The original Platypus hostel, one block away, has dorms and is popular with backpackers. It can be noisy.

🛈 17 🚭 🚭 🛇 AE, MC, V

RESTAURANTS

🍴 CRITERIÓN
$$$$$
CALLE 69A #5-75,
ZONA G
TEL 57-1/310-1377
criterion.com.co

In an area—Zona G (G for "Gourmet")—renowned for fine-dining restaurants, Criterión stands out for its award-winning French-inspired fusion cuisine—*francesa moderna*—served in sophisticated

PRICES

HOTELS
An indication of the cost of a double room in the high season is given by **$** signs.

$$$$$	Over $200
$$$$	$100–$200
$$$	$50–$100
$$	$25–$50
$	Under $25

RESTAURANTS
An indication of the cost of a three-course meal without drinks is given by **$** signs.

$$$$$	Over $35
$$$$	$20–$35
$$$	$10–$20
$$	$5–$10
$	Under $5

surroundings. Chef Mark Rausch and his brother Jorge (executive chef) run their restaurant with aplomb. Try the tasting menu, with a seven entrée sampler. Bogotá's elite gather here, and Mexico's President Felipe Calderón is rumored to order plates to go for his presidential jet.

🍴 80 🕐 Closed D Sun.
🛇 All major credit cards

SOMETHING SPECIAL

🍴 LEO COCINA Y CAVA
$$$$$
CALLE 27B #6-75,
PASAJE SANTA CRUZ DE
MOMPOX
TEL 57-1/286-7091
leococinaycava.com

Tucked in a cobbled alleyway near the Museo Nacional and Crowne Plaza Tequendama, this minimalist restaurant draws the big guns of Colombian business, politics, and celebrity life.

Chef-owner Leonor Espinosa hails from Cartagena. Her seafood menu fuses various African, Indian, and Spanish influences, such as appetizers of whitefish ceviche, or raw tuna, encrusted with *hormigas culonas* (see sidebar p. 120); and for main dishes, lobster tail with sweet red pepper sauce or flambéed shrimp with Antillean rum over risotto. The martinis are legendary. The sensual experience is made more so by the decor: contemporary erotic art.

60 Closed Sun. All major credit cards

SUNA
$$$$
CALLE 72 #5-09, CHAPINERO
TEL 57-1/317-7909
sunacolombia.com
Seeking health food? Then head to Suna, where sophisticated modernist decor provides an inspirational surrounding for enjoying a vegetable wok, roasted tofu with mushrooms, sea bass ceviche with passion fruit, or *tagliatelle napolitana*. The huge menu includes delicious desserts, such as tapioca pudding. It has a store stocked with quality health foods.

40 All major credit cards

SOMETHING SPECIAL

ANDRÉS D.C.
$$$
CALLE 3 #11A-56, ZONA ROSA
TEL 57-1/863-7880
www.andrescarnederes.com/andres-dc
Prepare to be astonished at this vast restaurant in the heart of Zona Rosa. Everything about this place is unique, from the four-tier industrial warehouse setting

(Hell, Earth, Purgatory, and Heaven) and the eclectic, bizarre, and kitschy decor to the dedicated troupe of actors there to stir up the fun. Service comes with more than a smile: Newcomers to Colombia are feted with the national anthem, a cocktail, and a tricolored sash. Although Andrés D.C. (for *de corazón*—from the heart) specializes in grilled meats (the barbecue is brought to your table), the 32-page menu includes delicious small-plate appetizers. No wonder Bogotáños consider Andres the place to celebrate birthdays and other special occasions. By night, it morphs into a wild party zone. This really is a must-visit.

700 All major credit cards

CASAS SANTA CLARA
$$$
CERRO DE MONSERRATE
TEL 57-1/243-8952
restaurantecasasanta clara.com
Hanging on the hillside by the tram station at Cerro de Monserrate, this belle epoque mansion offers fine views over the city. It serves gourmet Colombian dishes, from traditional appetizers like *patacones* (plantain chips) to chicken medallions in *maracuyá* sauce. Start with a drink of *canelazo*.

150 Closed Mon. All major credit cards

ANTIGUA SANTAFE
$$
CALLE 11 #6-20, LA CANDELARIA
TEL 57-1/566-6948
This cubbyhole just one block from Plaza de Bolívar is a tremendous option for savoring hearty *paisan* fare in a down-home environment with rustic tables and bench seats. Try a traditional *ajiaco santafereño*

(chicken and potato soup) or *cazuela de frijoles* (bean stew). It gets full at lunch, in which case try the identical La Puerta Falsa, next door; or, adjoining, the more upscale antique-filled La Puerta Real, also serving traditional fare.

82 None

CAPACHOS ASADERO
$$
CALLE 18 #4-68
TEL 57-1/243-4607
asaderocapachos.com
Specializing in grilled meats, this *llanero*-themed local favorite serves healthy portions with fried plantains and yucca. It also puts on country folkloric shows on weekends.

80 Closed Mon. MC, V

GAIRA CAFÉ
$$
CARRERA 13 #96-11, CHICÓ
TEL 57-1/746-2696
gairacafe.co
Known for its live music and comedy shows, this hugely popular and colorful restaurant-bar is a knockoff of Andrés D.C. It serves typical Colombian "food for the soul." The vast menu spans everything from seafood to *mazorcas* (corncobs) and *arepas de huevo* (corn cakes with egg). Bring friends and party!

200 Closed B All major credit cards

LA ROSCONERÍA
$$
CRA. 6A #117-32, USAQUÉN
TEL 57/320-231-0465
larosconeria.com
A colorful little café-restaurant, it specializes in *roscones*—large doughnut-like sponge breads, in this case stuffed with a wide choice of

options, from salmon with sour cream to mushrooms and mozzarella. It also has dessert options, including blackberry and cream cheese, plus flambéed bananas.

🪑 50 🚭 None

🍴 CREPES Y WAFFLES
$

CALLE 73 #10-83, CHAPINERO
TEL 57-1/676-7600 EXT. 750
crepesywaffles.com.co

This international chain has a dozen outlets in Bogotá. Clean, sharp, and efficient, they're great for filling up on crêpe de sal (savory crêpe), crêpe Gandhi (with tofu), and similar bargain-priced treats. Leave room for a vanilla ice cream and Nutella waffle. Also has health-conscious breakfasts.

🪑 40 🚭 All major credit cards

CHÍA

SOMETHING SPECIAL

🍴 ANDRÉS CARNE DE RES
$$$

VARIANTE A COTA
TEL 57-1/863-7880
www.andrescarnederes.com

The original Andrés restaurant is a pilgrimage site for Bogotános, who flock in sufficient numbers to pack this remarkable, one-of-a-kind restaurant extending for more than 125 yards (114 m). Imagine a crazed Hollywood director's interpretation of grandma's attic full of rustic furniture, chests, bells, lamps, illuminated stars, nude figures, puppets, and a veritable museum's worth of antique bric-a-brac. The huge menu, presented in the form of a magazine, ranges from traditional Colombian dishes to charcoal-grilled loin, rump steak with salad and new potatoes, and Chilean salmon

with coconut rice and salad. Hot dishes are served still sizzling on piping hot metal platters. The food is superb; flavors leap off the plate. Roving musicians and actors in costume entertain as you eat. A separate kid's zone across the street operates like a kindergarten, with face-painting, puppet shows, and educational programs for kids. Oh, and yes, it has its own kid's menu.

🪑 2,000 🕐 🚭 All major credit cards

GUASCA

🏨 HACIENDA BETANIA
🍴 $$

VEREDA TRINIDAD, CUNDINAMARCA
TEL 57/315-358-9877
hotelhaciendabetania.com

Deep in the countryside with magnificent views, this hillside hotel is named for its colorful owner, Berta López Martínez, who likes to wear a chef's hat. This rambling edifice is adorned with quaint knickknacks, many of a bovine theme. Simple bedrooms have thick comforters. The cozy and colorful restaurant specializes in trout and chicken dishes. Close to Guatavita. Horseback riding is also offered to guests.

ⓘ 5 🅿 🚭 AE, MC, V

SANTANDERCITO

🏨 ALTO DE LA PALMA
🍴 HOTEL BOUTIQUE
$$$

KM 1 VÍA BELLAVISTA
TEL 57/311-635-0906
altodelapalmahotel boutique.com

A grandiose and beautifully restored republican mansion dating from 1943 today houses this boutique hotel with individually styled rooms.

Hardwood floors gleam underfoot, and sunlight pours in through heaps of windows. Decor is understated yet cosmopolitan, playing up clinical whites, in Laura Ashley fashion. An open-air terrace lounge with cast-iron stove is ideal for relaxing with a good book. Sauna, whirlpool spa, plus trails and horseback riding. Close to the zoo.

ⓘ 11 🅿 🕐 🏊 🛏 🚭 DC, MC, V

SASAIMA

🏨 EL REFUGIO HOTEL SPA
🍴 $$$$

KM 80 CRA. BOGOTÁ, SASAIMA
TEL 57-1/805-4521
elrefugiohotelspa.com.co

Set in lush gardens surrounded by mountains, the former country mansion of a wealthy industrialist retains its original 1930s furnishings, including mahogany beds set off by rich tropical color schemes and gleaming hardwood floors. Trails lead past bamboo groves to a tennis court and a lake stocked with fish. Spa treatments are offered alfresco beside a cascade.

 14 P S ⓣ Ⓢ DC, MC, V

UBATÉ

🏨 CASA YUNQUE
$$$$$
VEREDA SAN LUÍS KM 1,
VIA CARMEN DE CARUPA,
UBATÉ
TEL 57-1/486-3398
casayunque.com

Style and sophistication are the watchwords at this small boutique hotel, fronted by a lake and backed by forests. Dramatic contemporary architecture provides a showcase for oversize rooms with huge picture windows and black-and-white in-vogue furnishings. Horseback riding and guided hikes are also offered.

ⓘ 6 cabins, 1 suite P Ⓢ
Ⓢ MC, V

ZIPAQUIRÁ

🏨 HOTEL CACIQUE REAL
$$
CRA. 6 #2-36 CENTRO,
ZIPAQUIRÁ
TEL 57-1/851-0209
hotelcaciquereal.com

Two blocks from the main plaza, and a short walk from the Catedral de Sal, it combines a colonial section dating from 1729 with a modern addition. The colonial rooms are quaint and simply appointed; for a good night's sleep, choose a room away from the street.

ⓘ 23 P Ⓢ Ⓢ MC, V

■ EASTERN HIGHLANDS

BARICHARA

SOMETHING SPECIAL

🏨 LA NUBE POSADA
🍽 $$$$
CALLE 7 #7-39
TEL 57-7/726-7161
lanubeposada.com

The owners (three Colombian siblings) have cleverly wed minimalist decor to colonial architecture in this chic historic gem near the center of town. Three rooms have windows onto the street; five windowless rooms face into a patio-garden with hammocks and loungers. Whitewashed and stone-paved throughout, the rooms almost monastic in their Zen-like serenity, but adorned with thoughtful touches. The shaded open-air restaurant delivers delicious fusion dishes and even serves *hormigas culonas* (see sidebar p. 120). Try the delicious cream of tomato soup, and appetizer of diced tofu and tomato seasoned with parsley, peppermint, olive oil, and chili; followed, perhaps, by fettuccine with shrimp in tomato and olive oil sauce, or a divine braised shank of goat with boiled potatoes. Holistic therapies are offered in a nearby spa.

ⓘ 12 P Ⓢ Ⓢ Ⓢ All major credit cards

🏨 HOSTAL MISIÓN SANTA BARBARA
$$
CALLE 5 #9-12
TEL 57-7/726-7163
hostalmisionsanta
barbara.com

Two blocks from the main plaza, this charming colonial-era hotel offers spacious,

modestly appointed yet comfy and gaily colored rooms around a flower-filled patio with fountain. Terracotta floors help to keep the rooms cool.

ⓘ 31 Ⓢ Ⓢ MC, V

BUCAMARANGA

🏨 HOTEL DANN CARLTON
🍽 BUCARAMANGA
$$$$
CALLE 47 #28-83
TEL 57-7/697-3266
dannbucaramanga.com.co

The city's most elegant option aims to wow patrons with its heaps of marble, Moorish-inspired architecture, and walls adorned with contemporary art. Guest rooms in various styles make bold use of mahogany, red brick, and sober or lively color schemes, according to room type. **Restaurante Brazza's** steak house, adjoining the lobby, has a warm and sophisticated ambience for enjoying sirloins, tenderloins, and whole roast pork cooked to perfection.

ⓘ 135 P Ⓢ Ⓢ ⓣ
Ⓢ All major credit cards

🏨 CLUB CAMPSTRE DE BUCAMARANGA
$$$–$$$$
CRA. 21 #30-02,
BARRIO CAÑAVERAL
TEL 57-7/680-3030
campestrebucaramanga.com

In Florblanca, on the upscale south side of Bucaramanga, close to major shopping centers and nightlife, this country club hotel has a complete complement of services, from tennis and near-Olympic-size pool to full spa services. The hotel rooms were transformed in 2011 into sophisticated digs, with avant-garde styling and state-of-the-art amenities (including 42-inch/107-cm flat-screen TVs), plus walls of glass offering views over the golf course. The open-air restaurant is a letdown with its somewhat bland food.

🏨 59 🅿 Ⓢ ⊜ Ⓢ ⊠ 🍴 Ⓢ All major credit cards

🏨 HOTEL LA TRIADA BUCAMARANGA
$$$–$$$$
CRA. 20 #34-22
TEL 57-7/642-2410
hotellatriada.com
The Hotel La Triada Bucamaranga is a stylish contemporary hotel; its rooms in various styles exude comfort, with tasteful turquoise, chocolate, and white color schemes and extensive modern amenities. Mediterranean dishes are the focus of its large, elegant restaurant, with paella specials on Friday. Terrace bar fitted with wrought-iron furnishings.

🏨 59 🅿 Ⓢ ⊜ Ⓢ 🍴 Ⓢ AE, MC, V

CÚCUTA

🏨 HOTEL BOLÍVAR
$$$–$$$$
AV. DEMETRIO MENDOZA, BARRIO SAN MATEO
TEL 57-7/582-8666
hotel-bolivar.com
This modestly upscale resort hotel on the southeast side of town features comfy and spacious accommodations in rooms and cabins surrounding two swimming pools. All have Wi-Fi. Junior suites and suites are of a high standard; some have king-size beds. It's a popular venue for business and social functions.

🏨 127 🅿 Ⓢ ⊜ Ⓢ ⊠ 🍴 🛜 Ⓢ AE, MC, V

🏨 ATLANTIS PLAZA HOTEL
$$$
CALLE 8 #7-55, CENTRO
TEL 57-7/582-1777
atlantisplazahotel.com
Appealing to travelers who prefer modishly Miami-style digs, this avant-garde hotel has stainless-steel railings and blue-tinted glass and draws a young crowd. Accommodations include a few gauche elements, but flat-screens, contemporary art, and clinical whites make amends. Sauna and steam room, and the restaurant takes a stab at gourmet cuisine.

🏨 61 🅿 Ⓢ Ⓢ ⊠ 🛜 In public areas Ⓢ MC, V

🍴 RODIZIO
$$$
AV. LOS LIBERTADORES #10-121
TEL 57-7/575-1719
OR
57-7/575-0095
rodiziocucuta.com
This elegant glass-walled restaurant offers a taste of Brazil with its signature meat dishes. It also has an excellent buffet, plus seafood and international dishes.

🍽 60 Ⓢ Ⓢ Most credit cards

GIRÓN

🏨 CHILL OUT
$$
CRA. 25 #32-06
TEL 57-7/646-1119
gironchillout.com
In a restored colonial mansion, this bed-and-breakfast-style boutique hotel offers plenty of comfort, having upgraded from hostel status. Furnishings blend antiques with more contemporary pieces. Its restaurant serves creative fusion cuisine.

🏨 7 Ⓢ Ⓢ MC, V

PRICES

HOTELS
An indication of the cost of a double room in the high season is given by **$** signs.

$$$$$	Over $200
$$$$	$100–$200
$$$	$50–$100
$$	$25–$50
$	Under $25

RESTAURANTS
An indication of the cost of a a three-course meal without drinks is given by **$** signs.

$$$$$	Over $35
$$$$	$20–$35
$$$	$10–$20
$$	$5–$10
$	Under $5

🍴 LA CROISSANTINA
$
CRA. 26 #31-03
TEL 57-7/646-1419
E-MAIL **croissantina@hotmail.com**
A tremendous budget option catty-corner to the main plaza, this bakery-café serves fixed-price *platos ejecutivos,* delicious croissant sandwiches, and enough fresh-baked desserts to keep a sweet tooth happy for months.

🍽 34 Ⓢ AE, MC, V

MESA DE LOS SANTOS

🏨 HOTEL HACIENDA EL ROBLE
$$$–$$$$
VEREDA EL CARIZAL, 18.6 MILES (30 KM) S OF BUCARAMANGA
TEL 57/310-273-3495
On a USDA-certified organic coffee estate, this deluxe colonial-era boutique hotel

---

🏨 Hotel 🏨 No. of guest rooms 🍴 Restaurant 🍽 No. of seats 🕐 Hours 🅿 Parking Ⓢ Nonsmoking

offers tranquillity and will especially appeal to birders and nature lovers for its birding and estate tours. Refitted with sophisticated contemporary styling, it combines delightful decor with modern amenities including flat-screen TVs and Wi-Fi.

🛈 6 P S 🛜 🅢 All major credit cards

PAIPA

SOMETHING SPECIAL

🏨 D'ACOSTA HOTEL
🍽 HACIENDA DEL SALITRE
$$$$

VÍA TOCA-PAIPA KM 3
TEL 57/317-362-5972
haciendadelsalitre.com
Also known as Casona de Salitre, this magnificent colonial hacienda dates from 1736 and featured prominently in the wars of independence: Simón Bolívar stayed here. Its deluxe accommodations play up the colonial feel with period furnishings but offer charming modern bathrooms, plus satellite TV. The candlelit **Restaurante El Mesón del Hidalgo** retains its aged chandeliers and serves local and international dishes, such as roast rabbit with herbs and stuffed lamb casserole. Then retire for cocktails beside the hearth in the cozy lounge. You can bathe on cool nights in the thermal swimming pool, and the hotel has a spa offering massage, exfoliation, and more. Staff dresses in period costume. Free use of mountain bikes.

🛈 23 P 🅱 🅢 All major credit cards

🏨 HOTEL SOCHAGOTA
$$$$

VÍA LAS PISCINAS
TEL 57-8/785-0011
hotelsochagota.com

Situated beside Lago Sochagota, this contemporary resort hotel has a lovely location, with pleasing views and gardens splashed with bougainvillea. Rooms combine modern and antique reproduction furnishings, plus vast views through walls of glass. Cabins have hearths. Thermal swimming pool, spa, horse-back riding.

🛈 45 rooms, 16 cabins
P 🅱 🅢 All major credit cards

PARQUE NACIONAL NATURAL EL COCUY

🏨 HOTEL CASA MUÑOZ
$–$$

CRA. 5 #7-28,
EL COCUY
TEL 57/313-829-1073
OR
57-8/789-0328
hotelcasamunoz.com
A two-story colonial structure on the main square in El Cocuy, this simple, bargain-priced hotel is the nicest of the basic options hereabouts. The simply appointed rooms have private hot-water bathrooms, and from one double bed to bunks for eight people.

🛈 10 S 🅢 None

🏨 CABAÑAS KANWARA
🍽 $

4.3 MILES (7 KM) NE OF GÜICÁN
TEL 57/311-231-6004
E-MAIL kabanaskanwara@gmail.com
A budget hostel for hikers, this no-frills place is up a steep and rugged dirt track northeast of Güicán. Each of four *cabañas* has a hearth, plus five bunk rooms with shared hot-water showers. You can also camp here. Superb mountain vistas are all around. Simple meals are served. Horses and guides are also available.

🏨 4 dorms P 🅢 None

🏨 HOTEL & RESTAURANTE
🍽 LOS MOLINOS
$

CALLE 8 & CRA. 4,
EL COCUY
TEL 57/312-352-9121
elcocuylaposadadelmolino.com
A similar option to Hotel Casa Muñoz, this hotel occupies a colonial building around a central courtyard with stream. Rooms feature colonial antiques. Its simple restaurant is the town's largest and specializes in three plates of the day of simple Colombian fare. It also serves trout.

🛈 11 S 🅢 None

SAN GIL

🍽 GRINGO MIKE'S
$$$

CALLE 12 #8-35
TEL 57-7/724-1695
gringomikes.net
Nirvana for U.S. tourists, this Tex-Mex restaurant offers a menu of all the to-be-expected favorites, from various burgers to Philly cheesesteak sandwiches plus quesadillas. Leave room for the chocolate brownie with vanilla ice cream and/or Oreo milkshake.

🍽 50 🅢 None

TIBANÁ

SOMETHING SPECIAL

🏨 HACIENDA BAZA 1638
🍽 $$$

1.9 MILES (3 KM) SW OF TIBANÁ
TEL 57-8/733-8033
haciendabaza.com
At a crisp 6,890 feet (2,100 m) elevation, this serene hotel is housed in a lovely conversion of a former Dominican convent built in 1638. The live-in owner, Doña Lucía Ospina Ordóñez, grew up

---

🛗 Elevator ❄️ Air-conditioning 🏊 Indoor pool 🏊 Outdoor pool 🏋️ Health club 🛜 Wi-Fi 🅢 Credit cards

here and has lavished impeccable taste in furnishing the classical building, with its wrought-iron chandeliers, open hearths, antique furnishings, spacious lounge, courtyards with aqueducts (the trickle of running water is a delightful constant), and manicured gardens set in grounds that include a lake with geese and ducks. All guest rooms are individually themed and have their own fireplace. The restaurant, candlelit at night, is a romantic setting for enjoying gourmet Colombian dishes.

🛈 14 🚭 AE, MC, V

TUNJA

🏨 HOTEL BOYACÁ PLAZA
$$$
CALLE 18 #11-22
TEL 57-8/740-1116
hotelboyacaplaza.co

The somewhat eclectic style here is modern and eye-catching, with the main draw a lush central patio with brushed steel railings. The decor is a combination of hip and contemporary with slightly dowdy and functional, but the overall mood is appealing. Large bedrooms, some with wooden floors; others are carpeted. All have Wi-Fi. Benefits from a steps-to-everywhere center of town locale, one block from Plaza de Bolívar.

🛈 38 🅿 🚭 📶 🚭 All major credit cards

VILLA DE LEYVA

🏨 LA POSADA DE SAN
🍴 **ANTONIO**
$$$$$
CRA. 8 #11-80
TEL 57-8/732-0538
hotellaposadadesan
antonio.com

Located in the heart of Villa de Leyva, this posada dates

from 1845, yet appears at least two centuries older. Today it's a national monument, centered on a stone patio with fountain. Terracotta floors, beamed ceilings, aged leather couches, and miscellaneous art pieces play up the colonial theme. The individually styled bedrooms combine similar yesteryear furnishings with stylish modern elements such as cable TV, Wi-Fi, and hair dryers; check several options, if possible, as rooms vary. The posada also offers horseback rides. The restaurant is a local favorite. The eclectic, globe-spanning menu ranges from paella and Hungarian goulash to grilled trout and even stretches to hamburgers. Live traditional music is also offered on the aural menu.

🛈 26 🅿 🚭 📶 🚭 All major credit cards

🏨 SUITES ARCO IRIS
$$$–$$$$
1.5 MILES (2 KM) E OF
VILLA DE LEYVA
TEL 57/310-873-3121
suitesarcoiris.com

No beauty prize at this ungainly redbrick hilltop hotel . . . but what rewarding views! Sunlight floods spacious suites through stained-glass-trimmed windows. Colorful yet modest furnishings stand atop terra-cotta tile floors, and suites have free Wi-Fi. The restaurant earns high marks for traditional and fusion dishes. A four-wheel-drive vehicle is recommended to ascend the narrow and steep access road.

🛈 23 🚭 📶 🚭 AE, MC, V

🏨 HOSTERÍA DEL MOLINO
🍴 **LA MESOPOTAMIA**
$$$
CRA. 8 #15A
TEL 57-8/732-0235
lamesopotamia.com

A gracious, rambling old

PRICES

HOTELS
An indication of the cost of a double room in the high season is given by **$** signs.

$$$$$	Over $200
$$$$	$100–$200
$$$	$50–$100
$$	$25–$50
$	Under $25

RESTAURANTS
An indication of the cost of a a three-course meal without drinks is given by **$** signs.

$$$$$	Over $35
$$$$	$20–$35
$$$	$10–$20
$$	$5–$10
$	Under $5

hacienda on the edge of Villa Leyva, it offers plenty of serenity. Older than the town itself, this former flour mill is stuffed with antiques, including religious icons. The spacious rooms surround a courtyard, are simply appointed, and have small bathrooms. An open-air terrace lounge has Wi-Fi, and the restaurant with creaky cowhide seats displays the original flour-crushing stones, or *molinos;* it serves Colombian staples. A highlight is the thermal stone-lined swimming pool in the woodsy grounds.

🛈 33 🅿 🚭 🏊 📶 Lounge
🚭 All major credit cards

🏨 HOTEL BOUTIQUE
IGUAQUE CAMPESTRE
$$$
VÍA AL HIPÓDROMO
TEL 57/311-521-6082
ecospaluxuryhotels.com

This self-styled spa and eco-lodge is just the ticket for a relaxing stay in the country. The gracious colonial ambience and calming gardens with Olympic-size swimming pool set the tone. Tangerine-toned accommodations have traditional hardwood furniture and range from large standard rooms to spa villas with fireplaces and romantic canopy beds. It has up-to-date amenities such as Wi-Fi. Its spa offers complete services.

🛏 13 rooms, 7 suites, 10 villas 🅿 🏊 🎽 🛜 🄰All major credit cards

🍴 MICOCINA
$$$
CALLE 13
TEL 57-8/732-1676
academiaverdeoliva.com /micocina-restaurante-villa -de-leyva

Renowned for the Verde Oliva cooking school, this airy and colorful restaurant just off the main plaza focuses on traditional Colombian fare but with a nouvelle touch, such as *ajiaco* (chicken and potato stew) and tongue in *salsa criolla*.

🪑 60 🄰MC, V

🍴 RESTAURANT ALBAHACA
$$
CRA. 8 #13-46
TEL 57/320-840-8673

This family-run restaurant offers a delightful country ambience aided by a wood fire. It serves American breakfasts but opt for the local fare, such as *cazuela boyacense,* a typical casserole; or creamy soup; plus *ajiaco* and cow's tongue with tomato and onion sauce. All dishes come with a choice of spaghetti or fries.

🪑 80 🄰MC, V

🍴 RESTAURANTE CAMALEÓN GOURMET
$$
CALLE 12, PLAZA MAYOR
TEL 57-8/732-1712
restaurantecamaleongourmet .inf.travel

On the main plaza, this conversion of a 300-year-old mansion is a delightful place for enjoying creative fusion dishes in artsy surrounds. Begin with garlic mushrooms or *crema de auyama* (cream of squash soup). Delicious entrées include Thai trout, and chicken in a choice of wine, mustard, or Roquefort sauce. Delicious.

🪑 24 🅿 🄰MC, V

▪ CARIBBEAN LOWLANDS

ALBANIA

🏨 WAYA GUAJIRA
$$$–$$$$
VÍA CUESTACITAS KM 1.5
TEL 57-1/508-2546
hotelwayaguajira.com

Striking for its "wow!" architecture, this recently launched and classily designed hotel (aiming principally at business travelers to the nearby coal mine) stands in marked contrast to the austerity of the landscape and *rancherías*. Furnishings are minimal yet suave, with colorful Wayúu fabrics, including hammocks, plus free Wi-Fi. The swimming pool provides relief from the heat, and the restaurant is the best for miles.

🛏 140 🄰 🏊 🎽 🛜 🄰AE, MC, V

ARACATACA

🏨 EL PATIO MÁGICO DE GABO
$$
CALLE 7 #5-57
TEL 57/310-571-7450

A pleasant little restaurant with tables arrayed around a patio. Attentive care provided by the owners, whose family were close friends to Gabriel García Márquez (aka Gabo). No surprise: The place is a mini-museum of memorabilia. The simple dishes include fried fish, and roast chicken with soup and platanos.

🛏 3 🅿 🄰 🄰 🄰None

BARRANCABERMEJA

🏨 HOTEL SANS SILVESTRE
$$$$
CENTRO COMERCIAL SANS SILVESTRE
CRA. 19 #58A-13
TEL 57-7/611-0100
hotelsansilvestre.com

Hidden within a large commercial mall (with cinema), this deluxe hotel combines sophisticated contemporary styling with state-of-the-art amenities, such as 42-inch (107 cm) flat-screen TVs, huge bathrooms, and contemporary chocolate-and-white color schemes. A food court and gourmet restaurant are steps away in the five-level mall.

🛏 48 🄰 🄰 🄰 🏊 🎽 🛜 🄰All major credit cards

BARRANQUILLA

🏨🍴 HOTEL DANN CARLTON BARRANQUILLA
$$$$$
CALLE 98 #52B-10
TEL 57-5/373-7777
www.danncarltonbaq.co

This deluxe redbrick high-rise, at the far north end of town, is topped by a disk-shaped restaurant overhanging the roof like the prow of Captain Kirk's starship *Enterprise*. The mammoth guest rooms have sober decor with autumnal color schemes, plus king-size beds, Wi-Fi (extra charge), cable TV, and all the desired amenities. The top-floor

Restaurante Bar El Giratorio (a Tony Roma's outlet) revolves through 360 degrees and offers sweeping vistas through its curved wall of glass.

ⓘ 142 🅿 🚭 💺 ⛄ 🏊 🍽 📶 Charge 🚭 All major credit cards

🏨 HOTEL EL PRADO
🍽 $$$$
CRA. 54 #70-10
TEL 57-5/369-7777
hotelelpradosa.com

A gracious republican-era hotel reminiscent of the Breakers in Palm Beach, Florida, this grande dame offers a superb locale in the heart of El Prado, plus heaps of elegance in its recently remodeled rooms. All have Wi-Fi and state-of-the-art amenities, although furnishings play on the period theme. Tennis, convention and business facilities, plus choice of restaurants, including the outdoor **Restaurante Pivijay,** which draws the local monied crowd for alfresco dining; the menu is international.

ⓘ 200 🅿 💺 🚭 ⛄ 🍽 📶 🚭 All major credit cards

🏨 HOTEL SONESTA BARRANQUILLA
$$$$
CALLE 106 #50-11
TEL 57-5/385-6060
sonesta.com/barranquilla

Set in a commercial mall on the far northern fringe of the city, this attractive, contemporary-themed hotel has spacious rooms with travertine floors and king beds with luxurious linens. Noise echoing up from the bar can be an annoyance in the atrium restaurant.

ⓘ 126 🅿 💺 🚭 ⛄ 🍽 📶 🚭 All major credit cards

🏨 HOTEL BARRANQUILLA PLAZA
$$$
CRA. 51B #79-246
TEL 57-5/361-0333
hbp.com.co

This modern high-rise offers modest elegance in its spacious rooms with IKEA-style furnishings and white-gold-and-blue color schemes, plus such conveniences as bathroom telephones. In the exclusive far north of the city.

ⓘ 176 🅿 🚭 💺 🚭 ⛄ 🍽 📶 🚭 All major credit cards

CABO DE LA VELA

🏨 RANCHERÍA UTTA
🍽 $
1.2 MILES (2 KM) W OF
CABO DE LA VELA
TEL 57/313-817-8076
rancheriautta.com

Perhaps the nicest among the area's many options, this Wayúu-run *ranchería* has a windsurf outlet on site and offers kayak rentals. Choice of hammocks alfresco or basic rooms with batik spreads for a dash of color. The airy restaurant offers American breakfasts, plus garlic shrimp, stewed goat, and similar traditional dishes.

ⓘ 96 🚭 None

🏨 RESTAURANTE &
🍽 HOSPEDAJE JARRINAPI
$
CABO DE LA VELA
TEL 57/321-600-2884
hospedajejarrinapi.com

This Wayúu-run beachfront hostel is one among two dozen or so almost identical options in traditional Wayúu fashion. Simple wooden huts here have poured concrete floors, cold-water showers, and hammocks in shaded patios. The restaurant serves

omelette breakfasts and simple yet filling meals.

ⓘ 19 🚭 None

CARTAGENA

HOTELS

🏨 DELIRIO HOTEL
$$$$$
CALLE DE LA IGLESIA #35-273,
CENTRO HISTÓRICO
TEL 57-5/660-2404
deliriohotel.com

In a city that claims many world-class boutique hotels, the Delirio Hotel stands out for its urbane South Beach–style sophistication and trendy decor. Cool white marble floors, whitewashed beamed ceilings, and clinically white walls in and out define the tone. Pine-colored hardwoods and tangerine pillows and cushions add splashes of color to this three-story minimalist conversion of a colonial town house. Top-of-the-line linens, state-of-the-art bathrooms with huge walk-in showers, and balconies (some with lounge chairs) highlight the rooms, with beds backed by floor-to-ceiling prints of yesteryear Cartagena. A wooden rooftop deck has loungers and a sofa.

🛗 17 ❄️ 🔲 🅿️ All major credit cards

SOMETHING SPECIAL

🏨 HOTEL LM
$$$$$
CALLE DE LA MANTILLA #3-56, CENTRO HISTÓRICO
TEL 57-5/664-9100
hotel-lm.com

Yet another luxury boutique hotel, this one exudes a distinctly individual style with its overwhelming attention to personalized service. Sumptuous comforts await behind its republican facade. The hoteliers here use chocolate, green, and mauve colors to great effect, combining minimalist decor with globe-spanning furnishings, such as Oriental rugs and signature embroidered linens. Travertine-clad bathrooms have huge freestanding tubs and motion-sensor lighting. Massage is offered on the rooftop sundeck. A kitchen and elegant dining room provide guests only with 24-hour service, with dishes prepared to order.

🛗 7 ❄️ 🔲 🏊 🅿️ All major credit cards

SOMETHING SPECIAL

🏨 SOFITEL LEGEND
🍽️ SANTA CLARA
$$$$$
CRA. 8 #39-29
TEL 57-5/664-4700
sofitel.com

Once the 16th-century Convento Santa Clara that

was a setting for Gabriel García Márquez's *Of Love and Other Demons* (coincidentally, the author's personal villa adjoins the hotel), this sumptuous French-run hotel features 21st-century styling behind its colonial facade. The once ascetic nun's quarters overlooking a lush courtyard with portico lounges today has two-level suites that ooze such comforts as plasma TVs and divinely comfy king-size beds. A modern addition wed to the original brick walls has 115 rooms overlooking a huge pool complex; many rooms have sea views. The 1621 restaurant serves gourmet dishes in a delightful setting that makes use of the convent's former dining hall. Main dishes include Angus beef with Camembert and mushroom sauce, and Chilean salmon with green risotto. The hotel also has a French bistro that serves homemade pastas, pizzas, breads, and croissants; an atmospheric bar with a crypt; plus deluxe full-service spa.

🛗 122 🅿️ ❄️ 🔲 🏊 🍽️ 📶 All major credit cards

🏨 ANANDÁ HOTEL
🍽️ BOUTIQUE
$$$$
CALLE DEL CUARTEL #36-77, BARRIO SAN DIEGO
TEL 57-5/664-4452
anandacartagena.com

Here are gorgeous suites in a tasteful contemporary remake of a colonial mansion in the heart of the old city. Behind the sturdy wooden door and historic 18th-century facade, this lovely boutique hotel has exposed redbrick walls, beamed ceilings, coralstone floors, and coral-and-chocolate color schemes throughout. Rooms are on three levels around the central courtyard, with a lounge deck

floating atop a pool. Stylish dark wicker furnishings are wed to state-of-the-art accoutrements, such as 42-inch (107 cm) flat-screen TVs, and divinely comfortable mattresses with luxurious linens and oodles of pillows. The 24-hour restaurant serves wholesome breakfasts with fresh-baked whole-wheat mini-loafs; plus tapas such as shrimp canapé in *alioli* sauce; and such appetizing entrées as grilled Chilean salmon with ginger mashed potatoes and orange sauce.

🛗 23 🅿️ ❄️ 🔲 🏊 📶 All major credit cards

🏨 HOTEL BÓVEDAS DE SANTA CLARA
$$$$
CALLE DEL TORNO #39-29, BARRIO SAN DIEGO
TEL 57-5/650-4469
bovedasdesantaclara.com

In a three-story republican-style mansion overlooking the city walls, this boutique hotel has been refitted with urbane deluxe rooms and loft suites boasting fashionable minimalist decor, modern comforts, plus balconies. Guests get privileges at the Hotel Sofitel Santa Clara, one block away. Rooftop solarium and Jacuzzi.

🛗 18 🅿️ ❄️ 🔲 🏊 📶 All major credit cards

SOMETHING SPECIAL

🏨 HOTEL CASA QUERO
$$$$
CALLE DEL QUERO #9-53, BARRIO SAN DIEGO
TEL 57/312-692-5027
hotelcasaquero.com

One of Cartagena's most adorable and intimate remakes, Hotel Casa Quero is a four-story boutique hotel with French provincial decor, including faux-faded eggshell blue Louis XIV–style furnishings. Every thoughtful extra has been provided for guests, from fluffy bathrobes and designer toiletries to 42-inch (107 cm) plasma TVs, DVDs, Wi-Fi, and iPod media players. The owners have also graced Casa Quero with a library, Turkish bath, and rooftop sundeck with plunge pool.

🛈 6 🛏 🌊 🛜 🚭 AE, MC, V

🏨 HOTEL HILTON CARTAGENA
$$$$
AV. ALMIRANTE BRION, EL LAGUITO
TEL 57-5/694-8000
hilton.com

For a beach vacation with the old city close at hand, the handsome high-rise Hilton outshines its many competitors, despite its unfavorable location at the tip of El Laguito, a ten-minute walk from the sands. Health-conscious travelers will appreciate such facilities as tennis courts and a well-equipped gym. It has a convention center and serves families with a watersports center and toboggan. Totally nonsmoking.

🛈 341 🅿 🚭 🛏 🛋 🌊 🛎 🚭 AE, MC, V

SOMETHING SPECIAL

🏨 TCHERASSI HOTEL & 🍴 SPA
$$$$
CALLE DEL SARGENTO MAYOR #6-21
TEL 57-5/664-4445
tcherassihotels.com

Acclaimed Colombian-born fashion designer Silvia Tcherassi is behind this stylish hotel, which fuses state-of-the-art amenities and comforts with the historic ambience of a completely restored 17th-century mansion. The seven spacious

suites are all individually styled by Tcherassi and feature partial bar-stone walls, glossy hardwood floors, plus private balconies. White-themed throughout, it is run with aplomb. The airy and ultrachic **Vera** restaurant opens onto a plunge pool and wall festooned with ferns. The Italian menu offers such divine dishes as *risotto al funghi* and decadent *giardino di chocolate* dessert.

🛈 7 🚭 🛏 🛋 🌊 🚭 All major credit cards

🏨 BANTÚ HOTEL
$$$–$$$$
CALLE DE LA TABLADA #7-62, CENTRO HISTÓRICO
TEL 57-5/664-3362
bantuhotel.com

This adorably stylish boutique hotel makes creative use of its aged architecture. Rooms vary widely from singles to a deluxe bi-level suite. Junior suites feature bare redbrick and limestone walls and terra-cotta floors inset with glass paving lit from beneath. All have cable TV, safes, and minibars. A lounge with rattan sofas opens to a cobbled, tree-shaded patio—one of three. Rooftop solarium with Jacuzzi and sauna.

🛈 11 🛏 🌊 🚭 AE, MC, V

🏨 HOTEL CASA LA FÉ
$$$
CALLE 2DA DE BADILLO #36-125
TEL 57-5/664-0306
casalafe.com

An exquisite colonial home festooned with flowering tropical vines and tucked behind nail-studded doors, this gracious nonsmoking boutique hotel opens to a narrow patio with colonial tile floors and fountain. Most rooms, on three levels, open to the courtyard; some have balconies overlooking Plaza Fernández de Madrid. The English/Colombian couple

---

PRICES

HOTELS
An indication of the cost of a double room in the high season is given by **$** signs.

$$$$$	Over $200
$$$$	$100–$200
$$$	$50–$100
$$	$25–$50
$	Under $25

RESTAURANTS
An indication of the cost of a three-course meal without drinks is given by **$** signs.

$$$$$	Over $35
$$$$	$20–$35
$$$	$10–$20
$$	$5–$10
$	Under $5

---

who own it have graced it throughout with period furnishings. The rooftop patio has a plunge pool.

🛈 14 🚭 🛏 🌊 🚭 AE, MC, V

🏨 HOTEL PORTAL DE SAN DIEGO
$$$
CALLE 2DA DE BADILLO #36-17
TEL 57-5/660-1083
portaldesandiego.com

Intimate is the watchword at this small boutique hotel located in the very center of the historic quarter, one block from Plaza Fernández de Madrid. Rooms are stylish albeit simply appointed, with tropical fruit colors offset against clinical whites. Some retain original colonial tile floors. All have the desired features: telephone, Wi-Fi, safe, and cable TV. If you're seeking a mid-priced hotel, this is as good as any.

🛈 11 🚭 🛏 🛜 🚭 AE, MC, V

🏨 Hotel 🛈 No. of guest rooms 🍴 Restaurant 🛏 No. of seats 🕐 Hours 🅿 Parking 🚭 Nonsmoking

🏨 MAKONDO HOTEL BOUTIQUE
$$–$$$
CALLE DEL CURATO #38-161, BARRIO SAN DIEGO
TEL 57-8/660-0823 OR 310-758-5493
hotelmakondo.com

Yet another remake of a lovely colonial home, this little bohemian gem is adorned with eclectic art, and bare brick walls add charm. You'd expect it to play on Gabriel García Márquez's *One Hundred Years of Solitude* . . . but no! Guest rooms are small; some are cramped. But decor is tasteful, and there's a small basement restaurant.

🛏 9 🆒 🅢 🅢 AE, MC, V

RESTAURANTS

🍴 CLUB DE PESCA
$$$$
FUERTE SAN SEBASTIÁN DEL PASTELILLO, MANGA
TEL 57-5/660-4594
clubdepesca.com

Founded in 1956, this acclaimed seafood restaurant occupies an 18th-century fortress lit by tiki lamps. Indoor and outdoor options. Couples can canoodle at a private table in a cannon embrasure that overhangs the harbor. Club de Pesca is famous for oysters *gratinado* with blue cheese and caramelized onions.

🍴 200 🕐 Closed B 🅿
🅢 All major credit cards

🍴 MONTE SACRO
$$$$
PARQUE BOLÍVAR #33-20
TEL 57/304-523-3701
restaurantemontesacro.com

Chef Abraham Dau conjures creative fusion dishes—with a focus on seafood—at this classy, brick-lined restaurant with walls of glass overlooking the plaza. Filet mignon in mushroom sauce and

seafood stew are house specialties.

🍴 60 🆒 🅢 All major credit cards

🍴 JUAN DEL MAR RESTAURANT
$$$
PLAZA DE SAN DIEGO #8-12
TEL 57-5/664-2782
juandelmar.com

A longtime favorite of local bohemians, this Peruvian seafood restaurant gets packed. A salsa band sometimes plays in an open courtyard with creeping vines and a well. You can peer into the open kitchen to view staff preparing your ceviche; *mofongo caribeño; langostino* in passion fruit sauce; or snails with coconut cream, ginger, lemongrass, and chili. Ceiling fans whir with enough speed to lift the roof off its beams!

🍴 80 🕐 Closed B 🅢 All major credit cards

SOMETHING SPECIAL

🍴 RESTAURANTE EL SANTÍSIMO
$$$
CALLE DEL TORNO #39-62
TEL 57-5/660-1532
restauranteelsantisimo.com

An über-chic restaurant with a contemporary cream-and-orange interior, plus leather seats, and a recherché menu. Various dining rooms surround a patio viewed through walls of glass. A perfect meal might feature salmon ceviche with honey, mustard, cilantro, and lime; and *la santísima* Trinidad—a traditional Caribbean dish with sautéed prawns and shredded white fish, stewed tomatoes, onions and garlic, cilantro, and lime, served with coconut rice. Leave room for the coffee custard with Baileys whipped cream.

🍴 100 🆒 🅢 All major credit cards

🍴 PACO'S RESTAURANT & TABERNA
$$
CALLE 35 #5, PLAZA DE SANTO DOMINGO
TEL 57-5/660-1638

Dine alfresco beneath red umbrellas while watching the flood of life as the crowds move through the plaza. Paco's mostly serves sandwiches and soups, but also stuffed crepes (try the mozzarella and spinach), plus garlic shrimp.

🍴 180 🆒 🅢 All major cards

🍴 RESTAURANTE CAFÉ SAN PEDRO
$$
PLAZA SAN PEDRO CLAVER #30-11
TEL 57-5/664-5121

This large, lofty, and airy space has massive windows all around. Industrial air-conditioning pipes. The fusion menu delights with such treats as Caribbean dumpling stuffed with black bean and curry paste, lemon shrimp with pork wonton on a base of squash, and Thai fish with coconut and citrus atop coconut rice. Also has patio dining.

🍴 200 🅢 AE, MC, V

GOLFO DE MORROSQUILLO

🏨 HOTEL PUNTA FARO
$$$
ISLA MÚCURA
TEL 57-5/356-5603
OR
57-1/616-3136
puntafaro.com

A two-hour boat trip from Cartagena, this beachfront hotel commands an exquisite tropical island to the northeast of the Golfo de Morrosquillo. It has daily boat transfers from Cartagena. Crafted entirely of timbers in indigenous

---

🔌 Elevator 🆒 Air-conditioning 🏊 Indoor pool 🏊 Outdoor pool 💪 Health club 📶 Wi-Fi 🅢 Credit cards

fashion, it's surrounded by palm trees. Spacious and comfy accommodations are graciously appointed in tropical style. French doors open to large balconies. Popular with Colombian families, the Hotel Punta Faro has water sports and other activities, plus nightly entertainment. (Transportation to the island costs an extra US$85. Pay at the dock.)

🛈 52 🅂 🅂 🅂 AE, MC, V

ISLAS DEL ROSARIO

🏨 **AGUA AZUL BEACH RESORT**
$$$$
CALLE STUART #7-46, ISLA BARÚ
TEL 57/311-420-2453
aguazulbeachresort.com
Combining Spanish colonial architecture (with gingerbread trim) and avant-garde tropical styling (including colorful batik spreads), this place oozes romance. Airy and luxuriously appointed rooms feature glazed hardwood or black-and-white checkered floors. The resort boasts its own beach, with water sports and volleyball available. A free shuttle is provided.

🛈 5 🅂 🅂 🅂 All major credit cards

🏨 **HOTEL SAN PEDRO DE MAJAGUA**
$$$$
ISLA GRANDE
TEL 57-5/650-4460 EXT. 4002
hotelmajagua.com
A peaceful and sophisticated island haven with stylishly rustic accommodations, this island hotel claims Pierce Brosnan, Mick Jagger, and other shutterbug-shy celebs as former guests. Its romantically appointed deluxe rooms and suites purposefully lack telephone, although flat-screen TVs were recently added. Fans take the edge off the heat,

as do cool limestone floors. Suites feature outdoor lounges with poured concrete sofas. It has a full-service dive center, plus kayaks and sailboats, and bike trips. The alfresco restaurant is shaded by dramatic strangler figs.

🛈 10 rooms, 7 suites
🅂 🅂 🅂 AE, MC, V

🏨 **HOTEL AGUA BARÚ**
$$$
ISLA BARÚ,
ENSENADA DE CHOLÓN
TEL 57-5/664-9431
hotelagua.com.co
This unpretentiously chic sister hotel to Cartagena's Hotel Agua has trendy bungalow suites with balconies offering views toward Isla Rosario, plus use of a boat to visit it. You'll sleep in a canopy bed beneath soaring needle-palm thatch in gleaming white rooms with navy blue cushions, and ocean vistas through shuttered French doors that peel back to huge verandas. Gourmet meals are served alfresco beneath a dramatic and lofty wooden canopy. A pebbled sundeck and horizon-edge pool overlook the hotel's small mangrove-lined beach, with a jetty for boat trips. Some bungalows are a steep climb from the main building.

🛈 3 🅂 🅂 🅂 MC, V

MINCA

🏨 **HOTEL MINCA**
$$
MINCA
TEL 57/315-519-3679
hotelminca.com
A lovely little hotel set in lush gardens, this conversion of a colonial-era convent formerly known as La Casona has colorful and simple decor and furnishings along with Wi-Fi in all rooms. Its appealing restaurant opens to a balcony with a view

of the wooded hills. It serves Colombian dishes.

🛈 14 🅿 🅂 📶 🅂 AE, MC, V, PayPal

🍴 **El MOX MUICA**
$$
BEHIND HOTEL MINCA
TEL 57/311-699-6718
This delightful art-filled little "restaurant" in the mountains is the home of Andres and Andrea, who conjure divine dishes from organic produce. Start perhaps with a fresh tomato, cheese, and basil salad, or chicken-stuffed crepe with a citrusy lulo and ginger sauce, as a prelude to specialty flavored chocolates. Wi-Fi is available.

🔢 4 🕐 Closed B 🅂 None

MOMPOX

🏨 **BIOMA MOMPOX HOTEL BOUTIQUE**
$$$

CALLE REAL DEL MEDIO #18-59
TEL 53-5/685-6733
bioma.co
This lovely property blends hip contemporary furnishings in a colonial mansion. Rooms feature flat-screen TVs, Wi-Fi, and iPod docking stations, plus elegant bathrooms. Rooftop whirlpool spa and sundeck.
🅘 11 🅢 🅒 🅐 🛜
🅢 MC, V

🏨 LA CASA AMARILLA
$–$$$
CALLE 13 #1-05
TEL 53-5/685-6326
lacasaamarillamompos.com
The choice budget option in town, this intimate charmer in the historic heart of town is owned by British travel writer Richard McColl and his Colombian girlfriend, Alba Torres. What started out as a hostel with two unisex dorms has expanded, with three simply furnished rooms with beamed ceilings and lovely murals, and eight spacious suites with flat-screen TVs and private bathrooms. McColl arranges interesting local tours. Howler monkeys sometimes frolic on the roof.
🅘 3 rooms, 8 suites
🅢 🅒 🅢 AE, MC, V, PayPal

PALOMINO

🏨 RESERVA NATURAL EL MATUY
$
PALOMINO
TEL 57/315-751-8456
elmatuy.com
A peaceful no-frills beachfront retreat popular with backpackers and birders, it has simply appointed, candlelit thatched cabins on stilts, with hammocks on broad verandas. Limited electricity.
🅘 10 cabins, 24 rooms
🅿 🅢 None

PUNTA GALLINAS

🏨 HOSPEDAJE ALEXANDRA
$
PUNTA GALLINAS
TEL 57/318-500-6942
OR
315-538-2418
E-MAIL hospedajealexandra@hotmail.com
You can sleep outside in hammocks at this no-frills, breeze-swept Wayúu *ranchería*. For privacy, opt for a comfy bed in a cactus-frame hut with private bathroom (your shower will be a scoop-and-pour from a bucket). Your friendly host, Ignacio "Chander" Alexander Arends, will take you on tours in his SUV, while his wife, Leonidas, whips up tasty garlic lobster or fresh-caught fish meals.
🅘 10 🅢 None

RÍOHACHA

🏨 TAROA LIFESTYLE HOTEL
$$$
CALLE 1 #4-77
TEL 57-5/729-1122
taroahotel.com
New in 2014, this boutique hotel is now by far the nicest hotel in town. The lovely contemporary-themed, gleaming white guest rooms feature local fabrics, including hammock, plus Wi-Fi and other amenities. The seafront pool and deck are highlights.
🅘 46 🅢 🅒 🛜 🅢 AE, MC, V

SANTA MARTA

🏨 HOTEL BE LA SIERRA
$$$$
CALLE 72 #6-30,
RODADERO
TEL 57-5/347-0099
hotelbelasierra.com
This beachfront resort hotel offers comfortable and eye-pleasing, yet understated, accommodations in somber autumnal tones. The Hotel be La Sierra's open-air terrace restaurant, complete with bamboo furnishings, serves a buffet and a la carte meals.
🅘 63 rooms, 11 suites 🅿 🔁 🅢 🅐 All major credit cards

🏨 IROTAMA RESORT
$$$
KM 14 VÍA A CIÉNAGA, 8.7 MILES (14 KM) W OF SANTA MARTA
TEL 57-5/438-0600
irotama.com
Family in tow? Then this large beach resort west of Rodadero may be just the ticket, with lots of facilities for both kids and adults, including tennis courts, nightly entertainment, water sports, a driving range and putting green, children's club, and convention facilities. It offers a choice of tree-shaded suites, bungalows, and villas, plus a high-rise apartment-hotel.
🅘 350 🅿 🔁 🅢 🅐 🐦 🅢 All major credit cards

🏨 LA CASA DEL FAROL
$$$
CALLE 18 #3-115
TEL 57-5/423-1572
Santa Marta's only true boutique hotel, this charming 18th-century property has been restored and fitted with modern accoutrements. The six individually styled rooms are delightfully furnished and have ceiling fans. Some rooms play on the historic theme; others are retro-modern, such as the Nueva York room with black and white furnishings by Philippe Starck. A rooftop terrace has a small pool and sundeck. Free Wi-Fi, plus use of laptop.
🅘 6 🅢 🅒 🅐 🛜 🅢 MC, V

🔁 Elevator 🅒 Air-conditioning 🅐 Indoor pool 🅐 Outdoor pool 🐦 Health club 🛜 Wi-Fi 🅢 Credit cards

▦ TAMACÁ BEACH RESORT HOTEL

$$$

CRA. 2A #11A-98, RODADERO
TEL 57-5/422-7015
tamaca.com.co

Facing the beach at Rodadero, this gleaming white, five-story modern resort hotel offers colorful accommodations, including junior suites, with complimentary Wi-Fi and a bevy of must-have amenities. Its spacious lobby opens to a pool complex. An annex—Torre Norte—is one block away and one block inland from the beach.

ⓘ 141 🅿 🛗 🚭 ♨ 🛜 🚭
All major credit cards

▦ ALUNA CASA & CAFÉ

$$

CALLE 21 #5-27,
CENTRO HISTÓRICO
TEL 57-5/432-4916
OR
310-709-3684
alunahotel.com

This small budget option is run to high standards by Irish expat Patrick Fleming. A five-minute walk from the waterfront, it occupies a converted 1920s town house in a working-class residential district and immediately earned rave reviews. Its lounge-café has a book exchange, cable TV, and free Wi-Fi, plus there's a roof terrace. Sleeping options include dorms, and singles and doubles. Reservations required.

ⓘ 14 🚭 🚭 🛜 🚭 None

🍽 DONDE CHUCHO

$$$$

CALLE 6 #2-61, RODADERO
TEL 57-5/422-1752
dondechuchorodadero
.inf.travel

One of the city's finest dining options, this elegant colonial-themed restaurant, recently relocated to Rodadero, offers

a choice of dining in an air-conditioned interior or the outside patio facing onto Parque de los Novios. The menu emphasizes seafood, such as garlic squid, and sea bass in tamarind sauce, and a delicious seafood stew, plus cannelloni, pastas, and risottos.

🪑 60 🕐 Closed Sun. 🚭 None

🍽 RESTAURANTE BAR MUELLE 8

$$$$

CRA. 1RA #10A-12,
MUELLE DE CRUCEROS
TEL 57-5/431-9896
OR
316-385-7476

This classy restaurant belongs to Chef Pincho Padilla, former mayor of El Rodadero, and draws the city's bigwigs for seafood dishes enjoyed in classy surrounds.

🪑 60 🕐 Closed B 🚭 None

🍽 CRÊPES EXPRESSO

$$$

CRA. 1 #18-67
TEL 57/317-280-5039

Needless to say, this French-owned landmark restaurant with redbrick walls and beamed ceiling specializes in crepes, stuffed any of 13 ways (e.g., with beef, mushrooms, or Rocquefort cheese), or as sweet crepes such as Suzettes. Hang out and linger over ice cream and coffee.

🪑 60 🕐 Closed Sat.–Sun & L 🚭 None

🍽 LAMART

$$

CRA. 3 #16-36
TEL 57-5/431-0797
lamart.com.co

Situated on a narrow pedestrian street free of traffic, this small bohemian restaurant with bare brick walls and simple wooden furniture serves excellent

---

PRICES

HOTELS

An indication of the cost of a double room in the high season is given by $ signs.

$$$$$	Over $200
$$$$	$100–$200
$$$	$50–$100
$$	$25–$50
$	Under $25

RESTAURANTS

An indication of the cost of a a three-course meal without drinks is given by $ signs.

$$$$$	Over $35
$$$$	$20–$35
$$$	$10–$20
$$	$5–$10
$	Under $5

Peruvian ceviche, pesto quesadilla, and a house special of muscle and clams in white wine sauce, with onion, garlic, and paprika.

🪑 20 🚭 AE, MC, V

SINCELEJO

▦ HOTEL BOSTON

$$$

CALLE 25B #31-14
TEL 53-5/280-4022
hotelbostonltda.com

This modern downtown hotel wins no prizes but is perfectly adequate thanks to spacious and comfy rooms with Wi-Fi and cable TV. Options include junior suites and a presidential suite. A small swimming pool tucked in a courtyard proves perfect for beating the heat. The restaurant offers Asian options, including sushi.

ⓘ 50 🅿 🚭 🚭 ♨ 🛜
🚭 AE, MC, V

🏨 Hotel ⓘ No. of guest rooms 🍽 Restaurant 🪑 No. of seats 🕐 Hours 🅿 Parking 🚭 Nonsmoking

TAGANGA

 HOTEL LA BALLENA
AZUL
$$$–$$$$
CRA. 1 & CALLE 18,
PLAYA TAGANGA
TEL 57-5/421-9009
hotelballenaazul.com

The best hotel in town overlooks the nicest section of beach, free of fishing boats. Recently remodeled in an exciting contemporary vogue, this property gleams white throughout, including the furnishings (some rooms are bedecked in tropical pastels). En suite bowl-shaped Jacuzzi tubs add a romantic touch, and ceiling fans are a plus. The blue-and-white beachfront **Restaurante Blue** is also Taganga's finest for alfresco dining; seafood and crepes highlight the menu.
🛏 30 P 🅿 None

 HOTEL OCEAN
TAGANGA
INTERNACIONAL
$$$
CALLE 14 #1B-75
TEL 57-5/420-3776
hoteloceantaganga.com

Facing the town's tiny plaza, half a block from the beach, this two-story hotel extends along an atrium courtyard. Rooms are modestly yet stylishly furnished with trendy chocolates and whites, with tropical fruit (lime, tangerine, and more) curtains and cushions. Porches have hammocks, and there is a rooftop terrace. Free Wi-Fi.
🛏 12 📶 🅿 AE, MC, V

BABAGANOUSH
RESTAURANTE & BAR
$$$
CRA. 1C #18-22
TEL 57/318-868-1476
E-MAIL restaurante
babaganoush@hotmail.com

Offering excellent beach views, this Dutch-run restaurant above Taganga Diver Center has a globe-spanning menu, from falafels and Thai green curry to local seafood and steaks. Go for happy hour and the ensuing party scene.
🍴 40 🕐 Closed Tues. & B 🅿 None

MOJITOS BEACH BAR
$$
CALLE 14 #1B-61
TEL 57-5/421-9187

Despite its name, there's no Cuban food here. Mojito specializes in a Mediterranean menu featuring Greek salad and various pasta dishes. It's known for its ceviches, from smoked fish to Thai, and for its parties fueled by cocktail specials and live DJs. A daily special includes a starter, main course, and drink. An Internet café adjoins.
🍴 30 🕐 Closed Tues. 🅿 None

TAYRONA

SOMETHING SPECIAL

 ECOHABS
$$$$$
ARRECIFES, PARQUE NACIONAL
NATURAL TAYRONA
TEL 57/311-600-1614
ecohabsantamarta.com

This deluxe hillside resort hotel enjoys a privileged position at the eastern gateway to Tayrona national park. Set amid a forested boulder field, its thatched circular huts adorn the hillside (the hotel is not appropriate for handicapped travelers), offering spectacular coastal vistas from balconies and open-air lounges. The resort has king-size lounge beds as well as a whirlpool spa on the sands. The circular open-air restaurant is topped by a soaring thatch roof and delivers gourmet fare, such as a delicious shrimp ceviche,

sancocho with coconut water, and fish filet wrapped in banana leaf with coconut rice and avocado salad. Staff dresses in uniforms inspired by the traditional Kogi costume.
🛏 20 P 🅿 All major credit cards

SOMETHING SPECIAL

 HOTEL PLAYA KORALIA
$$$–$$$$
PLAYA KORALIA, 29 MILES
(47 KM) E OF SANTA MARTA
TEL 57/310-642-2574
koralia.com

A perfect combination of luxury, simplicity, and eco-conscientiousness, this relaxing, ethnic-themed beachfront resort pays homage to globe-spanning deities. Hence, you might sleep in cabins named Ganesh or Nirvana. Cabins are spaced well apart amid forested grounds, guaranteeing secluded privacy—one reason Shakira and other Colombian paparazzi-shy celebs love it. Thatched whitewashed cabins with bamboo screen walls, colorful mosaic murals, and poured concrete patio wave-form sofas are utterly romantic—a mood enhanced by gauzy mosquito drapes hung around canopy beds. Roofless "rain forest showers." Campers can pitch their tents; meals are included in rates. You dine, literally, on the sands. Massage studio.
🛏 18 P 🍽 🅿 All major credit cards

TAIRONAKA
$$–$$$
RÍO DON DIEGO, 36 MILES
(58 KM) E OF SANTA MARTA
TEL 57/317-666-8836
taironaka.com

Occupying an old indigenous village with stone terraces, this riverside eco-resort offers a delightful mid-price alternative to the campgrounds of Tayrona national park, and the luxury of Hotel Playa Koralia and EcoHabs. The rustic cabins are simple but charming, and are set in lush grounds. Thatched open-air restaurant serves local dishes. Kayaks and tubes available.

🛏 11 🅿 🚭 🗎 All major credit cards

VALLEDUPAR

🏨 **CASA ROSALÍA**
$$$–$$$$
CALLE 16 #10-10
TEL 57-5/574-4129
lacasarosalia.com
This boutique hotel, on the main street in the heart of the historic downtown, is a converted 1950s modernist mansion with leafy garden patios. Tastefully decorated with contemporary furnishings and a scattering of antiques, it exudes comfort and good taste. Flat-screen TVs and Wi-Fi.

🛏 5 🅿 🚭 🗎 🛜
🚭 All major credit cards

🏨 **HOTEL SONESTA**
🍴 **VALLEDUPAR**
$$$–$$$$
DIAGONAL 10 #6N-15
TEL 57-5/574-8686
sonesta.com/valledupar
Striking for its stylish contemporary design and decor, this urban hotel (handily located in Guatapuri Plaza at the far north end of town) is also urbane enough to appeal to New York and London's city slickers. Aimed at sophisticated business travelers, it has Wi-Fi, full concierge service, and an executive floor. Guest rooms are furnished in trendy chocolates and gleaming whites. The **Manumkana Restaurant** is among the city's most upscale and serves fusion dishes.

🛏 108 🅿 🚭 🚭 🚭 🗎 📺
🛜 🚭 All major credit cards

🏨 **HOSTAL PROVINCIA**
$–$$
CALLE 16A #5-25
TEL 57-5/580-0558
provinciavalledupar.com
This clean, efficient Colombian-owned hostel, one block from Plaza Alfonso López, is run to international standards and offers a choice of dorm rooms or private rooms, each either with a fan or air-conditioned. Its many facilities include a laundry, TV room, free storage, and use of the kitchen, plus hammocks on a terra-cotta patio. It also offers its guests free Wi-Fi.

🛏 8 🚭 🛜 🚭 None

■ WESTERN HIGHLANDS

ALCALA

🏨 **FINCA HOTEL EL BOSQUE DEL SAMAN**
$$$$
VÍA ALCALA VEREDA KM 5, LA CAA
TEL 57-6/336-5589
bosquesdelsaman.com
This rustic yet delightful hacienda combines historic country ambience with a great setting, cozy comforts, and plenty of activities: It has forest trails and a zip line tour. At the heart of a working coffee estate and cattle farm, it offers guests a chance to milk the cows and learn about artisanal coffee production. Colorful guest rooms have gracious country-style furnishings.

🛏 32 🅿 🚭 🗎 🚭 MC, V

ARMENIA

🏨 **HACIENDA BAMBUSA**
$$$–$$$$
VÍA EL CAIMO–PROTUGALITO KM 93, LA TEBAIDA
TEL 57/311-506-9915
haciendabambusa.com

PRICES

HOTELS
An indication of the cost of a double room in the high season is given by $ signs.

$$$$$	Over $200
$$$$	$100–$200
$$$	$50–$100
$$	$25–$50
$	Under $25

RESTAURANTS
An indication of the cost of a a three-course meal without drinks is given by $ signs.

$$$$$	Over $35
$$$$	$20–$35
$$$	$10–$20
$$	$5–$10
$	Under $5

Set in lovely countryside at the heart of a multifaceted plantation, this ecolodge in the style of a traditional hacienda makes effusive use of bamboo. Contemporary artworks grace the walls. Bedrooms are sparsely furnished, but have terra-cotta floors plus satellite TV and terraces. A small pool studs the gracious palm-shaded grounds. Excellent birding. Four-wheel drive recommended to reach, about 15 miles (24 km) south of Armenia.

🛏 7 🅿 🚭 🗎 🚭 MC, V

🏨 **HACIENDA FINCA EL BALSO**
$$–$$$
VÍA ARMENIA AL AEROPUERTO EL EDÉN KM 5
TEL 57/300-656-5656
fincaelbalso.com
A century-old coffee estate. The hacienda is filled with

🏨 Hotel 🛏 No. of guest rooms 🍴 Restaurant 🪑 No. of seats 🕐 Hours 🅿 Parking 🚭 Nonsmoking

antiques. Breezes ease through glassless, shuttered windows. Wide, shady verandas on two levels have rockers. The owner, Julián Morales de la Pava, leads tours of the coffee fields.
🛏 5 🅿 🚹 ⛱ 🅢 None

🏨 HOTEL CAFÉ REAL
$$–$$$
CRA. 18 #21-32
TEL 57-6/744-3055
hotelcafereal.com
Billing itself as an "art and business hotel," the lively and colorful Hotel Café Real is festooned with contemporary art pieces. Its modern architecture and styling will suit young sophisticates. Facilities include steam room and massage, plus Internet cafe. Downtown, it's handy for sightseeing.
🛏 40 🅿 🚹 🔄 🅢 Café
🅢 All major credit cards

FILANDIA

🍴 HELENA ADENTRO
$$–$$$
CRA. 7 #8-01
TEL 57/321-873-9825
helenaadentro.com
Reason enough to visit Filandia, this sensational restaurant is run by a Paisa–New Zealand couple, who use fresh local ingredients to deliver delicious tapas, plus killer cocktails and coffees. It doubles as an art gallery and has Wi-Fi.
🍴 40 🕐 Closed Mon.–Tues.
& B 🅢 🅢 MC, V

IBAGUÉ

🏨 HOTEL DANN COMBEIMA
$$$$
CRA. 2 #12-37
TEL 57-8/261-8888
hotelesdann.com
The city's classiest digs are in this stylish contemporary

hotel, which sets the tone with a marble lobby featuring stainless-steel rails and dramatic contemporary art. The regal guest rooms have splendid views and elegant furnishings, including plump leather lounge chairs. All have Wi-Fi.
🛏 61 🅿 🚹 🔄 🅢 🅥 🅢
🅢 All major credit cards

🏨 HOTEL EL EDÉN BOUTIQUE SPA
$$$$
CRA. 45 SUR #161-180,
6.2 MILES (10 KM) S OF IBAGUÉ
TEL 57-8/269-5538
eledenhotelboutiquespa.com
First impressions can deceive at this upscale boutique hotel in an industrial zone on the southwest outskirts of the city. Beyond the guard gates, this colorful, two-story hotel is tucked in a valley. Spacious and sophisticated rooms have contemporary furnishings. The open-air restaurant and lounge-bar overlook a large swimming pool and tennis court.
🛏 9 🅿 🚹 ⛱ ⛱ 🅢 None

🏨 HOTEL INTERNACIONAL
🍴 CASA MORALES
$$$$
CRA. 3RA #3-47,
BARRIO LA POLA
TEL 57-8/261-9404
hotelcasamorales.com
This redbrick high-rise, located close to the city core, aims for both business and family-focused travelers. Its variety of junior suites and suites offer Wi-Fi, flat-screen TVs, tile floors, and Edwardian-themed furnishings. Facilities include a sauna, game room, and small cinema, and a pianist tickles the ivories in the large restaurant with bamboo furniture.
🛏 131 🅿 🔄 🅢 🅥 🅢
🅢 All major credit cards

MANIZALES

🏨 HACIENDA VENECIA
$$$
5 MILES (8 KM) W OF MANIZALES
TEL 57/320-636-5719
haciendavenecia.com
A throwback to a more peaceful era, this boutique hotel immerses you in country simplicity. It forms the heart of a coffee estate. Expect to share your room with moths as big as your hand. You'll dine well, if simply, on country fare such as potato soup and fried chicken breast with *papas* and salad. At night, sit in retro lounge chairs on the broad veranda and savor the chirping of insects and frogs.
🛏 8 🅿 ⛱ 🅢 MC, V

🏨 HOTEL CARRETERO
$$$
CRA. 23 #35A-31
TEL 57-6/887-9190
hotelcarretero.com
Standing over the main drag in town, the drab exterior of this five-story hotel hides an über-chic interior, with a combo of trendy chocolate, white, and bloodred decor. Suites have full office setups with the latest technology. Huge walk-in glass-and-marble showers. Twenty-four-hour business center. Friendly and helpful staff.
🛏 100 🅿 🔄 🅢 🅢 Business center 🅢 All major credit cards

🍴 ALTO PASTI TRATTORIA
$$$
CRA. 24A #58A-03,
LA ESTRELLA
TEL 57-6/881-2068
altopasti.co
Near the Zona Rosa, this well-managed Italian restaurant combines chic decor, eclectic music, and in or out dining. A full range of delicious pastas, risottos, lasagnas,

---

 🔄 Elevator 🚹 Air-conditioning 🅢 Indoor pool ⛱ Outdoor pool 🅥 Health club 🅢 Wi-Fi 🅢 Credit cards

and raviolis, plus pepper steak and seafood dishes.

🛏 70 🅿 🕐 Closed Sun. & B
⬙ All major credit cards

MEDELLÍN

🏨 ART HOTEL
$$$$
CRA. 41 #9-31,
ZONA ROSA
TEL 57-4/369-7900
arthotel.com.co

This loft-like boutique hotel has a superb position one block off Parque Lleras, in the heart of the city's epicenter of nightlife. Rooms and suites feature glazed concrete floors, beam ceilings, and sumptuous bathrooms with large walk-in showers. Hip decor caters to a young, sophisticated clientele, including flat-screen TVs and Wi-Fi. It features art galleries on its exposed red-brick walls.

🛈 54 🅿 🚭 ⬙ 🕐 📺 🛜
⬙ All major credit cards

🏨 HOTEL DANN CARLTON
🍴 MEDELLÍN
$$$$
CRA. 43A #7-50 &
AV. EL POBLADO
TEL 57-5/444-5151
danncarlton.com/medellin

In the heart of the financial, hotel, and entertainment district, the Dann Carlton sets a regal tone with its marble-clad lobby with sweeping staircase. Golds, taupes, and navy blues combine with Edwardian decor in spacious guest rooms that aim to please both business and leisure travelers. All modern conveniences are provided, including Wi-Fi (extra charge). Its choice of restaurants include a **Tony Roma's** in a cantilevered rooftop restaurant with all-around wall of glass for spectacular views as it revolves

through 360 degrees. The walk-in swimming pool has a fountain, and there's a sauna and Turkish bath.

🛈 200 🅿 🚭 ⬙ 🛁 📺
📷 Charge ⬙ All major credit cards

🏨 HOTEL PORTON
MEDELLÍN
$$$$
CRA. 43A #9-51
TEL 57-4/333-2020
hotelportonmedellin.com

A thoroughly avant-garde high-rise with dramatic architecture. Wi-Fi, cable TV, and hair dryers are all standard in elegantly furnished guest rooms. Choice of elegant club-room and traditional-style open-air restaurants. The spa includes a pilates studio. Located on the upscale Golden Mile close to boutiques, cafés, and businesses.

🛈 71 🅿 🚭 ⬙ 🕐 📺 🛜
⬙ All major credit cards

🍴 BASILICA
$$$
CRA. 38 #8A-4,
TEL 57-4/311-7366
restaurantebasilica.com

This airy Peruvian seafood restaurant on the south side of Parque Lleras impresses with the quality of its cuisine, which includes sushi (do try the Lleras rolls, with unagi). Get there early on weekends, when it gets packed. The open sides permit a grandstand view over the Zona Rosa action.

🛏 250 🅿 🕐 Closed B
⬙ All major credit cards

🍴 BONUAR
$$$
CRA. 44 #19A-100
TEL 57-4/235-3577
bonuar.com

To the side of the Museo de Arte Moderno, this

stylish café-restaurant will satisfy sophisticates with its urbane decor, including leather banquets and open-air wooden deck. It features a cocktail bar and hosts live blues and jazz. Go along for the Sunday brunch. The menu ranges from soups and ceviche to such entrées as creole lobster and shrimp gumbo.

🛏 60 🅿 🕐 Closed B
⬙ All major credit cards

🍴 RESTAURANTE
HACIENDA REAL
$$$
CRA. 49 #52-98, CENTRO
TEL 57-4/511-5330
restaurantehacienda.com

This downtown restaurant is renowned for its *bandeja paisa*—the national dish—prepared on an open grill. It also serves other meat plus seafood dishes in a casual ambience. It's

---

tucked-away upstairs, on the second floor, has an airy terrace for viewing the street life below.

🛏 132 🕐 Closed Sun. D
🌐 All major credit cards

MONTENEGRO

🏨 FINCA LOS GIRASOLES
$$$–$$$$
VÍA ARMENIA–MONTENEGRO KM 5
TEL 57-6/749-8528
OR
311-383-9885
fincalosgirasoles.com
A member of the Haciendas del Café group, this rustic blue-and-white colonial-era hacienda exudes yesteryear country charm. Furnished with antiques, including brass beds. The lounge-restaurant with chimney offers elegant place settings and has lovely views over the gardens vibrant with bougainvillea. It even has a chapel.

ℹ 20 🅿 🏊 🌊 🌐 MC, V

SOMETHING SPECIAL

🏨 CASA DE CAMPO EL DELIRIO
$$$
VÍA MONTENEGRO–PARQUE DE CAFÉ KM 1
TEL 57-6/741-5106
OR
310-438-9005
The decor at this delightful country quinta in classic *paisa* style whisks you back a century in time. Graced throughout with antiques, the public lounges are stuffed with charming porcelain pieces, dolls, and wrought-iron lanterns. Guest rooms are a striking counterpoint, with a gorgeous contemporary mood and luxurious linens. Wood-paneled ceilings and terra-cotta floors add to the mood. Handy for an early

morning visit to the Parque del Café, minutes away, but you can walk among the hotel's own coffee fields.

ℹ 8 🅿 🏊 🌊 AE, MC, V

PEREIRA

SOMETHING SPECIAL

🏨 SAZAGUA
🍴 $$$$$
VÍA CERRITOS KM 7, ENTRADA 4, URBANIZACIÓN QUIMBAYITA
TEL 57-6/337-9895
OR
313-649-4579
www.sazagua.com
An exemplary boutique hotel set in exquisite gardens, this contemporary hilltop two-story lodge is evocative of an antique *casona* (country mansion). Spacious and airy, its lounges and huge guest rooms feature wood beams, terra-cotta floors, and a wealth of antiques and Asiatic miscellany that recall the best of yesteryear. Furnishings also blend antiques with contemporary styling, exquisite artwork, and heaps of throw rugs. A lap pool with sundeck is framed by tall palms slung with hammocks. It has Wi-Fi and a business center, plus a stone-lined spa. The gracious restaurant, on an open-air garden-view terrace, fuses local ingredients with international inspiration and has an ever evolving menu. Try the salmon grilled with citric sauce on a bed of steamed veggies with croquettes; or langostinos with white rice and plantains bathed in a bean sauce. Divine!

ℹ 24 🅿 🏊 🌊 🏊 🌐
🌐 All major credit cards

🏨 HACIENDA SAN JOSÉ
$$$
VÍA DE PEREIRA–CERRITOS KM 4, ENTRADA 16, CADENA EL TIGRE
TEL 57-6/313-2612
haciendahotelsanjose.com
Built in 1888, this classical *casona* transports you metaphorically back to England with its interior decor, and to Tuscany in its lovely grounds with a pool inset in a stone patio. Bougainvillea clambers up the exterior walls, topped by an aged red-tile roof. Period antiques throughout. A broad veranda runs the length of the upper story.

ℹ 10 🅿 🏊 🌊 🏊
🌐 All major credit cards

🏨 HOTEL CASTILLA REAL
$$$
CALLE 15 #12B-15
TEL 57-6/333-2192
hotelcastillareal.com
A modern three-story, red-brick hotel with a yesteryear-themed interior, including curling wrought-iron staircase and Edwardian furnishings in public arenas. Carpeted bedrooms, however, have contemporary furnishings and a full roster of amenities, including in-room safes, mini-bars, and Internet modems. Charming English-style restaurant with barrel-vaulted ceiling mural. Café terrace offers fine cathedral views.

ℹ 24 🅿 🏊 🏊 🎦 🌐
🌐 All major credit cards

SALENTO

🏨 THE PLANTATION HOUSE
$–$$$
ALTO DE CORONEL, CALLE 7 #1-04
TEL 57/316-285-2603
theplantationhouse
salento.com
A delightful centenary farmstead in two parts,

this hostel is owned and run by a savvy English traveler who has settled in the coffee zone. Graced with flowerpots and terra-cotta tiles, it offers a choice of dorms and homey yet cozy private rooms (some with shared bathrooms). Hammocks are slung in patio gardens, and guests get use of two kitchens. A tremendous information source is the house's large English-language library.

🚹 15 🅿 🚭 🚭 None

🍴 CAFÉ JESÚS MARTÍN
$$
CRA. 6TA #6-14
TEL 57/300-735-5679
cafejesusmartin.com
This coffee shop, situated in an old mansion off the plaza is delightfully adorned with an eclectic miscellany, from pendant old bicycles to naïve art. Gourmet cappuccinos, espressos, and absolutely yummy baked goods can be enjoyed while listening to relaxing music.

🪑 30 🚭 None

SANTA FÉ DE ANTIOQUIA

🏨 HOTEL MARISCAL ROBLEDO
$$$–$$$$
CRA. 12 #9-70
TEL 57-4/853-1111
hotelmariscalrobledo.com
On Plazoleta de la Chinca, the Hotel Mariscal Robledo is the town's finest option. The owners have conjured a lovely hotel from an 18th-century mansion full of antiques and period detail, including exposed redbrick walls, beam ceilings, and broad verandas. The modestly furnished rooms vary; some have antique four-poster beds; others boast art nouveau pieces. The hotel has

free Wi-Fi throughout, and guests get use of a lovely swimming pool, Turkish bath, game room with Ping-Pong and pool tables, plus bicycles. Large swimming pool and sundeck. Bargain rates.

🚹 37 🅿 🚭 🚭 🏖 📺 🛜
🚭 All major credit cards

SOMETHING SPECIAL

🍴 QUEAREPAEN-AMORARTE
$$$
CARR. VÍA LAS PALMAS KM 30, EL RETIRO
TEL 57/542-0011
arepamor.com
Serving contemporary interpretations of classic country fare cooked over a traditional wood-fired stove, this open-air restaurant also has sensational contemporary decor. Gourmet dishes such as mixed-meat brochetta, and a mixed veggie tray with cheese, almonds, and vinaigrette, are served with an artistic flourish. The chef uses only fresh organic produce. TV personality Anthony Bourdain justifiably raved about it on his show *No Reservations,* and reservations are advised.

🪑 40 🕐 Closed Mon.–Tues.
🚭 None

🍴 COMEDIAÉ
$$–$$$
CALLE 11 #8-03,
PARQUE SANTA BARBARA
TEL 57/301-596-3032
A delightful spot to enjoy criollo dishes, including garlic trout or crepes stuffed with shrimp, and even apple pie. This brick-lined venue is festooned with colorful art. It hosts live music, including jazz, and sometimes screens movies in the plaza.

🪑 40 🅿 🕐 Closed Tues. in low season 🚭 None

PRICES

HOTELS
An indication of the cost of a double room in the high season is given by **$** signs.

$$$$$	Over $200
$$$$	$100–$200
$$$	$50–$100
$$	$25–$50
$	Under $25

RESTAURANTS
An indication of the cost of a a three-course meal without drinks is given by **$** signs.

$$$$$	Over $35
$$$$	$20–$35
$$$	$10–$20
$$	$5–$10
$	Under $5

■ SOUTHERN HIGHLANDS

BUGA

🏨 🍴 HOTEL GUADALA-JARA BUGA
$$$$
CALLE 1 #13-33
TEL 57-2/236-2611
hotelguadalajara.com.co
Billing itself as a California colonial-style hotel, this lovely boutique property invokes images of the Spanish missions with its cloistered arcades opening to a lovely patio garden with fountain. Spacious guest rooms are far from monastic, however, with gracious furnishings and modern amenities. Junior suites have high-speed Internet modems. Wi-Fi in public lounges. The wood-paneled restaurant has an open-air patio and serves local favorites such as chicken

stew and empanadas. A disco draws locals on weekend nights. Located just three blocks from the cathedral.

⬆ 67 🅿 ❄ ❄ 🏊 🏋
🛜 In public areas
🔑 All major credit cards

CALI

🏨 NH ROYAL CALI
$$$$
CRA. 100B #11A-99
TEL 57-2/330-7777
nh-hotels.com
This highly ranked Dutch chain offers steadfast service and contemporary elegance. The sophisticated mood of the curving atrium lobby carries to the guest rooms, with their whites and chocolate, flat-screen TVs, Wi-Fi, and other modern features. The hotel has a choice of restaurants, plus plenty of services to keep you amused on rainy days.

⬆ 145 🅿 ❄ ❄ ❄ ❄ 🏊 🏋
🛜 🔑 All major credit cards

🏨 HOTEL CASONA LA MERCED
$$$
CALLE 7 #1-65
TEL 57-2/489-4046
Perfectly situated for exploring the historic core, this charming historic property is perhaps the most intimate option in town and provides a cozy alternate to the large-scale chain hotels nearby. Lovely furnishings combine colonial and contemporary touches in the rooms. All have cable TV; some have Wi-Fi. A game room proves handy on rainy days.

⬆ 60 🏊 🛜 Some rooms
🔑 MC, V

🏨 SAN ANTONIO
🍴 HOTEL BOUTIQUE
$$$
CARR. 6 #2-51, BARRIO
SAN ANTONIO
TEL 57-2/524-6364

en.hotelboutiquesanantonio
.com
Located in the upscale San Antonio neighborhood, this colonial-era home has been spruced up with a contemporary remake. Old and new mix in guest rooms, with their antique reproductions, stylish design, and luxe linens. The Wi-Fi is free.

⬆ 10 ❄ 🛜 🔑 All major credit cards

🏨 JARDÍN AZUL
$$
CRA. 24A #2A-59,
BARRIO MIRAFLORES
TEL 57-2/556-8380
jardinazul.com
A lovely boutique hotel in the historic district, it has clinically clean rooms with a choice of modern or antique reproduction furnishings, all with Wi-Fi. The courtyard garden has a whirlpool spa.

⬆ 6 ❄ 🛜 🔑 All major credit cards

🏨 POSADA DE SAN ANTONIO
$$
CRA. 5 #3-37,
SAN ANTONIO
TEL 57-2/893-7413
posadadesanantonio.com
A colonial-style hotel centered on a patio with fountain and rockers. Infused with a delightful calm, it enjoys a splendid location in the heart of the historic district. Decorated with sturdy antique-style furnishings. Contemporary art abounds. Rates include breakfast and tax. A pleasant budget option.

⬆ 12 🅿 ❄ 🔑 AE, MC, V

SOMETHING SPECIAL

🍴 RESTAURANTE PATIO SANTO
$$$$
CALLE 18 #105-52,
CIUDAD JARDÍN

TEL 57-2/332-4410
facebook.com/patiosanto
In the heart of Cali's high-class Ciudad Jardín district, this open-air contemporary restaurant surrounds a tented patio with floodlit palms. One of the city's hippest eateries, it's favored for parties. The open kitchen delivers such gourmet treats as mushrooms in Gruyère, Tilsit, and blue cheese; and steamed sea bass on a bed of wok-sautéed vegetables with coconut sauce, wrapped in foil. Go for the live music, including Tuesday night jazz and a sensational Saturday night *salsa espectáculo*.

🍴 320 🅿 🕐 Closed Sun. D
🔑 All major credit cards

🍴 CARAMBOLO
$$$–$$$$
CALLE 14 NORTE #9N-18
TEL 57-2/667-5656
carambolo.com.co
The city's monied class is drawn to this classy, yet small, restaurant specializing in Mediterranean-inspired nouvelle cuisine. Start out with a warm arugula and Camembert salad with almonds and caramelized apples. Then retire to the martini bar. Owner Lona Serna is attentive.

🍴 80 🅿 🕐 Closed B & Sun.
🔑 All major credit cards

🍴 EL ESCUDO DE QUIJOTE
$$
CALLE 4 OESTE #3-46
TEL 57-2/893-2917
facebook.com
/elescudodelquijote
Tucked behind the Colegio La Sagrada Familia, this atmospheric restaurant specializes in tapas and fusion dishes, with an emphasis on Spanish cuisine, such as *gazpacho de pastor* (rabbit stew with bread and mushrooms).

🍴 65 🅿 🕐 Closed Sun.
🔑 AE, MC, V

GIRARDOT

HOTEL TOCAREMA
$$$

CRA. 5A #19-41
TEL 57-1/213-1308
hoteltocarema.com

This resort hotel, in the Magdalena Valley about 40 miles (60 km) east of Ibagué, rises in tiers over a large swimming pool with fountain and cascades. Comfy rooms have hair dryers. Facilities include tennis, a business center, and Wi-Fi in public areas.

🛏 150 P ⛽ 🆒 ⛶
🛜 In public areas
🆘 All major credit cards

LAGUNA DE LA COCHA

HOTEL SINDAMANOY
$$

1.9 MILES (3 KM) SW OF EL ENCANO
TEL 57-2/721-8222
hotelsindamanoy.com

Overlooking Isla La Corota, this lakeside Swiss-style hotel is reached by dirt road. It has a spectacular setting on a bluff above the lake. Rooms offer cozy, unfussy furnishings. Sunlight pours into the restaurant, with rich red-leather chairs and lime green sofas against rustic wooden walls. The menu features onion soup, plus trout, chicken in mushroom sauce, and other hearty local dishes.

🛏 23 rooms, 1 3-bedroom cabin P 🆘 AE, MC, V

NEIVA

HOSTERÍA MATAMUNDO
$$$–$$$$

CRA. 5 #3-51 SUR
TEL 57-8/873-0202
hosteriamatamundo.com

Far and away the nicest hotel in town, this gracious property evokes the past with its 1940s neocolonial architecture and period furnishings. Rooms are comfortable and inviting and have Internet modems, while public areas have Wi-Fi. Wide shaded verandas. Within the grounds of an historically important hacienda just off the *circunvalar* (city bypass), overlooking the Río del Oro.

🛏 30 P 🆒 🏊 🛜 In public areas 🆘 AE, MC, V

HOTEL CASA PABLO
$$$

CALLE 5 #12-45,
SECTOR EL ALTICO
TEL 57-8/872-3100
hotelcasapablo.com

This modest three-story hotel sits on a hill overlooking town and caters to a span of budgets. Cheaper ground-floor rooms have fans only; upper-level rooms boast cable TV and en suite bathrooms. All are crisp and clean with free Wi-Fi.

🛏 36 P 🆒 🛜 🆘 All major credit cards

RESTAURANTE LA CASA DEL FOLCLOR
$$

CALLE 33 #5P-59
TEL 57-8/875-3040
lacasadelfolclor.com

This rustic open-air charmer specializes in *comida típica huilense*–typical dishes of the region–such as chicken with wine, and *róbalo* (sea bass) with shrimp. The owner is a famous composer and performer of local *bambuco* music and dance, and folkloric dances.

🪑 180 P 🆘 All major credit cards

PASTO

LOFT HOTEL
$$$

CALLE 18 #22-2

TEL 57-2/722-6737
lofthotelpasto.com

A dramatic counterpoint to Pasto's historic core, this mid-range avant-garde hotel would fit well in New York's SoHo. Its modernist planar white facade with blue-tinted glass balconies sets the tone. Huge rooms are arranged around an atrium over the restaurant. They are decorated in tangerine, chocolate, and white colors; all feature pine floors and have luxurious linens warmed by a nightly hot-water bottle. The hotel offers free Wi-Fi and in-room condiments, plus business center and sauna. One block from both the main plaza and Gold Museum. The equally stylish restaurant serves regional and international dishes, with an eager and capable waitstaff.

🛏 24 P 🆒 ⛶ 🛜
🆘 All major credit cards

PITALITO

🏨 HOTEL TIMANCO
$$$
AV. PASTRANA
TEL 57-8/836-6500
hoteltimanco.com

A bright and airy modern hotel located just a 30-minute drive away from San Agustín's archaeological sites. Caters to business travelers and has a nightclub. Spacious rooms have modish contemporary furnishings plus Wi-Fi. An elegant, café-style restaurant has views. Weekend poolside barbecue.

ⓘ 20 P 🅢 ⚐ 🛜
🅢 MC, V

POPAYÁN

🏨 HOTEL DANN MONA-
🍴 **STERIO POPAYÁN**
$$$–$$$$
CALLE 4 #10-14
TEL 57-2/824-2191
hoteldannmonasterio
popayan.com

The cream of the Popayán crop, Hotel Dann Monasterio occupies a former Franciscan monastery that is a city landmark. Dating back to 1570, its dramatic architecture is a perfect venue for deluxe abodes four centuries later. There's nothing ascetic to the carpeted bedrooms, today regally appointed with antiques and Oriental throw rugs. Airy cloisters open to lovely gardens and a very non-monkish swimming pool. Plus, guests get golf and tennis privileges at the Popayán Country Club. The restaurant is also perhaps the city's finest, serving gourmet local and international dishes.

ⓘ 47 P ⚐ 🅢 All major credit cards

🏨 HOTEL CAMINO REAL
🍴 **$$$**
CALLE 5 #5-59
TEL 57-2/824-3595
hotelcaminoreal.com.co

A mid-price alternative to the ritzy Dann Monasterio, this delightful hotel is a 16th-century convent school a stone's throw from the main park. Exuding period character, it recalls the grace of yesteryear. Rooms have Wi-Fi (and squeaky floorboards). The restaurant opening to a peaceful courtyard is a stand out for its eclectic menu, specializing in nouvelle French cuisine. *Tiradito de tilapia*, spaghetti, and beef stroganoff are also featured.

ⓘ 28 P 🛜 🅢 All major credit cards

🍴 RESTAURANTE ITALIANO
$
CALLE 4 #8-83
TEL 57-2/824-0607

This simple restaurant with creaky wood-and-leather seating is one of very few in town that opens on Sunday. It serves filling and tasty local dishes, such as garlic trout, roast chicken, and tongue in tomato sauce. On weekdays, budget hounds—and those with big appetites—will appreciate the *almuerzo ejecutivo*—the prix fixe set lunch.

🍴 60 P 🕐 Closed B
🅢 None

SAN AGUSTÍN

🏨 HOTEL YALCONIA
$$$
VÍA AL PARQUE ARQUEOLÓGICO
TEL 57-8/837-3001
OR
316-304-8353
E-MAIL hyalconia@gmail.com

Although far from luxurious, the motel-style Hotel Yalconia is the only modern hotel of international standard located in San Agustín. It offers clean, spacious rooms with bamboo frame beds, and has a handsome restaurant serving local and continental dishes.

ⓘ 32 P 🅢 ⚐ 🅢 MC, V

🏨 SAN AGUSTÍN INTERNACIONAL HOTEL
$$$
VÍA VEREDA LA ESTRELLA
TEL 57-8/837-3807
hotelsanagustin
internacional.com

Here's something different. This upscale hotel has rooms in five structures, each themed on a destination: American, Colombian, Mediterranean, Scandinavian, and indigenous. All are tastefully and thoughtfully furnished. However, some are bare-bones family rooms with multiple beds. The three-story, circular Maloka Estílo Indígena has contemporary rooms with indigenous motifs and is the setting for the hotel's open-air restaurant. Live folkloric music.

ⓘ 20 P 🅢 🅢 🅢 MC, V

🏨 HACIENDA ANACAONA
$$–$$$
VÍA EL ESTRECHO KM 2,
VEREDA LA CUCHILLA
TEL 57-8/837-9390
OR
311-231-7128
anacaona-colombia.com

This colonial-era hilltop hacienda now functioning as a rustic hotel is set in lovely gardens. Spacious, sparsely furnished rooms on two levels have beam ceilings and traditional Colombian furnishings. Hammocks and rockers on broad verandas.

Simple meals are served in an open kitchen-lounge with fireplace. Horseback riding is a specialty. The hacienda also sells homemade jams, natural chocolate, and organic estate-grown coffee.

🏨 10 🅿 🚭 ♿ MC, V

🏨 HOSPEDAJE EL JARDÍN
$

CRA. 11 #4-10
TEL 57-8/837-3455
E-MAIL eljardincasa
colonial@hotmail.com
hosteltrail.com/eljardin

Perhaps the nicest of the colonial-era lodgings actually located in town, this clean hostel is run by live-in owner Ismenia. Meals are served in an atrium courtyard festooned with potted plants, plus hammocks and aviary. Choose from bunk-rooms, or private rooms with a choice of shared or private hot-water bathrooms.

🏨 10 🅿 🚭 ♿ None

🍴 RESTAURANTE DONDE RICHARD
$$

CALLE 5 #23-45, VIA PARQUE ARQUEOLÓGICO
TEL 57/312-432-6399

Open air and cross ventilated, this simply furnished restaurant is a favorite of locals, who come for the *asado huilense*—slow-roasted pork. Ten dollars buys you lunch: pork, chicken, or a large, soft-fleshed fish called *bagre*, with fries, plantains, and a side of tomatoes and shredded lettuce.

🪑 100 🅿 ♿ None

SAN ANDRÉS DE PISIMBALÁ

🏨 LA PORTADA
🍴 $$

SAN ANDRÉS DE PISIMBALÁ
TEL 57/311-601-7884
laportadahotel.com

The nicest of several budget options in this mountain hamlet close to Tierradentro archaeological site, this hotel made of bamboo and concrete has spacious, simply appointed rooms with hot-water showers. Tasty, filling criollo meals are served alfresco in the town's only restaurant. The owner, Don Leonardo Velasco Bolanos, is a charming and talkative character.

🏨 11 🅿 🚭 ♿ None

🔲 PACIFIC & SAN ANDRÉS

BAHÍA SOLANO

🏨 MAPARA CRAB
🍴 ECOLODGE
$$$

PLAYA PARIDERA, 20-MIN. BOAT RIDE N OF BAHÍA SOLANO
TEL 57-2/312-815-3026
maparacrab.com

The finest option around, this ecolodge sits on a partially landscaped hill backed by forest, a 20-minute boat ride from Bahía Solano. Its five simply appointed yet cozy and spacious cabins stand on stilts and have large balconies with hammocks and bamboo-framed lounge chairs. Activities include kayaking, fishing trips, and guided hikes. The airy restaurant offers a modicum of elegance and, needless to say, specializes in seafood.

🏨 5 ♿ None

🏨 EL ECOLODGE REFUGIO DE MR. JERRY
$$

PLAYA HUINA
TEL 57-4/682-7233
OR
311-340-1923
mrjerrychoco.jimdo.com

Surrounded by coconut

PRICES

HOTELS

An indication of the cost of a double room in the high season is given by **$** signs.

$$$$$	Over $200
$$$$	$100–$200
$$$	$50–$100
$$	$25–$50
$	Under $25

RESTAURANTS

An indication of the cost of a a three-course meal without drinks is given by **$** signs.

$$$$$	Over $35
$$$$	$20–$35
$$$	$10–$20
$$	$5–$10
$	Under $5

palms, this colorful two-story wooden beachfront ecolodge is run by an equally colorful Dutchman, who settled here two decades ago. Rooms are basic but stocked with hundreds of fading paperbacks—perfect for rainy days in one of the hammocks slung in the restaurant-bar. El Ecolodge Refugio de Mr. Jerry is located only a 20-minute boat journey away from Bahía Solano.

🏨 40 🚭 ♿ None

BUENAVENTURÁ

🏨 HOTEL BALCONES DE LA BAHÍA
$$$

CALLE 1 #6-53
TEL 57-2/241-9913
facebook.com/hotelbalcones.bahiabuenaventura

The hotel of choice, this striking contemporary option offers surprisingly hip and

---

🏨 Hotel 🏨 No. of guest rooms 🍴 Restaurant 🪑 No. of seats 🕐 Hours 🅿 Parking 🚭 Nonsmoking luxurious styling. Towering eight stories, its lofty perch overlooking the ocean guarantees breezes while lounging on your balcony. Just steps from the tourist dock. Flat-screen TVs, mini-bars, and Wi-Fi, plus rooftop whirlpool spas.

🏨 24 🔌 🅰️ 🛜 🛟 All major credit cards

🏨 HOTEL TEQUENDAMA
🍴 ESTACIÓN INN
$$$
CALLE 2 #1A-08
TEL 57-2/241-9512
hotelestequendama.com
This historic grande dame hotel harkens back to a golden era and is the city's main historic landmark. Operated by the Tequendama hotel group, it offers plenty of old-style comfort, plus modern amenities. Its restaurant offers an ocean view and serves international and local fare, with a logical emphasis on seafood.

🏨 79 🔌 🅰️ 🏊 🛟 All major credit cards

CAPURGANÁ

🏨 HOTEL NAUTILOS
$$$
PLAYA CALETA
TEL 57-4/436-6262
OR
57-4/444-6264
almar.com.co
Nestled up to white sands, Hotel Nautilos is popular with families for its comfy air-conditioned pine-log rooms, with ceramic floors. Far from deluxe, it nonetheless offers massage, scuba diving, and guided hikes and birding.

🏨 48 🅰️ 🛟 🏊 None

🏨 CASA BLANCA
$$–$$$
CAPURGANÁ

TEL 57-4/413-7926
lodgecasablanca.com
This simple two-story beachfront hotel is perhaps the nicest place in Capurganá. Modestly appointed rooms each have TV, small refrigerator, and private cold-water bathrooms, plus hammocks on a wraparound shared balcony. It specializes in three- to six-night packages.

🏨 11 🅰️ 🛟 None

🍴 DONDE JOSEFINA
$$
PLAYA CALETA
TEL 57/316-779-7760
This palm-shaded beachfront restaurant sets a high standard for gourmet seafood dining, courtesy of cook Josefina, who conjures such delights as lobster or octopus with garlic and coconut sauce.

🍴 12 🕐 Closed B 🛟 None

EL VALLE

🏨 EL ALMEJAL ECOLODGE
& RAINFOREST RESERVE
$$$–$$$$
PLAYA EL ALMEJAL,
EL VALLE
TEL 57-4/412-5050
almejal.com.co
Offering the choice digs in the region, this beachfront ecolodge is set amid palm-shaded lawns backed by forested mountains. Cross ventilated, with folding doors on two sides, the spacious two-bedroom cabins are simply appointed and have open-air decks with lounge chairs and hammocks. The alfresco restaurant uses homegrown organic vegetables, with filling criollo meals. Guided hikes, kayaking, rappelling, and other activities. Butterfly garden plus turtle conservation program. Accessible by boat only.

🏨 11 🛟 All major credit cards

NUQUÍ

🏨 EL CANTIL ECOLODGE
$$
35-MIN. BOAT RIDE S OF NUQUÍ
TEL 57-4/255-7355
elcantil.com
A great base for exploring the rain forest or for water activities, this well-run lodge offers multiday packages. Its simple yet charming cabins stairstep a hill and have ocean views, plus net-draped beds. A generator guarantees electricity. Kayaks, scuba diving, and surfboards. Ferry transportation needed.

🏨 7 🅰️ 🛟 AE, MC, V

PROVIDENCIA

🏨 DEEP BLUE
🍴 $$$–$$$$
MARACAIBO BAY
TEL 57-8/514-8423
OR
321-458-2099
hoteldeepblue.com
By far the stand-out accommodations are at this chic boutique hotel overlooking Maracaibo Bay. Coralstone walls and floors combine with flat-screen TVs, king-size beds, snow-white linens, and colorful local fabrics exuding good style and comfort. Deep Blue has a lap pool, plus a private boat for excursions and dive trips. The hotel's casually elegant oceanfront restaurant has an eclectic menu featuring creatively prepared local favorites plus international staples, including traditional American breakfasts.

🏨 12 🅰️ 🛟 🏊
🛟 All major credit cards

🏨 CABAÑAS MISS MARY
$$$
SOUTHWEST BAY
TEL 57-8/514-8454
www.decameron.co
This charming little beachfront

is marketed as a Decameron affiliate and includes the chain's all-inclusive option. Albeit small and with only cold-water showers, the rooms stretch out in front of palm-shaded sands and have hammocks on porches. Take the ocean-view cabins; three to the rear appeal less. Amiable and conscientious staff is a plus.

🛈 7 🅿 🎁 🚭 All major credit cards

🏨 SIRIUS HOTEL & DIVE CENTER
$$$
BAHIA SUR OESTE,
ISLA DE PROVIDENCIA
TEL 57/318-743-5367
siriushotel.net

Filled with character, this rambling beachfront hotel is run by Paulino Gamboa, a friendly and knowledgeable host whose wife, Carolina, is a professional underwater photographer. It has an on-site dive center and specializes in dive packages. Rooms vary, but most are spacious and feature white furnishings; some have bamboo king-size beds and flat-screen TVs; all rooms have ceiling fans.

🛈 9 🎁 🚭 V

🏨 SOL CARIBE PROVIDENCIA
$$$
BAHÍA AGUADULCE
TEL 57-8/514-8036
OR
1-650-1400
solarhoteles.com

Done up in blazing tropical colors, this mid-range beach resort is considered the island's most upscale, although it has its faults (such as unreliable water and questionable sewers). Still, it offers plenty of homey Caribbean character. Wind chimes on balconies add to

the charm. It specializes in all-inclusive packages and has a dive center.

🛈 35 🅿 🎁 🚭 🎁 All major credit cards

SAN ANDRÉS

SOMETHING SPECIAL

🏨 CASA HARB
🍽 $$$$$
CALLE 11 #10-83, 1 MILE/1.6 KM
SW OF SAN ANDRÉS TOWN
TEL 57-8/512-6348
casaharb.com

Serving deep-pocket guests, this exclusive boutique hotel causes a double take with its sublime architecture and decor. And you thought San Andrés would be a sleepy backwater. The inspiration is part Bali, part New York styling. The result is the kind of chic hotel that you expect Hollywood's shutterbug-shy A-list to seek. Casa Harb is the very epitome of intimacy, with just five loft-like suites, each as distinct as a thumbprint and fitted with contemporary craft furnishings such as artsy wicker beds. The mood carries into the restaurant-bar serving fusion dishes.

🛈 5 🅿 🎁 🎁 🚭
🎁 All major credit cards

🏨 DECAMERON
🍽 BOUTIQUE LOS DELFINES
$$$$
AV. COLOMBIA #16-86
TEL 57-8/512-4083
decameron.com

Transporting you metaphorically to Miami's South Beach, this motel-style hotel in the Decameron chain has a hip, youthful ambience, trendy decor, and puts you steps from the nightlife and shopping. Guest rooms, on two levels, wrap around a

free-form swimming pool. They're nicely appointed, but small; mattresses are second rate, and soundproofing is lacking (honeymooners next door could be cause for your own sleepless nights). The **El Muelle** restaurant sits over the waters and serves quality fusion dishes. Wi-Fi costs extra.

🛈 36 🅿 🎁 🚭 🎁 Charge
🎁 All major credit cards

🏨 COCOPLUM
🍽 $$$
VÍA A SAN LUÍS #43-39,
SAN LUÍS
TEL 57-8/513-2121
cocoplumhotel.com

Seeking a pleasant beachfront hotel outside town? With its tropical fruit colors and plantation rails, this low-rise Caribbean-style resort is tucked among palms behind snow white sands. Steeped in sunlight, guest rooms have ceiling fans and pleasant, albeit modest, furnishings; some are family suites. The plunge pool complements the turquoise ocean, just steps away. Open to the public, its beachfront restaurant specializes in seafood and Caribbean dishes.

🛈 42 🅿 🕃 ⛱ 🅲 All major credit cards

🏨 HOTEL CASABLANCA
$$$

AV. COLOMBIA #3-59
TEL 57-8/512-4115
**hotelcasablanca
sanandres.com**

Competing with Los Delfines for chic boutique stylish, this hotel has the advantage of a beachfront location and has the edge over its competitor for ambience. Guest rooms wrap around the kidney-shaped pool. Travertine floors are a bonus, as is free Wi-Fi in all rooms, which are spacious and tastefully furnished. Choice of a hip café and two restaurants.

🛈 91 🕃 ⛱ 🛜 🅲 All major credit cards

🏨 HOTEL MS SAN LUIS VILLAGE
$$$

CIRCUNVALAR,
SOUND BAY N°71-27,
SAN LUÍS
TEL 57-8/513-0500
hotelsanluisvillage.com

This unpretentious, mid-price all-suite beach hotel has a Mediterranean-style aesthetic. Choice of junior suites or two types of suites in five blocks surrounding a lap pool; three are oceanfront. King-size beds, walls of glass, and terraces, plus tasteful turquoise and chocolate highlights against gleaming white floors.

🛈 18 🅿 🕃 🕃 ⛱ 🅲 AE, MC, V

🏨 CARSON'S PLACE
$$

EL COVE KM 10
TEL 57-8/513-0352
**posadacarsonsplace.inf.
travel**

Perfect for escaping the overdeveloped North End beach scene in favor of local intimacy, this tiny place on the peaceful southwest side of San Andrés is part of the *posada nativas* program (see sidebar p. 241). It has two family-size wooden cottages. Broad verandas with hammocks.

🛈 3 🅿 🅲 None

🏨 POSADA CLI'S PLACE
$$

AV. 20 DE JULIO
TEL 57-8/512-0591
**facebook.com
/PosadaNativaClisPlace**

One of the best budget options in town, Cli is named for friendly Raizal owner Cleotilde Henry. This homey *posada nativa,* one block from the beach, has rooms with kitchenettes. It's popular and often full. Cli's brother also rents rooms next door.

🛈 8 🕃 🅲 All major credit cards

🏨 POSADA LICY DUKE
$$

FLOWERS HILL #39-19,
LA LOMA
TEL 57-8/513-3972
**facebook.com
/posadalicy.duke**

This simple yet delightful *posada nativa* offers a chance to immerse yourself in local Raizal lifestyle with owner Reolicia Duke Santana, whose two-story clapboard home overlooks a pretty garden. Reolicia prepares *rondón* and other Caribbean meals upon request.

🛈 16 🅿 🕃 🅲 None

▇ LOS LLANOS & AMAZON BASIN

LETICIA

🏨 DECAMERON DECALODGE TICUNA
$$$$

CRA. 11 #6-11
TEL 57/098-592-6600
decameron.com

The Decameron is an all-inclusive hotel that offers the best comfort in the region. Just a five-minute walk from Parque Santander. Spacious guest rooms surround a pool and are a visual delight with contemporary styling, cool washed cement floors, and comfy king-size beds. A soaring *palenque* restaurant features a huge faux snake suspended from above. Food is of average quality and the menu is limited, although meals are filling.

🛈 28 🅿 🕃 ⛱ 🅲 All major credit cards

🏨 HOTEL MALOKAMAZONAS
$$$

CALLE 8 #5-49
TEL 57-8/592-6642
OR
313-822-7527
**facebook.com
/hotelmalokamazonas**

Although in the heart of Leticia, this small hotel plays up the jungle theme with its thatch roofs, rough-hewn timber furniture, and shaded grounds. The comfortable cabins each have private bathroom and hammocks, and pleasant Amazonian decor. There's a TV room and open-air Jacuzzi. Wheelchair accessible.

🛈 8 🅿 🕃 ⛱ 🅲 MC, V

HOTEL YURUPARY
$$$
CALLE 8 #7-26
TEL 57-8/592-4743
OR
312-542-5900
hotelyurupary.com
The most salubrious hotel
in town, this hotel surprises
visitors to the Amazon with
its Wi-Fi, satellite TV, and
modestly upscale urban-style
furnishings, such as leather
sofas atop gleaming floor tiles.
The restaurant serves buffet
and à la carte dishes.
🛏 42 🅿 🚭 🏊 🛜
🚭 AE, MC, V

KURUPIA CABAÑ FLOTANTE
$$$
LA MILAGROSA, 3 MILES
(5 KM) NW OF LETICIA
TEL 57/311-508-5666
amazonheliconia.com
/kurupira
Tethered riverside close to
the park, this rustic, thatched
floating wooden lodge offers
an authentic Amazonian
experience at one with
nature. Barebones open-air
dorm rooms include beds
with mosquito nets, plus
hammocks. Fresh-cooked
meals are served in the open
kitchen and dining platform.
🛏 5 rooms, 20 beds 🚭 None

ALBERGUE TACANA
$$
8.7 MILES (14 KM) N OF LETICIA
TEL 57/313-872-3207
on.fb.me/1JMkKhX
A 20-minute taxi ride north
of Leticia, this simple lodge is
owned by live-in British expat
Steve McAlear, who leads
hiking excursions through
the rain forest and to nearby
molokasi (indigenous com-
munities). Macaws on the
property. Backpackers are
offered an eight-bed dorm
in the house. Two of three

outside cabins have private
cold-water showers and flush
toilet, plus netted porch with
hammock.
🛏 3 🅿 🚭 None

SOMETHING SPECIAL

RESERVA NATURAL TANIMBOCA
$$
7 MILES (11 KM) VÍA LETICIA
TARAPACÁ, ZONA RURAL DE
LETICIATEL
TEL 57/310-791-7470
OR
321-207-9909
tanimboca.com
Although you can sleep in a
hammock in an open-air dorm
beneath a soaring *maloka*, try
one of the two treetop cabins
where you're magnificently
alone in the heart of the rain
forest, 0.6 mile (1 km) from
the lodge. These sturdy cabins
(one sleeps three people;
the second sleeps five) have
simple mattress beds with
mosquito nets, plus showers
and flush toilets. The chirrup-
ing of frogs and rasping of
insects is your lullaby. Unseen
mammals prowling the night
might wake you as they scam-
per along the branches. The
food, prepared by indigenous
guides and served in a simple
bare-earth kitchen, is basic
and bland.
🛏 2 treehouses, 4 cabins,
hammocks 🚭 None

RESTAURANTE A.ME.K.TIA
$
CRA. 9 #8-15
TEL 57-8/592-6094
E-MAIL amektiar@yahoo.es
A popular and clean heart-
of-town Leticia restaurant
where you can sit beneath
fans on the patio and watch
the quiet street life. A wide-
ranging menu, from burritos,
burgers, and sandwiches to

PRICES
HOTELS
An indication of the cost of
a double room in the high
season is given by **$** signs.

$$$$$	Over $200
$$$$	$100–$200
$$$	$50–$100
$$	$25–$50
$	Under $25

RESTAURANTS
An indication of the cost of a
a three-course meal without
drinks is given by **$** signs.

$$$$$	Over $35
$$$$	$20–$35
$$$	$10–$20
$$	$5–$10
$	Under $5

shrimp-filled crepes and
fish dishes.
🍴 60 🅿 🚭 MC, V

PUERTO LÓPEZ

SOMETHING SPECIAL

LAGOS DE MENEGUA COMLEJO AGROTURÍSTICO
$$$
VÍA PUERTO LÓPEZ–PUERTO
GAITÁN KM 17
TEL 57/315-326-6068
OR
57-1/616-0439
lagosdemenegua.com
This modern resort hotel
with lakeside setting has
only modest accommoda-
tions, but the overall expe-
rience at the hacienda is
enriching. Bogotaño families
come for the swimming pool,
fishing, horseback riding,
mountain biking, nighttime
crocodile tours, and other

activities, such as the cattle ranching demonstrations. Guest rooms, on two levels, enjoy comfy albeit minimal furnishings, plus TV. *Joropo* music and dance is hosted on Sunday.

🛈 24 🅿 🚭 ❄ ♒
🅢 MC, V

PUERTO NARIÑO

🏨 HOSTAL ALTO DE ÁGUILA
$$
SALIDA DE PUERTO NARIÑO KM 2
TEL 57/313-239-7944
OR
311-502-8592
altodelaguila.wordpress.com

This comfortable, no-frills budget option, riverside outside the village, is run by a Franciscan missionary, Friar Hector, and his son (and a troop of semi-tame monkeys). Meals are prepared in a communal kitchen, and it has kayaks.

🛈 3 cabins 🅢 None

🏨 HOTEL CASA SELVA
$$
CRA. 2 #6-72
TEL 57-3/320-233-7318
OR
311-212-6043
E-MAIL casaselvahotel@yahoo.com

The nicest place in the village, this two-story option has large rooms with painted concrete floors, ceiling fans, and private cold-water bathrooms. It's simple, yet perfectly adequate and comfortable.

🛈 12 🅿 ❄ ♒ 🅢 None

🏨 MALOCA NAPU
$$
CALLE 4 #5-72
TEL 57/315-607-4044
malocanapu.com

This delightful, well-run two-story thatched *maloca* (guesthouse) offers simple accommodations with shared bathrooms and hammocks, a stone's throw from restaurants. Excursions are offered to the "flooded jungle" of Lago Tarapoto by dugout canoe.

🛈 8 🅢 None

VILLAVICENCIO

🏨 GHL HOTEL VILLAVICENCIO
$$$
CRA. 39C #19C-15
TEL 57-8/668-0666
ghlhoteles.com

By far the classiest hotel in town, this contemporary themed option offers spacious, elegantly appointed rooms with Wi-Fi. It is popular as a business hotel and has convention facilities, plus a rooftop pool and solarium.

🛈 120 🅿 ❄ ♒ 🎽 📶
🅢 All major credit cards

🏨 HOTEL DON LOLO
$$$
CRA. 39 & CALLE 21
TEL 57/078 670-6020
donlolohotel.com

This ten-story tower hotel is perhaps the city's finest. Bedrooms here come in various styles. Some are elegantly furnished; others verge on being merely functional, but all have cable TV and Wi-Fi. Families can opt for two-bedroom suites. Facilities include a sauna and conference room.

🛈 57 🅿 🚭 ⬍ ❄ ♒ 📶
🅢 All major credit cards

🏨 HOTEL PALOVERDE
$$$
6.2 MILES (10 KM) VIA PUERTO LÓPEZ–VEREDA APIAY
TEL 57-8/310-609-3729
hotelpaloverde.com

This small resort hotel is part of a residential complex away from the city hubbub. Its modestly furnished rooms face onto the swimming pool and have huge walk-in showers, plus Direct TV. Also four-person villas with private pools. It can be noisy on weekends, when the music cranks up to please the weekend party crowd.

🛈 80 🅿 🚭 ❄ ♒
🅢 MC, V

Shopping

Colombia is a great destination for both shopaholics and casual shoppers, who will find plenty of fabulous bargains. Visitors come for the cut emeralds and emerald jewelry, for the latest in designer fashions, and for the authentic simplicity of indigenous crafts, ideally bought directly from the artisans. The major cities have plenty of cosmopolitan boutiques as well as art galleries selling contemporary pieces.

Emeralds

If there is one item that is synonymous with Colombia, it's emeralds and emerald jewelry. Every major city in the country has a wide range of upscale jewelry stores specializing in fine emeralds, sold loose or set in gold or silver as rings, brooches, earrings, and necklaces.

Colombian gem cutters and gold designers are considered among the best in the world. Nonetheless, their relatively low salaries translate into relatively low prices for finished jewelry. Plus competition is stiff, and people roam the streets handing out business cards to tempt you to buy at particular stores.

Expect savings of between 10 and 50 percent over retail prices charged in the United States for quality emeralds. If the savings are greater, you'll get what you pay for in terms of quality. However, note that extra discounts are offered during summer low season. Do your homework before you leave home. You'll be better informed to figure out if the salesperson is stretching the truth or not.

The epicenter of the emerald trade is the junction of Carrera 7 and Calle 15, in Bogotá, where several dozen jewelry stores are located. Street emerald traders congregate on the southwest corner of the junction and sell loose emeralds from the palms of their hands. Unless you're a gemologist, the best motto here is look but don't buy, as you're almost assuredly going to pay through the nose. Stick to the reputable stores.

All shops selling emeralds are licensed by the Colombian government, which is concerned to protect the country's reputation as the source of the world's finest gemstones.

Cruise-ship passengers visiting Cartagena will be better off buying in town than aboard ship. Companies such as Colombian Emeralds usually have shipboard stores, but the high cost of retail space and of advertising in the ship's literature are factored into the cost of the jewelry.

Indigenous Products

Colombia's other strong suit is indigenous crafts. Most upscale hotels have gift stores selling high-quality crafts, although artisans markets have by far the widest choice. However, you'll have more fun if you buy direct from the artisans themselves—which has the added benefit of contributing directly to the artisan community.

Almost every town has an artisans market selling intricate **woven baskets,** colorful **bead necklaces,** or intricately knitted *mochilas*—the woven shoulder bags used by many indigenous peoples throughout Colombia. These are bright and colorful, and usually woven with imaginative and interesting abstract patterns.

Hammocks come in every shade of the Pantone chart. Expect to pay from US$30 up to US$100 for the more complex and well-made hammocks. Ask whether the fabric was colored with natural dyes; the more garish examples are typically made from industrially manufactured dye.

La Guajira is the place to buy exquisite hammocks, mochilas, and colorful bracelets that are a specialty of the Wayúu people.

In Chocó, look for **tagua nut carvings** of native wild animals made by the Emberá people. About the size and shape of a golf ball, these ivory-like carvings are usually exquisitely crafted and painted. The more upscale crafts stores nationwide will also carry tagua nut carvings, as well as beautiful carvings hewn from lignum vitae, rosewood, mahogany, or other tropical hardwood.

In Colombia, all such craft sales are final. Most crafts are small enough to fit in your suitcase, but if you're buying art pieces, remember to take into account the size of your luggage and how much you can carry.

One of the most Colombian of crafts souvenirs is a *sombrero vueltiao*—the trademark wide-brimmed straw hat of the country. It has the added advantage of being practical, and comes in all shapes and sizes for men and women. Leave room in your luggage for the country's renowned **coffee.**

Although large furniture items are not an option for most travelers, if you're prepared to ship an item by air or sea freight, consider a beautiful wood-and-leather or wicker **rocking chair,** such as those made by the craftsfolk of Mompox. Typical **Antioquian doors, windows, and metal window grilles** are other possible items that can be shipped.

Colombia has a vibrant art scene, and you might be tempted to shop for a work by an up-and-coming artist such as Adriana Vargas Ferero. And it's impossible to walk down any urban street in Colombia without being presented with bootleg music CDs or DVDs of iffy quality for sale.

Colombia is a fashion-conscious nation, and Medellín is one of the world's foremost fashion design centers. The major cities don't lack for upscale fashion boutiques, often concentrated in large malls, where international name-brand stores stand shoulder-to-shoulder with shops selling fashions by local designers such as Pepa Pombo and Francesca Miranda. Or opt for a *ruana*—traditional woolen poncho.

Precautions

Be cautious of any scams, such as passing off mass-produced items as handcrafted goods, including artfully forged historic artifacts. Note that the sale of pre-Columbian antiquities is illegal and any item offered as such is either stolen or a fake. Don't encourage the trafficking of historic items by criminals. The same goes for items involving protected species, such as macaw feathers or bird-feather headdresses, stuffed frogs or caiman, and the like. In remote areas, you may occasionally come across impoverished people selling parakeets, songbirds, or even tiny monkeys. Such trade adds to the plight of endangered species—don't support it.

Count your change carefully when shopping at outdoor markets or with individuals in the street. The latter requires particular caution, especially if your trade includes an exchange of foreign currency. It's best to ensure you have enough Colombian currency to pay the correct amount. If you need to exchange foreign currency, do so in advance at a bank or official exchange bureau, to avoid the sleight of hand that often leaves foreigners shortchanged.

Haggling

Haggling is not a tradition in Colombia except in crafts markets and indigenous communities. Most shops—even crafts shops—and boutiques stick to their fixed, posted prices, but once you start purchasing off the street and at open-air stalls, things are more fluid. Don't come to Colombia thinking you can pick up astonishing bargains. Expect to bargain a price down no more than 20 percent from the original asking price, and remember that no matter how far you've talked down a seller, he or she won't go down to breakeven. Remember that in many indigenous communities, the item you're interested in may already be a true bargain at its asking price, and beating down the price for the sake of it may be insensitive. This is their livelihood, not a game.

Payment

Colombia is a thoroughly modern nation and most department stores will accept payment by credit card (Visa is the preferred card). Many crafts merchants also accept credit cards and will have a portable scanner on hand to process your payment. Most artisans markets, however, operate on a cash-only basis, as do all the indigenous communities. Markets are often crowded and pickpockets often work the crowd, so take the usual precautions to guard your money.

Sales Tax

All purchases in Colombia are subject to a value-added sales tax (IVA) of 16 percent. If you've visited the country for less than 60 days, you can request a refund at the airport upon departure for merchandise purchased with a credit card and valued at more than $250,000 COP.

Shops & Stores

All the cities have large-scale shopping malls and areas where upscale shops are concentrated. The following list of stores represents only a small fraction of Colombia's shopping opportunities. For many visitors, the act of exploring artisans markets in remote colonial hamlets and indigenous communities is the most exciting part of the shopping experience.

Art & Antiques

Colombia's homegrown art scene is vibrant. Don't expect to be able to buy a Fernando Botero sculpture (unless you're a millionaire), but fantastic works by lesser known artists adorn galleries nationwide. Colonial towns such as Villa de Leyva and Barichara are good sources for antiques.

Antigüedades

Cra. 10 #10-21,
Santa Fé de Antioquia
Tel 57-4/853-1111
In the Hotel Mariscal Robledo (see p. 294), this shop sells all manner of antiques, including those displayed throughout the hotel. Looking for an original Spanish suit of armor? No problem.

Galería Casa Cuadrada
Cra. 7 #83-20, Edificio Saturno,
Bogotá
Tel 57-1/257-6541
casacuadrada.com
A tremendous collection of
modern art representing six
leading artists.

La Tienda Feroz
Cra. 8 #11-32,
Villa de Leyva
Tel 57/317-435-5202
latiendaferoz.com
A fabulous collection of
contemporary art and crafts.

Books
Colombians are highly literate
book lovers, and every town has
at least one major bookstore.
Colombia's own publishing
industry is well developed.
Look for beautiful coffee-table
books about the country.

Librería del Fondo de Cultura
Calle de la Enseñanza 11 #5-60,
Bogotá
Tel 57-1/283-2200 ext. 122
fce.com.co
In the Centro Cultural Gabriel
García Márquez, it has a superb
selection of coffee-table books
about Colombia.

Librería Lerner
Av. Jiménez #4-35,
Bogotá
Tel 57-1/334-7826
librerialerner.com.co
An excellent resource for travel-
related books to Colombia.

Panamericana
Cra. 43A #6S-150,
Medellín
Tel 57-4/448-0999
This large bookshop/office supply
store sells maps, as well as a very
modest range of English-language
titles.

Fashion & Accessories
Bogotá's Chicó and Chapinero
districts are ground zero for
über-contemporary designer
stores. Cartagena, Cali, and
Medellín also have plenty of
high-end fashion shops. The big
names have outlets in the major
malls, but many of the up-and-
coming designers have shops in
the backstreets.

Bettina Spitz
Cra. 122 #25-04,
Usaquén, Bogotá
Tel 57-1/213-7699
bettinaspitz.com
The store offers glamorous
female fashions from one of
Colombia's top designers. It
has five stores in Bogotá and
one in Cartagena.

Mario Hernández
Cra. 68D #13-74,
Bogotá
Tel 57-1/294-8181
mariohernandez.com
Shop sells unique, handcrafted
leather items, including
ostrich-skin purses. Also
eye-catching jewelry.

Miguel Caballero
Calle 71 #15-28,
Bogotá
Tel 57-1/347-8199
miguelcaballero.com
The self-styled "Armani of bullet-
proof clothing" can fit you with
cool duds that can take a bullet
at point-blank range.

Pepa Pombo
Cra. 14 #83-46,
Bogotá
Tel 57-1/236-5958
pepapombo.com
Fashion designer Pepa Pombo
is acclaimed for her avant-garde
haute couture, sold at three
stores in Bogotá.

Sombrería San Miguel
Calle 11 #8-88,
Bogotá
Tel 57-1/243-6273
lacalle11delsombrero.com
This is the place in the capital city
to buy a fedora or cowboy hat,
pressed to shape while you wait.

Taller Manuel del Cuero
Cra. 5 #26A-18,
Macarena, Bogotá
Tel 57-1/342-8964
cesargiraldo.com.co
Since 1988, César Giraldo has
been crafting quality hand-
stitched leather bags, briefcases,
and belts in a rainbow of colors.

Jewelry
The two major centers for
jewelry stores are Bogotá and
Cartagena; the finest jewelry
pieces are sold there.
Mompox is famous for
its artisanal silverwork.

Galería de Cano
Plaza de Bolívar #33-20,
Local 679, Cartagena
Tel 57-5/664-7078
galeriacano.com.co
Craftsmen at this family-run
gallery reproduce pre-Columbian
gold figurines using the age-
old lost-wax technique. Also
has quality crafts. Has stores
in Bogotá.

Joyería Caribe
Calle 5 #2-51,
Cartagena
Tel 57-5/665-4625
jcemeralds.co
For emeralds and fine jewelry,
visit this museum and shop.

Lucy Jewelry
Calle Santo Domingo #3-19,
Cartagena
Tel 57-5/664-4255
lucyjewelrycartagena.com

A good place in the historic center of Cartagena for emerald shopping.

Museo Internacional de la Esmeralda
Calle 16 #6-66,
Edificio Avianda 23rd fl.,
Bogotá
Tel 57-1/482-7890
museodelaesmeralda.com.co
This large store also has a small museum, plus an exhibition center of fine emeralds.

Taller Artesanal de Esmeraldas
Plaza Mayor,
Chivor
This small artisanal workshop on the main square of Chivor sells exquisite craft items using locally mined emeralds and gold. Combine it with a tour of the emerald mines.

Taller y Joyería Orvilla Hermanos
Calle Real del Medio #17A-76,
Mompox
Tel 57-5/684-0130
An artisanal studio that crafts earrings, and more from silver.

TuEsmeraldo
Emerald Trade Center,
Av. Jiménez #5-43,
Local 104, Bogotá
Tel 57/300-743-8007
tuesmeralda.com/en
This store is one of eight emerald stores in the high-rise Emerald Trade Center.

Outdoor Clothing & Equipment

Amarelo
Calle 57 #9-29,
Bogotá
Tel 57-1/211-8082
campingamarelo.com
A good place to stock up on camping gear before heading off to hike the Andean peaks.

Monodedo
Cra. 16 #82-22,
Bogotá
Tel 57-1/616-3467
monodedo.com
The premier shop catering to alpinists, campers, and hikers. Also has an outlet at Suesca.

Traditional Crafts
You're never far from a source of crafts in Colombia, be it ceramic miniatures of *chivas*, colorful *chinchorros* (hammocks), or a handmade drum from Guapí. The Guambiano of Silvia, Wayúu of La Guajira, Ticuna peoples of Amazonia, and Kuna of the Golfo de Urabá all produce quality crafts. Certain colonial cities are known for specific crafts: Pasto for decorative wood panels, for example, and El Cocuy for woolen *ruanas*.

Almacén Calle 86
Calle 86A #13A-10,
Chicó, Bogotá
Tel 57-1/691-7149
This store has three floors with a tremendous collection of quality crafts by indigenous communities.

Almacén Centro de Convenciones
Cra. 8 Local 5,
Getsemaní, Cartagena
Tel 57-5/660-9615
Within the Convention Center, this upscale shop sells top-quality traditional crafts, from hammocks to mochilas.

Artesanías de Colombia
Cra. 2 #18A-58,
Bogotá
Tel 57-1/211-9364 or 310-4437
artesaniasdecolombia.com.co
One of the best high-end collections of indigenous and other crafts in Bogotá, this government-sponsored showcase for pottery, handmade masks, and more has one store in Bogotá and five elsewhere in the country.

Feria de San Alejo
Parque Bolívar,
Medellín
This flea market is held every first Saturday of the month—a chance to browse for collectibles, from antiques to modern crafts.

Las Bóvedas
Plaza de las Bóvedas,
Cartagena
This row of crafts stores has a great selection, but prices are high. Don't expect any bargains.

Mercado de Pulgas Los Toldos de San Pelayo
Cras. 6 & 119,
Usaquén, Bogotá
This flea market one block from the plaza in Usaquén is a good place to browse the eclectic offerings, from handmade jewelry to carvings.

Entertainment

Colombians are supreme party animals and like nothing as much as music and dance, from the scratchy sounds of *vallenato* to sizzling hot salsa. Every city is bursting with informal bars and trendy nightclubs. Bogotá, Medellín, and Cali have something for everyone, from theater and movies to casinos and discos. Folkloric and contemporary music festivals are hosted nation-wide, and each department has its own cultural festivals—from Medellín's flower festival to Barranquilla's wild Carnaval—while all-important beauty contests culminate with the crowning of Señorita Colombia—Miss Colombia—in Cartagena.

Colombians are proud of their rich and diverse cultural history, and despite the country's modernity and sophistication, traditional entertainment and festivals are supported enthusiastically. Colombia's musical culture has been defined by its fusion of disparate cultural traditions—those of old-world Spain wed to the influences brought by African slaves, and to those of the nation's various indigenous peoples. Exploring Colombia's traditional and contemporary cultures—whether it be live theater or a *salsa espectáculo*—can give a better insight into the character of the nation, while guaranteeing that you'll have fun.

Bullfighting (see sidebar p. 181) is a key element of the cultural scene. While the gory spectacles are not to everybody's taste, many Colombians are passionate supporters and elevate the best matadors to the level of national heroes.

Bars

Every major city in Colombia has its Zona Rosa (Pink Zone), where the trendiest bars concentrate. Bogotá's Zona Rosa revolves around Calle 82 and Carrera 13. Medellín's Zona Rosa is centered on Parque Lleras. In Cartagena, many of the trendiest bars and nightclubs are in Getsemaní. Do not walk at night; take a taxi, regardless of distance or destination.

Andres Carne de Res
Variante de la Luna,
Chía
Tel 57-1/861-7880
andrescarnederes.com
The perfect venue for groups, this wacky bar is truly one of a kind. Patrons often dance on the tables.

Bogotá Beer Company
Cra. 12 #83-33,
Zona Rosa, Bogotá
Tel 57-1/702-9999
bogotabeercompany.com
As close to an English pub as you'll find, this company—affectionately known as BBC—has 27 outlets, but the Zona Rosa pub is the liveliest. Connoisseurs will delight in the eight custom-brewed beers, including a hearty stout and porter.

Café del Mar
Baluarte de Santo Domingo,
Centro Histórico,
Cartagena
Tel 57-5/664-6515
facebook.com/cafedelmar cartagena
Sitting atop the old wall of the city, this is a great place for a drink at sunset and to enjoy the evening with the breeze coming off the ocean.

Café Havana
Calle Media Luna & Calle del Guerrero, Getsemaní,
Cartagena
Tel 57/315-556-3905
cafehavanacartagena.com
This Cuban-theme bar is one

of the city's coolest watering holes, and partyers spill into the street.

Trilogia Live Bar
Cra. 43G #24-08
Tel 57-4/204-0562
trilogiabar.com
One of Medellín's liveliest bars, it has live music and great food.

Chivas

A nocturnal tour of the city aboard a roving party bus, or *chiva rumbera,* is a great way to experience a uniquely Colombian institution. Most tours end at a disco where you can continue the party.
See sidebar page 78 for more information.

Chivas Tours de Colombia
Calle 100 #49-07,
Bogotá
Tel 57-1/481-4444
chivastours.com

Excursiones Rafael Pérez
Av. 1ra #6-130,
Cartagena
Tel 57-5/655-0086
excursionesrafaelperez.com

Cultural Festivals

JANUARY

Festival Internacional de Música
Cartagena
Tel 57-1/217-9970
web.cartagenamusic
festival.com
A week-long series of classical

music concerts and theater by international performers.

FEBRUARY
Carnaval
Barranquilla
Tel 57-5/319-7616
carnavaldebarranquilla.org
Colombia's wildest, most colorful festival. Only Brazil does it better.

APRIL
Festival de la Leyenda Vallenata
Valledupar
Tel 57-5/573-8393
festivalvallenato.com
The town explodes into life for the Festival of the Vallenato Legend, which keeps the *vallenato* music (from the North coast) tradition alive.

JUNE
Festival Folclórico
Ibagué
Tel 57-8/262-0314
festivalfolclorico.com
The city's plazas are venues for traditional Colombian rhythms.

Festival Nacional del Joropo
Villavicencio
This five-day event features plenty of traditional *joropo* music and dance.

Rock al Parque
Parque Metropolitano Simón Bolívar, Bogotá
rockalparque.gov.co
Each June, rock bands (and fans) from around the world descend on Bogotá for a week of live music.

Wayúu Culture Festival
Uribia, La Guajira
Demonstrations of traditional music, dance, crafts, and legends of the Wayúu people.

AUGUST
Feria de las Flores
Medellín
Tel 57-4/444-4144
feriadelasfloresmedellin.gov.co
The Flower Festival celebrates Colombia's status as a major exporter of flowers and features floral, classic car, as well as horseback parades.

NOVEMBER
Concurso Nacional de Belleza
Cartagena
Tel 57-5/660-0779
srtacolombia.org
Cartagena comes to a halt for the Señorita Colombia (Miss Colombia) beauty pageant. See sidebar page 135 for more information.

Live Music
Many bars and restaurants in Bogotá, Medellín, and Cali have music, and all three cities have major live-music venues. Bogotá's Parque Metropolitano Simón Bolívar is a major outdoor setting for megamusicians to perform, as are each of the cities' major sports arenas.

Nightclubs
Colombia's nightclubs don't get in the groove until after midnight; many are still pulsing when the sun comes up. So plan an afternoon siesta before hitting the clubs for a long night of lively *cumbias* and sensual salsa.

Babylon
Cra. 41 #9-22, Medellín
Tel 57-4/266-2126 or 381-8169
On Parque Lleras, this small yet hugely popular disco is adorned with pop cartoon hero decor.

Delirio
Cra. 2A Oeste #13-34B
Barrio Santa Teresita, Cali

Tel 57-2/893-7610
delirio.com.co
One of Colombia's hottest salsa shows puts you in the mood to dance on one of the stages.

Radio Berlín
Cra. 6 #26-57,
Bogotá
facebook.com/RadioBerlinBogota
Considered by night-owls to be *the* place to get your late-night groove on.

Theater & Performance
Colombia's cities are blessed with theaters, and the country has a strong tradition of plays and a keen appreciation for ballet, classical music, and opera. The country's major orchestras offer seasonal concerts.

Orquestra Filarmónica de Bogotá
Tel 57-1/288-3466
filarmonicabogota.gov.co

Orquestra Sinfónica Nacional
Tel 57-1/350-5325
sinfonica.com.co

Teatro Heredia
Plaza de la Merced #38-10,
Cartagena
Tel 57-5/664-6023

Teatro Jorge Eliécer Gaitán
Cra. 7 #22-47,
Bogotá
Tel 57-1/379-5750 ext. 213
teatrojorgeeliecer.gov.co

Teatro Metropolitano de Medellín
Calle 41 #57-30,
Medellín
Tel 57-4/232-2858
teatrometropolitano.com

Teatro Municipal
Cra. 5A #6-64,
Cali
Tel 57-2/883-9106
teatromunicipal.gov.co

Outdoor Activities

Away from the cities and beaches, Colombia is as thrilling a destination as anywhere in the world when it comes to outdoor activities. Take your pick from sensational Andean hiking and thrilling white-water rafting, plus horseback riding, rappelling, paragliding, rock climbing, and more.

Colombia's varied and rugged landscapes—from lowland deserts and Amazonian rain forests to snowcapped Andean peaks—allow for a wide variety of outdoor activities. On the Caribbean coast, there are ample opportunities for snorkeling, windsurfing, and kiteboarding; scuba diving is world-class at Bahía Solano and Isla de Malpelo, on the Pacific, and at Colombia's Caribbean isles of San Andrés and Providencia. The towering peaks and *páramo*-carpeted valleys of the Cordilleras Central and Oriental are ideal places for high-altitude hikes and multiday treks, with El Cocuy and Los Nevados national parks the key venues. San Gil is Colombia's main center for outdoor activities, with a repertoire of options that ranges from rafting to paragliding.

You don't have to venture far from the major tourist centers before you find yourself in pristine, untouched wilderness ripe for exploring. Check local security conditions, however, before venturing into any wilderness zone that's off the beaten tourist path.

In addition to the companies listed below, many hotels are willing and able to organize excursions for their guests. For information on scuba diving, see sidebar p. 235.

ATV & Motorcycle Tours

ATV Rentals Van Den Enden
Santa Marta
Tel 57/317-436-6930
E-mail atvrentals@hotmail.com
atvrentals.blogspot.com
Fourtrax tours through the foothills of the Sierra Nevada.

Cuatri Tours ATVS
Medellín
Tel 57/301-673-9698
cuatritoursatvs.com

Motolombia
Av. 6 bis, Calle 26N,
Cali
Tel 57-2/392-9172
motolombia.com
Guided motorcycle day excursions and multiday trips.

Golf

Colombia boasts more than 50 golf courses, many laid out by legendary designers such as Robert Trent Jones, Jack Nicklaus, and Gary Player. About half are in or around Bogotá. Others, tucked into folds of the Andes, offer the challenge of steep slopes against dramatic backdrops. Alas, almost all the courses belong to private social clubs or tourist resorts. Few courses offer carts, but caddies are always available.

Club Campestre Bucaramanga
Anillo/Vial km 2.5, Bucaramanga
Tel 57-7/680-3030 ext. 600
campestrebucaramanga.com
The Casa de Campo course is a nine-hole, 3,600-yard (3,290 m) layout. The club has a driving range.

Club Campestre Medellín
Calle 16A Sur #34-950,
Medellín
Tel 57-4/325-9000
clubcampestre.com.co

Club de Golf La Cima
Vía Bogotá–La Calera km 13,
Bogotá
Tel 57-1/860-9857
on.fb.me/1P7F8BU

Federación Colombiano de Golf
Cra. 7 #72-64,
Bogotá
Tel 57-1/310-7664
federacioncolombianadegolf.com
The Colombia Federation of Golf website profiles 48 golf courses nationwide.

Hiking & Trekking

Asociación Ecoturística de Güicán y Cocuy (ASEGÜICOC)
aseguicoc.com
This guides association provides guide services.

El Cocuy Sierra Nevada
Calle 11 #6-10,
El Cocuy
Tel 57/310-618-2094
Guided hikes of Parque Nacional Natural El Cocuy.

Guaicani
Cra. 27 #70-76,
Alcazares, Bogotá
57-1/314-336-3099 or
311-492-7631
Offers guided tours of the Parque Nacional Natural El Cocuy circuit.

Kumanday Aventuras
Calle 66 #23B-40,
Manizales
Tel 57/315-590-7294
kumanday.com
Guided hikes to Parque Nacional Natural Los Nevados.

Turcol: Turismo Colombiano
Cra. 13 # 313, Centro Comercial San Francisco Local 115,
Santa Marta
Tel 57-5/421-2256
turcoltravel.com/en
Specializes in the six-day trek to the

Ciudad Perdida (Lost City); see sidebar p. 152; also shorter treks.

Walking & Biking Tours

Bogotá Bike Tours
Cra. 3 #12-72,
Bogotá
Tel 57-1/281-9924
bogotabiketours.com

Candelaria
Cra. 8 #11-39,
Bogotá
Tel 57-1/281-5569 or
310-311-9845
lacandelaria.info
Guided walking tours, plus
romantic rides in classic cars.

Cuadrante Cultural
Tel 57/316-239-9927
cuadrantecultural.com
Guided historical walking tours.

La Chiva de Jaime
Villa de Leiva
Tel 57/312-450-5856
Offers four distinct tours of the
town and surrounding sites in
La Chiva in the Eastern Highlands.

Tierra Magna Tours
Cartagena
Tel 57-5/655-1916
tierramagna.com
Offers a self-guided audio tour:
Gabriel García Márquez—
Gabo's Cartagena.

Velo Tours
Calle Don Sancho #36-125,
Cartagena
Tel 5/664-9714
Guided bicycle tours of Cartagena
and environs.

Zebra Trips Adventure Travel
Tel 57/311-870-1749
zebratrip.com
Offers adventure trips by Land
Rover or on foot throughout the
Eastern Highlands.

Water Sports

With its Andean ranges and high
rainfall, Colombia is a white-water
nirvana. Scores of rivers cascade
from the mountains, and several
have evolved as well-established
runs for white-water enthusiasts.
The key centers are San Gil, San
Agustín, and Santa Fé de Antioquia. The Caribbean coastline also
provides opportunities to get into
the water and even dive.

Colombia Rafting Expediciones
Cra. 10 #7-83,
San Gil
Tel 57/311-291-2870
colombiarafting.com

Dive & Green
Capurganá
Tel 57-4/682-8825 or
311-578-4021
diveandgreen.com
Dive off the Caribbean shores
and Golfo de Urabá.

Magadalena Rafting
Calle 5 #16-04,
San Agustín
Tel 57/311-271-5333
magdalenarafting.com

Naturaventura
Calle 10 #16-70,
Santa Fé de Antioquia
Tel 57-4/853-1969 or
313-667-8150
facebook.com/naturaventura
.ecoturismo
Specializes in white-water rafting.

Octopus Dive Center
Taganga
Tel 57-5/421-9332
Dive center near Santa Marta.

Sport Barú
Cartagena
Tel 57/314-506-6520
sportbaru.com
Day boat excursion to Isla
Rosario.

Sunset Sailing
Cartagena
Tel 57/315-755-5386
sunsetsailingcartagena.com
Caribbean day tours and three-hour
night tours by luxury catamaran.

Tayrona Dive Center
Taganga
Tel 57/315-638-3307
tayronadivecenter.com
Caribbean diving.

Windsurfing & Kiteboarding

Colombia's two centers for
windsurfing and kiteboarding
are windswept Lago Calima,
near Cali, and Cabo de la Vela,
in La Guajira.

Calima Kitesurf School
Lago Calima,
Cali
Tel 57/317-821-4889
calimakitesurf.com

Escuela Pescao
Lago Calima, Cali
Tel 57/311-352-3293

Kite School Aquanaútica
Cra. 9 #22-802, Anillo Vial,
Cartagena
Tel 57/311-410-8883
kitesurfcolombia.com

Kiyakite
Calle 2 #22-2 Prado Mar,
Puerto Colombia
Tel 57/310-727-1110
kiyakitesurfing.com
Instructor David Ibern teaches at
this school outside Barranquilla.

INDEX

Bold page numbers
indicate illustrations.
CAPS indicates
thematic categories.

ACKNOWLEDGMENTS

National Geographic wishes to thank all the organizations and individuals that have made this book possible including: Proexport Colombia and the Ministerio de Comercio, Industria y Turismo, Colombia; the staff of Parques Nacionales Naturales; Margarita Gaitan, MarViva; Nate Skinner, ProAves; Andrés Delgado, Kaishi travel; Tim Buendia, Buendia Tours and the Gypsy Residence; Diego Montañez, Pamplona Cultural; Richard McColl, La Casa Amarilla; Maria Motta, Boyacá Tourism Board; Juliana Niño Pilonieta, Bucaramanga Tourism Board; Marcela Madrid, El Almejal Reserve; and all the other departmental and local tourism boards across the country.

ILLUSTRATIONS CREDITS

All photos by Christopher P. Baker unless otherwise noted below:

Cover: Eva Kaufman/Getty Images; spine: Blake Kent/Design Pics/Corbis; 4, courtesy of PROEXPORT COLOMBIA; 11, AWL Images/Aurora Photos; 23, Cesar Carrion, Presidency of Colombia; 26, Library of Congress, LC-USZ62-104354; 33, Laurence Griffiths/Getty Images; 63, Stephen Ferry/Redux; 92, Thornton Cohen/Alamy Stock Photo; 126, courtesy of PROEXPORT COLOMBIA; 138, "Action of Cartagena, 28 May 1708" (detail), Samuel Scott, 18th century, oil on canvas, National Maritime Museum, Greenwich, London; 207, Dennis Drenner/Getty Images; 210, Carlos Angel/Getty Images; 211, Steve Raymer/National Geographic Creative; 222, Christian Escobar Mora/epa european pressphoto agency b.v./Alamy Stock Photo; 231, Tomas Kotouc/National Geographic My Shot; 254, Mariya Bibikova/iStockphoto.

National Geographic
TRAVELER
Colombia
SECOND EDITION

Since 1888, the National Geographic Society has funded more than 12,000 research, exploration, and preservation projects around the world. National Geographic Partners distributes a portion of the funds it receives from your purchase to National Geographic Society to support programs including the conservation of animals and their habitats.

National Geographic Partners
1145 17th Street NW
Washington, DC 20036-4688 USA

Become a member of National Geographic and activate your benefits today at natgeo.com/jointoday.

For information about special discounts for bulk purchases, please contact National Geographic Books Special Sales: specialsales@natgeo.com

For rights or permissions inquiries, please contact National Geographic Books Subsidiary Rights: bookrights@natgeo.com

ISBN: 978-1-4262-1702-9

Printed in Hong Kong

16/THK/1

The information in this book has been carefully checked and to the best of our knowledge is accurate. However, details are subject to change, and the National Geographic publisher cannot be responsible for such changes, or for errors or omissions. Assessments of sites, hotels, and restaurants are based on the author's subjective opinions, which do not necessarily reflect the publisher's opinion.

THE COMPLETE TRAVEL EXPERIENCE

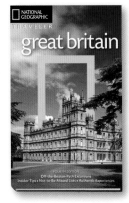

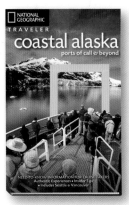

With more than 75 destinations around the globe; available wherever
books are sold and at www.shopng.com/travelerguides

for iPhone®,
iPod touch®,
and iPad®

TRIPS
natgeoexpeditions.com

MAGAZINE

APPS